Blasphemy and Exaltation
in Judaism

Blasphemy and Exaltation in Judaism

The Charge against Jesus in Mark 14:53–65

Darrell L. Bock

Baker Books

A Division of Baker Book House Co
Grand Rapids, Michigan 49516

Reprinted 2000 by Baker Books
a division of Baker Book House Company
P.O. Box 6287, Grand Rapids, MI 49516-6287
with permission of the copyright holder

This book first appeared in 1998 as Blasphemy and Exaltation in Judaism and the Final Examination of Jesus, volume 106 in Wissenschaftliche zum Neuen Testament, 2d series, published by J. C. B. Mohr (Paul Siebeck), P.O. Box 2040, D-72010 Tübingen.

Printed in the United States of America

Library of Congress Cataloging-in-Publication Data

Bock, Darrell L.
  [Blasphemy and exaltation in Judaism and the final examination of Jesus]
  Blasphemy and exaltation in Judaism : the charge against Jesus in Mark 14:53–65 / Darrell L. Bock
      p. cm.
  Originally published: Blasphemy and exaltation in Judaism and the final examination of Jesus. Tübingen : Mohr Siebeck, c1998, in series: Wissenschaftliche Untersuchungen zum Neuen Testament. 2. Reihe.
  Includes bibliographical references and indexes.
  ISBN 0-8010-2236-3 (pbk.)
  1. Jesus Christ—Trial.   2. Trials (Blasphemy)—Jerusalem.   3. Bible. N.T. Mark XIV, 53–65—Criticism, interpretation, etc.   I. Title.

BT440 .B63 2000
226.3'067—dc21   00-030405

For information about academic books, resources for Christian leaders, and all new releases available from Baker Book House, visit our web site:

http://www.bakerbooks.com

Preface

This monograph presents my study of an event that has long fascinated me. My previous labors in Luke's use of the Hebrew Scriptures in the New Testament revealed that Jesus' examination by the Jewish leadership played a central role in the evangelists' representations of Jesus. I have always wanted to take a closer look. My research took place at the Eberhard-Karls-Universität Tübingen during my sabbatical in 1995-96. Notes of gratitude are appropriate, as such an endeavor is never a soliloquy.

I thank the Dallas Theological Seminary for granting me a year's absence to pursue this study. Special mention goes to Hall Harris and Harold Hoehner, who regularly kept in touch about my progress by email, keeping up with me from thousands of miles away. Such collegiality is most appreciated. In addition, my graduate assistants, Greg Herrick and James Davis, read the entire manuscript and engaged in fruitful reflection about the topic. Greg also converted my files into the proper computer format. Finally, I wish to thank those who gave helpful comment to earlier portions of this work: David Capes, Bruce Chilton, Craig Evans, Larry Hurtado, and Carey Newman. Their feedback improved the study. Whatever shortcomings remain are mine.

I extend heartfelt thanks to the German government and to the Alexander von Humboldt Stiftung, whose generosity helped to underwrite my research and allowed my family to accompany me. It is rare to find countries that value the serious study of the humanities as the Bundesrepublik Deutschland does. Doing research in a different culture with people who are serious about the pursuit of genuine interaction in their field has been a privilege. The Humboldt program's vision for international cooperation and interaction in education is worthy not only of commendation but emulation. Special mention must be made of Juliane Brenner and Cäcilia Nauderer, who handled all the details of our stay for the Stiftung with grace and promptness.

I thank my host university at Tübingen and the faculty and staff at the Institut für antikes Judentum und hellenistische Religionsgeschichte. Prof. Hermann Lichtenberger and his support staff made me feel welcome and provided all the assistance I needed. Dr. Friedrich AveMarie not only gave me my original tour of the campus but also generously helped me locate resources when I was mired deep in Jewish source material.

When it comes to kindness, a special place must be given to my Humboldt hosts, Prof. Dr. Martin Hengel and Prof. Dr. Otto Betz. Both interacted with this work in its roughest form. Prof. Betz consistently encouraged me through his well-known English language colloquium. Prof. Hengel met with me on several occasions to discuss the study's progress step by step. His suggestions opened new avenues for reflection. His and Frau Hengel's concern was that our family would have a good experience. Their desire bore fruit because they were hosts in every sense. To say thank you does not say enough.

I also must note our German friends in Neckartailfingen, the village where we lived. The Werths, Brauns, Rehms, and Canals kept a considerate eye on us answering all the questions a different cultural experience raises. The teaching staff of the local Gymnasium in Neckartenzlingen and most especially the Sportverein of Neckarhausen/Neckartailfingen made sure our three children not only remained busy but well educated. My son experienced the beauty of engaging in competitive Fußball as only the Germans play it. Our fellowship community at the International Baptist Church of Stuttgart also made certain that we never felt too isolated. I thank them all.

A note of appreciation must also go to my family. My wife, Sally, was willing to repeat a journey to Germany that called on her to take classes in a foreign language, returning to the classroom again after twenty years. My three teenage children, Elisa, Lara, and Stephen deserve special credit because they left friends and functioned in a new culture for a year.

This work is dedicated to a German lady who helped raise me, Greta Hock. She came to our family in Canada from Mannheim in 1953, having lost her husband to a sniper during World War II. She remained an adopted family member since the time I was born. In the middle of our sabbatical in Germany she suffered two major heart attacks, but managed to survive a quadruple bypass at the tender age of eighty-three. Her survival was a special testimony of God's grace. This dedication is especially appropriate because I grew up listening to her stories about German life, including her accounts of living through two world wars. She sparked my initial interest in this part of the world. What better symbol of appreciation could there be to her for her life of love and service than to dedicate to her the work I was able to do in her home country. I believe such a dedication represents the very kind of relationship and reconciliation the Humboldt scholarships were designed to foster.

Darrell L. Bock
Neckartailfingen, Germany
June 19, 1996

Table of Contents

Abbreviations

For biblical and extra-biblical books, standard abbreviations are used.

AB	The Anchor Bible
ABRL	The Anchor Bible Reference Library
AGAJU	Arbeiten zur Geschichte des Antikes Judentums und des Urchristentums
AHAW	Abhandlungen der Heidelberger Akademie der Wissenschaften Philosophisch- historische Klasse
ANRW	*Aufstieg und Niedergang der römischen Welt*
Apoc	Apocrypha
ArB	The Aramaic Bible
ATD	Das Altes Testament Deutsch
b	*Babylonian Talmud*
BBR	*Bulletin for Biblical Research*
BECNT	Baker Exegetical Commentary on the New Testament
Bib	*Biblica*
BIS	Biblical Interpretation Series
BJS	Brown Judaic Studies
BZNW	Beihefte zur Zeitchrift für die neutestamentliche Wissenschaft
BZRG	Beihefte der Zeitschrift für Religions- und Geistesgeschichte
CBQMS	Catholic Biblical Quarterly Monograph Series
CBSC	Cambridge Bible for Schools and Colleges
CRINT	Compendia Rerum Iudaicarum ad Novum Testamentum
CSHJ	Chicago Studies on the History of Judaism
DJDJ	Discoveries in the Judean Desert of Jordan
FB	Forschung zur Bibel
FZPT	*Freiburger Zeitschrift für Philosophie und Theologie*
GCS	Die Griechischen Christlichen Schriftsteller der ersten drei Jahrhundert
H	Jerome's Vulgate

Herm	Hermenia- A Critical and Historical Commentary on the Bible
HKNT	Herders theologischer Kommentar zum Neuen Testament
HT	Hebrew term
ICS	*Illinois Classical Studies*
JC	*Judaica et Christiana*
JJS	*Journal of Jewish Studies*
JQR	*Jewish Quarterly Review*
JSHRZ	Jüdische Schriften aus hellenistisch-römaischen Zeit
JSNT	*Journal for the Study of the New Testament*
JSPS	Journal for the Study of the Pseudepigrapha Supplement Series
JStJud	*Journal for the Study of Judaism*
JTS	*Journal of Theological Studies*
K	Kethiv
KTVU	Kleine Texte für Vorlesungen und Übungen
LSJ	Liddell-Scott-Jones Lexicon (1940 ed.)
LXX	Septuagint
m	*Mishnah*
MM	Moulton-Milligan, *The Vocabulary of the Greek Testament* (1930 ed.)
MT	Massoretic Text
NCC	New Century Commentary
NovT	*Novum Testamentum*
NTOA	Novum Testamentum et Orbis Antiquus
NTS	*New Testament Studies*
OTL	Old Testament Library
OTP	*The Old Testament Pseudepigrapha*
p	*Palestinian Talmud*
PN	Passion Narrative
Q	Qere
RAC	Reallexicon für Antike und Christentum (ed. Ernst Dassmann)
RB	*Revue Biblique*
RBen	*Revue Bénédictine*

RQ	*Römische Quartelschaft für Christliche Altertumskunde und Kirchengeschichte*
RSR	*Recherches de science religieuse*
RT	Rabbinische Texte
SBLDS	Society of Biblical Literature Dissertation Series
SBLMS	Society of Biblical Literature Monograph Series
S-B	Strack/Billerbeck's *Kommentar zum Neuen Testament aus Talmud und Midrasch*
SHR	Studies in the History of Religion: Supplements to NUMEN-Religions in Antiquity
SJ	Studia Judaica: Forschungen zur Wissenschaft des Judentums
SJLA	Studies in Judaism in Late Antiquity
SNovT	Supplements to Novum Testamentum
SPAW	*Sitzungsberichte der (königlichen) Preussischen Akademie der Wissenchaft*
SPB	Studia Post Biblica
StUNT	Studien zur Umwelt des Neuen Testaments
SVTP	Studia in Veteris Testamenti Pseudepigrapha
TANZ	Texte und Arbeiten zum neutestmentlichen Zeitalter
TDNT	*Theological Dictionary of the New Testament*, eds. G. Kittel and G. Friedrich (10 vols.; 1964-76)
TLI	*The Talmud of the Land of Israel* (ed., J. Neusner), vol. no. follows (35 vols.)
TSAJ	Texte und Studien zum Antiken Judentum
TWAT	*Theologisches Wörterbuch zum Alten Testament*, eds. G. J. Botterweck and H. Ringgren; 7 vols., 1970-)
TU	*Texte und Untersuchungen zur Geschichte der altchristlichen Literatur*
TynB	*Tyndale Bulletin*
ÜTY	Übersetzung des Talmud Yerushalmi (= Der Jerusalemer Talmud in deutscher Übersetzung)
VT	*Vetus Testamentum*
WBC	Word Biblical Commentary
WUNT	Wissenschaftliche Untersuchungen zum Neuen Testament
x	times (with a numeral in word counts)
YJS	Yale Judaica Series
ZNW	*Zeitschrift für die Neutestamentliche Wissenschaft*

Introduction

Mark 14:61 πάλιν ὁ ἀρχιερεὺς ἐπηρώτα αὐτὸν καὶ λέγει αὐτῷ· σὺ εἶ ὁ χριστὸς ὁ υἱὸς τοῦ εὐλογητοῦ; 14:62 ὁ δὲ Ἰησοῦς εἶπεν· ἐγώ εἰμι, καὶ ὄψεσθε τὸν υἱὸν τοῦ ἀνθρώπου ἐκ δεξιῶν καθήμενον τῆς δυνάμεως καὶ ἐρχόμενον μετὰ τῶν νεφελῶν τοῦ οὐρανοῦ. 14:63 ὁ δὲ ἀρχιερεὺς διαρρήξας τοὺς χιτῶνας αὐτοῦ λέγει· τί ἔτι χρείαν ἔχομεν μαρτύρων; 14:64 ἠκούσατε τῆς βλασφημίας· τί ὑμῖν φαίνεται; οἱ δὲ πάντες κατέκριναν αὐτὸν ἔνοχον εἶναι θανάτου.

These words allegedly report one of the most significant cross-examinations in legal and religious history. According to the evangelist Mark, the key question is, "Are you the Christ, the Son of the Blessed One?" It comes from the Jewish high priest, who Mt 26:57 tells us is Caiaphas. Before this leading Jewish figure stands a popular but strongly controversial Jewish Galilean teacher, Jesus. He comes from a small village named Nazareth.

Jesus' reply in response to this query started the decisive stage to the most famous crucifixion ever performed. Jesus' subsequent death and the events that followed it launched the Christian church and produced a split within Judaism that produced a history of tension between the old and new religion.

The key conflict of the scene centers around the leadership's perception that blasphemy took place because Jesus claims that he will be exalted to God's right hand and come on the clouds. Three questions dominate this study. Why would such a claim for exaltation be considered worthy of death to the Jewish leadership? How did the early church, as represented by Mark, portray the nature of the disagreement that led to this execution? Could such an account credibly reflect the original examination scene, revealing to us the gap of perception that existed between Jesus and the Jewish leadership?

The Jewish examination of Jesus has been studied for centuries. It has even been visually memorialized in epic paintings like the "Christ before the High Priest" by Gerrit van Honthorst (c. 1617). In this powerful portrayal one bright candle illuminates the face of the high priest as he asks Jesus if he is the Christ, and the same light shows a cynically pensive Jesus waiting to give his dramatic reply. The painting, which resides in the National Gallery of London, artistically depicts the moment that blasphemy and exaltation became united in a conflict of opinion that has been alight ever since. Yet surprisingly no comprehensive study of this event presents a focused consideration of the Jewish background to the two major conflicting themes that Jesus' reply raises, namely, blasphemy and exaltation. It is time to fill this gap. Renewed attention on the value of Jewish materials for New Testament study, the extent of such material now made more widely available, and a fresh direction in the history of religion's approach to Jesus studies make the time ripe for such a study. The Marcan pericope of the examination scene raises many issues. However, this study is concerned only with the philological and religious-historical background of the high priest's question and Jesus' reply — a reply that led the high priest to tear his garments and proclaim that Jesus had uttered a blasphemy that was worthy of death. Other issues will surface and be examined, but only as they help us identify what Mark was trying to say in this portion of his presentation and whether that presentation ultimately has roots in the religious-cultural context of Jesus' life. In an era when many New Testament studies are moving away from careful philological-historical study in the earliest, most relevant sources, it is important to see if such a study still has merit. Can such a study help us understand an important and extremely controversial text better? In an era when literary readings are on the rise, should we give up on what historical study can teach us? Though I welcome the new trend as helpful, it is not advisable to ignore questions of history, especially as a new wave of research is opening up fresh avenues in these disciplines as well.

As we shall see, those who have studied this text have challenged this report's historicity, because Jesus did not commit the crime of blasphemy as it is outlined in the *Mishnah*. Jesus apparently did not utter the divine name in an offensive way that would have invoked the penalty mentioned in *m Sanh* 7.5: "The blasphemer is not culpable unless he pronounces the Name itself." This narrow definition of blasphemy, clearly attested as well in the later Jewish material, has raised the question whether this report of Jesus' trial fits the historical-cultural background it portrays, rather than being a piece of early church rhetoric and propaganda.[1]

So key questions surround this account. What was Mark trying to say? Can we know what might have really happened? Only a comprehensive survey of blasphemy in Judaism can answer the question whether a broader definition

---

[1] For a recent declaration that the Marcan Jewish examination evening scene "derives from a Christian hand" and is, in fact, "a kind of christological compendium," see Simon Légasse, *The Trial of Jesus* (London: SCM Press, 1997), p. 41. He concludes, "there is little in this narrative which can be said to have a historical origin." Rather, he says, "Jesus' reply is none other than the confession of faith of the first Christians." Légasse, typical of discussions of this text, emphasizes the confession as the Son of God and does no historical work of any detail. He says, "this dialogue is Christian; it is an *ad hoc* composition aimed at bringing out the mystery of Christ the Son of God, uniting in his person the glory of the divinity and a destiny which consigns him to suffering and death." I shall examine this kind of reading of Mark in chapter 4.

or expression of blasphemy existed in the first century. Could Jews see other types of utterances, claims, or acts as blasphemous? The second chapter of this study focuses on this specific issue after the first chapter considers recent views about the nature of the blasphemy at the examination of Jesus as portrayed by Mark. This survey of the discussion of the Marcan text in this century raises the question whether a consensus is starting to emerge about where the crucial and controversial part of the reply in Mark is.

Jesus' reply centers in a claim to be seated at the right hand of power and to return as a figure that rides the clouds. The response evokes exaltation imagery that also needs careful study. Though Judaism was not united on this concept, almost all strands of this ancient religion wrestled with these questions. In Jewish thinking, who gets exalted directly into God's presence and how were such exaltations viewed? Here is the focus of the third chapter. Both human agents and angelic figures will be considered to see how often one is said to sit next to God. How common is it for these figures to be able to go directly into his presence? How long do they stay? What are they said to be doing when they are there? These questions put Jesus' reply and claims into a cultural context where the emotive force of his response can be appreciated. Such study also allows us to assess its potential uniqueness.

The fourth chapter returns to the examination scene to see if this cultural background helps to define the nature of the blasphemy charge from a Jewish point of view. Our first goal is to understand the event as Mark has presented it and to treat some of the fundamental historical-legal questions his description of events has raised. The issue of possible sources for his report also needs consideration. Next the nature of the blasphemy charge will be treated. Can we define as precisely as possible what concerns stood at the base of the charge? Is there a case for the scene's authenticity? Does the description of the trial possess historical credibility? Five aspects of objection to the scene not already covered will conclude the final part of the chapter.

The study of ancient events is an elusive affair. First, often it is the case that written sources are few. Second, the events often are recorded in texts some distance in time from the original events. Third, sometimes the report involves a language different from the events themselves, with only one side's perspective being present. All of these limitations apply to Jesus' examination as presented by Mark. Nonetheless, the best starting place for such study is to consider the historical evidence and cultural perspective(s) reflected in the documentary sources. This study concentrates on the Jewish understanding of blasphemy and exaltation. It is one way to see how the perspective and report of a Christian document compares to a Jewish perspective. For this reason, other Christian documents are excluded from consideration when it comes to the major issues of blasphemy and exaltation.[2] Every effort is made to pay attention to terminology, to date the documents cited and to detail the internal differences between the views raised. If the study of Judaism in the last half-century has taught us anything, it is that first century Judaism was a complex, multi-faceted entity. Some of these conflicts surface in the differing perspectives these Jewish documents reveal on both blasphemy and exaltation. Nonetheless, a certain consistency emerges in these two themes that can illumine our understanding of this event. That consistency explains what issues drove the response to Jesus that emerged.

The question of who Jesus is and who he claimed to be has been of significance for two millennia, but such a question was never as important as it was in this examination before the Jewish leadership. The question will surely continue to be examined, as it ought to be, given its historical significance. But, it is always valuable to consider the roots of such an event and to know what claims may have led to such a historic parting of the ways. At the least, this study seeks to understand how one Christian evangelist, namely Mark, understood the nature of the disagreement and whether his portrayal makes sense in the cultural setting of the trial. Is it possible that this text gives insight into what ultimately led to this most famous of executions?

In sum, our pursuit of the understanding of this crucial event can be reduced to one question: What can the Jewish views of blasphemy and exaltation tell us about the Jewish examination of Jesus as presented by Mk 14:61-64? I believe that careful historical-cultural study of this background tells us a great deal about what originally brought about the theological separation of Christians from Judaism, providing a far more illuminating portrait of the nature of this event than even the most moving of paintings on the subject.

---

[2]The exclusion of Christian material in the chapters on the Jewish background to blasphemy and exaltation is purposeful. Though the earliest Christianity still saw itself as Jewish, the evaluation of the trial scene's cultural background with regard to blasphemy and exaltation should not be overly colored by evidence that is already touched by potentially earlier, similar disputes over Jesus' identity.

Chapter I

The Charge of Blasphemy in Mark 14:53-65: Recent Interpretation and a Move Toward Consensus

1. Out of Many Questions, One

Surely one of the most discussed texts concerning the life of Jesus is Mk 14:53-65, where Jesus comes before the Jewish leadership for examination. It also is a potentially important text. This event, if nailed down historically, would provide great insight into why Jesus was crucified and the nature of the controversy surrounding his ministry and mission. As a result, much energy has been expended on the careful analysis of this one scene.

A thorough examination of this text's history of interpretation, just in this century alone, would show that many questions swirl around the account. In fact, a consideration of this passage demands that at least fifteen major questions be answered. 1) What was the nature of the blasphemy portrayed in this scene? 2) Was the meeting a trial or an examination? 3) Did the Jews have authority over capital cases? 4) Was there a Sanhedrin then? 5) What would the examination procedures have been? 6) Could there have been an evening examination so close to a feast day and as part of an investigation of a capital offense? 7) Were there one or two trials (evening/morning)? 8) Where would it have met? 9) Who could have served as the transmission chain for what happened at such a meeting? 10) Would Jesus have made the Son of Man remark as reported on the occasion? 11) Is the account Mark's creation or rooted in genuine tradition? 12) Does "the temple to Messiah" movement in the questions make any sense? 13) What was the nature of the false testimony, since Jesus did discuss the fall and rebuilding of the temple? 14) What is the connection of the blasphemy verdict to the charges eventually brought before Pilate? 15) Does the major historical information for this scene, if it exists, come only from Mark's account?

Just reading the list of questions the passage raises is intimidating, since each question has its own set of additional sub-questions, some of which demand careful searching of ancient materials that are not always full of detail about the secrets being pursued. The goal of this study is quite modest in the face of this array of queries. I wish to focus on the first question in the list, that is, the nature of Jesus' blasphemy. I seek to cover a representative sample of the significant studies of the question made since the scene received its most thoroughgoing critique at the hands of Hans Lietzmann in 1931.[1]

I begin with the blasphemy question, since in some ways this question is the most central one raised by the scene, regardless of how we view its historical character. If every other question in this list could be answered, and yet we could not find the answer to the nature of Jesus' blasphemy, a major key to the subsequent passion events would still be missing.

To look at the answers offered for the nature of the blasphemy, we will inevitably find ourselves running into several of the other questions the passage raises, but the studies I examine in this historical overview are chosen because of how they treat the blasphemy question and the steps they take to resolve it or treat it as insoluble. A careful, similar study of the question by David Catchpole in 1965 noted that five solutions had been proposed for the blasphemy.[2] Our examination will concentrate on the period since Catchpole's work, supplementing it and attempting to show that the discussion has been largely narrowed down to variations on two of the categories he raised. They are: 1) Jesus' discussion of the temple, and 2) Jesus' claim about the Son of Man seated at God's right hand and returning on the clouds, with its combined allusion to Ps 110:1 and Dan 7:13.

Lietzmann is the starting point for our study because his 1931 study largely dictated the discussion of this scene for almost fifty years. It is only in the last decade or so that the discussion has emerged from his shadow.[3] In fact, an element of consensus is surfacing from more recent study that may represent one of the more significant achievements of the so-called "Third Quest" for the historical Jesus. Nevertheless, our survey will show that this consensus still needs development when it comes to the historical background of blasphemy in Judaism. I will proceed one study at a time, making the significant assessments and connections along the way.

---

[1] Hans Lietzmann, "Der Prozeß Jesu," SPAW 14 (1931). This short twelve page study has had an influence that far surpasses its brevity.

[2] David R. Catchpole, "'You Have Heard His Blasphemy,' TynB 16 (1965):10-18. The data in this article reappears in his comprehensive study, *The Trial of Jesus: A Study in the Gospels and Jewish Historiography from 1770 to the Present Day,* SPB 18 (Leiden: E. J. Brill, 1971). The five options he noted were: 1) the claim to be Messiah, 2) the claim to be the Son of God, 3) the word against the temple, 4) the use of the divine Name in Jesus' "I am" reply in Mark, and 5) the claim to sit at God's right hand.

[3] Since I am focusing on this century, two studies need noting as falling before Lietzmann's work but as making a contribution to this discussion, as the subsequent allusions to them will show. They are Jean Juster, *Les Juifs dans l'empire Romain: Leur condition juridique, economique et sociale,* 2 vols. (Paris: Geuthner, 1914), which raised many of the historical challenges that Lietzmann noted seventeen years later, and the 1926 discussion of blasphemy by Paul Billerbeck in S-B, vol. 1, pp. 1007-19. Billerbeck's summary is still one of the best brief discussions of blasphemy from a Jewish perspective in print.

2. Hans Lietzmann, "Der Prozeß Jesus" (1931)

This powerful little study was a serious attempt to bring Jewish backgrounds into the discussion of the scene in a way that also raised serious questions about the Marcan scene's credibility. Lietzmann's study alternately defended and challenged the historicity of aspects of the gospel accounts' portrayal of certain passion events, especially as presented in Mark. He argued that Mark's account of Peter's denials is historical, rooted in Peter's memory, but suggested that one can divide up the trial scene into constructed units that give evidence of its creative Marcan character. He then made the case that this "stitched together character" is corroborated by a consideration of the historical evidence that comes from a list compiled by Juster. He argued, using six Jewish examples taken mainly from Josephus, that the Sanhedrin had the right to capital punishment. The examples are: 1) the execution of James (Josephus, *Ant* 20.200), 2) the execution of Stephen (Acts 6:12 — 7:60), 3) the right to slay Gentiles who come into the temple (citing Josephus, *JW* 6.124, though the relevant portion is 6.124-28); 4) the execution by burning of a Jewish priest's daughter who committed adultery (*m Sanh* 7.2, a text that also accuses the Sadducees of not having right knowledge in doing what they did, and *b Sanh* 52b), 5) a theoretical discussion of the execution of any priest — even a high priest — if he goes into the Holy Place (Philo, *Embassy to Gaius* 307 has Agrippa II's letter to Caligula explaining the law as a protest against hanging Roman shields there) and 6) the Essene practice of executing blasphemers (Josephus, *JW* 2.145). These texts appeared to many to give some merit to Lietzmann's case.

For Lietzmann, Mark is the only source for gospel trial accounts, a position that should not be surprising given the recent emergence of the Two Source hypothesis as the prevailing solution to the Synoptic problem. He saw Peter as responsible for the Passion Narrative (henceforth PN) up to the Jewish trial scene, but Mark created the Jewish trial, as is seen by the fact that Jesus is not executed by stoning (the Jewish custom according to Lev 24:10-16), but by crucifixion. Since the Jews had authority to issue death sentences (as the six examples noted above show), the presence of a crucifixion shows that Rome, not the Jewish leadership, was responsible for Jesus' execution. Lietzmann's position represented a repudiation of Jn 18:31, that the Jews did not possess authority to issue a guilty verdict for a capital crime and then administer the execution. Lietzmann argued that since the Jews possessed this authority, had they held a trial and issued the death sentence, stoning would have resulted. So the fact of crucifixion stood against a Jewish trial.[4] For Lietzmann, the PN

---

[4]As we shall see, Paul Winter, *On the Trial of Jesus,* 2d rev. ed., SJ 1 (Berlin: DeGruyter, 1974), developed this approach and argued that any Jewish response was the result of Roman pressure. The first edition appeared in 1961, while many of the essays appeared in 1959.

is religious poetry. Historically, the Jews arrested Jesus but gave him over to Rome. The movement to the cross from the Jewish trial scene is formed from the OT and has parallels with the trial before Pilate and the scene of Stephen's martyrdom. In fact, the blasphemy question by the high priest in the scene is not Jewish, nor is Jesus' reply believable as blasphemy. Had Jesus spoken in this way, it would have been detested as senseless fantasy and as pernicious superstition, but not as blasphemy. Here is what Lietzmann says about the blasphemy remark as it appears in Mark:

> Auf diese Messiasfrage gibt Jesus eine bejahende Antwort: diese erklärt der Hohepriester für eine qualifizierte Gotteslästerung, die ipso facto die Verurteilung zum Tode begründe, und das Synedrion beschließt demgemäß. Auch hier stehen wir vor einem Rätsel: denn es ist völlig unverständlich, worin die Lästerung bestehen soll, zumal wenn man weiß, wie nachdrücklich die Rabbinen der Mischna das Aussprechen des göttlichen Namens bei der Lästerung als Voraussetzung der Verurteilung fordern [(m Sanh. 7.5)]. Und Jesus sagt hier weiter nicht als: "Ich bin es, und ihr werdet sehen den Menschensohn zur rechten der Kraft sitzen und kommen mit den Wolken des Himmels." Das mochte man als wahnsinnige Phantasie verabscheuen, als volksverderblichen Aberglauben bekämpfen, aber eine Lästerung war es nicht— selbst der Name Gottes, die Bezeichnung "Gott", war mit jüdischer Korrektheit in der Antwort Jesu ebenso vermieden wie in der Frage des Hohenpriesters. So bleibt die Geschichte an ihrem entscheidenden Punkte lückenhaft, wenn man sie als eine auch nur annähernd getreue Wiedergabe eines historischen Vorgangs zu begreifen versucht.[5]

Here the problem of the nature of the blasphemy is introduced in as clear a form as possible. If, as the Mishnah says, one must pronounce the Divine Name to blaspheme, then where is Jesus' blasphemy in this scene? This fundamental question about the blasphemy would bedazzle many interpreters of this scene for years to come, while others would simply see the discrepancy as telling evidence of the scene's creation by Mark. As noted above, much of Lietzmann's work actually parallels a 1914 work by a French lawyer, Jean Juster (*Les Juifs dans l'empire Romain*). Lietzmann's six examples of possible Jewish authority for execution would become a major feature of future discussion, as debate swirled over whether Rome or Jerusalem was responsible for Jesus' death.

At this point, proceeding chronologically through the interpretive history gets difficult. Blinzler's study was issued in various editions, but his most comprehensive edition came in 1969.[6] Meanwhile Paul Winter was writing a series of essays that finally came together in a book in 1961 and was released

---

[5]Lietzmann, "Der Prozeß Jesu," SPAW 14 (1931), p. 6.

[6]Josef Blinzler, *Der Prozess Jesu*, 4th ed. (Regensburg: Verlag Friedrich Pustet, 1969). A reworked second edition was released in 1961, while the original, much shorter study, goes back to 1951.

in a second edition in 1974 (see n. 4 above). So Blinzler and Winter interact with each other. We will discuss Winter before Blinzler because Blinzler's fourth edition, which regrettably has never been translated into English, is the fullest statement of his views and provides the fullest interaction on the issues.[7] This order also has the advantage of showing Lietzmann's continued influence as Winter is basically an elaboration of the direction Lietzmann began.

3. Paul Winter, *On the Trial of Jesus* (1961 and 1974)

This work represents a collection of studies on the trial of Jesus that argued for a reduced amount of Jewish responsibility in the events that led to the condemnation of Jesus. Studies include: discussion of the meeting place of the Sanhedrin and Mark's nocturnal session, identity of the High Priest (an attempt to argue that the gospels did not know who the involved High Priest was), the arrest (argued for a basically Roman arrest), Pilate in history and in Christian tradition, the penalty of crucifixion (the Jews never used crucifixion as a capital punishment), and Jewish death penalties (how strangulation came to be noted as a form of execution). Winter argued that the Jews did have authority to execute, so he challenged Jn 18:31-32, as Lietzmann had done. He also questioned the Paschal amnesty and Barabbas scene (the privilege was a figment of the imagination and Barabbas was involved but not clear how and in what way). The other details of his studies fall outside our scope.

The claim that the Jews did not execute by crucifixion during the Roman rule is important and we shall return to it later. But it needs to be remembered that it is one thing to say the Jews did not execute by crucifixion and another to consider whether they could pass on some of their felons to Rome for crucifixion. The possibility of such a distinction is never noted by Winter. So just because official Judaism may not have crucified Jews does not mean that the leadership could not have a role in cases where Jews ended up being crucified by Rome. The outstanding examples here are numerous and involve the various cooperative instances where Zealots of various types or opponents of the Jewish regimes were removed from the scene, not to mention the very

---

[7]A similar phenomena will surface when we discuss August Strobel, *Die Stunde der Wahrheit*, WUNT 21 (Tübingen: J. C. B. Mohr [Paul Siebeck], 1980), and Otto Betz, "Probleme des Prozesses Jesu," in ANRW, series II, vol. 25.1 (Berlin: Walter De Gruyter, 1982). They worked independently of each other, though their studies overlap at many points. In fact, Betz's article was written long before Strobel's book was released, as the Betz supplement to his ANRW article indicates. Betz wrote this supplement because his work took some time to be released. Nevertheless, we shall discuss Strobel first, and then Betz, so as to reflect their publication dates. This means that though Betz appears to supplement Strobel in the flow of the scholarly discussion, this is much more a matter of appearance than reality.

robbers of the Judean region hanged alongside Jesus (Josephus, *JW* 1.97-98-Alexander Janneus' use of this type of execution to slay 800 opposing Pharisees; *Ant* 13.379-83- the parallel discussion of Alexander; 11QTem 64:6-13, esp. 64:8, 11- crucifixion of those who deceive the people or put them at risk).[8] In discussing crucifixion, Winter did discuss some key texts like *4QpNah* 1:3, 7-8 from Qumran, which notes the execution of those "hanged alive on wood," something he claims that was not formerly done in Israel (but see n. 8 above). Winter also treated the *AsMos* 8:1, where a note is made of the persecution of Jews who are crucified for confessing circumcision.[9] He argued that the Nahum pesher's note that crucifixion was not performed before in Israel reveals both the "abhorrence" that it had taken place and thus, it seems Winter implies, a rejection of such a procedure. But Winter still argued that had Rome "merely ratified a sentence which had been passed by a local Jewish court, the sentence would not have been carried out by crucifixion, but in a manner specified in the regulations governing Jewish penal code."[10] So his work attempts to supplement Lietzmann in light of new evidence that was emerging. Winter proceeded very much along the lines of Lietzmann and showed that some continued along this direction, even to the point of extending it into other portions of the PN. Needless to say, for such an approach, the issue of the original nature of the blasphemy before the Jews becomes irrelevant, since they issued no sentence.

4. Josef Blinzler, *Der Prozess Jesu* (1969 edition)

The latest edition of a classic study on the trial of Jesus becomes among other things, an attempt to answer Lietzmann by defending much of the gospel accounts' portrayal of the trial scene, especially as it appears in Mark and as it appears in John's chronology. The blasphemy for him is tied to the messianic claim (and not in the "right hand" remark). In a line of argument I shall trace from here on, Blinzler noted that the key seems to come in the reply which

---

[8]The significance of the crucial temple scroll text has been developed by Betz, "Probleme des Prozesses Jesu," pp. 606-08. Its importance for our topic will become evident as our study proceeds, especially in our final chapter. For how crucifixion came to be read as a fulfillment of Deut 21:22, see David J. Halperin, "Crucifixion, the Nahum Pesher, and the Rabbinic Penalty of Strangulation," JJS 32 (1981):32-46 and M. Hengel, *Crucifixion in the Anicent World and the Folly of the Message of the Cross* (Philadelphia: Fortress, 1977), pp. 71-76, 84, and his *Rabbinische Legende und frühpharisäische Geschichte: Schimeon b. Schetach und die achtig Hexen von Askalon*, AHAW (Heidelberg: Carl Winter/Universitätsverlag, 1984), pp. 27-36, esp. 31-33.

[9]For the *Assumption of Moses* text, Winter noted that it gives evidence of awareness of crucifixion, but not that Jews practiced it. His argument here seems correct about the *AsMos* text, but not about the larger discussion. For this text, see OTP 1:930-31.

[10] Winter, "On the Trial," p. 62.

linked two messianic texts: Ps 110:1 and Dan 7:13, where Jesus says in Mk 14:62 that, "I am, and you will see the Son of Man seated at the right hand of the Power and coming with the clouds of heaven." As Blinzler says,

> Unter Anspielung auf zwei messianische Texte des Alten Testaments stellt er seine machtvolle Wiederkunft zur Rechten Gottes in Aussicht. Damit begegnet er dem zwar nicht direkt ausgesprochenen, aber, wie wir gesehen haben, vorauszusetzenden Einwand, daß sein Messiasanspruch der jeden Zweifel ausschließenden göttlichen Legitimation ermangle . . . .. Da auch das Judentum seinem als Menschen aufgefaßten Messias das Sitzen zur Rechten Gottes und das Kommen auf den Wolken des Himmels zuschrieb, verbietet sich die Annahme, daß die Synedristen aus den Worten Jesu mehr heraushörten als den Anspruch auf die messianische Würde.[11]

So for Blinzler, the key is the claim to be the returning judge at the end. He argued that the rending of the garments after this remark shows how crucial it is. Blinzler preferred Mark's account; argued for one evening meeting; defended the variations from the Mishnah, like *m Sanh* 7.5, as expressive of Sadducean differences from the more benevolent Pharisaic Mishnaic code[12]; expressed uncertainty about an additional Lucan source; critiqued Lietzmann and Winter heavily; and, most significantly, argued that a capital crime could be investigated by the Jews but that they could not execute. This distinction he presented in a long and important excursus.[13] One of the points he made is particularly telling.[14] Citing a discussion that goes back to Friedrich Büchsel, Blinzler noted that the right, which did exist, to execute Gentiles who came into the temple is granted as a clear exception. This is evident from Josephus *JW* 6.126, who notes that Titus is reported to have said, "Have we not given you leave to kill such as go beyond it [i.e., into the temple area], though he were a Roman?" Here Blinzler says "die Ausnahme, die nur die Regel

---

[11]Blinzler, *Der Prozess Jesu*, 4th ed., pp. 158-59.

[12]Blinzler, *Der Prozess Jesu*, 4th ed., pp. 197-98, 227.

[13]Blinzler, *Der Prozess Jesu*, 4th ed., pp. 229-42 (Excursus no. 10).

[14]He also raised the controversial CD 9.1, but this text's translation is too disputed to make much of it. One of the translation options would clearly mean that execution rights are in the hands of Gentiles. Dupont-Sommer, *The Essene Writings from Qumran*, trans. G. Vermes (Gloucester, Mass.: Peter Smith, 1973), p. 148, translates the line, "In all cases when anathema is pronounced against a man, it is by order of the Gentiles that this man shall be put to death." Dupont-Sommer's note suggested a parallel to the remark of Jn 18:31. For the dispute, see also the changed translation of E. Lohse, *Die Texte aus Qumran*, 2nd ed. (München: Kösel, 1971), p. 83 from his first edition in 1964, also p. 83. In the first edition, he translated it much as Dupont-Sommer, but in the second edition he opted to translate it to the effect that any Jew who testifies against a Jew before a gentile judge should be killed. Blinzler notes another translation from Rabbinowitz, "The Meaning and Date of 'Damascus' Document IX,1," RQ 6 (1968):433-35, which goes, "Any man who devotes and destroys a man —'of mankind' [Lev 27,28-29]— because of 'the customs of the nations' [Lev 20,23] is himself to be put to death." The ambiguity of the text means that not much can be made of it.

bestätigt, daß die Juden keine uneingeschränkete Blutgerichtsbarkeit besaßen."[15]

He raises as possible blasphemy texts: *Sifre Num* § 112 on 15:30-31 and *Sifre* § 221 on Deut 21:22. These texts discuss "sins of a high hand," which is the point of the Numbers text. The Num § 112 text notes King Manasseh as an example of blasphemous activity. The text on Deuteronomy notes that death is the sentence for those who threaten "a fundamental principle of faith." Blinzler's discussion is widely regarded as having answered Lietzmann on the issue of Jewish authority over capital crimes.[16] It also began the movement toward considering the historical value of the scene anew.

5. David Catchpole, *The Trial of Jesus* (1971)

This detailed historical study is really an examination of the history of interpretation of the trial scene within Judaism in the last two hundred years. In a departure from other studies, Catchpole turned fresh attention to Luke's account, discussed the issue of the various interpretations of the blasphemy in some detail, and engaged in a tradition historical examination of the material.[17] Unlike many, Catchpole argued that Luke had access to some fresh traditional material that supplemented what Mark used. In fact, he believes that Luke's account is the most careful one historically. This position has

---

[15]Blinzler, *Der Prozess Jesu*, p. 238. See also F. Büchsel, "Die Blutgerichtsbarkeit des Synedrions," ZNW 30 (1931):202-210, esp. 206-07. Blinzler merely paraphrased Büchsel here. The Büchsel article goes through the Lietzmann examples. Another key text that he noted is Josephus, *JW* 6.300-09, where Jesus, son of Ananus, issued prophecies against the people, so the leadership, after flogging him, brought him to the Romans hoping to get a sentence of execution, but they only flogged him. Büchsel argued that had the right of execution existed, there was no need to take the man before the Romans. He also notes that in the case of the execution of James, *Ant* 20:197-203, Josephus speaks of the view of some present that a breach of laws had taken place at his execution and notes that such a gathering of the Sanhedrin was not allowed without Roman permission. This last incident Büchsel discussed again in "Noch einmal: Zur Blutgerichtsbarkeit des Synedrions," ZNW 33 (1934):84-87.

[16]Two summations will suffice. David Catchpole, *The Trial of Jesus: A Study in the Gospels and Jewish Historiography from 1770 to the Present Day*, SPB 18 (Leiden: E. J. Brill, 1971), p. 403 writes, "In sum, the distinction asserted by Blinzler between the right to pass and the right to execute a sentence must be maintained against Winter's amalgamation of the two." The classic historian, A. N. Sherwin-White, *Roman Society and Roman Law in the New Testament* (Oxford: Oxford University Press, 1963), p. 110, states, "The theory of Juster about the capital jurisdiction of the Sanhedrin collapses. And much of the interpretations of Lietzmann and Winter, which are built on it, collapses with it."

[17]David Catchpole, *The Trial of Jesus: A Study in the Gospels and Jewish Historiography from 1770 to the Present Day*, SPB 18 (Leiden: E. J. Brill, 1971), and his "You Have Heard His Blasphemy," TynB 16 (1965):10-18.

received more attention and acceptance in Britain and in North America than in Germany, where discussions still tend to concentrate on Mark.[18] Catchpole, like Blinzler, saw the blasphemy as tied to the Ps 110:1 and Dan 7:13 remark as it relates Jesus' claim to be seated at God's right hand. However, he did not develop in any detail here exactly how this would be seen as blasphemous, except through noting the possible analogy of the rebuke of rabbi Akiba in *b Sanh* 38b, a text I shall discuss in more detail later. Catchpole's work is important, because he raised the question of whether some independent pieces of information about Jesus' meeting with the leadership might be found from tradition outside of that which is present in Mark. In addition, his survey of the options on the nature of the blasphemy represented the state of the discussion at the time he wrote.

6. August Strobel, *Die Stunde der Wahrheit* (1980)

Strobel's study of the trial worked two angles.[19] First, it sought to challenge Lietzmann. Second, it tried to tighten Blinzler's case. Strobel argued that one can make sense of the background to the trial scene from a Jewish perspective by reviewing the evidence Lietzmann tried to bring forth to argue for Jewish authority to issue a capital crime death sentence.[20] Strobel argued that such authority did not exist. He listed a long series of texts and discussed most of them (Josephus, *JW* 6.126; 6.300-09; *Ant* 20.199-206; *Megillat Taanit* 6; *p Sanh* I,18a[37]; VII,24b[43]; *b Aboda Zara* 8b; *m Sanh* 7.2b; Philo, *Embassy to Gaius* §§ 306-07).[21]

---

[18]An exception is G. Schneider, "Gab es eine vorsynoptische Szene "Jeus vor dem Sanhedrin"?" NovT 12 (1970):22-39 and his *Verleugnung, Verspottung, und Verhör Jesu nach Lukas 22,54-71* (München: Kösel, 1969), pp. 105-34. However, he saw a more limited influence of an extra source than Catchpole, seeing its main impact in Lk 22:63-68 rather than running through the whole scene. Catchpole's position was anticipated by J. Tyson, "The Lucan Version of the Trial of Jesus," NovT 3 (1959):249-58. It needs to be noted that the case of whether Luke has access to independent material for the scene that could give more detail is a distinct question from whether Luke is a later, more reflective gospel about Jesus than Mark's. The traditional connection between Peter and Mark is one reason Mark has figured so prominently in recent discussion, along with the view that Mark is the earliest gospel. The debate about whether Mark or Matthew is the earliest gospel does not significantly impact the blasphemy discussion, since in this reply the two accounts are parallel in the essential points. The differences in the gospels in the trial scene center on issue of setting and the prominence given to the temple issue. For these issues, see Darrell L. Bock, *Luke 9:51-24:53* BECNT 3 (Grand Rapids: Baker, 1996), pp. 1775-77.
[19]August Strobel, *Die Stunde der Wahrheit*, WUNT 21 (Tübingen: J. C. B. Mohr [Paul Siebeck], 1980).
[20]Strobel, *Die Stunde der Wahrheit*, pp. 21-45.
[21]For example, he argues that the case of the execution of the priest's daughter as noted in *m Sanh* 7.2 was a case of Judea being between procurators during Agrippa's rule from AD

In an effort to strengthen the case Blinzler made, Strobel added that Deut 13:1-13 is a key text, since it calls for the removing of anyone who deceives the people.[22] He argued for the advantage of this approach to the text in that it need not posit any difference between Sadducean and Pharisaical judicial practice, which he thinks is hard to confirm in a particular instance. In other words, the concern the leadership had about Jesus was not confined to a particular party, and the basis for action had Old Testament roots. The text in Deuteronomy is especially related to the worship of false gods, but as we shall see shortly through Betz's work, its application in the first century was associated with a broader set of concerns. The problem in Strobel's proposal is the stress it puts on the prophetic identification of Jesus' ministry, when there is little of this theme concretely expressed at the trial. For example, the Marcan mocking in 15:16-20 stresses his claim as King of the Jews (so also Mt 27:29), but Lk 22:64 has the mockers call on Jesus to offer prophecy as they blindfold him. The Lucan text comes the closest to connecting to Strobel's emphasis. Also problematic is his hesitation to credit the Sadducees with a harsher position on criminal punishment when Josephus acknowledges their reputation for harshness on such matters (*Ant* 20.199). On the other hand, it must be noted that a strong case can be made from Jesus' ministry as a whole, that he was seen as a prophet and that he had his credentials at this level challenged within official Judaism so that a plausible case can be made for this concern being a factor entering the trial.[23]

Strobel saw the blasphemy as centered in the claim to sit at the right hand from Ps 110:1 and Dan 7:13.[24] He also noted that blasphemy is one of the

---

41-44. See also J. Jeremias, "Zur Geschichtlichkeit des Verhörs Jesu vor dem Hohen Rat," *ZNW* 43 (1950-51):145-50, esp. 146. Jeremias's discussion has much that appears both in Blinzler and Strobel.

[22]Strobel, *Die Stunde der Wahrheit*, pp. 46-61.

[23]Three recent British studies develop this point. D. Neale, "Was Jesus a *Mesith*? Public Response to Jesus and His Ministry," *Tyndale Bulletin* 44 (1993):89-101; G. Stanton, "Jesus of Nazareth: A Magician and a False Prophet Who Deceived God's People?" in *Jesus of Nazareth Lord and Christ: Essays on the Historical Jesus and New Testament Christology* (Grand Rapids: Wm. B. Eerdmans, 1994), pp. 164-80; N. T. Wright, *Jesus and the Victory of God* (Minneapolis: Fortress Press, 1996), pp. 149-474, esp. 439-42. Stanton, who is more circumspect than Strobel, argues that Mark and Q independently attest to a charge against Jesus of being a magician, while Matthew, John, and probably Luke are aware of the charge. He suggests that though the specific charge of being a false prophet-deceiver is lacking, the cumulative evidence makes it a "strong probability" (see p. 179). It should be noted that something like this charge may well be reflected in Lk 23:2.

[24]Strobel notes Paul Billerbeck's position in S-B vol. 1, pp. 1017. Billerbeck focuses on the Ps 110:1 reference and says, "Daß im Gegensatz hierzu Jesus scheinbar aus eigener Machtvollkommenheit heraus u. ohne göttliche Autorisation in der übersinnlichen Welt den ihm gebührenden Platz zur Rechten des Allmacht einnehmen u. von dort aus überweltlich, kommend auf den Wolken des Himmels, seine Herrschaft als Messias ausüben will— das ist

reasons one rends clothing, as indicated in *b Moed Katan* 26a. In placing himself as judge over the Jewish high court, Jesus makes a remark that is seen as an affront against the Torah and the leadership.[25] The remark was also a prophetic warning. A key element of the reply is the binding of exaltation and return. Jesus is condemned for blasphemy and is hanged according to Deut 21:23 as a blasphemer and idolater. Deut 13 stands in the background as a key text. He concludes, "Aus solcher früher Auslegungsgeschichte von Deut 21,23 geht ebenfalls hervor, daß die Kreuzigung Jesu (in Verbindung mit der Aufhängung für einen Tag!) zwingend auf den jüdischen Verurteilungsgrund Jesu, Lästerer und Götzendiener nach Deut 13 gewesen zu sein, zurückweist."[26]

7. Otto Betz, "Probleme des Prozesses Jesu" (1982)

This detailed survey of Jewish background and its contribution to the trial accounts serve independently to supplement and strengthen aspects of Strobel's study.[27] He decisively defended the unity of Mark in the face of Lietzmann's attempt to reject Mark. Betz noted how well the account fits in the context of Jewish background and explained how the temple question leads logically into the messianic question. He surveyed the work of Josephus and Qumran and then turned to the NT. He argued that Jesus' teaching risked bringing Roman power more comprehensively into Jerusalem and the temple, putting the people of Israel at risk. Jn 11:48-50 reveals the fear explicitly, when Caiaphas argues that a released Jesus means that all will turn to him and Rome will come and take away what power and rights remain in Judea.[28] This risk to the people meant that Jesus' remarks about a claim of Messiah could be called blasphemy. Betz presented *11QTem* 64:7-13 as a key text, since it calls for those who slander or curse the people or bring the people into danger to be "hanged on wood" and then die. The allusion in the Temple scroll is to a combination from Deut 13 and 18:15-19; as well as to 21:22-23. The text from Deut 21:22-23 has the order of death and then hanging for display, but

---

es, was dem Hohenpriester als eine Antastung der göttlichen Majestät erscheint u. ihn zu dem Urteil veranlaßt: er hat (Gott) gelästert."

[25]On this point Strobel follows R. Pesch, *Das Markusevangelium*, HKNT II, 1-2 (Freiburg: Herder, 1976-1977), 2.437-38.

[26]Strobel, *Die Stunde der Wahrheit*, p. 94.

[27]Otto Betz, "Probleme des Prozesses Jesu," in ANRW II. 25.1 (Berlin: Walter De Gruyter, 1982). As n. 7 already discussed, Betz worked independently of Strobel and actually wrote his material before Strobel did, so the description of "supplement" for this work portrays the effect of Betz's work given the timing of its publication. In fact, what seems to have taken place was an independent parallel development of this theme.

[28]Betz, "Probleme des Prozesses Jesu," pp. 601-03.

the order of death by hanging was accepted by the time of the Temple scroll. This first century reading meant that a crucifixion could reflect this penalty and would be seen as an equivalent to what Deuteronomy calls for as punishment.[29] Betz's point about those putting the people at risk being subject to death introduced an important variation to Strobel's approach. The particular risk Jesus' teaching brings for the nation, alongside his messianic pretensions, places him, in the leadership's view, within the scope of Deut 13. Thus, it is not the claim to be messiah that is blasphemous, but the particularly threatening form of messianism that is the point of contention. For Betz, Jesus is seen as a false prophet through *the risk* his messianic claim and actions raise for the nation as a major disturber of Roman peace. The interrogation at the trial only underscores this perception of him; so, for Betz, the details of the interrogation are not as important as its logical unity in moving from the question of temple to Messiah. He concludes,

> Das nächtliche Verhör ergab, daß Jesus sich tatsächlich für den Messias hielt und von dieser als gefährlich beurteilten Vorstellung selbt dann nicht abließ, als alles gegen sie sprach. Nach Ansicht der Richter bezog er die Weissagung 2. Samuel 7 zu Unrecht auf sich, weil in ihr vom davidischen Gottessohn verheißen wird, Gottes Gnade solle nicht von ihm weichen (2. Samuel 7,15). Deshalb mußte der verhaftete Jesus als ein falscher Prophet und Verführer gelten, der nach der Tora keine Schonung verdient (Deuteronomium 13,9). Von diesem Urteil der sadduzäischen Justiz wurde er von allem deshalb betroffen, weil sein Anspruch den Tempel und das jüdische Volk in ihrer Existenz bedrohten.[30]

As a result, Betz also noted the expectation that Messiah will rebuild the temple (2 Sam 7:13-14-with its movement from temple to sonship; *Shemoneh Esreh* [18 Benedictions] 14- calls on God to rebuild everlasting Jerusalem and raise up David's throne; *b Pesaḥ* 5a).[31] This expectation led Betz to argue that the temple-Messiah sequence of Mark makes consummate sense historically. In Mark the temple charge, even though it collapses in the light of the variant testimony, naturally raises the question, Is Jesus the Messiah who will rebuild the temple (*4QFlor*)? Jesus' reply is blasphemous in general terms, because it shows how dangerous Jesus is (in the tribunal's view) as he makes such a false claim of authority. Jesus is hanged as a seducer of Israel. For Betz, Mark is the oldest, most significant account. Betz's work makes two key points: 1)

---

[29]Betz, "Probleme des Prozesses Jesu," pp. 603-12. See n. 8 above.

[30]Betz, "Probleme des Prozesses Jesu," p. 639.

[31]Blessing 14 reads, "And to Jerusalem, thy city, return with mercy and dwell in its midst as thou hast spoken; and build it soon in our days to be an everlasting building; and raise up quickly in its midst the throne of David. Blessed are thou, Lord, who buildest Jerusalem." For this translation, see Schürer's *The History of the Jewish People in the Age of Jesus Christ*, rev ed., G. Vermes, F. Millar, M. Black, eds. (Edinburgh: T & T Clark, 1979), 2:458.

it shows the unity and coherence of the Marcan account in its historical context and 2) it reveals a better point of contact with the nature of the blasphemy, since the messianic aspect of Jesus' claim comes more into view than any prophetic association. What is not as clear is why the high priest rips his clothes when he does within the trial scene. What specifically triggers this reaction? Betz's study sets some of the background for the reaction, but is more detail possible?

8. E. P. Sanders, *Jesus and Judaism* (1985)

Sanders' study represents the best recent summary of an approach that is still heavily critical of the Marcan scene.[32] He rejected the historicity of the trial scene in the tradition of Lietzmann, showing that recent developments have not stopped the debate.

He claims there are 7 difficulties.[33] They are: 1) Nothing in Jesus' ministry (except the problematic triumphal entry) explains the raising of the question, "Are you the Christ, the Son of God?"; 2) The gospels are reluctant to have Jesus admit to the charge of being the Christ and the Son of God, though the evangelists certainly believed it. Only Mk 14:62 makes a clear affirmation. Though one could argue a motive that seeks to prevent Jesus being seen as guilty, it is more likely that blasphemy was not firmly rooted in the tradition; 3) The exchanges between Jesus and the high priest, especially in Matthew and Mark, do not carry conviction. Sanders' focus on Matthew and Mark shows how Catchpole's raising of the partial independence of Luke has registered in some later discussions. The examination is likely to have started with the temple charge, but it ends up being dropped. No basis exists for a blasphemy charge in the trial scene. Sanders says, "The issue in which Matthew and Mark is said to lead to the charge of blasphemy, Jesus' being Christ (Messiah) and Son of God, is not compelling."[34]; 4) What chain of

---

[32] E. P. Sanders, *Jesus and Judaism* (Philadelphia: Fortress, 1985), pp. 296-306

[33] Sanders, *Jesus and Judaism*, pp.297-99.

[34] Sanders, *Jesus and Judaism*, p. 297. On pp. 297-98, Sanders continues to explain, "For one thing, the combination of the two appellations looks more like a Christian one than a Jewish one: outside the Christian movement there is no evidence for the combination of 'Messiah' and 'Son of God'. Further, as is widely recognized, neither phrase points towards blasphemy. We need not accept the Rabbinic definition of blasphemy, (pronouncing the explicit name: Sanh. 7.5) in order to rule out 'Messiah' and 'Son of God' as blasphemous claims. Subsequent would-be Messiahs were not charged with blasphemy, and 'son of God' might mean almost anything. All Israelites can be said to be 'sons of God' (see e. g. Rom. 9.4), and it is only the subsequent Christian claim that Jesus himself was divine that clearly constitutes blasphemy." It should be noted, however, that none of the studies claiming to be able to describe the blasphemy see the blasphemy as merely present in the adoption of a title, but in the function and context in which that title is used. It is a valuable characteristic of the

transmission existed for the trial? It is hard, though not impossible, to imagine what that chain would be. No disciples were present; 5) Would a formal court actually convene on the first night of Passover, as Matthew and Mark have it? Luke has only a morning meeting, while John has no Sanhedrin trial at all; 6) Two trials, as Matthew and Mark suggest, is even less likely. In fact, for many, all the night trial of Matthew and Mark looks like is an expansion of the summary note about a trial in Mt 27:1 and Mk 15:1; and 7) The gospels have a theological motive to incriminate the Jews and exculpate the Romans. The account serves to shift the blame in an official way.

Sanders is aware of Blinzler, Strobel, and Catchpole (he notes them as among those who still defend the scene today), but he does not really engage their argument in any substance, except for attempting to challenge, through Harvey's critique, Strobel's understanding of the deceiver charge.[35] Sanders and Harvey argued that there is no reason to suggest that "false prophet" was the formal charge sustained by the Sanhedrin, and they went on to note that the Talmudic passages that treat Jesus as a deceiver also say that he was hanged. (The key text is *b Sanh* 43a). Sanders asks, "Is the conviction as deceiver more likely than execution by hanging?"[36] What the question begs, however, is whether what the Talmudic texts meant by hanging involved using the biblical expression "hang" for any type of execution that represented a capital crime.[37] Sanders summarizes his view as follows: "All we need do is to accept the obvious, that we do not have detailed knowledge of what happened when the high priest and possibly others questioned Jesus. We cannot know even that 'the Sanhedrin' met. Further, I doubt that the earliest followers of Jesus knew . . .. Scholars will continue to dissect the

---

third quest not to isolate sayings and titles from their context or their functional role, as is often done in such arguments about authenticity.

[35]A. E. Harvey, *Jesus and the Constraints of History* (Philadelphia: Westminster, 1982), p. 59.

[36]Sanders, *Jesus and Judaism*, p. 408, n. 29.

[37]It is true that the Sanhedrin text mentions stoning when the herald is announcing the sentence and is looking for defense witnesses, none of which are found after forty days. But both times the text describes the death of Jesus in summary form, it uses the term hanged, as it also mentions the death's timing in association with the Passover feast. On the possibility of having this meaning, see David J. Halperin, "Crucifixion, the Nahum Pesher, and the Rabbinic Penalty of Strangulation," JJS 32 (1981): 32-46, who notes that the phrase in texts like the *4QpNah* 2:11-13 means to "hang alive" (*yitleh 'anashim hayyim*), which is clearly an allusion to crucifixion. He also refers to the Palestinian Targum to Num 25:4 (= *Neofiti, Ps-J,* and *Frag Targ.*) and to Targum Ruth 1:17 and notes that the Temple scroll (v. 22) would permit such a reading. He notes on p. 45 that the talmudic text sees stoning and then the crucifixion as "a suspension following execution by stoning." Interestingly, Halperin takes Winter on directly at this point (see pp. 36-37, 45, n. 66). On this, see also Hengel, *Rabbinische Legende und frühpharisäische Geschichte*, pp. 31-33.

accounts of the 'trial', but I fear that our knowledge will not be greatly advanced."[38]

Sanders rejected the deceiver category as significant because there is no evidence in the Marcan trial scene itself that this category was applied. But one must be careful to distinguish between the thought world of what the leadership might be fearing (the risk to Israel that Betz mentions) and the formal charge raised to get Jesus before Rome. The very political charge of Lk 23:2 suggests that the deceiver charge framed in a political way *does* show up in the tradition. It becomes the concrete way to express the blasphemy of the initial trial. Catchpole's argument about the possibility of independent tradition in Luke may well indicate that we should be careful of an unwritten rule that says, "if it is not in Mark, it cannot count in the historical discussion."

9. Martin Hengel, "'Sit at My Right Hand!': The Enthronement of Christ and the Right Hand of God" (1991, 1995)

Hengel's work involves a careful survey of the uses of the "seated at the right hand imagery" throughout Judaism and early Christian tradition. He works from Old Testament texts like Ps 110:1 through the New Testament to heavenly throne tradition in Judaism.[39] Hengel argued, as Catchpole did, that the key to the blasphemy is found in the Ps 110:1 and Dan 7:13 remark. He argued for the value of 1 Enoch and the Similitudes section for showing the Jewish character of the imagery (*1 En* 51:3; 55:4; 61:8; 62:2).[40] Here is a figure whose authority becomes like that of God in exercising end time judgment. That this section of 1 Enoch (*1 En* 37 – 71) was missing at Qumran is no problem for a first century AD dating of 1 Enoch's Similitudes material, since many Jewish documents were not found there. There may even be mutual influence. Though Hengel does not note it in his article, he reminded me in one of our discussions on this issue, that such a combination is possible within Judaism and available to Jesus as can be seen by Akiba's reflection on Dan 7:9 in *b Sanh* 38b. This text is also noted in the next study by Gundry and shall receive careful attention in chapter three.

The reply at the trial is not a construct of Mark, but reflects an old form of christology, connecting exaltation and parousia. Indications of its age are: 1)

---

[38]Sanders, *Jesus and Judaism*, p. 299.

[39] Martin Hengel, "Setze dich zu Meiner Rechten. Die Inthroniation Christi zur rechten Gottes und Psalm 110.1," in M. Philonenko, ed., *Le Thrône de Dieu* WUNT 69 (Tübingen: J. C. B. Mohr [Paul Siebeck], 1991). It was translated for his *Studies in Early Christology* (Edinburgh: T & T Clark, 1995), pp. 119-225. I will refer to the latest English edition, for which the key portion for this topic is pp. 175-203.

[40]Hengel, *Studies in Early Christology*, pp. 185-89.

the use of a circumlocution for God and 2) the statement that Sanhedrin members will see Jesus as coming on the clouds, which does not reflect an AD 70 perspective. So the reply is part of a pre-Marcan PN. Whether these are the words of Jesus or he said something similar cannot be proven, but he "seems to have provoked them with an indication of his 'messianic-judgmental' authority that they delivered him as a messianic pretender to Pilate . . . . The statement is   . . . not only a claim to authority, but at the same time a word of the accused to his accusers."[41] Thus, without necessarily defending the *ipsissima verba* here, Hengel argued that the account reflects a summarization that certainly fits well into Jewish background, a point that would counter Sander's rejection of the possibility of a plausible ground for the blasphemy existing in the account. Hengel shows us a zeroing in on Ps 110:1 and Dan 7:13 as the key point when it comes to the blasphemy. He also noted Jesus' attack on the leadership as a key additional factor to consider, a combination Strobel also observed.

10. Robert Gundry, *Mark: A Commentary on His Apology for the Cross* (1993)

This commentary contains a particularly full discussion of the trial scene and thus merits inclusion, even though it is not a special study of the question.[42] Gundry argued that the divine Name was pronounced at the trial, but was suppressed as is common in public reports of blasphemy (*m Sanh* 7.5).[43] The mishnaic text notes that a euphemism, "may Jose smote Jose," is used in the public portion of the trial, while the actual blasphemy using God's name is only repeated by the witnesses in private. This means that the divine Name could have been used during the citation of Ps 110:1, but that it may not have been reported as used when the scene was summarized. Thus we read the use of the circumlocution "right hand of the Power" in Mk 14:62.

The juxtaposition of sitting at the right hand and coming on the clouds is unattested in non-dominical NT materials and so is likely to be authentic. Jesus arrogated to himself divine roles in claiming to be able to destroy the temple and build another one, but the temple charge is characterized as false. So this is not key, though such sayings may have been the occasion for arresting Jesus.[44] Gundry concludes, "We may think that the high priest and the rest of the Sanhedrin judge Jesus to have verbally robbed God of

---

[41]Hengel, *Studies in Early Christology*, p. 187.

[42]Robert Gundry, *Mark: A Commentary on His Apology for the Cross* (Grand Rapid: Wm. B. Eerdmans, 1993), pp. 883-922.

[43]Gundry, *Mark: A Commentary on His Apology for the Cross*, pp. 915-18.

[44]Gundry, *Mark: A Commentary on His Apology for the Cross*, pp. 900-06.

incommensurateness and unity by escalating himself to a superhuman level, by portraying himself as destined to sit at God's right hand and come with the clouds of heaven . . .."[45] He also notes the Akiba parallel from *b Sanh* 38b, where the rabbi says that David is said to sit by the Shekinah, a remark that gets a stern rebuke from rabbi Jose. Again it is Ps 110:1 and Dan 7:13 that are seen as key.

What is emerging is a developing consensus that the key to the blasphemy resides not in the mere use of a title, but in the juxtaposition of Ps 110:1 with Dan 7:13 to apply to a human figure an unusually high level of heavenly authority. The Akiba parallel is significant in showing how such a claim to sit by God was viewed. However, it should also be noted that others saw Akiba's contemplation of exaltation for an old luminary as dangerous and highly offensive. Still it was less than immediate blasphemy, because it was merely reported as a held view that required a warning. The possibility of such an exaltation would seem to fit even more with the case of the positive presence of the seated imagery in 1 Enoch, where the thought of one positioned in heaven to render judgment is affirmed because a luminary of old is in view (apparently Enoch according to 1 En 71:14). It should be noted, however, that there is no explicit seating language used for Enoch; the association of him with the seating of the Elect One/Son of Man implies it.

11. Raymond Brown, *The Death of the Messiah* (1994)

In his full study of the passion, Brown listed the options scholars have suggested for the basis of the blasphemy, a list similar to the one Catchpole made in 1965.[46] He discussed five options.

1) Some argue it is in the claim to be Messiah. But Brown argued that this is not blasphemous, as the numerous messianic claimants of the period show.

2) Some suggest the claim of Son of God is the source of the charge. But Brown rejects the use of the title by Jesus or his followers during his lifetime, so this claim is also rejected.

3) Others see the blasphemy in the claim to be Son of Man. This title, Brown thinks, Jesus did use in his lifetime, but it is not clear what he meant by it. In addition, the claim to sit might be a point of departure, but the Akiba remark in *b Sanh* 38b shows that this is not blasphemous to claim. More potential exists for an exalted claim related to Dan 7 and the clouds, but it alone is not enough. Brown says, "One would be imprudent to base the

---

[45]Gundry, *Mark: A Commentary on His Apology for the Cross*, p. 917.

[46]Raymond E. Brown, *The Death of the Messiah*, 2 vol., ABRL (New York: Doubleday, 1994), pp. 520-47, esp. pp. 534-44.

historicity of the Jewish charge of blasphemy on that alone."[47] He suggested that since the idea for such a figure exists in Dan 7, the idea itself, and thus Jesus' claim, is not blasphemous. Even 1 Thes 4:17 suggests that believers will be taken up in the clouds. This last argument is not particularly persuasive, since it is a Christian claim and there is only ascension into God's presence in view, not an exercise of judicial authority as Jesus claimed.

4) Others argue for a key in the destruction of the temple claim. Here Brown cited Betz's work, though with not quite the nuance Betz gave this argument. Brown argues that this temple element was a part of the proceedings, but that "none of the parallels cited above where serious action was taken on Temple issues states that blasphemy was involved."

5) Then there is the charge of false prophet. Brown noted Strobel's case in detail, but also discussed the lack of direct evidence of Jesus presenting himself as a prophet, though one should note that Jesus is mocked as a false prophet by those who detained him (Mk 14:65). This critique of Strobel, which Sanders had noted already, seemed to be a gap in Strobel's view that Betz's view attempted to fill. Both Sanders and Brown seem to have missed this development in the argument, which turns the charge in a more messianic direction and relates it to threats against the nation. Brown concludes: "In summation, it is possible that the main blasphemous charge against Jesus, especially in the mind of religious Jews, was that he was a false prophet; but once again evidence falls far short of establishing this point."[48] However, as was noted already in the discussion of Strobel, work subsequent to the critique of Sanders and Brown has addressed this question of a lack of evidence for charges against a prophetic Jesus in a more substantive manner and has provided a stronger basis for considering this approach.[49]

Earlier in his lexical survey of the meaning of blasphemy in Judaism Brown had argued, "From the attested meanings of the *blasphēm-* words, *the only likely historical charge would have been that Jesus arrogantly claimed for himself status or privileges that belonged properly to God alone and in that sense implicitly demeaned God* (italics his)."[50] However, since none of the trial remarks seem exactly to fit, where could the charge lie? Brown ended his discussion with a list of things from Jesus' ministry that together might by

---

[47]Brown, *The Death of the Messiah*, p. 538.

[48]Brown, *The Death of the Messiah*, p. 544.

[49]See n. 23 above for the work of Neale, Stanton, and Wright, all of whom address this question in detail.

[50]Brown, *The Death of the Messiah*, p. 531. Brown cites Lev 24:16, Ex 22:27, Num 15:30, CD 5.11, Tosefta *Sanh 1.2*, *b Sanh 56a*, *Sifre* on Deut 21:22 (#221), Philo, *Life of Moses* 2.206, Bel 9 ϴ, Philo, *Special Laws* 1.53, Philo, *Decalogue* 19.93, Josephus, *Apion* 2.237, 2 Macc 9:28, 2 Kgs 19:4, 6, 22, Philo, *On Dreams* 2.123-31, and Philo, *Embassy to Gaius* 368. This is the best short survey of blasphemy in Judaism currently in print and it stands behind Brown's definition noted here.

implication lead to a feeling he had blasphemed if he did or said most of them: amen sayings, claims to forgive sin, healing while claiming arrival of God's kingdom, proclaiming judgment if one does not respond to him, teaching on law, teaching on temple, his refusal merely to be portrayed as a prophet, his use of Abba, and his use of son language. Nevertheless, Brown's conclusion to this discussion is very vague regarding the specifics of the blasphemy. He seems to have opted for blasphemy at the level of Jesus' ministry considered as a whole, an even broader variation of a type of generalized blasphemy like Betz argued for when he focused on the messianic threat and not any particular saying in the Jewish examination scene. Brown concludes his entire discussion with, "If in his lifetime Jesus plausibly did or said most of these things, I see little reason to doubt that his opponents would have considered him blasphemous (i.e., arrogantly claiming prerogatives or status more properly associated with God), even as the Gospels report at the trial."[51] One has the sense that the blasphemy question is not entirely resolved for him, except in a general way, though, in contrast to Sanders, he does not seem to rule out the possibility of finding the question's resolution in the sources we possess.

12. J. C. O'Neill, *Who Did Jesus Think He Was?* (1995)

J. C. O'Neill's work is a study of the self-consciousness of Jesus that argues that the tendency of New Testament scholars to assume an adoptionistic christology from texts like Rom 1:2-4 and Acts 2:36 has led christology down the wrong path for the last hundred years.[52] In making his case that Jesus had a messianic consciousness, O'Neill inevitably turned to the trial scene. For O'Neill, the key to the blasphemy was that Judaism possessed an expectation that the Messiah would remain "hidden;" he could not claim for himself to be the Messiah until the Father had clearly spoken.[53] The Messiah was to be revealed, and so people had to look for the "signs of the times." As Josephus shows, messianic claimants performed acts, but did not claim to be Messiah (Athronges, *Ant* 17.280 dons a diadem). A claimant approached Jerusalem like a king and went into the temple wearing royal robes (Manahem, the son of Judas the Galilean, *JW* 2.433-34, 444); or ruled their band like a king (Simon bar Giora, *JW* 4.510). They might claim prophetic gifts, but would make no messianic claims (The Samaritan figure of *Ant* 18.85-89 or Jesus, son of Ananus, who prophesied the temple's destruction, *JW* 6.300-09). So

---

[51]Brown, *The Death of the Messiah*, p. 547.
[52]J. C. O'Neill, *Who Did Jesus Think He Was?* BIS 11 (Leiden: E. J. Brill, 1995).
[53]O'Neill, *Who Did Jesus Think He Was?*, pp. 42-54, esp. p. 48.

O'Neill argues that, "The blasphemy lay in *saying* one was the Messiah."[54] Jesus is "guilty of the capital crime of saying himself that he was the Messiah."[55] O'Neill argued for a morning trial that the gospels make look like an evening trial because the evangelists weave it together with Peter's evening denials. He noted that the predicting of the temple's destruction was not blasphemous, as prophets had done that before (or Jesus, son of Ananus, did later).

In responding to the idea that the blasphemy is tied to Jesus' claim to be seated at the right hand of God, he rejected the claim I made about the blasphemy being related to the Son of Man's seating. His premise was that the idea exists in 1 Enoch, so it would not be a blasphemous idea.[56] This critique, which on the surface appears to have merit, however, understated the view I hold, since it is not the claim alone that is the issue but the fact that a current living person, who is perceived as deceiving the people, is making the claim. Such a claim might be possible for a previously exalted luminary like Elijah (or for that matter, David or Moses), but not for a living, Galilean teacher. Three texts, out of several which discuss exalted figures, stand closest to Jesus' claim. One is the Akiba text from *b Ḥag* 14a and *b Sanh* 38b, which was noted above. It involved David. The second is the 1 Enoch texts that O'Neill noted and the third is a text concerning Moses, where he sits on God's throne to observe some events and serve as judge in *The Exagoge of Ezekiel* 67-89. All these texts look to past luminaries to perform the special role. None involve direct self-claims, but at most they report the experiences that placed the person in the role described.[57] O'Neill is right to discuss and

---

[54]O'Neill, *Who Did Jesus Think He Was?*, p. 49.

[55]O'Neill, *Who Did Jesus Think He Was?*, p. 48. It is the self claim that is offensive.

[56]O'Neill, *Who Did Jesus Think He Was?*, p. 52, n. 23. My approach to the problem was introduced in my essay in "The Son of Man Seated at God's Right Hand and the Debate over Jesus' Blasphemy" in *Jesus of Nazareth Lord and Christ: Essays on the Historical Jesus and New Testament Christology* (Grand Rapids: Wm. B. Eerdmans, 1994), pp. 181-91. Written in 1992, it was the first study that led me into this monograph's topic. In it I argued, as several others have, that the key to the blasphemy is the combination citation of Ps 110:1 and Dan 7:13. Then I argued that in the conceptual world of Judaism, the claim *by a contemporary* to sit by God in heaven would be seen as blasphemous, because it was worse than claiming that he would walk into the Holy of Holies and sit by the Shekinah. The article discussed the concept of God's holiness, blasphemy in the first century, and the fact that the temple was seen as a model of God's heavenly presence. These conceptions stand as the world view basis behind the perception of offense. I still think the substance of the article, in terms of the background perceptions, is sound, though more nuancing is necessary, which this monograph seeks to develop.

[57]These texts receive careful treatment and evaluation in chapter 3. I hope to show how rare the claim to sit at God's side in heaven is in the face of many Jewish texts that discuss exalted figures. It will develop lines of argumentation that Martin Hengel made in his study of exaltation to the right hand noted above.

focus upon the importance of a self-claim, but I am not sure the messianic element is the entire key to the equation.

O'Neill correctly observed that blasphemy is not limited to just using the divine Name (*m Sanh* 7.5), since idolatry was seen as blasphemous (Isa 65:7; Ezek 20:27-28). Here the violation is of Deut 13:5, which is codified in *m Sanh* 11.5 – "he that prophesies what he has not heard and what has not been told him" is to be put to death. Interestingly, O'Neill, in citing this line and applying it to Jesus' messianic claim, has to add a phrase to the line to make his point, i.e., "what has not been told him *to tell*."[58] He argued that Jesus "was condemned as a false prophet who blasphemed by saying what God had decreed he was not to say."[59] He went on to argue that Jesus was misunderstood, since the reply using the Son of Man was ambiguous, rather than being a clear self reference.[60]

Accepting for the moment O'Neill's premise about a silent messiah, one can still ask questions to challenge his point. Had not Jesus been revealed by his acts by this point, so he would now be free to speak (not only baptism, and acts of ministry, especially those tied to works of forgiving sins, but also triumphal entry and temple cleansing)? O'Neill has some important things to say about the background of blasphemy for the trial scene, adding points of support to Strobel's and Betz's emphasis on the messianic offense, but his "silent" Messiah approach does not seem viable. In other words, if concepts like those in *m Sanh* 11.5 — concerning a false prophet — were applied to Jesus, it was not because Jesus merely dared to make a messianic claim, when he needed to be silent, but because his messianic claim was perceived for clear reasons to be false and risky.

13. C. A. Evans, "In What Sense 'Blasphemy'?: Jesus before Caiaphas in Mark 14:61-64" (1995)

Evans' essay is part of a collection of studies that treat a variety of historical issues tied to Jesus.[61] He argued that the blasphemy was not the promise of temple destruction, as that charge had conflicting witnesses and comes to nothing in the account; nor was it a messianic seating at the right hand, since he could have been understood to be speaking only in a messianic sense; nor was it the possible use of the divine Name in the reply, since it would have

---

[58]O'Neill, *Who Did Jesus Think He Was?*, p. 53.

[59]O'Neill, *Who Did Jesus Think He Was?*, p. 54.

[60]O'Neill, *Who Did Jesus Think He Was?*, pp. 122-32.

[61]C. A. Evans, "In What Sense 'Blasphemy'?: Jesus before Caiaphas in Mark 14:61-64," in his *Jesus and His Contemporaries: Comparative Studies*. AGAJU 25 (Köln: E. J. Brill, 1995), pp. 407-34.

only appeared as part of the citation of Scripture.[62] The key to the charge must be found elsewhere.

That key is the juxtaposition of Ps 110:1 with Dan 7:13, of sitting and coming: ". . . it is in this odd juxtaposition that we probably have found our solution, for surely Jesus' claim to share God's throne and to come in judgment upon Caiaphas and the Temple establishment would have prompted the High Priest to accuse Jesus of blasphemy, whether or not the Divine Name was pronounced." He adds, " . . . such a claim would have qualified as blasphemy according to the usage of the word in the writings in Philo and Josephus."[63] Unfortunately, Evans did not note which specific blasphemy texts he had in mind, and his earlier summation of blasphemy did not note any texts that directly apply, unless they are contained within the article references he made to the lexical study of Beyer or to Sander's summary.[64] He did cite four examples from *Against Apion* that he says argue that "blasphemy constituted words or actions contemning [*sic-* condemning] what was regarded as sacred, particularly God himself."[65] Yet these citations, along with the others he noted from Josephus and Philo, lack a single reference that is being applied to God (*Apion* 1.59- refers to slanders against Israel; 1.223- to Israel; 1.279- to Moses; 2.143- to Apion). Though his point is, I believe, correct, his citations do not show it. Evans concludes, "Jesus' claim would have been understood as denigrating God and as threatening the High Priest, Israel's ruler."[66] He also saw a potential parallel in the Akiba example from *b Ḥag* 14a and *b Sanh* 38b.

Evans' study is another indication of a growing consensus among many scholars that the key to the blasphemy resides in the functions Jesus claims through the combination of Ps 110:1 and Dan 7:13. Among many students of this history, there is a growing sense that this saying is a crucial key to the solving the riddle of Jesus' blasphemy.

14. Conclusion

We have traced the major lines of study concerning the nature of Jesus' blasphemy through much of this century. Lietzmann's shadow of skepticism is receding as the possibility of a potential answer to the blasphemy question

---

[62]The issue of how the divine Name is quoted from Scripture in this period will be considered in chapter 4.

[63]Evans, "In What Sense 'Blasphemy'?: Jesus before Caiaphas in Mark 14:61-64," p. 423.

[64]Evans, "In What Sense 'Blasphemy'?: Jesus before Caiaphas in Mark 14:61-64, pp. 409-11; H. W. Beyer, βλασφημέω, κ. τ. λ., TDNT 1: 621-25 and E. P. Sanders, *Jewish Law From Jesus to the Mishnah: Five Studies*" (London: SCM Press, 1990), pp. 57-60.

[65]Evans, "In What Sense 'Blasphemy'?: Jesus before Caiaphas in Mark 14:61-64," p. 410.

[66]Evans, "In What Sense 'Blasphemy'?: Jesus before Caiaphas in Mark 14:61-64," p. 423.

emerges. The juxtaposition of Ps 110:1 and Dan 7:13 is being repeatedly pointed to as a key productive avenue for study. However, caution is still required. Three factors still need careful consideration. First, a thorough study of blasphemy is required. Beyer in TDNT, 1:621-25, did the last full-scale study. What is lacking in many discussions is a detailed look at blasphemy in Judaism, something beyond a handful of references. A comprehensive survey is needed to show the character of what is culturally conceived of as blasphemy. Brown's examination comes the closest to giving a survey, while Beyer in TDNT fails to discuss the evidence from Judaism thoroughly enough with reference to this scene. Second, there needs to be consideration of how Jesus' claim of exaltation fits within the sphere of Judaism. How unusual was his claim? Third, it must be remembered that the idea of a single reason for the charge of blasphemy may risk oversimplifying the problem. What may need more serious consideration is not the mere use of a title or presence of a claim, but recognition that such claims were processed through the sieve of worldview issues as well as a sequence of events within the life of Jesus. The complex interplay of several factors together may explain why the text sets the story out as it does.[67]

The tendency of Jesus scholarship today to divide stories into small units and analyze them in small, independent pieces may break up these larger life sequences in ways that obscure the complexity of the background rather than enabling us to see it more clearly. It is here that the more general approach of Betz, Strobel, and Brown, with their sensitivity to considering how a unit fits into a larger social and cultural whole, issues a warning as we pursue the answer to this question. The fact that this study focuses on an event at the end of Jesus' ministry gives us some advantage in overcoming the difficult historical questions the gospels often leave unanswered about the relationship

---

[67]One example of another attempt to be sensitive to such multiple concerns is the work by Bruce Chilton, *The Temple of Jesus: His Sacrificial Program Within a Cultural History of Sacrifice* (University Park, Penn: Pennsylvania State University Press, 1992). His pursuit of the role of purity, table fellowship, and sacrifice as a key background to what the Jews found offensive about Jesus pursues a perspective that interacts with the thrust of his entire ministry as it surrounds key events. He argues that in the background to the temple scene and the Jewish reaction to it stood Jesus' challenge on the issue of purity, fellowship and sacrifice. Such a challenge led Jesus to institute an alternative meal which represented a pure meal in contrast to the impure sacrifices of the Temple. Chilton sees Jesus as guilty of blasphemy in the leadership's eyes because he was constructing an alternative cult. In the midst of his argument, Chilton suggests that blasphemy had a broader scope in early Judaism than either the formal criterion of *m Sanh* 7.5 suggests or the attempt to find the answer at the level of christology (see pp. 153-54, and n 31). The question about the scope of blasphemy is the burden of the next chapter. On the issue of christology and method, see n 69 below. I treat Chilton here, because his discussion, though important, only treats the examination scene tangentially. His work may suggest a reason why the leadership was so disturbed by Jesus as the scene begins.

of events to one another, since the decisive events that led to Jesus' death belong to a rather tight sequence of the last week of his life. The chapters that follow will take up each of these three concerns in turn, considering blasphemy, exaltation and the Jewish examination of Jesus. The study hopes to demonstrate that the Marcan scene possesses a coherence that fits historical verisimilitude. That is not to argue that the case is proved that all the details of this text are historical, for that requires pursuing the answer to the many additional questions I raised at the start of this chapter.[68] However, it does mean that one can show that at the point of the scene's highest controversy, it makes historical sense in the world of second temple Judaism.

In sum, I am going to agree with the line taken by Catchpole, Hengel, Gundry and C. A. Evans, the roots of which go back at least to Billerbeck. I shall argue also that the key to understanding the blasphemy is the juxtaposition of Ps 110:1 and Dan 7:13. Jesus' claim to be a heavenly judge is not only an example of personal self exaltation in the leadership's view, but it also represents an attack on the Jewish leadership as implicitly guilty for putting Jesus on trial. *Both* elements would be seen as blasphemous, an attack on God's unique honor *and* an attack on his leaders. I also think that the fear of risk to the nation, as Betz has noted, is very much in play in the background. For the leadership Jesus was extremely dangerous, not just to them, but potentially to the nation. Such fear reflects the way the leadership is reading Jesus *politically and religiously* at the trial. In addition, the general impression made by Jesus' ministry created the backdrop for the leadership's nervousness and concern, as Brown has suggested.[69] I am not sure that we can

---

[68]Many of these additional questions will be considered in chapter four, including the issue of potential sources for this scene. There is an almost forty year period of tension between Annas' family, with its row of high priestly descendants, and the Christians. The consistency of this leadership is important because this had become by the tradition's inscripturation a family struggle against the Jewish Christians in Jerusalem. The consistency of the Jewish leadership between the trial and subsequent early church events would have kept the same issues raised at this trial before the public, as other Christians were also put to death for blasphemy or "law breaking." See Stephen in Acts 7 and James' trial in Josephus, *Ant* 20.200 (ὡς παρανομησάντων). I thank Prof. Hengel for making me aware of this argument which he is currently working on and which I shall develop in chapter 4.

[69]I also think that some of the social, religious purity issues raised by Chilton's study of sacrifice noted above in n. 67 also contributed significantly to the leadership's unease. I do have one caveat for Chilton's framing of the argument, which I believe underplays an important principle his study actually is attempting to uphold. When Chilton plays christology down in favor of an emphasis on issues of purity and sacrifice (pp. 148-54), he risks slipping into a focus on a single cause which his study as a whole seems sensitively to avoid (note his careful statement about authenticity on p. 113-21). It may be that what Chilton observes about the diversity and complexity of the sources needs more careful attention as he reminds us that a text is not a "tell" where we can simply dig down and pare away late material to find the earlier stuff. Chilton argues for the reality that earlier meanings may well be conveyed within later meanings. But one other possibility must also be seriously

dissect all of these elements totally from one another and isolate a single cause for the blasphemy, though the scriptural combination of Ps 110:1 and Dan 7:13 certainly appears as the most obvious, decisive catalyst to the ultimate response. In other words, the clothes rending by the high priest at the scene speaks volumes about the specific act that put things over the edge.

I wish to make the case for this complex understanding of the scene. I want to take a careful look at blasphemy in Judaism and then consider a specific set of exalted figure analogies as they surface in texts where humans or angels are described as sitting next to God. What is important to us is not merely being exalted and present in heaven, but in having a position that places one at God's side. For some Jews, a few select luminaries of old could be considered for such an honor by a direct invitation from God. However, the lack of good, clean parallels for contemporary figures making such a self claim serves as evidence for the offense when a contemporary like Jesus makes such a statement. Here, in the view of the leadership, is no great luminary like those of old, but an untrained Galilean Jew, a trouble-maker, who claims *not only* the ability to sit at God's side, *but also* to possess the authority to be their judge. In looking for the answer to the nature of Jesus' blasphemy in a specific titular claim or in one place alone, we may have missed the fact that his claim was offensive at many levels.

---

entertained, namely, that events themselves can have multiple meanings, which the various evangelists each draw from in their own way. The tendency of each gospel to focus on an aspect of an event should not prevent an attempt to ascertain the possibility of the multiplicity of causes of offense or perspective in the way those events were read. It is the complex nature of defining what "historical" is and how it works that makes the discussion of the nature of the sources so complicated. See my "When *Jesus Seminar* Meets *Jesus Under Fire*: On Whose Side Does History Fall?" *Princeton Theological Review* 4 (1997): 3-8. In this particular case, surely if Jesus was seen as constructing an alternative cult by the leadership, the issue of his person and the kind of authority he bore to attempt this bold step in an eschatologically charged environment would also be a very relevant concern. If Jesus himself consciously constructed such an alternative approach and engaged in a public, frontal challenge of the leadership, then the question of who he was also would have occurred to him. Whatever the answer is, it is likely to be more than Jesus was a herald or advocate of a kingdom that would be renewed with a fresh purity in response to his call of the opportunity of forgiveness. This interaction with Chilton is concerned with the nuancing, relationship, and emphases in the historical argument, but it is a complexity that is worth engaging in with some care. A full presentation of Chilton's view of the kingdom is found in *Pure Kingdom: Jesus' Vision of God*. Studying the Historical Jesus (Grand Rapids: Wm B. Eerdmans, 1996).

Chapter II

Blasphemy in Judaism

The study of blasphemy is a complex undertaking, since an array of terminology exists that can express the idea. In addition, the concept, as I hope to show, involves both utterances and actions. So pursuing only certain lexical terms is a limitation in finding references to the idea. Sometimes blasphemy is described and not explicitly named. As John Hartley has noted, "In fact, trying to gain a precise understanding of the ancient view of blasphemy is itself very difficult, for the ancient Hebrews wished to avoid any hint of cursing God in speaking about cursing God. This perspective, therefore, led them to employ all sorts of euphemisms in referring to blasphemy . . . ."[1]

As shall become clear, the ancient Hebrews and their successors tried to avoid cursing God, even while describing it. This meant they tended to report it in summarizing ways, rather than getting into its offensive details. This also means that they rarely named it when discussing it. In some cases they used substitute terms, including terms like "to bless," that outside of a euphemistic force would give no hint that blasphemy was present. Finally, while several Hebrew terms can mean to curse, there is no technical term in Hebrew that means, "to blaspheme."[2] In this chapter I shall point out the variety of terminology that can point to blasphemy as I examine a wide range of texts where the concept is also in evidence. Our textual survey will proceed from the Hebrew Scriptures through the midrashim.[3] However, the study begins with a survey of the key terms that contribute to the semantic field of

---

[1]John E. Hartley, *Leviticus* WBC 4 (Dallas: Word, 1992), p. 408.

[2]Hartley, *Leviticus*, p. 408.

[3]The listing of texts in this chapter makes no claim of completeness when it comes to rabbinic references, as the Jewish material is vast and the possibility of allusion to blasphemy is so great that such a claim cannot be made. However, the major, rabbinic blasphemy texts are discussed and the entire list is representative of rabbinic discussion, as the various concordances on a wide array of rabbinic materials have been examined for the most central terms, which are noted in each unit. At the base of this survey stands the fundamental texts of the Hebrew Scripture plus a collection of over one hundred fifty extra-biblical references. New Testament references are not included in this count, nor are they brought into consideration in this chapter. The survey reflects a complete examination of the most central terms in the earliest extra-biblical materials (i.e., through the Mishnah).

blasphemy in Hebrew and Aramaic.[4] These surveys introduce the key terms
and discuss the frequency of use. The more detailed handling of specific texts
and usage comes in the consideration of the texts themselves. The survey of
Greek terms comes with the discussion of the Septuagint and Pseudepigrapha,
as does the noting of key Latin terms. The key terms will be noted as each
unit of material is covered.

1. The Hebrew Scriptures

The Key Terminology

The concept of blasphemy appears in the Hebrew Scriptures through the use
of seven different terms. Some of them have a major role, while others appear
only briefly with such force. Surprisingly, one of the sets of terms that are not
used are the verbs, קבב, "to curse" and ארר, which has the same meaning. In
these sacred texts God is never the object of these verbs. The absence of the
use of these two terms is significant and a good place to begin, because the
respect for God was so great that the combination of cursing God was never
used with the most explicitly available terms. Such respect for God and the
absence of direct reference to cursing him explains the variety of terms that
do address the concept.

Four terms are important to the presentation of the concept in the Hebrew
Scriptures. They appear in passages that become central in later Jewish

---

[4]The variety of terms that can point to blasphemy is briefly discussed in Beyer, *TDNT*
1:621-25, esp. 621. See also the entry "blasphemy" in the Jewish Encyclopedia vol. 4, cols.
1073-74 and Wallis, *TWAT* 1, cols. 956-58 on גדף. Our list in the next section of the semantic
field for blasphemy in the Hebrew Scriptures is one we have constructed in the midst of
perusing our survey. For consideration of the related Semitic terms to be noted there, see
TWAT 1:811-42 (ברך); 3:223-29 (חרף); 4:582-86 (לעג); 5:129-37 (נאץ); 5:589-91 (נכב); 6:1138-
39 (קבב); 7:40-49 (קלל). As we shall see in discussing the LXX, there are also a variety of
Greek terms that can point to the concept or related ideas besides βλασφημέω (especially
ὀνειδίζειν- to reproach, revile and παροξύνειν- to provoke, as well as καταλαλεῖν- to speak against
and παροργίζειν- to provoke). The first two Greek terms refer to a concept that is less severe a
charge than blasphemy. See also H. Währisch, C. Brown, "βλασφημέω," *NIDNTT* 3:341-45; M.
Jastrow, *A Dictionary of the Targumim the Talmud Babli and Yerushalmi and the Midrashic
Literature* (New York: Pardes Publishing House, 1950 [1903]), vol. 1, p. 214; J. Levy, H. L.
Fleischer, L. Goldschmidt, *Wörterbuch über die Talmudim und Midrashim* (Darmstadt:
Wissenschaftliche Buchgesellschaft, 1963), vol. 1, pp. 303-04; M. Sokoloff, *Jewish
Palestinian Aramaic of the Byzantine Period* (Jerusalem: Bar Ilan University Press, 1990), p
121; and E. C. Dos Santos, *An Expanded Hebrew Index for the Hatch-Redpath Concordance
to the Septuagint* (Jerusalem: Dugith Publishers Baptist House, n.y.), pp. 35, 127.

discussion of the idea and are often associated with incidents that become the model examples of blasphemy.

The first term is גדף in the piel stem and its related noun form, גדוף. It means "to revile or slander," while the noun refers to slanderous words. The verb appears seven times in the Hebrew Scriptures (Num 15:30; 2 Kings 19:6, 22 = Isa 37:6, 23; Ezek 20:27; Ps 44:17). The noun appears only three times (Isa 43:28; 51:7; Zeph 2:8). In some cases, as in Isa 51:7 and Zeph 2:8, it is Israel being reviled by other people. But more often it is God who is the object of such slander (Num 15:30; the 2 Kings-Isaiah complex; Ezek 20:27; Isa 43:28). The key example texts will be Num 15:30, which discusses high handed sin, and the Sennacherib-Hezekiah confrontation in 2 Kings-Isaiah.

The second key term is קלל in the piel stem, which also means "to revile" or "to make small," so that it can in certain cases have the sense of cursing someone by showing them dishonor. The noun, קללה, appears often as well. The verb is used 40 times plus additional appearances in two qere texts. The noun appears 33 times. Usually the curse involves man (Gen 12:3- Abraham; Jos 24:9- Balaam of the nation; 6x plus two qere readings in 2 Sam 16, where Shimei curses David) or nature (Gen 8:21-the ground). This term will introduce us to our first euphemism, "to blaspheme the Name and curse" in Lev 24:11, a text that will become a key example passage for later discussions. The verb appears four times in this passage. In Lev 24:15 appears one of the few cases where one is said to "curse God." The term also appears in the important passage of Exod 22:27, where the referent is more uncertain as to whether God or the leadership is meant. The resolution of that question awaits our discussion of the verse.

The third key term is חרף, "to reproach." This verb appears 39x overall, with 4 uses in the Qal stem. Its usage in the piel is important to our study, for it includes two key example passages. Five of the uses of the verb occur in the passage where David meets Goliath in 1 Sam 17. Eight other uses occur in the already noted Sennacherib-Hezekiah confrontation of 2 Kgs 19 = Isa 37 (4x in each book). Thus a significant amount of uses occur in two texts, while the Sennacherib passage shows a collection of related terms in the semantic field appearing side by side.

The final key term is a slightly broader word, נאץ, which in the piel means "to despise." The noun and infinitival forms appear twice and three times respectively. The two substantival uses come in the 2 Kgs 19-Isa 37 complex, giving us a third key term in that one text. Two of the infinitival uses describe the nation's serious rebellion in the desert (Neh 9:18, 26). The verb appears 24x overall, with 15 of those in the piel stem. Sometimes, it is Israel that is despised as in Isa 60:14, but the majority of references speak of serious malicious acts against God (the nation's rebellion in the desert- Num 14:11, 23; Deut 31:20; the incident involving Korah, Dathan, and Abiram- Num

16:30; Eli's sons' sacrifices- 1 Sam 2:17; David killing Uriah- 2 Sam 2:14; Israel's later unfaithfulness- Isa 1:4; 5:24; of actions by the enemies of God- Ps 10:3, 13; 74:10, 18). These kinds of actions will often coincide with discussions of blasphemy in later texts, raising the question whether blasphemy is only verbal.

Three other terms play a minor role in the concept as they represent more euphemistic ways to express the idea. The use of נקב, "to mark out, name, or curse" appears 19x in these texts, but three of the uses bear a special negative nuance as they refer to "cursing the Name" in Lev 24:11-16, and combines with references to "reviling the Name." The passage, noted already, points intensively with this combination of expressions to a misuse of the name of God. The verb לעג, "to mock," appears 18x as a verb, while the noun appears 7x. God is described as mocked in 2 Kgs 19:21 = Isa 37:22, making yet a fourth conceptual term that appears in the description of that event. The final term, ברך, "to bless," shows just how far the euphemisms can go. This verb is used 6x to indicate cursing against God, expressed in a way that is not offensive (Job 1:5, 11; 2:5, 9; 1 Kgs 21:10,13- the false charges against Naboth).

One can see the variety of terms applied to describe the presence of blasphemy. Just listing the associated terms of the semantic field indicates that blasphemy has to do with insulting or shaming another through some utterance. Whether a broader type of blasphemy involving actions also exists requires an examination of the texts.

Exodus 22:27 (22:28 Eng.)

אלהים לא תקלל ונשיא בעמך לא תאר:

This text appears in the midst of a series of short legal statements related to social and religious laws that are designed to lead the people into holiness (20:22 — 23:33).[5] In 22:27, the people are not "to revile" God. The verb קלל in the piel refers to cursing.[6] This verb appears in several texts of the Hebrew

---

[5]This portion of Exodus has been called "The Book of the Covenant," as 24:3 and 7 suggest. See John I. Durham, *Exodus* WBC 3 (Dallas:Word, 1987), p. 315.

[6]This verse will alternately be referred to as Exod 22:27 or 22:28, depending on the traditional versification of Jewish texts discussing it. The versification of some later Jewish resources alluding back to this text retains the versification as it is reflected in English. These I shall not alter, so the references can be directly located.

The stem קלל often means "to make light of" or "to show disrespect to." Some, in fact, argue that blasphemy is not in view originally in Exodus, but merely a showing of disrespect toward God; H. Brichto, *The Problem of "Curse" in the Hebrew Bible*, SBLMS 13 (Philadelphia: Society of Biblical Literature and Exegesis, 1963), pp. 150-65. That is conceivable, but there is no doubt that in the history of interpretation this text was seen as a primary text on blasphemy, and for our study that prevailing reading is the most important factor to consider. Cassuto, *A Commentary on the Book of Exodus*, trans by I. Abrahams

Scriptures including the important text of Lev 24 that shall be examined shortly. It is primarily a term that refers to utterances, as opposed to acts, but there is some ambiguity in its use as God's remarks about the flood in Gen 8:21 show. There God "cursed" the ground, but the curse is really a divine command that led to the act of the Flood. Gen 12:3 reflects a similar ambiguity, when those who curse Abraham are cursed by God. In both cases the term alludes certainly to an attitude, not just remarks, that results in action. The verbal thrust of the term appears in Exod 21:17, where the cursing of father or mother is a crime worthy of death (also Lev 20:9; Prov 20:20, 30:11). The same force appears in Lev 19:14, where the deaf are not to be cursed. The example of God's turning Balaam's cursing into blessing shows, through the use of linguistic antonyms, the presence of intended respect or the lack of it. The utterance expresses an attitude that is the real issue (see also Jos 24:9; Neh 13:2).[7]

These Torah texts share the same verb and call for a showing of respect by their prohibition of verbal disrespect. One should not defame someone through speech that reflects an attitude of disrespect. So Cassuto summarizes the force of this Exodus verse as, "This admonition includes every utterance or act that detracts from the Divine glory . . . ."[8] In addition to the prohibition of disrespect shown to God comes a warning not to curse the leader, who within the portrayal of Exodus would not have been a king, but merely an administrative figure. Later in Israel's history, this prohibition would have extended to the king (1 Kgs 21:10; Isa 8:21), priests (Acts 23:3-4), and any other figures of significant leadership in Israel.

Isa 8:21 indicates an early view of this Exodus text as referring to the reviling of gods and leadership. That text echoes the Exodus text, but in a sense of rebuke for the nations' unfaithfulness, suggesting that Isaiah read the

---

(Jerusalem: Magnes Press, 1967 Eng. ed. of 1951 Heb. ed.), p. 293, argues for blasphemy in this original context.

[7]Individuals can also be cursed as Abimelech was (Judg 9:27) or as David was by Goliath (1 Sam 17:43) and by Shimei (2 Sam 16:5, 7, 9, 10, 11, 13; 19:22; 1 Kings 2:8). Nehemiah issues a curse against those who engage in mixed marriage (Neh 13:25). Elisha's curse on the Bethel youth led immediately to the act of their being mauled by the bears, also showing the connection between word and action (2 Kings 2:24). One can even "curse oneself" by their actions, as Samuel's sons did (1 Sam 3:13), a text the LXX translates as blaspheming or speaking evil of God (κακολογοῦντες θεόν). The frustration of the mediums in judgment will lead the nation to curse God and king, a clear allusion back to this Exodus text (Isa 8:21). One can also curse a time, like the day of one's birth, a curse directed at the self for having been created (see also Job 3:1). One wisdom texts calls its readers not to take everything said about them too seriously as they may hear their servants curse them. The reason for the call for more indifference is that the reader knows he has also cursed others (Eccle 7:21). A second wisdom text warns against cursing the king or the rich, lest they hear about it (Eccle 10:20).

[8]Cassuto, *A Commentary on the Book of Exodus*, p. 293.

text as a call of faithfulness to God himself. Nonetheless, there developed early a somewhat natural extension of the sense of this text to include other gods as well, often as part of an apologetic desire to show Israel's respect for other gods in a more pluralistic context. The LXX, Philo, and Josephus give evidence of this understanding of the passage. The LXX translates the passage with the plural θεούς and even puts it in the emphatic position. Josephus, *Ant* 4.207 and *Ag Apion* 2.237 reflect this broader reading of the text, as do Philo's *Life of Moses* 2.205; *Special Laws* 1.53 and his *Questions and Answers on Exod* Book 2.5 on Exodus 22:28a. This reading assumes a respect for the God of Israel, as Josephus's *Ag Apion* reference makes the point that this is done out of respect for the name of God.[9] Philo's exposition of Exodus argues that it is a sign of the Law's desire to breed peace and prevent war.[10] This reading plays on the ambiguity in the term אלהים, which can refer to God or to the gods (Exod 18:11; 20:3; 23:13; 32:23). This broader interpretation, which clearly was present by the first century, may simply be the result of a natural extension of the passage's force, which as part of the Law of Israel, referred to both God and man. In fact, a further extension to preventing blaspheming of rulers appears in the Targums and Midrashim (*Onq* on Exod 22:27; *Mek* on Exod 22:27). In the Talmud, *Sanh* 66a encompasses all of these options.

The importance of the text for us is that it shows the verbal primacy of blasphemy. In short, blasphemy is something spoken in disrespect against God. However, it must also be noted that the word often carries with it the connotation of an attitude manifesting itself in action beyond the mere uttering of harsh words. The text also indicates a close linkage between utterances against God and those against the people's rulers. This close association in the earliest texts on reviling God is significant. It may well reflect the view that to speak against God's rulers is to speak against the

---

[9]*Ag Apion* 2.237 reads, "Our legislator has expressly forbidden us to laugh at or revile those that are esteemed gods by other people, on account of the very name of God ascribed to them." The apologetic nature of these remarks is clear when one considers how many Jewish texts deride the idolatry around them as part of defending the concept of the one true God.

[10]*Questions and Answers on Exod* Book 2.5 on Exod 22:28a reads in part, "Do they then still accuse the divine Law of breaking down the customs of others? For, behold, not only does it offer support to those of different opinion by accepting and honoring those whom they have from the beginning believed to be gods, but it also muzzles and restrains its own disciples, not permitting them to revile these with a loose tongue, for it believes well spoken praise is better." Philo then goes on to note that to do otherwise results in war. For a discussion of the early interpretation of these verses, see A. Le Boulluec and P. Sandevoir, ed., *La Bible d' Alexandrie* (Paris: Éditions du Cerf, 1989) 2:230-31. They attribute the interpretation of a singular "God" in Exodus to Rashi. But the apologetics and sarcasm of Isa. 8:21 suggests the reading is older. See below for Isa 8:21.

wisdom of the God who chose them.[11] Of course, the prohibition's practical goal was to produce support for the nation's leadership and thus promote national stability.

Leviticus 24:10-23

This text involves an incident more than applying specific terminology used in a prohibition. In fact, it illustrates the Exodus law. The text in v. 11 discusses "one who named the Name and cursed" (בן־האשה הישראלית את־השם ויקלל ויקב). The text's exact force is disputed. Should the verse be rendered as in the *RSV,* "he blasphemed the Name and he cursed"? Or should it be read as *NEB,* "he uttered the Holy Name in blasphemy," a reading that molds the two verbs together into one action, but that as a result treats the first verb as more neutral?[12] The text involves a man of mixed descent; he has an Israelite mother and Egyptian father. In v. 14 he is described through the participle as the blasphemer (המקלל). The ruling about what to do with him comes in vv. 15-16. The one who curses God is held responsible for the sin and the one who blasphemes the Name ("names the Name" = ונקב שם ־יהוה) must be put to death. Such a person is to be stoned, whether he is alien or native born. The mixed descent of the man was probably what raised a question, but his racial roots are treated as irrelevant, revealing that the scope of blasphemy extends to all.[13] Anyone can be subject to a penalty for the act. So in v. 23 the culprit is stoned.

The passage could appear to make a distinction between cursing and naming the name[14], but this ignores the nature of the linkage of the two verbs

---

[11]Brevard Childs, *Exodus* OTL (London: SCM Press, 1974), p. 479. He notes that the passage is an extension of the fifth commandment of Exod 20:12.

[12]Though the two readings are only slightly different in sense, the case for the latter reading has been well made by J. Weingreen, "The Case of the Blasphemer (Leviticus XXIV 10ff.)," VT 22 (1972):118-23. He notes that parallelism in v. 16 shows that the initial verb here is נקב־ "to name," not קבב־ "to curse." For the claim that the story as it now stands is a redactor's attempt to narrow the definition of blasphemy to pronunciation of the name, see J. B. Gabel and C. B. Wheeler, "The Redactor's Hand in the Blasphemy Pericope of Leviticus XXIV," VT 30 (1980):227-29. I am less confident of spotting such a result simply in the juxtaposition of the verbs. Dennis H. Livingston, "The Crime of Leviticus XXIV 11," VT 36 (1986): 252-54, sees the crime as calling on Yahweh to destroy Yahweh using his name. But he uses later rabbinic evidence from *m. Sanh* 7.5 as key. This renders his conclusion as too specific an application of the verse's language.

[13]Hartley, *Leviticus*, p. 406 and Fishbane, *Biblical Interpretations in Ancient Israel* (Oxford: Clarendon Press), p. 101, argue that the question arose because of the mixed race of the offender and whether he deserved the same penalty as someone from totally within the nation.

[14]So Hartley, *Leviticus*, pp. 407, 410. The problem with Hartley's contention is that he takes the verb "to name" in the neutral sense noted earlier, while correctly noting that the second verb gives to the first a harsh sense. This means that in this context it is hard to make the first verb by itself the bearer of a technical force. Had the verbs been reversed the case for

that open the passage showing that the two expressions are merely two parts of the same act. The parallelism allows the example to be told with a literary flair.

The passage is interesting because in the midst of giving a sentence of death for blasphemy it repeats the note that to murder means to face death and that the basis of the penalty is an eye for eye type of justice (*lex talionis*). The implication is not very great that to speak against God is the equivalent of verbal murder.[15] The text indicates how seriously speech against God was viewed and forms the basis of the mishnaic instruction in *Sanh* 7.5 that the Name be used in capital cases of blasphemy. This verbal aspect of naming the Name became so strong in some later tradition that blasphemy and naming the Name were equated or combined into a single act.[16]

Numbers 15:30-31

This text is not about blasphemy, but it is an important discussion of the death penalty, which allows it in later exposition to become related to blasphemy, since blasphemy also carries this penalty. The text relates how the death penalty is issued for anyone, alien or native, who "sins with a high hand." A man who violated the Sabbath by collecting sticks on the holy day illustrates it in the next passage (Num 15:32-36). The parallelism of the death penalty and the reference to native or alien serve to create the basis for a connection of this passage to Lev 24. The passage actually appears in a context where various offerings are discussed; yet it serves to give an example of when an offering is rejected, so that judgment, not forgiveness, is demanded.

The key point of the passage for our concern is that it is the high handed sin, an act of affront against the Lord (אֶת־יְהוָה הוּא מְגַדֵּף)[17], that prevents one

---

a distinction would be stronger. The debate in the end makes little difference in the verse's point as the blasphemer who misuses God's name is put to death in either reading. The debate only effects whether technical terminology helps to make the point.

[15]As is well noted by Erhard S. Gerstenberger, *Das Dritte Buch Mose: Leviticus* ATD (Göttingen: Vandenhoeck & Ruprecht, 1993), p. 330, "'den Namen zu verletzen/zu durchbohren', d.h. zu 'fluchen'." God's Name is the object of damaging disrespect.

[16]*Onq* on Lev 24:11ff. combines the two key verbs in this Leviticus text to render the key phase as "pronounced the Name in provocation." This is actually a good sense, as was noted above, given the way the act is seen as linked to an attitude. It will lead to a debate, however, whether the name is absolutely required or whether verbal provocation can occur without the explicit use of the divine Name.

[17]Jacob Milgrom, *The JPS Commentary: Numbers* (New York: The Jewish Publication Society, 1990), p. 125, describes the "upraised hand" as rooted in the picture of Ancient Near Eastern deities who are "sculpted with an uplifted or outstretched right hand, bearing a spear, war ax, or lightening bolt . . .. The upraised hand is therefore poised to strike; it is a threatening gesture of the Deity against his enemies or of a man against God Himself." See Num 33:3, Exod 14:8 and Job 38:15.

from being able to offer sacrifice and leads to being "cut off" (v. 30), that is, executed or "utterly cut off" (v. 31) from the people.

The term for an act of affront against the Lord comes from the root גדף. In the piel stem it means to "revile" or "blaspheme." But, as was already noted in the survey of key terms, it is a rare word, appearing only seven times in the Hebrew Scriptures. The bulk of those references (four of them) come in the 2 Kgs 19 – Isa 37 parallel text discussing Sennacherib's encounter with Hezekiah (2 Kgs 19:6, 22; Isa 37:6, 23). In these passages, Sennacherib has blasphemed God by challenging God's power and protection of Israel. By saying he will overrun Hezekiah, he has actually blasphemed God (2 Kgs 19:6 = Isa 37:6, 2 Kgs 19:22 = Isa 37:23). Worthy of note here is the close connection between God and his ruler, a view very much like Exod 22:27.

One other use of the term is also revealing. Ezek 20:27 refers back to the fathers blaspheming of God, a text that looks at their entire record of unfaithfulness in the wilderness, especially acts like creating the golden calf. In fact, in this text to blaspheme God is to forsake him for another, an allusion to their involvement with idolatry.[18]

In later Judaism, high handed sin was put into three classes: (1) impudent speech against Torah and so against God, where Manasseh is the example in *Sifre* §112 on Num 15:30-31; (2) idolatry, especially the golden calf incident as noted in the same Sifre text or in Philo's *Life of Moses* 2.159-66; or (3) the blaspheming of God's Name, which also leads to death by hanging (*m Sanh* 6.4). Given the use of the term גדף for speaking and preparing to act in a disrespectful way against God, these three categories are not surprising.

Related to this death penalty (or the penalty to be "cut off")[19] is another text, Deut 21:22-23. It notes that one who dies is hanged on a tree (after the execution) for public display and is the object of God's curse (קללת אלהים תלוי כי). Here the noun קללה is used to describe the presence of a curse. The passage reads, "When someone is convicted of a crime punishable by death and is executed, and you hang him on a tree, his corpse must not remain all night upon a tree; you shall bury him that same day, for anyone hung on a tree

---

[18]The final use of the term in Ps 44:17 involves the insults hurled at a righteous sufferer and so does not apply as the term has a human object.

[19]The penalty of being cut off, the *"karet,"* is debated. Is it a death penalty or is it God cutting off the line of the man as a result? On this, see the excursus by Milgrom, *Numbers*, pp. 405-08. He argues that it is more than mere death, but includes either an extirpation of the man's line or a denial to him of the afterlife. In other words, man executes, but God extirpates. Again, the distinction is a fine one, since God's act is seen as an extension of the execution. See also Philip J. Budd, *Numbers* WBC 5 (Waco: Word, 1984), p. 98. He opts for a third choice, "excommunication," but gives no reason for the view. The distinction between a death penalty and the divine cessation of the line as a result makes little difference to our study, since a death is involved either way. On the term כרת, see the article by Hasel in *TWAT* 4: 355-67.

is under God's curse." This text originally looks to hanging in public after being stoned, as Lev 24:16 makes it clear that the means of carrying out the penalty for death was stoning. Yet it came to be associated with other forms of hanging death, including crucifixion. Every form of such a death was viewed as one suffering a curse from God.[20]

With these three key texts from Exod 22, Lev 24, and Num 15 come the legal roots to the discussion on blasphemy. The remaining texts from the Hebrew Scriptures describe examples where God or a ruler is cursed or is contemplated as being cursed — acts which connect to Exod 22. They are treated briefly.

1 Kings 21:13

Although he was falsely accused, Naboth is executed for speaking against God and the ruler Ahab. This text uses a euphemism to describe the event as Naboth is said to have cursed God and the king, but the verb used to describe the act is ברך, to bless. The alteration shows how much care is given to expressing the idea of cursing God. Later in this survey, we shall treat other texts that will indicate the great care with which blasphemous testimony is taken in public (*m Sanh* 7.5).

Job 2:9-10

The same bless-curse idiom shows up in Job, when Job's wife advises the patriarch to curse God and die (v. 9- ברך אלהים ומת). The scene closes by noting that Job did not sin by anything that he said. The verbal character of blasphemy is underscored in this text.

Isaiah 8:21

This text was noted above.[21] The text may give us a major clue as to how Exodus was read in the period of Isaiah, as the prophet urges the nation not to seek mediums as the other nations do, but to read the Law and fear God. Those who mislead the people in this way fall under a judgment that causes them to speak against their king and their God or gods (וקלל במלכו ובאלהיו). The key phrase could be rendered "by his king and god," which means that the curse in anger invoked the deity and the leader, whichever deity the medium-using sinner had associated to himself. A similar expression appears in 1 Sam 17:43. The ambiguity of the term for God appears here as well, just as it did in Exod 22:27. Is it a reference to God or gods? If the verse refers to God, then

---

[20]David J. Halperin, "Crucifixion, the Nahum Pesher, and the Rabbinic Penalty of Strangulation," JJS 32 (1981): 32-46. For the history of the debate in Judaism over whether "curse of God" is a subjective or objective genitive, see Moshe J. Bernstein, "כי קללת אלהים תלוי (Deut 21:23): A Study in Early Jewish Exegesis," JQR 74 (1983): 21-45.

[21]See n. 10.

there is a clear allusion to Exod 22:27 that represents a prophetic critique of the nation for unfaithfulness. The time frame looks at a time of judgment when God has acted in judgment. As a result, the judged are angry with him. This seems the more likely sense. However, even if the reference is to gods, which is also possible, then a similar sense obtains. For if the text discusses gods, then the context appeals to spiritism (Isa 8:19). The resultant sense would be a sarcastic prophetic appeal to the nation's transgression of the warning of Exod 22:27. They have reacted poorly to judgment. Even in their anger they ignore God's actions. It is God that is rejected here by the appeal to gods through spiritism and by the leader's attributing the powers of judgment to them. Whether God or gods is meant, unfaithfulness to him is the point. Sin begets more sin of the same type. The ultimate result of their unfaithfulness is that they are thrust into utter darkness. This text shows the close connection that emerges between pagan practices and the tendency to blaspheme.

The examples considered so far have either used the key terms of קלל, גדף, or euphemistic ברך. These are not the only terms that can point to blasphemy's presence, though the first two are the key terms in the legal literature. Attention now turns to other texts where the nature of the description points to blasphemy's presence. Once again the key terms will be noted, but these examples are cited, not because a technical term for blasphemy is used, but because the event's description makes it clear that blasphemy is present or that something equivalent to it is present at a more national level. Thus, this survey will indicate the semantic field in which blasphemy operates.

Numbers 14:11, 23

This passage speaks of "despising God" using the piel stem of נאץ. The incident involves the people grumbling against God as they complain about Moses and Aaron bringing them into the desert. They regard it a better thing if they had died or never left Egypt. The remarks repudiate God's gift of deliverance. The indication that blasphemy is present comes in the response by Joshua and Caleb, who tear their clothes upon hearing the complaint, an act that indicates that God has been insulted and that they are grieving as a result (v. 6; Gen. 37:29; Judg. 11:35; 2 Sam. 1:11). In Num 14:11 and 23 God describes the people's remarks as indications that he is despised by them (יֹנַאֲצֻנִי- v. 11/מֲנַאֲצַי-v. 23). God issues a judgment of death for those who reject his goodness. When Joshua and Caleb address the people, they call on the people not to rebel against God and to see that the Lord is with them. God's remarks to Moses express the commentary that to despise the Lord is not to believe in him, despite all the signs he has performed. The remarks look at a kind of national blasphemy, dishonoring God by questioning his goodness and deliverance.

Numbers 16:30

Similar in tone is the incident involving Korah, Dothan, and Abiram. They also question Moses and Aaron about where the nation is being taken and suggest that these servants of God have exalted themselves. What results is God issuing an instant judgment as the ground swallows up the complainers. The incident comes with a lesson for the people summed up in vv. 28-30, where Moses declares that the people can know that he is sent because "if the Lord creates something new, and the ground opens its mouth and swallows them up, with all that belongs to them, and they go down alive into Sheol, then you shall know that these men have despised (נאצו) the Lord."

Two points are significant about this text. First, the sin is a virtual replication of the rejection of God's goodness in Num 14. Second, the attack on God is present in the rejection of the leaders he has appointed, a connection that reaches back to texts like Exod 22:27.

Other passages using the concept of God being despised include Deut 31:20, where God predicts that the nation will turn to idols, an action that reflects despising God and breaking covenant by engaging in idolatry; 1 Sam 2:17, where Eli's sons make an offering and then feast on portions that are not theirs, despising God's offering; and 2 Sam 12:14, where David sends Uriah into battle and takes his wife, despising the Lord. In each case, a judgment of God follows or is predicted as his response to the action. They reflect the range of action, which is not formally, called blasphemy, but that indicates intense disrespect toward God to which some type of response is made.

2 Kings 19:3 = Isaiah 37:3/Ezekiel 35:12/Nehemiah 9:18, 26

The noun form of the verb just discussed, נאצה, means to insult. Three texts can be treated briefly, because they indicate the force of this term and show how this concept overlaps with texts noted earlier as explicitly tied to blasphemy. The semantic overlap surfaces in the parallelism.

The 2 Kgs 19 = Isa 37 incident involving Rabshekah's words and insults on behalf of Sennacherib have already been noted. Hezekiah describes these words as reflecting "a day of insult" (ונאצה היום הזה). The wording in the parallel texts is the same. The remarks lead to the foreign king's defeat in judgment. The challenge to God was expressed in the confidence that Hezekiah's armies would not be able to defeat Sennacherib's forces. Again God and leader are tied together closely. To defame one is to dishonor the other.

Ezek 35:12 is similar. Here Edom is personified as speaking with abusive speech against God by rejoicing in the devastation that has fallen on Israel. To speak against Israel with abusive speech (נאצותיך) is to magnify oneself against God and speak against him. So Edom will be judged with desolation. Here is another example of a national form of blasphemy. Here the point is that to speak against God's people is to speak against God.

The final example with this noun is the Neh 9 text. Here actions like making the golden calf and acts of unfaithfulness in the wilderness are seen as great insults against God (vv. 18, 26-נאצות גדלות). The entire set of actions is called casting the law behind one's back leading to these great insults against God.

These three passages show what we have already seen elsewhere, that speech and action are both included as reflecting blasphemy. Particularly singled out are acts that challenge God's uniqueness, such as acts of idolatry or words that suggest a limitation on his power, as in the claim of a foreign king to be stronger than Israel's God is.[22]

Summary

The Hebrew Scriptures indicate that blasphemy represents speech or action that shows disrespect to God, by insulting his power, uniqueness, or goodness. In such speech or action, God is reviled, insulted, or taunted. To attack those who are God's appointed leaders or even his people can also be seen as indicative of disrespect toward God. Such actions are worthy of judgment, whether it is stoning by the community in the case of individuals, or by God acting directly to remove the culprit, or through the threat of national judgment for more corporate expressions of blasphemy. To insult God using his Name is explicitly cited as worthy of such judgment in Lev 24, but the use of the Name does not seem to be a requirement to see the need for judgment. God sometimes undertakes such judgment directly, as in the case of Korah, Dothan, and Abiram (Num 16). Thus, more than speech can constitute a blasphemous event.

2. Qumran

The texts from Qumran, Josephus, and Philo are extremely important, since they represent, along with the Hebrew Scriptures and the LXX, the witnesses closest in temporal proximity to the first century. The fact that these witnesses come from distinct parts of Judaism is also significant, since the opinions

---

[22]Conceptually similar is the idea of taunting God (חרף). Here, texts like Goliath's taunt of Israel in 1 Sam 17:10, 25-26, 36, 45 come to mind. This terminology also surfaces in the Sennacherib incident in 2 Kgs 19:4, 16, 22-23 = Isa 37:4, 17, 23-24 (see also 2 Chron 32:17). The cluster of terms pointing to the insult of God makes this text a significant example. However, there are no new developments in this additional terminology.

expressed cover an array of Jewish communities. The Qumranian evidence itself is not extensive, involving only four brief passages.

The Key Terminology

There are three terms that belong to the semantic field associated with blasphemy at Qumran.[23] They are all related to terms already observed in the Hebrew Scriptures.

The first key term is גדף, which is used three times in texts noted in the textual discussion (*1QpHab* 10.13; *1QS* 4.11; *CD* 5.12). The latter two references are to the blaspheming tongue, while the first one is a more general reference to unfaithfulness.

The second term is נאץ, "to despise." Here three references also appear, but two of them are in texts that are so fragmentary that the force and reference of the term are not clear (*4Q381* 19 1.6; *4Q381* 13.1). The other reference is a citation in the *Isaiah Scroll* from Isa 5:24 (4Q162 col. 2.7-8 = 4QIs^b), where allusion is made to some who "despise the Word of the Holy One of Israel." This charge is made against those who are unfaithful in Jerusalem and reflects the tension that existed between those in Qumran and those in more official roles in Jerusalem. Thus this reference falls short of a specific charge of blasphemy, but reflects serious sin. The tone of this text is like other Qumranian texts, where those in Jerusalem are castigated for other, additional sins.

The third term is קלל, "to curse," which also appears three times. Two of these texts are also unclear, because of the condition of the text (*4Q176* 21 1.2) or because the reference itself appears to be allusive (*3Q15* 6.4).[24] But the remaining passage is directly related to our theme, and so is discussed in detail below (*1QS* 7.1)

1QpHab 10.13

The Habakkuk commentary is one of the better known Qumran texts with its pesher style of exegesis, assigning many biblical texts to fulfillment in contemporary events.[25] In a section explaining Hab 2:12-13, the pesher applies the prophet's language about idolatry to the subjects of Hyrcanus who have joined in his unfaithfulness and thus face the judgment of fire for having "insulted and outraged the elect of God" (גדפו ויחרפו הא בחירי אל). The presence here of the key root גדף is the indication that serious sin is in view. The text may indicate a kind of corporate blasphemy by much of the nation. What is

---

[23]James H. Charlesworth, *Graphic Concordance to the Dead Sea Scrolls* (Tübingen: J. C. B. Mohr, 1991), pp. 101-02, 419, 478.

[24]On the *3Q15* text, see DJDJ III:252, 290, esp. n. 138 on p. 252.

[25]M. P. Horgan, *Pesharim: Qumran Interpretations of Biblical Books* CBQMS 8 (Washington D.C.: Catholic Biblical Association of America, 1979).

significant is that the unfaithful action is equated with pagan idolatry and the attack is seen as coming against God's people, his elect, or the Qumranians in their own reading. It is understandable that a separatist wing of Judaism would have a broader use of the concept of blasphemy as support for their withdrawal and opposition.

1QS 4.11

The Rule scroll, also sometimes called The Manual of Discipline, is one of the significant community documents in the collection.[26] In 3.13 — 4.26 comes the discussion of the "two Spirits," a key doctrine that underlies much of the community's view of itself and the world. In the midst of this presentation of these contrasting Spirits of light and darkness comes the reference in 4.11 to "a blaspheming tongue" (ולשון גדופים).[27] This is one of the attributes of the spirit of perversity. The remark is significant, because it helps to show that the remark in the Habakkuk pesher should also be read as reflecting a view that the opponents to the sect are guilty of blasphemy. The stark contrast between good and evil is the basis for the hope of the ultimate redemption of the truly righteous and the ultimate fall of the wicked (4.12-14). Thus as one crime among many, blasphemy will be judged by God. The association of blasphemy with the tongue again highlights the sin's fundamental verbal character.

1QS 7.1

This is one of the few texts to mention verbal slander in a legal context. It is in a section that is outlining penalties for various violations in the community. However, its meaning is not entirely clear, partially because of the context in which it is mentioned. To show the contextual problem, here is the text starting from 6.27b:

> [And whoever makes any mention whatever of the name of the Being venerated above all other beings, [shall be put to death.] 7.1 But if he has spoken a curse (ואם קלל או) from fright or under a blow of distress, or for any other reason whatever while reading the Book or pronouncing the blessings, he shall be separated 7.2 and shall return no more to the Council of the Community.

---

[26]For arguments why Manual of Discipline is not the best name for the document, see A. Dupont-Sommer, *The Essene Writings from Qumran*, trans by G. Vermes (Gloucester, Mass.: Peter Smith, 1973), p. 69.

[27]The translation of A. R. C. Leaney, *The Rule of Qumran and Its Meaning*, The New Testament Library (London: SCM Press, 1966), p. 144, of "abusive tonque" is too soft for this context. See J. Charlesworth, *The Dead Sea Scrolls: Hebrew. Aramaic, and Greek Texts with English Translations. Vol. 1: Rule of the Community and Related Documents* (Tübingen: J. C. B. Mohr [Paul Siebeck], 1994), pp. 16-17, who reads correctly "a blasphemous tongue."

Here two offenses appear one after the other. One apparently bears a death penalty, the other excommunication from the community. The text is missing which describes the penalty of the first offense, but given its relationship to the second example, it looks as if its penalty would be harsher, since the second example appears to consider attenuating circumstances that would lessen the sentence. If this is correct, then only death could be harsher than excommunication. (Thus the wording that appears in brackets before 7.1) The penalty would also fit with the punishment of Lev 24:16, provided it is blasphemy against God that is meant here — a view that is more likely than that the Teacher of Righteousness is meant.[28]

This text indicates that the misuse, even pronunciation (!), of the divine Name is a serious enough offense to mean death, unless there are circumstances that suggest that the misuse has been forced. The difference in penalty recognizes the possibility of such a remark being forced, but it still is a severely punishable offense. This is yet another indication of how serious an offense blasphemy is regarded. Blasphemy is framed in very specific, verbal terms here, when death is the penalty. What is less clear is whether in the second case, in the uttering of a "curse" from fright or distress, there is included expression other than simply a pronunciation of the Name.

CD 5.12

Another key community document is the Damascus Scroll, which is a shortened title for the more descriptive, "The Document of the New Covenant in the Land of Damascus." The title is in all likelihood a reference to the community's earlier days of exile outside of the land in the Damascus region.[29] It is mostly a collection of ordinances for the community. In a section extending back to 4.12b, the document outlines the three nets of Belial, a concept perhaps related to the seven evils of Belial appearing in the *Testament of the Twelve Patriarchs* (*TReub* 2:1-9; *TBen* 7:1-3) and noted by the document's author as connected both to Levi (*CD* 4:15; *TLevi* 18:12-13? — in a reference to the eschatological Priest) and to the judgment to come on those who are caught in its web. The three sins are lust, riches, and defiling

[28]A. Dupont-Sommer, *The Essene Writings from Qumran*, p. 87, n. 2. Dupont-Sommer raises the possibility that the Teacher of Righteousness is meant. He cites the remarks of Josephus, *JW* 2.145, that for the Essenes "the name of the Lawgiver is, after God, an object of veneration and if any man blasphemes against the Lawgiver, he is punished with death." He notes as well that Moses' name is mentioned in these documents without any sense of limitation, so that the restriction could apply to the Qumran lawgiver, that is, to the Teacher. But the description in 6.27 b of "the being venerated above all other beings" seems too lofty and exclusive to apply to a person. It is the type of euphemism one would expect for a respectful reference to God.

[29]P. R. Davies, *The Damascus Document: An Interpretation of the Damascus Document,* JSOTSS 25 (Sheffield: Sheffield Academic Press, 1983).

the sanctuary (*CD* 4:17-18). The text then outlines sins of marrying more than one wife (including a niece, the conceptual-linguistic allusion appears to combine Lev 18:6 and 13 [the MT text is about an aunt]!). It also treats defiling the temple. As a result they "have defiled their Holy Spirit and with a blaspheming tongue have opened their mouth against the precepts of the covenant of God, saying, They are not true!" (*CD* 5:11-12; ובלשון גדופים פתחו). To approach such blasphemers is to face certain punishment. Again, these texts support our contention that blasphemy is more than speech, for in this context, blasphemy, though primarily verbal, has taken on the element of being expressed in unfaithful action as well.

So Qumran evidences a rather wide view of blasphemy as it extends to actions that represent the denial of God's precepts. Both shameful utterance and unfaithfulness to Torah are in view.[30]

3. The Septuagint

The Key Terminology

In turning to the Greek translation of the Hebrew Scriptures, it is the Greek terms βλασφημεῖν/βλάσφημος/βλασφημία that need attention. The term refers to some type of hostile speech or slander.[31] This Greek text is important because Mark and Luke use the LXX. These three terms appear 9x as a verb, 6x as βλάσφημος, and 7x as βλασφημία for a total of 22x. Eleven of these appearances are in the deutero-canonical texts. If one adds the hexapla, then the verb occurs another fourteen times, while βλασφημία appears on three more occasions. Among the Hebrew terms represented by the translation of the verb are: גדף in the piel stem (2x for the verb- 4 Kgds 19:6, 22), יכח in the hiphil (1x- 4 Kgds 19:4 apparently), נאץ in the hithpolel (1x- Isa 52:5), and then a disputed Semitic term in Dan 3:29 (perhaps either אמר שלה [K] or שלו

---

[30]It should be noted before leaving the Qumran material that, though it is not tied explicitly to blasphemy terminology, the Temple scroll from cave 11 does refer to the death penalty using Deut 21:22-23 in *11QMiqdasch* 64.6-13. Death is required for anyone who slanders, leads the people astray or does evil against the people of God, including putting them at grave risk. The importance of this text to the overall discussion has been well developed by Otto Betz, "Probleme des Prozesses Jesu," in ANRW vol. II. 25.1 , pp. 603-10. See the discussion of Betz in chapter 1. The examples we see in the contemporary texts, particularly in Josephus, will often reinforce this connection and suggest that Qumran is not the only place it was held. The importance of this passage shall emerge in our discussion in chapter 4.

[31]LSJ, pp. 318-19. MM, p. 112 has a set of references from the papyri of *Vettius Valens* 44.4; 58.12; 67.20.

אמר [Q]).[32] It should also be noted that that the key verb גדף is rendered in the LXX by the following terms besides its two mentions with βλασφημεῖν: καταλαλεῖν (1x- Ps 43:16 LXX [A, S²]), παραλαλεῖν (1x-Ps 43:16 LXX [B, S¹]); παροξύνεῖν (2x- Num 15:30; Isa 37:23); and παροργιζεῖν (1x- Ezek 20:27). For the noun βλασφημία, the Semitic terms are נאצה (1x- Ezek 35:12) and a disputed term in Dan 3:96 Theodotion (= 3:29MT; either שלה [K] or שלו [Q]). Put differently, the various Semitic terms that render the Greek noun forms of blasphemy include מברך (1x- Isa 66:3 apparently), נאצה (1x-Ezek 35:12) and the disputed שלה [K] or שלו [Q] in Dan 3:29. Again the variation and slim distribution of the various terms confirms how the concept is rendered in a variety of ways. Blasphemy has a wide semantic field in both Hebrew and Greek.

Of the texts discussed already, the Greek term appears in 4 Kgds 19:4, 6, 22 = Isa 37:6, 23, in the fourth column of the Hexapla for Lev 24:11, and in Ezek 35:12. To this list should be added Tob 1:18S, which looks back at the Sennacherib incident of 4 Kgds and Isaiah as an example of someone fleeing when God judged blasphemy (περὶ τῶν βλασφημιῶν, ὧν ἐβλασφήμησεν). Sennacherib serves as an example of blasphemy that does not fit the limited technical definition that later emerged in the Mishnah, though the idea of those outside the nation blaspheming God should not be seen as surprising.

Since we are covering the Old Testament and its canonically disputed books, this is a good time to consider the Latin terminology of the Vulgate as well. The relevant terms here are *blasphemia* (12x OT, 5x Apoc- Tob 1:21; 1 Macc 7:38; 2 Macc 8:4; 10:35; 15:24), *blasphemo* (28x OT; 4x Apoc- Tob 13:16; Dan 14:8; 1 Macc 7:41; 2 Macc 12:14), and *blasphemus* (1x OT-Lev 24:14; 3x Apoc- 2 Macc 9:28, 10:4; 13:11). Most of the key Old Testament uses have already been discussed: Num 16:30; 2 Kings 19:3, 6, 22; Isa 37:3, 4, 6, 17, 23; Lev 24:11, 14, 16 (2x); and Neh 9:18, 26. Some new texts appear but refer to already discussed events: 2 Sam 12:14 (David's sin against Uriah); 2 Chron 32:17 (Sennacherib), Isa 5:24; 43:28, 48:11, Jer 23:17, and Ezek 5:15; 20:27 (in all six Israel's unfaithfulness leads to her being delivered over to "blasphemy"). A few texts are new references such as Jonathan's slaying a giant from Gath for blaspheming (2 Sam 21:21 = 1 Chron 20:1); Eliphaz's and Elihu's condemnation of Job as blaspheming (Job 15:5; 34:37), Zephaniah's condemnation of foreign blasphemy (2:8, 10), and numerous references in the PsalterH (9:24, 34; 43:17; 73:10, 18; 106:11). These references are for the most part verbal or reflect the description of corporate activities that reflect intense disrespect towards God. What remains is to look

---

[32]The dispute over the reading explains why we did not discuss this text when considering the Hebrew Scriptures. For more detail, see the discussion of Dan 3 below.

at the most significant texts in this material. The Semitic text appears with the
verse entry where it is present.

Isaiah 66:3 מזכיר לבנה מברך און

This text shows the close relationship between unfaithfulness and blasphemy.
The passage comes in a context where God describes the various acts of the
unfaithful who have not listened to him even as they continue to offer worship
(66:3-5). The relevant line in the Hebrew text involves one of four illustrative
comparisons made in v. 3, where positive actions are compared to negative
ones. The key phrase translates as "whoever makes a memorial offering of
frankincense, [is] like one who blesses an idol." The LXX renders this as ὁ
διδοὺς λίβανον εἰς μνημόσυνον ὡς βλάσφημος. The translator has apparently
paraphrased the passage and has noted that the act of blessing an idol is
similar to blasphemy, an association not at all surprising given the example of
the golden calf incident in the Pentateuch.

Daniel 3:96 (3:29 Eng.) די-יאמר שלה על אלההון די שדרך מישך ועבד נגוא

This text is unusual in that it is an instruction from a king outside of Israel to
show respect toward Israel's God, the very reverse of the Sennacherib
example of 2 Kings and Isaiah. In discussing the key terminology the Kethiv-
Qere problem of the Aramaic was already noted, but the reference to
blasphemy in the LXX is not disputed.[33] Though expressed somewhat
differently in the Septuagint's textual tradition, the idea is that
Nebuchadnezzar issued a decree stating that anyone who blasphemes the God
of Shadrach, Meshach, and Abednego shall be torn limb from limb and have
their house laid waste since there is no other god who delivers as their god
does.[34] The interesting thing about this text is that it is not an endorsement of
monotheism from the mouth of a foreign king, only a recognition of high
respect for Israel's God. What exactly constitutes blasphemy is not defined,
which is the case with many of the blasphemy texts.

---

[33]Some suggest the reading should be שאלה ("thing," see 4:14), while others opt for a Qere
of שלו ("remissness," see 6:5) or a Kethiv of שלה ("insult," "blasphemy"). See John Goldingay,
Daniel WBC 30 (Dallas: Waco, 1989), p. 67.

[34]The wording does differ. Θ reads, "ἣ ἂν εἴπῃ βλασφημίαν κατὰ τοῦ θεοῦ Σεδραχ . . .,"
while the bulk of the LXX tradition reads, "ὃς ἂν βλασφημήσῃ εἰς τὸν κύριον τὸν θεὸν Σεδρακ
. . .. The idea in both cases is the same. The rendering "god" is purposeful, since it is clear
that the king is arguing only for a show of respect toward the God of Israel in a world filled
with national gods. For the nature of the stylistic variation in these two Greek constructions in
the LXX, see Winifried Hamm, *Der Septuagine A-Text des Buches Daniel: Kap. 3-4 nach
dem Kölner Teil des Papyrus 967* (Bonn: Rudolf Habelt, 1977), p. 159.

1 Maccabees 2:6/ 2 Maccabees 8:4, 9:28, 10:4, 15:24

These texts are grouped together because they all discuss actions during the traumatic Maccabean period. Their conceptual unity indicates the value of considering them together.

1 Macc 2:6 follows the naming in 2:1-5 of the priest Mattathias and his five sons, including the hero Judas Maccabeus. The passage itself introduces a lament over Judah and Jerusalem as the father Mattathias surveys the devastation of a fallen Jerusalem with its holy temple in foreign hands.[35] The entire event is summarized by the introductory phrase of the verse: καὶ εἶδεν τὰς βλασφημίας τὰς γινομένας ἐν Ιουδα καὶ ἐν Ιερουσαλημ.[36] The fall of Jerusalem itself is seen as an act of blasphemy and the priest cries out asking why he should live to see this. In fact, he wonders why should he continue to live. The scene is reinforced in v. 14 as the patriarch and his sons tear their clothes, put on sackcloth, and mourn greatly. The sight of the capital of God's people fallen into foreign hands is an insult to God as far as these priests are concerned (2 Macc 8:2-4). This text thus associates blasphemy with the fate of the people and their holy places.

2 Macc 8:4 is part of a summary description in vv. 2-4 of what motivated Judas Maccabeus to take up the cause of the nation with six thousand loyalists. The verses read, "They implored the Lord to look upon the people who were oppressed by all; and to have pity on the temple that had been profaned by the godless; to have mercy on the city that was being destroyed and about to be leveled to the ground; to hearken to the blood that cried out to him; to remember also the lawless destruction of babies and the blasphemies committed against his name (καὶ περὶ τῶν γενομένων εἰς τὸ ὄνομα αὐτοῦ βλασφημῶν); and to show his hatred of evil." What is difficult to be certain of in this text is whether blasphemies refer to utterances against God or serve as a summary description of the wide variety of actions described here. Goldstein prefers the latter suggesting that, "Antiochus IV committed blasphemy in his arrogance after the sack of Jerusalem (5:17, 21), repeating the sin of an earlier king of (As)syria (see II Kgs 19:22-24; Isa 37:23-25). He also did by presuming to set aside the Torah (cf. Dan 7:25, 11:36) and by forcing Jews to violate it, for violation of the Torah by Jews leads Gentiles to speak of the ineffectiveness of God's command and thus constitutes blasphemy (Ezek 36:16-27)."[37]

---

[35]The lament in vv. 7-13 recalls the laments of the Psalter (44, 74, 79) and of Lamentations.

[36]J. A. Goldstein, *I Maccabees*, AB (Garden City, New York: Doubleday & Company, 1976), p. 231, notes that the Greek root blasphemy appears at Isa 52:5 and Ezek 35:12, but suggests a conceptual parallel from Neh 9:18, 26.

[37]J. A. Goldstein, *II Maccabees*, p. 325

The clues to the answer may well come from other texts in 2 Maccabees, for in *2 Macc* 9:28 and 10:4, the term appears in a broad sense. In 9:28, Antiochus is described as a murderer and blasphemer (ἀνδροφόνος καὶ βλάσφημος), who suffered greatly for his crimes when God struck him down with a disease that brought him great internal pain.[38] Blasphemy here surely refers to more than his utterances, as he is described as an abominable fellow in v. 13. In 10:4, the occasion is the regaining and repurification of the temple. Maccabeus and his followers prostrate themselves and pray that they might never again be handed over to blasphemous and barbarous nations (μὴ βλασφήμοις καὶ βαρβάροις ἔθνεσιν παραδίδοσθαι). In this context as well, the term blasphemy is clearly a broad description of a general attitude and set of actions like those by Antiochus.

These Maccabean texts reveal the broad use of blasphemy to describe someone who has shown great disrespect to God in the way the people of God and his holy place have been treated. The example is significant in indicating that a technical sense of specific utterances is not the only way the term was used. The actions of Antiochus demanded a reaction. The Maccabean revolt is seen as an attempt to defend God's honor and be faithful to God and the holy city of his presence.

Similar in force is *2 Macc* 15:24. Here the setting is the opposition of the gentile ruler Nicanor to Maccabeus. The warrior-priest prays that Nicanor be opposed in battle, just as God had done to Sennacherib, the king of old who serves as the arch example of the gentile blasphemer.[39] Maccabeus asks that, "By the might of your arm may these blasphemers who come against your holy people be struck down (μεγέθει βραχίονός σου καταπλαγείησαν οἱ μετὰ βλασφημίας παραγινόμενοι ἐπὶ τὸν ἅγιόν σου λαόν)." In this text, blasphemy also carries a broad force and is focused on the opposition to God's people.[40]

---

[38]On this pattern of punishment for the flagrant sinner paralleling what the persecuted Judas and his men had suffered, see Goldstein, *II Maccabees*, p. 371; *2 Macc* 5:27; 10:6, and *1 Macc* 6:13.

[39]On Nicanor, one of the military leaders who tired and failed to restrain Judas in 165 BCE, see Goldstein, *I Maccabees*, p. 116.

[40]Two more Maccabean texts remain. In *2 Macc* 12:14 the use focuses on verbal remarks. Blasphemy is tied to the remarks from Gentiles in the town of Caspin. They are said to have railed at Judas Maccabeus, even blaspheming and saying unholy things. That blasphemers end up being punished is seen as they are buried alive in *2 Macc* 10:34-36. It is a judgment like that expressed in *Wis* 1:6, where blasphemers will not be freed from their words by wisdom. Another reference to blasphemy in the LXX material is *Sir* 3:16, which teaches that to forsake a father is like blasphemy. Obviously the point of comparison is seen as a forsaking of God. Finally, a reverse example appears in *Bel* 9, where Daniel is accused of blasphemy against Bel.

These texts about the Maccabean period indicate a consistent usage related to the disrespectful behavior of the nations towards God, his temple, and his people. It is both actions and utterances that are in view.[41]

4. The Pseudepigrapha

The Key Terminology

Blasphemy texts are rare in this material and tend to be general references. The relevant terminology can be covered more briefly as they have all been discussed. The verb and substantive forms of the Greek for blasphemy are rare, as each appears twice (*AsMos* 8.163 has one use of both the verb and noun, while the noun also appears in 9.1).[42] The remaining use is in the *TJob* 16:7.

Latin terms for blasphemy appear in six texts (*blasphemare-TMos* 8.5; *blasphemaverunt-LAB* 38.3; *blasphemabunt-LAB* 50.5; *blasphemantes-4 Ezra [= 5 Ezra]* 1.22; *blasphemiis- 4Ezra* 1:23; *blasphemi-FVisElijah Z* 10).[43] These Latin texts are largely general references, such as the reference to blasphemy in *FVisElijah Z* 10. For example, it simply lists blasphemy as one of the sins for which one is judged and suffers greatly in hell.[44] The two texts from *4 Ezra* allude to Israel's unfaithfulness in the wilderness, blasphemies for which God did not punish Israel. *LAB* 50.5 has Hannah of 1 Sam 1 fear that if her prayers are not answered those around her will blaspheme God. In 38.3, a certain Jair, who has ordered worship of Baal, has seven faithful men placed in a fire of judgment for failing to participate in the sacrifice and rebuking the pagan for his false worship. They are said to have blasphemed

---

[41]For consideration of another Maccabean text that does not use βλασφημός but τῶν δυφημιῶν, see *1 Macc* 7:38, which is discussed below in relationship to Josephus, *Ant* 12.406. This text shows the close relationship between a perception of blasphemy and insulting the priesthood.

[42]For these references, which belong to the fragments portion of the Testament, see the appendix to A.-M. Denis, *Concordance grecque des Pseudépigraphes d'Ancien Testament* (Louvain-la-Neuve: Université catholique de Louvain, 1987), p. 901. The fragments do not appear in *OTP*.

[43]For these references, see Wilfried Lechner-Schmidt, *Wortindex der lateinisch erhalten Pseudepigraphen zum Alten Testament*, TANZ 3 (Tübingen: A. Franke, 1990), p. 21. For discussion of *TMos* text (also sometimes called *Assumption of Moses*), see next note. I have not noted the terminology in some of these passages, since they are not in Greek, Latin, or a Semitic language. None of the fragments of *1En* from Qumran cover the relevant portions of the verses from that book.

[44]This text is found in line 12 of the *Apocalypse D'Elie* in the edited version by D. Be Bruyne, "Nouveaux Fragments: Des Actes de Pierre, de Paul, de Jean, d'André, et de l'Apocalype d'Élie," RBen 25 (1908):153-54.

Baal. Their refusal to worship and explanation for it is seen as blasphemous. This is a reversal of the normal usage since a foreign god is meant. The seven are preserved from perishing much as Shadrach, Meshach and Abednego were.

Most texts are simple warnings against blasphemy (*TIsaac* 4:52; *TJacob* 7:19) or note that those who blaspheme are cursed or are judged. For example, *2 En* 7:1 [J] has the blasphemer hanging, according to the pattern of the Hebrew Scripture. *1 En* 91:7, 11 predict blasphemy's increase before the end when judgment for it will result. Similar in thrust are *2 En* 42:14[J], 52:4, and *SibO* 2.260. This last text simply notes that blasphemers and ravagers of the pious will be judged. Here, as in the Maccabean material, there is a link between blasphemy and persecution of God's people. *2 En* 42:14[J] speaks of "lying blasphemies." The note indicates that something broader than formal pronunciation of the name is in view. *2 En 52:4* merely notes that a curse exists for the one who opens his mouth for cursing or blasphemy before the Lord. The results of these actions will be revealed in the judgment (*2 En* 52:15).

More revealing is *1 En* 27:2. The angel Uriel speaks to Enoch as part of his discussion of what future events will be like. The angel describes the accursed as those who speak with their mouth unbecoming words against the Lord and harsh words against his glory. A Greek rendering of latter part of this passage reads, καὶ περὶ τῆς δόξης αὐτοῦ σκληρὰ λαλήσουσιν. In Enoch, this expression is an alternative way to express blasphemy (*1 En* 1:9; 5.4G, 101.3; note also *En^a* 1 ii 13).[45] Once again blasphemy is verbal. It is seen as an attack on the person of God and is broader than merely saying the divine name. These sins will be judged at the final judgment as the wicked will reside in the accursed valley, a place they remain forever.[46]

So the few references of the so-called Pseudepigrapha also suggest a broad definition of the term blasphemy. It is primarily verbal, but is not limited to utterances involving the divine name (*1 En* 27:2; *2 En* 42:14[J]).

---

[45]M. Black, *The Book of Enoch or 1 Enoch: A New English Edition*. SVTP 7 (Leiden: E. J. Brill, 1985), p. 174.

[46]Four other pseudepigraphical texts remain. *JosAsen* 13:9 (Philonenko numbering; 13:13 in *OTP*) has Aseneth acknowledge that she had spoken blasphemies against her lord Joseph, a good example of the more secular use of slander. The *TMos* 8:5 predicts persecution so severe for Jews that they will engage in blasphemy. No details of what the blasphemy consists of are given. *TJob* 16:7 reports Job's claim that he did not blaspheme (ἐβλασφήμησα). Two passages appear in the fragmentary *AsMos* 8.163 (βλασφημοῦντος and βλασφημίαν) and 9.1 (βλασφημίας). Here Michael and the evil angel fight over Moses' body, a theme also present in Jude 9. The devil blasphemes Moses and Michael, with the angel simply replying, "the Lord rebuke you." There is no context to work with to determine exactly what was in mind. However, the text also indicates a verbal focus.

5. Josephus

The Key Terminology

The ancient Jewish historian Josephus covers a wide period of history in his works, extending from the origins of humanity and of the nation of Israel up to the recent events of the fall of Jerusalem to Rome. Without his writings, we would know significantly less about first century, second temple Jewish practice. So his testimony is among the most important witnesses we shall consider, especially given his knowledge of the center of Jewish power.[47] The major examples we shall consider all come from his *Antiquities*.

Josephus reflects a wide use of the various terms for blasphemy. The noun, βλασφημία, occurs 24x, while βλάσφημος appears 4x.[48] The verb, βλασφημέω, shows up in 39 texts. Before turning to the religious uses of the term βλασφημέω, it is worth noting that Josephus often sees this term in a less technical, more secular sense of slandering or hurling insults at a person. Among those insulted are Moses (*JW* 2.145, but those who do so faced a penalty of death, an allusion to what Exod 22:27 commands), Agrippa (*JW* 2.406), Tiberius (*JW* 2.493), Josephus (*JW* 5.375, 393 — Jeremiah as an example of what Josephus is going through), Caesar (*JW* 5.458), the nation's leaders (*Ant* 4.215 — like Exod 22:27), the blind and dumb [are not to be slandered] (*Ant* 4.276), Abimelech (*Ant* 5.242), Jonathan (*Ant* 6.237), and David (*Ant* 7.207, 265, 388 [by Shimei]). The noun βλασφημία is similar in predominating with secular usage. Among those blasphemed are David ([by Saul] *Ant* 6.238; [by Nabol] 6.300), Antigonus and Herod (*Ant* 14.405), Jews (*Ag Apion* 1.2, 59 [verb], 223; 2.32), the law of his own country (*Ag Apion* 2.143 — of Apion) and Moses (*Ant* 3.307 — with Aaron; *Ag Apion* 1.279). The term βλάσφημος appears most frequently with reference to Josephus himself as the object of such invective (*Life* 158, 320).

However, several texts address situations beyond these more mundane uses. The important examples follow.

Antiquities 3.180

This passage is interesting as Josephus is defending Jewish theology from the attack of those who argue that the Jews are "despising the divinity" (ὡς ἐκφαυλιζόντων ἡμῶν τὸ θεῖον) that the critics profess to honor (3.179).

---

[47]For a helpful summary of current attitudes towards Josephus, see H. Attridge, "Josephus and His Works," in *Jewish Writings of the Second Temple Period: Apocrypha, Pseudepigrapha, Qumran Sectarian Writings, Philo, Josephus*, CRINT, Section Two (Philadelphia: Fortress Press, 1984), pp. 185-233.

[48]K. H. Rengstorf, *A Complete Concordance to Flavius Josephus*, vol. 1 (Leiden: E. J. Brill, 1973), pp. 327-28.

In particular, Josephus is considering the vestments of the priests and high priests before turning to ask his readers to consider the tabernacle. He writes, "For if one reflects on the construction of the tabernacle and looks at the vestments of the priest and the vessels which we use for sacred ministry, he will discover that our lawgiver was a man of God and that these blasphemous charges (τὰς βλασφημίας ἀκούοντας) brought against us by the rest of men are idle."

Two points are significant. First, the blasphemy that the Jews slight God is really seen as an attack against the lawgiver, Moses, who is seen as speaking for God. Thus the blasphemy of the nations against Israel is an attack on a venerated leader of the nation, as well as against God. Second, the reply, dealing as it does with the place of worship, indicates that in Judaism this sacred locale was seen as a model and microcosm of what the universe is like (3.181-87). In the midst of this discussion there is the remark that the three fold division of the tabernacle reflects the earth, the sea, two places accessible to all, and then a third inaccessible area, representing heaven "reserved for God alone, because heaven is also inaccessible to men" (3.181). The remarks are designed to defend the Jewish sense of worship and their view of God's holiness as a sign that the charges are false. They also indicate how uniquely Judaism viewed God and his presence, a crucial theme to be considered in the next chapter in detail.

Antiquities 4.202, 207

In book, 4, chapter 8 of the *Antiquities* Josephus reviews the law that Moses gave. It is only here that he formally mentions blasphemy. Interestingly, the remark comes in between the discussion of the holy city where there is to be only one temple and a discussion of the feast at that temple. So Josephus is moving through laws related to God's presence.

In 4.202 he notes, "Let him that blasphemes God (ὁ δὲ βλασφημήσας θεόν) be stoned, then hung for a day, and buried ignominiously and in obscurity." The remark summarizes the blasphemy law by combining Lev 24:16 and Deut 21:22-23. It also indicates that whatever the debate is about the original meaning of Lev 24, in the first century this text was clearly read as a passage on blasphemy. Now there are no details here as to what blasphemy is, but a clue comes later in the same passage when Josephus turns to consider how other gods should be treated. In 4.207 he also summarizes the Law and presents an explanatory reading of Exod 22:27, "Let no one blaspheme the gods (Βλασφημείτω δὲ μηδεὶς θεούς) which other cities revere, nor rob foreign temples, nor take treasure dedicated in the name of any god." The issue of respect, whether in words or in things associated with the presence of deity, is the central concern. Blasphemy is seen as the verbal element, but the underlying concern is offense against things closely associated with the god in question. This view of respecting other gods is rooted in Exod 22:27 as expressed in the LXX, and is repeated by Josephus elsewhere (*Against Apion* 2.237) and is also noted by Philo (*Life of Moses* 2.38—as noted in the pagan example of Ptolemy II's respect for Yahweh in allowing the Torah to be translated).[49] Israel's painful experiences in seeing these actions done against her had made Israel sensitive to not treating others in a similar manner.

Antiquities 6.183

Josephus is considering the David-Goliath incident in one of the few texts that provide an explanation of the nature of the blasphemy in question. Josephus is dramatically presenting the view of David as he prepares to face the giant and compares it to an earlier battle David had with a bear. The key text, 6.183, reads, "Let this enemy then be reckoned even as one of those wild beasts, so long as he has insulted our army and blasphemed our God (ὀνειδίζων ἐκ πολλοῦ τήν στρατιὰν καὶ βλασφημῶν ἡμῶν τὸν θεόν), who will deliver him into our hands."

Important here is the explanation and the relationship between the elements of the insult-blasphemy. First, the remarks distinguish the attack on the army and that against God, but in a way that clearly relate the two. In fact, the connection is very much like the 2 Kgs 19 = Isa 37 passage, where Sennacherib's attack against the strength of Israel's army is seen as blasphemy against God. Since God is the greater figure, the crime against him is seen as the greater. So men are insulted, but it is God's power and honor that are blasphemed. The people in view are God's people, so that what is said about them is also said against the One they represent. Second, for David it is a matter of religious honor to respond to such a shameful act, and though he is small in stature, the youngster is confident that God will deliver the blasphemer into the young boy's hands. To make this point Josephus has David say to Goliath "I, in coming against you, have God for my armor" (6.187).

Antiquities 10.233, 242

Later in his history, Josephus is reviewing the story of Daniel and is coming to the end of the Babylonian line of Nebuchadnezzar. This leads him to discuss Baltasar, better known as Belshazzar. In relating the end of this king before the onslaught of Cyrus, king of Persia and Darius the Mede, Josephus relates a key portent of defeat that took place as he was engaged in festal revelry. The king was using the vessels of the temple that Nebuchadnezzar

---

[49]For the LXX reading of Exodus, see the discussion of this passage in the section on the Hebrew Scriptures above. Note also Philo's discussion of Exod 22:28a [Eng] cited in n. 10 above. For the *Ag Apion* text, see n. 9 above.

had brought from the conquering of Jerusalem and its temple. The conquering king had shown respect and had merely deposited the spoil in one of his temples, but the heir, Belshazzar, was different. In 10.233, Josephus notes, "Baltasar, however, went so far in his audacity to use them [the vessels], and while drinking and blaspheming God (μεταξὺ πίνων καὶ βλασφημῶν εἰς τὸν θεόν), he saw a hand coming out of the wall and writing certain syllables on (another) wall."[50]

Once again the offense is seen in a combination of verbal remarks and actions. For the reference to the king's audacity is surely a sign that the profane use of these holy vessels is part of what constitutes the offense (see *Ant* 4.202, 207 above). The whole affair is told in such a way that Josephus is suggesting that the king's arrogance is part of what has led to the sign pointing to his demise. In fact, this inference is confirmed later in the account in 10.242, which reads, "on the contrary, though Nebuchadnezzar's way of living had been changed to that of beasts because of his impieties, and only on obtaining mercy after many supplications and entreaties had he been restored to a human way of living and to his kingdom and had therefore until the day of his death praised God as the possessor of all power and the guardian of men, Baltasar had forgotten these things and had grievously blasphemed the Deity (καὶ πολλὰ μέν ἐβλασφήμησε τὸ θεῖον) and had allowed himself with his concubines to be served from His vessels." The description of the "severe" blasphemy and of the use of the vessels at the end of the citation is tied closely together in the remark with a Greek μέν - δέ construction, indicating the interrelationship between the blasphemy and the slanderous means of celebration. As Josephus goes on to discuss, the entire affair had brought the wrath of God down upon the king (10.243). Once again words and deeds are seen as forming the core of a blasphemy.

Antiquities 12.406

Josephus has now reached the Maccabean period and is discussing the encounter with the military leader Nicanor that was already noted above in the discussion of *2 Macc* 15:24.[51] Nicanor has brought Judas into his trust, only to betray him and try to arrest him. But the attempt fails and the foreign leader is tracking Maccabeus down, arriving at the temple, where the priests note their sacrifices made to God on behalf of the king. The important text follows. This text is quite ambiguous, so the Greek is noted and then possible translations are discussed. It reads, "ὁ δὲ βλασφημήσας αὐτους ἠπείλησεν, that unless the people delivered up Judas to him, he would pull down the temple when he returned." Now the question is whether the verse should read, "the one who

---

[50]A few manuscripts (R, O) read πρός, not εἰς in this line, but it makes no difference in the sense.

[51]See also *1 Macc* 7:26-43.

slandered them threatened," in which case there is no blasphemy noted in the passage, or should the line read "The one who blasphemed threatened them," in which case the remark about pulling down the temple summarizes the blasphemy. Put grammatically, is the accusative αὐτους to go with the participle or with the verb?

It must be admitted that the decision is not a clear one. Nevertheless, as we saw in several of these texts from Josephus, there often is a temple-blasphemy association. In addition, the pattern is that one who acts arrogantly is judged, as the Belshazzar incident shows. What follows in the account is the discussion of Nicanor's defeat, a defeat that led to the establishing of an annual festival that was still celebrated in the first century. In addition, the account has a strong parallel in *1 Macc* 7:33-38. There it is clear that the insults are directed at the priests, since Nicanor mocks, derides, and defiles the priests as well as speaking arrogantly. It is also possible the insults included spitting at them. Now this reading, it must be admitted, favors taking the accusative with the participle. Yet in a detail that Josephus does not give, *1 Maccabees* notes that the priests went in and appealed to God on the basis of the fact that God chose this house to be the place where his name dwelled. So his people prayed that divine vengeance should be taken on this man and that he should be slain in battle, "remembering their defamations (τῶν δυσφημιῶν) and let them live no longer" (*1 Macc* 7:37-38).[52] What this means is that apparently the priests saw the attack on them as ultimately an attack on God, as Exod 22:27 suggests, as the David-Goliath incident showed, and as the Sennacherib incident indicates. Thus, one could still read the text in a more secular way, as the priests being insulted by Nicanor, and yet still be quite justified in regarding the action as blasphemous, because of the setting where it took place and who it was who was slandered. Of course, if the other reading is adopted, then the presence of blasphemy is more explicit.

This text is included in this survey, then, because it has a strong claim to be another example of blasphemy, regardless of how the grammatically ambiguous line is read. The passage is significant because it reflects a pattern that has been seen of a particularly significant connection between blasphemy and attacking the people of God, especially the leadership. In addition, the association of the locale of God's presence and offense is also present in this text. The act of arrogance is met with God's judgment, another sequence Josephus likes to note.

---

[52]Again reflecting the ambiguity and difficulty in intepreting the scene, the *NRSV* translates the *1 Macc* phrase as "their blasphemies." On this text and the possibility of spitting being in view, J. A. Goldstein, *1 Maccabees*, p. 340 on vv. 34-35. The model for the prayer is 1 Kings 8:29-30, 43, 9:3. See also F. M. Abel, *Les Livres des Maccabees*, Études Bibliques (Paris: J. Garbalda, 1949), p. 141.

Antiquities 20.105-17

Yet one more incident associated with the temple presents the final example
from Josephus. Here the issue is not one of terminology, but of action and
response. The incident described here takes place during the procuratorship of
Cumanus (48-53 CE). All the elements for a major clash are present, as it is
Passover and the scene takes place at the temple, so religious feeling is high.
Josephus introduces the account by noting that he is describing an "uprising"
(στάσεως), during which "many of the Jews lost their lives" (20.105).[53]

On the fourth day of what was a week of celebration, one of the soldiers,
guarding the temple and showing a tremendous lack of cultural sensitivity,
exposed his private parts (αἰδοῖα) to the crowd (20.108). The reaction was
immediate. The crowd was angry and raging, for they said "it was not they
who had been insulted, but that it was an act of impiety against God (τὸν θεὸν
ἠσεβῆσθαι)." The result was that the crowd also started to slander (i.e.,
blaspheme) Cumanus. The crowd's reaction required the leader to call out the
entire army from the fortress Antonia to quell the disturbance. Many were
crushed to death as they sought to escape the city. Upon reaching the narrow
gates they trampled over each other trying to flee. Josephus closes the account
noting, "Such were the calamities produced by the indecent behavior of a
single soldier" (20.112).

Now this might not seem like an incident that qualifies for the survey,
except that two additional factors need to be noted. First, Josephus follows
this first account with a second soldier incident, where one of the soldiers
finding a copy of Moses' law tears it "in two while he uttered blasphemies
and railed violently" (ἐπιβλασφημῶν καὶ πολλὰ κατακερτομῶν; 20.115). The Jews
made an embassy to Cumanus "to avenge not them but God, whose laws had
been subjected to outrage. For they could not endure to live, since their
ancestral code was thus wantonly insulted." Cumanus beheaded the solider
and thus avoided an upraising from surfacing a second time.[54]

The description of this second event to Cumanus is key in understanding
both incidents, since the second incident is told in a way that makes it parallel
to the first. In addition, the description of the action to Cumanus in the second
incident never uses the term blasphemy though that is what is being
described. God needed to be avenged and the acts were insults against the
Law.

---

[53]The term could well be translated "a revolt." In the sentence Josephus throws it forward
to make the point emphatically and dramatically.

[54]It is perhaps significant, given the interpretive disputes that exist today concerning
whether Jews had the right to exercise capital punishment, that the Roman procurator carried
out this execution, even though it was Jewish religious sensitivities that had been violated.
Thus this text suggests Jews did not have the right, at least at this time.

The second clue that both of these incidents should be read as blasphemous in Jewish eyes is that in the parallel description of the exposure incident in *JW* 2.223-26, it is noted that many of the more rash in the crowd (i.e., the youth) picked up stones and threw them at the soldiers. This detail is significant, since the penalty for blasphemy is stoning (Lev 24:11-16, 23). It is also noted there that the soldier spoke as he revealed himself to the crowd.

This shocking pair of incidents again shows how respect for the Law and for God's presence as reflected in the temple could be the ground for seeing blasphemy as present. Again, as we have seen consistently, it is action as well as word that can be the basis for this perception.

The texts from Josephus are among the most detailed and contemporary that shall be considered. Their importance is that they show that blasphemy can come from words or from acts. Three particular associations are viewed with sensitivity: the people-leadership, the temple, and the Law. God's intimate relationship with all three fuels the sensitivity. Thus offensive remarks or actions against the people, the temple or the Law can result in the view that blasphemy is present and that judgment will come either directly from God or that honoring His Name requires that action must be taken.

6. Philo

The Key Terminology

Philo is the second significant individual witness from our period. His writings span both the biblical text and the currents of ancient philosophy.[55] His remarks also show the range that the Greek term for blasphemy can possess, as his uses range from secular uses that mean slander (*Flac* 5.33-35, 17.142) to one of the longest developed discussions of blasphemy that we have for the period (*Dec* 61-64).[56] Philo uses the verb βλασφημέω on ten occasions, while the noun, βλασφημία, also appears 10x.[57] The term, βλάσφημος shows up only twice.

The discussion of Philo below involves two types of texts. The first three citations cover actions that are seen as offensive to God, but are not explicitly called blasphemy. The remaining texts treat blasphemy directly. Philo also

---

[55]Peder Borgen, "Philo of Alexandria," in *Jewish Writings of the Second Temple Period: Apocrypha, Pseudepigrapha, Qumran Sectarian Writings, Philo, Josephus* CRINT, Section Two (Philadelphia: Fortress Press, 1984), pp. 233-82.

[56]The two texts from *Flaccus* involve Flaccus speaking against the king in 5.33-35 and Isadorus speaking against Flaccus in 17.142.

[57]Günter Meyer, *Index Philoneus* (Berlin: De Gruyter, 1974), p. 58.

moves across a broad range of events, moving from the incident at Babel in Gen 11 to more recent controversies of his own time. What he reveals is a range of actions like that seen at Qumran and in Josephus.

On the Confusion of Tongues 154

Philo is discussing the Gen 11 Babel incident, which he describes as "daring to set foot on heavenly matters" (152, καὶ τῶν ὀλυμπίων ἐπιβαίνειν ἐτόλμησαν). Those who conspire to build the tower are called "revilers." In 154, he describes their action:

> For when, insatiate in wrongdoing, they had taken their fill of sins against all that is of earth and sea and air whose allotted nature is to perish, they thought it well to turn their forces against the divine natures in heavens. But on them nothing that exists can usually have effect except evil speech (τὸ βλασφημεῖν), though indeed even the foul tongue does not work harm to those who are its objects (for they still possess their nature unchanged) but only brings disasters beyond cure on the revilers.

He then goes on to note that God acted before they finished their impiety (ἀσεβείας, 155).

The text is significant, because it equates the action with blasphemy through the comparison of the attempt to harm through evil speech. Philo also sees God dealing quite directly with the act. In fact, Philo's emotion of revulsion for the crime comes through quite clearly, something many of the Philonic texts will evidence. The multiplication of languages as a punishment may also indicate a comparison. If one sees a principle of justice being applied where the punishment is like the crime, then the act is punished in a verbal way, because the crime was like speaking against God. This means that blasphemy would involve both speech and act.

On the Migration of Abraham 115-117

In this passage, Philo is reviewing the Balaam incident and explains how God turned cursing into blessing. The illustration is actually the basis of a principle Philo wishes to argue: one must look at the heart, not just the utterance. To make his point, he reverses the illustration to a negative-positive example. He notes that people such as proctors, tutors, schoolmasters, parents, and magistrates often revile or offer accusation in order to give blessing. This means that the test of an utterance is its intention.[58] So he says in 117, "Let no treatment, then, that is marked by prayers and blessings on the one hand, or by abusing or cursing (εἰς βλασφημίας καὶ κατάρας) on the other hand, be

---

[58]In *On Joseph* 74, Philo gives a similar example using only parental criticism. There he says, "it is against all morality to call such treatment evil-speaking or outrage (βλασφημίαν οὔθ᾽ ὕβριν) instead of friendliness and benevolence."

referred to the way it finds vent in speech, but rather to the intention; for from this, as from a spring, is supplied the means of testing each kind of spoken words." Now Philo's point here is that Balaam's words alone do not mean that he really wanted to bless, but the exact opposite. Only God was responsible for the reversal.

This text raises the possibility that speech, even hostile speech or positive speech, needs to be interpreted. The question is whether this concern, in fact, reflects how threatening speech was viewed. It will take other examples to see if this kind of distinction appears and is important.

Special Laws 4.197

This text treats the teaching of Lev 19:14, which commands a person not to revile the deaf. It is an excellent example of an everyday use of the concept. The start of the discussion reads in 4.197, "Another excellent injunction is that no one is to revile or abuse any other (μηδεὶς μηδένα βλασφημῇ καὶ κακηγορῇ), particularly a deaf-mute who can neither perceive the wrong he suffers nor retaliate in the same way, nor on equal footing." He notes that God protects those who cannot protect themselves and argues that such acts are punished with God's wrath. These three examples show how evil speech in general was viewed. While the examples from *The Migration of Abraham* and from *Special Laws* discuss slander in general, the example of Babel shows how easily it is to move from utterance to action and associate the concepts. The remaining examples treat blasphemy more directly and surface Philo's intense feelings about the offense.

Embassy to Gaius 368

The first of the examples to treat blasphemy more directly summarizes a diplomatic mission of five Jews before the ruler Gaius (349-67). One of the participants was Philo. The problem was that Gaius was angered that they refused to address him or regard him as a god. The five were angrily examined by the ruler, but were released with Gaius's judgment, "These men do not appear to me to be wicked so much as unfortunate and foolish, in not believing that I have been endowed with the nature of God" (367).

Philo describes the relief at having escaped "a theater and a prison rather than a court of justice." But their departure led to ridicule from the crowd that even came to the point of their being struck and tortured by the mob. Also disturbing were:

> the blasphemies which those around us uttered against the Deity (διά τε τῶν εἰς τὸ θεῖον βλασφημιῶν), and the threats they breathed forth against ourselves, and which the "autocrat" poured forth with such vehemence, being indignant with us not in behalf of anyone else, for in that case, he would have soon been appeased, but because of himself and his great desire to be declared

a god, in which desire he considered that the Jews were the only people who
did not acquiesce, and who were unable to subscribe to it (368).

Once again the blasphemies are not detailed, only noted. Yet there is a
depraved irony between what "breathed forth" from the crowd against God
and what came from the ruler, who also poured forth his own threats and
indignities because the Jewish captives would not acknowledge the ruler as a
god. Conceptually related verbs are used for the utterances of both
(ἐπανατάσεων/ἐπαντείετο). Clearly the refusal to give the emperor such honor
suggests that part of the offense for Philo was the leader's desire to be
associated with the only higher power, something the faithful ambassadors
refused to do. Significantly, this is one of three such passages where Philo
mentions blasphemy and equality with God. The consistency with which the
two topics of blasphemy and a person equating themselves to the divine are
mentioned suggests that, for Philo, an important linkage exists between the
two.

On Flight and Finding 84

Philo is considering cities of refuge as an example of God's mercy. But what
of the possibility of someone misusing the protective haven of a city of
refuge? Such an abuse is Philo's concern in this short discussion. He equates
the action with accusing God as the cause of the offense and concludes, "But
to pronounce Deity the cause of evil is a spot which is hard to cure, or rather
which is altogether incurable" (80). Such offenders should be punished. Then
in 83 Philo discusses Exod 21:15 as an example of the type of punishment
required, "Therefore having further commanded the unholy man who is a
speaker of evil against divine things to be removed from the most holy places
and to be given up to punishment, he proceeds to say, 'He who hates his
mother and father, let him die.' And in a similar manner he says, 'he who
accuses his father or mother, let him die.'"

The analogy leads to a conclusion in 84, also made by analogy, with one's
human parents: "He here all but cries out and shouts that there is no pardon
whatever to be given to those who blaspheme the Deity (ὅτι τῶν εἰς τὸ θεῖον
βλασφημούντων). For if they who bring accusations against their mortal parents
are led away to death, what punishment must be thought that those men
deserve who venture to blaspheme the Father and Creator of the Universe
(τοὺς τὸν τῶν ὅλων πατέρα καὶ ποιητὴν βλασφημεῖν ὑπομένοντας)?" In a classic
lesser to greater argument, Philo takes the Exodus command and applies it to
false accusation against God, so that the inference is that to falsely accuse
God is blasphemy. Such an act is subject to the same penalty one faces when
one accuses parents wrongly.

What is significant about the example is that it clearly shows that
blasphemy is not a technical term for Philo that involves the use of a specific

term for God. That is not to say that Philo's views are automatically those of others, but we have seen a similar breadth of application for the concept of blasphemy at Qumran and in Josephus. These three Jewish sources do not share in the same particulars, but all apply the term in the sense of certain actions being blasphemous because they are an inherent offense against God.

On the Life of Moses 2.205-06

As Philo tells the story of the great ancient figure, Moses, he also relates some of the nation's key legislation. Included in that list at this point is the origin of the ruling from Lev 24:10-23 (2.192-208). Some of his detail goes beyond the text, yet his views are an indication of how the text was interpreted.

In 2.196, the man is said to have "cursed it [heaven] with his accursed, and polluted, and defiled soul, and his wicked tongue." Philo's sense of indignation is expressed in his judgment in 2.197 "that no man could possibly devise any punishment adequate to such enormous impiety." The emotion rises further in 2.199 with the exclamation and explanation, "O man! Does anyone curse God? What other god can he invoke to ratify and confirm the curse? Is it not plain that he must invoke God to give effect to his curses against himself? Away with such profane and impious ideas!" So Moses tossed the man into prison until he heard "what the author of such a monstrous and unprecedented impiety and unholy crime ought to suffer" (2.201).

In reviewing the Leviticus text, Philo distinguishes between cursing God leading to guilt for sin and naming the Name, which calls for death (2.203-04). He then extends the application to foreign gods out of respect for the name of God (2.205). In fact, he reads this point as the passage's primary application. But the naming of the Name is not the only blasphemy, just the most offensive, as he declares in 2.206, "But if anyone were, I will not say to blaspheme against the Lord of Gods and men, but were even to dare to utter his name unseasonably, he must endure punishment of death (εἰ δὲ τις οὐ λέγω βλασφημήσειεν εἰς τὸν ἀνθρώπων καὶ θεῶν κύριον, ἀλλὰ καὶ τολμήσειεν ἀκαίρως αὐτοῦ φθέγξασθαι τοὔνομα, θάνατον ὑπομεινάτω τὴν δίκην)." The way the penalty is spelled out is quite interesting, since Philo makes a comparison and cannot even dare to contemplate someone blaspheming God. Yet even the inappropriate use of the Name is so offensive that it also will yield a judgment of death.

Four features of this passage merit attention. First, there is a focus on the use of the divine Name, a factor that shall become increasingly important. Second, this passage gives probably as no other to be considered the sense of revulsion that blasphemy raised for those who sought to honor God. Third, the distinction between cursing God and using his Name in an utterance is made, though how the distinction works is not spelled out. Fourth, and this point is interesting in light of the previous one, there still remains using the Name unseasonably and then blaspheming God. Yet both are seemingly worthy of death. In fact, so sensitive is the use of the Name that its unseasonable use outside of explicit blasphemy can be punished.

On Dreams 2.130-31

In his discourse on dreams, Philo is considering the dreams of Joseph and explaining how one can interpret them. In an aside, Philo turns to what he calls afterward "dreams of vain opinion" (2.155). It is here that he mentions an unnamed Egyptian prefect and governor, who tried to suspend Jewish law and claimed to be divine. This governor argued that he was the whirlwind, war, deluge, thunderbolt, the calamity of famine, the misery of pestilence, and an earthquake (2.129).

Philo's commentary follows in 2.130-33. Here is the full citation, as its significance is obvious:

> (130) What then can we say that a man who says, or who merely thinks such things as these, is? Is he not an evil of an extraordinary nature? He surely must be some foreign calamity, brought over from the sea, or from some other world, since he, a man in every respect miserable, has dared to compare himself to the all-blessed God. (131) We must likewise add, that he is daring here to utter blasphemies against the sun (τοὺς ἄλλους ἀστέρας βλασφημεῖν), and the moon, and the rest of the stars, whenever anything which has been looked for according to the seasons of the year, either does not happen at all, or is brought about with difficulty; if, for instance, the summer causes too much heat, or the winter too excessive a cold, or if the spring or autumn were unseasonable, so that one were to become barren and unfruitful, and the other to be profile only in diseases. (132) Therefore, giving all imaginable license to an unbridled mouth and abusive tongue, such a man will reproach the stars as not bringing their customary tribute, all but claiming for the things of earth the reverence and adoration of the heavenly bodies, and for himself above them all, in proportion as he, as being a man, looks upon himself as superior to the other animals. (133) Such men then are classed by us as the very teachers of vain opinion.

Among the values of the citation is that once again Philo's revulsion for someone making such arrogant claims comes through. The claim to be like God is "evil of an extraordinary nature." It also serves as an insult to the heavenly bodies, who are seen, as is common in the ancient world, to possess their own spheres of influence. Such claims are empty, but still are shocking. For Philo, God's honor, and even that of the heavens, demand some sense of respect for the distance between human and heavenly beings. One can "dare" to make such comparisons, but it is the rambling of "vain opinion" and of "imaginable license" given to "an unbridled mouth and abusive tongue."

Decalogue 61-69

The theme of the claim to be equal to deity also comes up in Philo's exposition of the Decalogue. Here Philo is appealing to his audience not to worship rulers, who claim to be like God. A part of this discussion, 61-65, is also significant, so it deserves a full citation as well:

> (61) As, therefore, if any one were to assign the honors of the great king to his satraps and viceroys, he would appear to be not only the most ignorant and senseless of men, but also the most fool-hardy, giving to slaves what belongs to the master; in the same manner, let the man who honors the Creator, with the same honors as those with which he regards the creature, know that he is of all men the most foolish and the most unjust, in giving equal things to unequal persons, and that too not in such a way as to do honor to the inferior, but only to take it from the superior. (62) There are again some who exceed in impiety, not giving the Creator and the creature even equal honor, but assigning to the latter all honor and respect, and reverence, and to the former nothing at all, not thinking him worthy of even the common respect for being recollected; for they forget him whom alone they should recollect, aiming, like demented and miserable men as they are, at attaining to an intentional forgetfulness. (63) Some men again are so possessed with an insolent and free-spoken madness, that they make an open display of impiety which dwells in their hearts, and venture to blaspheme the Deity (προφέροντες βλασφημεῖν ἐπιχειροῦσι τὸ θεῖον), whetting an evil speaking tongue, and desiring, at the same time, to vex the pious, who immediately feel an indescribable and irreconcilable affliction, which enters in at their ears and pervades the whole soul; for this is the great engine of impious men, by which alone they bridle those who love God, as they think it better at the moment to preserve silence, for the sake of not provoking their wickedness further. (64) Let us, therefore, reject all such impious dishonesty, and not worship those who are our brothers by nature, even though they may have received a purer and more immortal essence than ourselves (for all created things are brothers to one another inasmuch as they are created; since the Father of them all is one, the Creator of the Universe); but let us rather, with our mind and reason, and with all our strength, gird ourselves up vigorously and energetically to the service of that Being who is uncreated and everlasting, and the maker of the universe, never shrinking or turning aside from it, nor yielding to a desire of pleasing the multitude, by which even those who might be saved are often destroyed. (65) Let us, therefore, fix deeply in ourselves this first commandment as the most sacred of all commandments, to think that there is but one God, the most highest, and to honor him alone; and let not polytheistic doctrine ever even touch the ears of any man who is accustomed to seek for the truth with purity and sincerity of heart...

The explanation goes on to rank the sins of polytheists as those who worship the heavenly objects. They are in lesser error than those who worship and fashion idols.

The citation reveals that the key to Philo's view is his commitment to the first commandment. In his view, there is no possibility of equal honor being given to creature and Creator.[59] As with other texts, the sense of deep offense is expressed openly. In fact, even one's ears are to be protected from anything that rings with polytheistic implications (65). Nothing is more fundamental than the unique position God occupies within his Creation.

This *Decalogue* text reflects a consistency in Philo's views and makes it clear why three of the four texts discussing blasphemy turn to cases where a human is claiming divine-like authority. Humans are not able to breach the gulf that exists between their created nature and the unchangeable, eternal essence of God. Claims to do so are not only arrogant and vain; they are blasphemous. Though the *Decalogue* text makes this point in the most detail, this is a view that dominates the Philonic description of blasphemy's implications. Philo reveals an understanding of blasphemy grounded explicitly in the theology of the first commandment. His concern is the tendency of rulers to demand the ascription of divinity, an act that represents a grave offense against the only true God.

7. The Mishnah and Tosefta

The Key Terminology

The survey now moves beyond the key first century period. Nevertheless, the Mishnah, as a late second century collection of rulings of oral torah, is significant as it often reflects older practices and also shows which concerns dominated later periods.[60] The examples can be covered more briefly, since most of the instances merely state a position as a matter of legal principle. Also important for illustrative purposes are the three examples from the Tosefta, the supplement to the Mishnah. The various forms of the key term גדף appear seven times in the Mishnah (*Ker* 1.1-2 [2x in 1.2]; *Sanh* 6.4; 7.4-5; 9.3) and three more times in the Tosefta (*Sotah* 3.18; *Meg* 3.41; *Kerit* 1.1). The forms of קלל appear twenty-eight times in the Mishnah, but most of them do not refer to blasphemy but to cursing the father or mother (e.g., *Sanh* 7.8; *Yeb* 2.5) or to reading of the Blessings and Cursings (e.g., *Meg* 3.6; 7.5, 8). The one relevant example using this term is *Sanh* 9.6. It is discussed below.

---

[59]There is dispute about how consistent Philo is here, given the language of exaltation and deity surrounding Moses in *Questions and Answers on Exodus* 2.40-45. This significant passage will receive detailed treatment in our next chapter. It will be seen that Philo's remarks can be read in a way that does not reflect inconsistency but rather coherence.

[60]*The Literature of the Sages, First Part: Oral Tora, Halakha, Mishna, Tosefta, Talmud, External Tractate*, ed. Shmuel Safrai, CRINT (Philadelphia: Fortress Press, 1987), pp. 211-62.

m Sanhedrin 6.4

The Mishnah discusses how a capital execution, that is, stoning, takes place. It notes that some of those who are stoned are hanged afterward until the end of sunlight when they are removed for burial. There is a difference of opinion about those who qualify for the hanging. Rabbi Eliezar (c 90 CE) argues that all who are stoned are hanged, while the Sages limit hanging only to blasphemers and idolaters. "No one is hanged excepting the blasphemer and the idolater (אינו נתלה אלא המגדף והעובד)." Then after discussing and mostly rejecting the possibility that women are hanged, the passage closes with, "Why was this man hanged? Because he blasphemed the Name (שביירך את-השם מפני), and the Name of Heaven was profaned (ונמצא שם שמים מתחלל)."

Several points are worth noting. First, the text is developing teaching about hanging the one executed from Deut 21:23, which is cited just before the concluding remark. Second, the Sages' limiting the hanging to blasphemers and idolaters shows how they sought to limit the passage's application, but also, thirdly, indicates that blasphemy and idolatry are seen as two heinous sins.[61] The linkage of blasphemy and idolatry is something that will frequently occur in the rabbinical material. It should be noted that crucifixion came to be associated with the hanging in a later period, though it took place simultaneously with the execution, not subsequent to it.[62] Fourth, the importance of uttering the Name, as Lev 24 mentioned, also becomes more prominent. Fifth, the offense of blasphemy is described as profaning the Name. In one of the uses, the euphemism "to bless" occurs. Nevertheless, the issue, as always, is dishonoring God.

m Sanhedrin 7.4-6, 10

We group several units together because they reflect the close association between blasphemy and idolatry. The discussion begins in 7.4 with a list of who is subject to stoning indicating the various types of sin that qualify. Certain sexual sins (various forms of incest and bestiality) are included. In addition, others subject to death are the blasphemer (והמגדף), the idolater in a variety of expressions, the profaner of the Sabbath, those who curse parents, overpower a woman engaged to another, entice or mislead into idolatry, engage in sorcery, and the rebellious son.

The discussion then proceeds to detail each of these violations, explaining when culpability exists. For the blasphemer (המגדף) the culpability emerges upon his "pronouncing the Name" (עד שיפרש השם; 7.5). This remark goes back to Lev 24 as well. There follows detail about how such testimony is to be taken in public trial. The witnesses are not to repeat the blasphemy in public,

---

[61]The severity of these crimes is also discussed in *m. Sanh.* 9.3, a text to be noted below.

[62]David J. Halperin, "Crucifixion, the Nahum Pesher, and the Rabbinic Penalty of Strangulation," JJS 32 (1981): 32-46.

but use a euphemism like "may Jose smote Jose" to indicate that blasphemy was uttered. Only when everyone is excused and the chief witnesses are left with the judges do they repeat exactly what was said. If blasphemy is reported, then the judges stand up and rend their garments. Such testimony needs corroboration. The next unit (7.6) discusses the kinds of idolatry that make for culpability. Included is participating in idolatrous worship, while mentioned later is one who "instigates" idolatry (7.10).

This text is important, because it is the one place where trial procedure for blasphemy is discussed. The focus on the Name has a limiting effect on how many people can formally be convicted of blasphemy. It is so limiting, in light of the other texts raised, that one wonders if the most limited example is discussed here. Other texts to be considered indicate there was debate about what had to be pronounced (*m Scheb* 4.13 — involving R. Meir, c. 140 CE).[63] J. Blinzler has argued that the mishnaic code reflects the more humanitarian approach of the Pharisees to such questions, in contrast to the harsher example of Sadducean authority. The Sadducean approach surfaces in the various examples of execution present during the time they exercised political control before 70 CE.[64] Blinzler's view has not gone unchallenged.[65] Strobel prefers to argue that the case can be made that mishnaic procedures were not yet in effect in the period before 70 CE.[66] He follows with a careful discussion of eleven examples to defend the point. Given what is yet to be seen about debate on this naming question and the previous examples of blasphemy already noted, it seems likely that the *m Sanh* 7.5 text represents the narrowest interpretation of this law, a restricting of capital punishment during a period when capital punishment was a largely theoretical discussion anyway, given how the nation had been overrun. As other texts will show, there seems to be evidence of controversy on this matter and the decision ultimately came down in favor of a more limiting exercise of power, not a surprise when real power has been limited already. The fact that the debate continues into the Talmudic period, as will be seen, indicates just how persistent the discussion remained.

---

[63]This text will be considered below. Another indication of the respect with which the Name is treated appears in *m. Yom* 3.8, 6.2 and *m. Sot* 7.6. In 6.2, the personal name of God is pronounced by the priests in benediction, but the people use a euphemism "the name of the glory of the kingdom" in their response. In 7.6, it is noted that at temple blessings the Name is pronounced as written, while in the provinces a substitute is used. All of this shows how much care was given to using the Name.

[64]*Der Prozeß Jesu,* 4th ed. (Regensburg: Friedrich Pustet, 1969), pp. 216-29.

[65]August Strobel, *Die Stunde der Wahrheit* WUNT 21 (Tübingen: J. C. B. Mohr [Paul Siebeck], 1980), pp. 48-61.

[66]On p. 50, Strobel argues that "Eine Reihe von Beobachtungen soll die These stützen, daß allgemein zur Zeit Jesus die mischnische Gesetzgebung noch nicht in Kraft war."

m Sanhedrin 9.3

This passage shows just how serious a crime blasphemy is. There are four different kinds of death penalty discussed: stoning, burning, beheading, and strangling. The debate in this mishnah is which penalty is more severe. Rabbi Simeon argues that burning is more severe than stoning, but he is overruled by the Sages who argue that idolatry and stoning show stoning to be more severe, since these crimes require stoning.[67] The assumption of the argument is that these two crimes are among the worst and therefore demand a more severe punishment: "If stoning were not the more severe, it would not have been prescribed for the blasphemer and idolater (לא נתנה למגדף ולעובד גלולים)." In fact, the note in the Blackman edition of the Mishnah reads, "Blasphemy and idolatry are deemed the most heinous of all transgressions."[68] This reflects an attitude already seen in the texts from Philo, where the theology of the first commandment takes a paramount position.

m Sanhedrin 9.6

This text can be considered briefly, but is potentially significant. The passage is considering when "the zealots may lay hold" of a person, that is, slay them for a serious offense.[69] Among the punishable offenses are stealing a service vessel and having sexual intercourse with an "Aramaic woman" (an idolatress). Second on the list of three offenses is והמקלל בקוסם, or "the one who curses by the Kosem." The term Kosem is disputed.[70] Many take it as another way to refer to the name of God or as a reference to the disguised name for God. So speech that misuses or insultingly refers to God is subject to instant justice. The Messianic reference is important, because it could suggest a view other than the one seen in *m Sanh* 7.5, where the Name must be explicitly used. However, the reference is so brief and uncertain enough in character that one must be careful how much to make of it.

m Schᵉbuoth 4.13

This text gives the first indication of debate within the rabbinical tradition over the use of the divine Name in cases of blasphemy. The passage is

---

[67]The rabbi Simeon referred to here is probably Gamaliel II, a rabbi of the second generation after Hillel (c 140 CE). As we cite traditional material, the date of the rabbi tied to the tradition will always be noted. In doing so, this does not mean that the passage necessarily dates from that time, but only indicates how the tradition presents the material. The date given represents an approximate date for the beginning of the ministry unless otherwise noted.

[68]Philip Blackman, *Mishnayoth: Order Kodashim*, vol. 5 (London: Mishna Press, 1954), p. 283, n. 8.

[69]Blackman, *Mishnayoth: Order Nezikin*, vol. 4, pp. 284-85, esp. n. 4.

[70]Blackman, *Mishnayoth: Oder Nezikin*, p. 284, n. 2 and H. Danby, *Mishnah*, p. 396, n. 4.

discussing what kinds of oaths to God make one responsible for the oath and then extends to consider blasphemy. Here is the whole discussion:

> 'I adjure you,' or 'I command you,' or 'I bind you,' these are liable. By heaven or earth, these are exempt. By *'Aleph-Daleth,'* or, by *'Yod-He,'* or, by *'the Almighty,'* or, by *'Hosts,'* or, by *'the Gracious and Merciful'*, or, by *Him Who is longsuffering and of great lovingkindness,'* or, by any one [of God's] attributes, they are culpable. If one blasphemes by all [= any one of] these, he becomes liable [to stoning].[71] This is the view of Rabbi Meir (c 140 CE); but the sages say he is exempt.

The last comment could return to the issue of exemption from oaths, since exemption is mentioned earlier. However, it may also sum up the entire discussion. The text is significant to us for the array of alternative names noted for God and the aside applied to blasphemy, as well as the clear indication of a dispute about whether other expressions apply. One can see the debate over differing standards here, with the more narrow view of the sages having the last word. The passage indicates that sensitivity could extend to the use of the various alternative names for God, a situation that is not unusual given how rarely the actual name of God was being used.[72]

m Kerithoth 1.1-2

This passage lists the sins that require extirpation, that is, being cut off or being put to death. The list is very much like *m Sanh* 7.4. Blasphemy (המגדף) is on the list and the allusion is probably to Num 15:30. In 1.2, there is a discussion of "sin with a high hand" or wanton sin. The rabbis distinguish between a wanton sin, which requires excision and unwanton sin, which calls for a sin offering. If there is doubt, then a guilt offering is required. The discussion closes with the remark that the same applies to the blasphemer, which means that if there is unwanton blasphemy or doubt there is no offering required, since there is no act involved. This situation is treated as less serious because it is seen as speech that had no "intent" behind it. This distinction much like one noted in Philo's *On the Migration of Abraham* 115-17. Of course, blasphemy with intent means excision, something *m Sanh* already made clear.

Pirke Aboth 4.4 b (Strack), 4.5 (Herford), 4.7 (Taylor, Goldin)

This final text represents one of the supplemental tractates to the Mishnah and has a disputed versificaton, which is why the various references above are

---

[71]The key phrase here is המקלל בכולן חייב.
[72]See n. 63 above.

given.[73] It does not add much to our understanding of blasphemy, other than possibly to help explain the enigmatic *ARN* 32 text, which is examined below. The *Pirke* text reads, "Rabbi Johanan ben Barokah (c 110 CE) said: He who profanes the Name of Heaven (כל-המחלל שם) in secret they exact the penalty from him openly. Ignorant and willful are all one in regard to profaning the Name (בחלול השם)." The new term חלל refers to desecrating the Name, which is to treat the Name as a common thing.[74] The misuse of God's name will be punished. The text also suggests another contrast: what is done in secret is taken care of in public.[75]

The Mishnaic texts and the supplemental tractate reflect a concern to explain when blasphemy applies. It is seen as a serious sin, ranked with idolatry. The discussions lack any specific examples, only the rules are given. Pronouncing the Name inappropriately is certainly blasphemous. Some debate centers on whether alternative names can also yield a judgment of blasphemy. The code reflects a care to see that only the clearest cases result in death, but judgment will come one way or another.

The three texts from the Tosefta supply evidence of the type of examples of blasphemy or how the crime was viewed. All use a form of גדף.

t Sotah 3.18

The 2 Kgs 19 = Isa 37 passages on Sennacherib have represented one of the most frequently cited examples of blasphemy. It is also the example of this passage. It reads, "Sennacherib shamed and blasphemed God (חירף וגידף ע''י) through a messenger, as it is said, "By your messengers you have mocked the Lord (2 Kgs 19:23)." The use of two verbs to describe the act only serves to highlight the severity of the crime. In Kings what follows is Sennacherib's boast about ascending the mountains with his chariots and drying up the

---

[73]Charles Taylor, *Sayings of the Jewish Fathers: Sefer Dibre Aboth Ha-Olam Comprising Pirque Aboth in Hebrew and English with Critical Notes and Excursuses* (Amsterdam: Philo Press, 1970), p. 99-100, and Judah Goldin, *The Fathers according to Rabbi Nathan* Yale Judaica Series, ed. Julian Obermann, vol. 10 (New Haven: Yale University Press, 1956), p. 66. They both number the text as 4.7. But see R. Travers Herford, *The Ethics of the Talmud: Sayings of the Fathers: Pirke Aboth* (New York: Schocken Books, 1962 printing of 1925 ed.), p. 99, who places it at 4.5 and H. L. Strack, *Die Sprüche der Väter: ein ethischer Mischna-Traktat* (Karlsruhe: Reuther, 1882), p. 33, who places it at 4.4b.

[74]M. Jastrow, *A Dictionary of the Targumim, the Talmud Babli and Yerushalmi, and the Midrahic Literature*, vol. 1 (New York: Pardes Publishing House, 1950), p. 469-70; J. Levy, *Wörterbuch über die Talmudim und Midraschim* (Darmstadt: Wissenschaftliche Buchgesellshaft, 1963, vol. 2, pp. 58-60.

[75]This might suggest the reverse contrast for the *ARN* 32 text — what is done in public is dealt with privately, which may well mean that God takes care of it directly. See discussion below.

streams of Egypt with the sole of his foot, expressions that declare his total victory. The passage goes on to note that God exacted punishment for him through a messenger as well by the slaying of 185,000 in the camp. The blasphemer, who had insulted both God and the Lord's nation, met God's judgment against his own nation. The tradition noted here is quite popular in the rabbinical material (*b Sanh 94* a/b; *NumR* 9.24 on 5:27; *Tanḥ Beschallah* 88b).[76]

t Megillah 3.41

The note in Megillah comments on the proper reading of the sacred texts. Among the instructions is one coming from R. Judah (c. 200 CE), "But the one who adds to what is written, lo, this person is a blasphemer (ה'' ז מגדף)." The instruction shows the respect with which Scripture was treated in its reading. It also is a clear example of blasphemy attributed to an act or speech that need not involve the divine Name. Like other texts, where respect is shown for the temple or for God's people, this passage shows that things associated with God can produce actions viewed as blasphemous.

t Kerithoth 1.1

This passage merely comments on *m Ker* 1.1. In discussing the term "he who blasphemes (המגדף), which appears in the mishnaic text, R. Judah (c. 200 CE) notes that a blasphemer is liable for an offering as a result of his sin. This text adds nothing new to our understanding of blasphemy.

The Tosefta confirms what we have already seen. Attacks on God's people or distorting the divinely rooted Scripture are viewed as blasphemous in the broad understanding of the term.

8. The Targums

The Targums are significant, since they are mostly paraphrases. Many of the texts we have discussed in the sections on the Hebrew Scriptures and the LXX are also represented here, but the discussion is not merely a repetition. For this section, the discussion considers together the various targums for a particular text and only considers those texts that go beyond merely translating the passage. The multiplicity of targums available, especially for the texts from the Law, and their tendency to serve as expanded texts or to give explanation makes them an important source to consider in detail.

---

[76]H. Bietenhard, *Der Tosefta-Traktat Soṭa: Hebräischer Text mit kritischem Apparat, Übersetzung, Kommentar* Judaica et Christiana 9 (Frankfurt: Peter Lang, 1986), p. 62 n. 153.

Exodus 22:27 [22:28 Eng]

In *Onqelos*, this text is rendered in a way that makes it refer exclusively to humans: "Do not slight a judge, do not curse the leader of your people."[77] It appears similarly in *Neofiti*, where the passage reads, "My people, children of Israel: do not despise your judges and do not curse the lord who is in your people."[78] *Pseudo-Jonathan* also goes this way rendering the verse, "My people, children of Israel, do not slight your judges, and do not curse the leaders who have been appointed rulers of your people."[79] This rendering prevents the text from warning about blasphemy, though the same penalty as blasphemy was applied in such cases.

Leviticus 24:11-23

Pseudo-Jonathan is largely a paraphrase, but it reads the vv. 15-16 as indicating a distinction of offense: "(15b) Any young man or any old man who reviles and blasphemes a substitute name of his God (וחרף שום כינוי אלהיה) shall incur his guilt. (16) But any one who pronounces and blasphemes the name of the Lord ('דמפרש ומחרף שמא דה) shall be put to death; the whole congregation shall pelt him with stones. The sojourner as well as the native shall be put to death when he blasphemes the proper Name (דיחרף שמא)."[80] The text agrees with *m Sanh* 7.5 and with the Sages in *m Sch^{e}b* 4.13. Blasphemy involves the pronunciation of the divine Name.

Targum Neofiti renders v. 11 with "And the son of an Israelite woman expressed the holy Name with blasphemies [HT- ויקב] and reviled [HT- ויקלל] (it)."[81] The key term in the text reads in the key phrase וחרף. An object is missing in the text, but the context makes it clear from v 12 that the "holy Name" is meant. Then follows a long addition that appears in several Neofiti texts in only slightly differing forms. It teaches that Moses had four cases to

---

[77]Bernard Grossfeld, *The Targum Onqelos to Exodus* The Aramaic Bible, vol. 7 (Edinburgh: T & T Clark, 1988), p. 65

[78]Martin McNamara, Robert Hayward, and Michael Maher, *Targum Neofiti 1: Exodus/Targum Pseudo-Jonathan: Exodus* The Aramaic Bible vol. 2 (Edinburgh: T & T Clark, 1994), p. 97.

[79]Martin McNamara, Robert Hayward, and Michael Maher, *Targum Neofiti : 1 Exodus/Targum Pseudo-Jonathan: Exodus* The Aramaic Bible, vol. 2, p. 227. A similar reading is noted in *b Sanh* 66a. For the last command, *Onqelos* has לא תלופם, while *Ps-J* and *Neof* have לא תלומן.

[80]The translation is from Michael Maher (with M. McNamara on Neofiti), *Targum Neofiti 1: Leviticus/Targum Pseudo-Jonathan: Leviticus* The Aramaic Bible, vol. 3 (Edinburgh: T & T Clark, 1994), p. 198. He notes that the term "reviles" is literally "provokes" and so the reading agrees with *Onkelos* here. The double translation of "reviles and blasphemes" renders the HT *qll*, while the key phrase of v. 16 renders a HT *nqb*. See v. 11. See also *b Sanh* 56b below.

[81]McNamara's translation in *Targum Neofiti 1: Leviticus/Targum Pseudo-Jonathan: Leviticus* The Aramaic Bible, vol. 3, pp. 95-96.

decide, two of which he handled slowly and two of which he dealt with quickly.[82] The Num 15 incident and the Lev 24 incident were the two cases handled slowly, because one distinguished civil cases from the more slowly handled capital cases. In addition the man is described as one who "expressed his holy Name with blasphemies." In v. 14, the Lord instructs Moses to bring the blasphemer (דמחרף) outside the camp. Then the ruling is summarized in vv. 15-16: "(15b) Anyone who pronounces the name of God in blasphemy (שמה דאלה בנדפין) will receive (the punishment of) his sins. (16) And whoever pronounces the name of the Lord in blasphemy (שמיה דייי בנדפין) shall surely be put to death; all the people of the congregation shall stone him. Sojourners as well as natives, when one pronounces the name of God in blasphemy (בנידופין שמה דאלהה) he shall be killed." This text is like *Pseudo-Jonathan* in its perspective. One must use the divine Name explicitly to be guilty of capital blasphemy.

Targum Onqelos on this passage follows the same pattern.[83] In v. 11, the man "pronounces the Name in provocation." In v. 14, the "blasphemer" is taken outside the camp. In vv. 15-16, the man "who causes provocation before his God," bears his guilt; while "whoever pronounces the Name of the Lord" shall surely be put to death. Later in v. 16, one "upon pronouncing the Name of the Lord" shall surely be put to death. The targum follows the approach of the others as well.

These targums focus on blasphemy involving the divine Name as worthy of death. It is the consistent and official rabbinical view of Lev 24, distinguishing the crime of v. 15 from v. 16. What "bearing the sin for blasphemy" in v. 15 requires is never specified in any of these translations. However, to misuse the Name means automatic death. The silence here on the penalty for other types of blasphemy might include the possibility of being subject to death[84]; however, what the distinction does indicate is that death is not automatic. Certainly, at the least, certain sacrifices would have been required. The distinction in the text is important for indicating the view of this later period that pronunciation of the Name in an inappropriate manner is a

---

[82]*Neofiti* on Num 9:8, 14:12; 15:34 and 27:5.

[83]The discussion here follows Bernard Grossfeld, *The Targum Onqelos to Leviticus and the Targum Onqelos to Numbers* The Aramaic Bible, vol. 8 (Edinburgh: T & T Clark, 1988), pp. 54-55. Note 5 is particularly helpful, "The targum, in an attempt to avoid using the term "curse" (Aramaic *lyṭ*) in conjunction with God, renders *qll* by the *aphel* of *rgz* with the meaning of "to provoke" and *nqb* by *prʾs* "to pronounce." . . . , Tg. Neof. uses *prʾs* for *nqb* but adds *bgdpyn* "with blasphemous remarks" and *qll* by *ḥrp* "to blaspheme/revile" in vs. 14, but the same translation as for *nqb* in vs. 15, while Tg. Ps.-Jon. is very inconsistent, using a combination of *prʾs* and *ḥrp for* nqb in vss. 11 and 16; *rgz* for *qll* in vs. 14; *rgz* in combination with *zwd/zyd* ("to be presumptuous") in v. 11 and *ḥrp* in vs. 15 for this same Hebrew root."

[84]See below on *Onqelos* Num 15:30-31

grave offense, while the silence about what punishment other types of reviling required leaves us less than certain about how such cases could have been handled.

Numbers 15:30-31

This text discusses the sin of the high hand and the violation of the Sabbath. Extirpation is a result of acting defiantly against the Lord. *Onqelos* reads, "(30) If a person, whether native born or alien, acts defiantly, he provokes anger before the Lord, that person will be cut off from among the people. (31) For he has despised the word of the Lord and has altered his commandments; that man shall surely be cut off from the people; he bears his guilt."[85] What is fascinating about this text is that "bearing the guilt," a phrase we saw in Lev 24:15 involves extirpation, a sentence of removal.[86] The variation of terms between the texts, the seeming shifting of penalties in some passages, and the lack of specific penalties in other texts show how complex the discussion is, as it is not clear if phrases carry a technical force or not. Though this text does not refer to blasphemy directly, it is a passage that was often related to the concept as was noted in the discussions of the Mishnah (*m Ker* 1.1-2).[87]

Targum *Pseudo-Jonathan* also discusses the "high hand" situation without using the term blasphemy.[88] The quite expanded translation in vv. 30-31 reads,

> (30) But anyone who performs a premeditated sin, whether he be a native-born or a stranger, and does not repent from his sins before the Lord, he causes the anger of the Lord, and that man shall be destroyed from among his people. (31) For he has despised the initial word of the Lord commanded at Sinai and

---

[85]Grossfeld, *The Targum Onqelos to Leviticus and the Targum Onqelos to Numbers*, p. 112. Note 8 by Grossfeld on p. 113 adds the relevant comment, "The Hebrew 'he blasphemes the Lord' is here paraphrased using the buffer particle *qdm*—"before," in order to avoid the direct association between the act of blasphemy and the divine Name. This resulted in the paraphrase "he provokes anger before the Lord," the act of blasphemy also being toned down to an act of provoking anger." He cites Ezek 20:27 and Isa 37:6 as doing the same thing. The notes ends, "The same is true for the verb *qll* in conjunction with someone directly cursing God, which the targum likwise paraphrases by "provoking anger before the Lord," for which cf. Lev 24:11 and esp. v 15."

[86]Grossfeld's comment on p. 113, n. 10, is again apropos, "Lit. "his guilt is upon him," a variant formula for "he/she/they bear his/her/their guilt," for which cf. Lev 5:1, 17; 17:16; 19:8; 20:17; Num 18:23; 30:16."

[87]See also below the discussion of *Neofiti* on Num 15:30-31. These texts indicate that the penalty varies depending on the violation. Lev 5:17 looks to the bringing of sacrifice for unwillful sin, while 19:8 looks to extirpation for improperly eating part of a fellowship offering, a sin that is very much like that of Eli's sons in 1 Sam 2:29. Lev 20:17 looks to extirpation for incest. Here is one example where the penalty is altered.

[88]Martin McNamara, Ernest G. Clarke and Shirley Magder, *Targum Neofiti 1: Numbers/Targum Pseudo-Jonathan: Numbers* The Aramaic Bible, vol. 4 (Edinburgh: T & T Clark, 1995), pp. 231-32.

has negated the commandment of circumcision; that man will be destroyed in this world (and destroyed) in the world to come, because he shall give an account of his sins on the day of the great judgment.

Like *Neofiti*, it has the "four cases" discussion involving Moses, though it lacks a direct reference to the blasphemer in discussing it, mentioning only "cases concerning life." Moses' careful deliberation is said to be an example to future rulers. Here extirpation and "bearing the sin" have a double force, both death now and a severe judgment of destruction in the end. The penalty for Sabbath violation could not be more comprehensive.

Targum *Neofiti* runs similarly:

> (30) But a person who does anything with a head uncovered, whether he be from the citizens or the sojourners, is a blasphemer before the Lord (יי הוא מחרף ובגיוריה קדם), and that person shall be blotted out from the midst of the people. (31) Because he despised the word of the Lord and has desecrated his precept, that person shall be blotted out: he shall receive (the chastisement of) his sin.[89]

Here the Sabbath violation is explicitly called blasphemy.

Targum Jonathan on 1 Kings 21:10,13

This text discusses where Naboth is falsely accused of blasphemy and is executed. No detail is given to the nature of the charge other than to say in both v. 10 and v. 13 that he "blasphemed before the Lord and [you- v. 10 only] have cursed the king."[90] The MT in this text used the euphemism bless in both verses. The interesting thing about the charge is the God and king combination, which recalls Exod 22:27. It is not at all clear that the name of God was portrayed as the issue here as much as a violation of the Exodus text.

The targums reflect an interesting ambiguity. On the one hand, it is clear that blasphemy involving the use of the Name was seen as deeply offensive and required a judgment of automatic death. On the other hand, texts like *Neofiti* on Numbers suggest a broader reading of the concept of blasphemy, involving explicitly a Sabbath violation, with a penalty just as severe. Traces of any internal discussion on this question do not surface in the targums as much as they do in other rabbinical material, since these are translations, not expositions of oral legal discussion. Nevertheless, the overlapping terminology between the various texts, reflected also in the targums, makes it very difficult to develop a clear sense of where the lines were drawn for

---

[89]Martin McNamara, Ernest G. Clarke and Shirley Magder, *Targum Neofiti 1: Numbers/Targum Pseudo-Jonathan: Numbers*, pp. 91-92. The "uncovered head" is another euphemism for blasphemy.

[90]Daniel J. Harrington and Anthony J. Saldarini, *Targum Jonathan of the Former Prophets* The Aramaic Bible 10 (Edinburgh: T & T Clark, 1987), p. 258.

blasphemy and what the penalty for it was in this period. But "bearing responsibility for guilt," when applied to the cases of other sins, could involve anything from bringing a sacrifice for unwillful sin to extirpation. It is possible that blasphemy outside of using the name would have a similar range of penalty. If so, then death came automatically with blasphemy using the divine Name. Death also could be the result of other types of blasphemy as well. This additional possibility is a potentially important finding of this survey. If this possibility reflects the Jewish view, then these texts serve as an additional confirmation that a broad definition of blasphemy existed.

9. The Midrashim

These ancient expositions of Scripture are often important because they can contain explanation and development that allow us to understand the thinking behind a view.[91] There are numerous texts that mention blasphemy. The less important discussions will be briefly summarized while citations will occur in the more important texts. We will divide between tannaitic and amoraic midrashim.

Tannaitic Midrashim

Sifra Leviticus Emor Parashah 14 on 24:11-14 and Emor Pereg 19 on Lev 24:15-23. These two passages develop the Lev 24 discussion, as well as *m Sanh* 7.5.[92] The *Sifra* 14 text notes that the son of an Israelite woman spoke the Name (ויקוב . . . את השם), a name (שם המפורש) God had given on Sinai in the first commandment. Earlier the text had noted the man had "cursed" (וניךף).[93] The passage also cites a significant portion of *m Sanh* 7.5 as proof that the divine Name must be pronounced to face death. The examination takes place inside the camp, but the execution of stoning occurred outside the camp. The next text then details how the stoning should occur: with witnesses and judges laying hands on him and declaring that "Your blood be on your head, for what you have caused." Then he is to be stoned. Next comes a discussion noting

---

[91]For a summary of this literature, see H. L. Strack and G. Stemberger, *Introduction to the Talmud and Midrash* (trans., M. Bockmuehl; Edinburgh: T & T Clark, 1991) and Craig A. Evans, *Noncanonical Writings and New Testament Interpretation* (Peabody, Mass.: Hendrickson, 1992), pp. 114-48. This material has quite a date range, from fourth century for *Sifre* to the eleventh century for parts of *Rabbah*.

[92]The most readily available access to a discussion of this text can be found in Hermann L. Strack and Paul Billerbeck, *Kommentar zum Neuen Testament aus Talmud und Midrasch* (München: C. H. Beck, 1926), 1:1013-14, which is part of a long summary discussion on blasphemy covering pp. 1008-19. More recent is the translation by J. Neusner, *SIFRA: An Analytical Translation* BJS 140, vol. 3 (Atlanta: Scholars Press, 1988), p. 284-86.

[93]This is the only use of נדף in *Sifra*.

the equal culpability of Jews and non-Jews. This is followed by debate over whether substitute names are permissible. Rabbi Meir (c. 140 CE) thought so, but the Sages argue that substitute names yielded a warning. As shall be seen, the discussion here is very parallel to *b Sanh* 56a and recalls the debate of *m Sch^eb* 4.13. In the mishnaic text, the phrase המקלל אביו ואמו appears right after the discussion of blasphemy. So the discussion of cursing the parents and blasphemy are treated as parallel when it comes to the issue of using substitute names. The mishnaic text treats the two situations as parallel, noting the dispute between Meir and the rabbis in each case. This midrash in *Sifra* maintains the rabbinical view that blasphemy requires the Name, though what is not stated is what happens if one continues to dishonor God after a warning with substitute terms.

Yet it is quite likely that the result of a repeated offense was execution, as that would be a likely procedure. A potentially important parallel example comes from *m Sanh* 8.4. It treats the parallel capital case of the rebellious son, an analogous circumstance. In this case, a repeated offense could lead to a carrying out of the full penalty, provided the three judges initially present were also present in the second hearing.

The *Sifra* 19 text is similar in emphasis. It considers whether a Gentile is liable when one curses God like Israel (על קללת השם כישראל). Yes, they are liable but only to be slain with a sword as all the children of Noah, because whoever curses his God (כי יקלל אלהיו) shall bear his sin. The passage then notes Lev 24:16 that those who "also pronounce the name Lord (' ונוקב שם ה), shall be put to death." The midrash then asks if euphemisms make one liable as well. The positive answer of Rabbi Meir is cited, whoever curses his God (יקלל אלהיו) is liable, followed by a notation of the more limiting view of the rabbis that only fully pronouncing the Name makes one liable (אומרים על שם והחכמים), while others are admonished. A final set of remarks deals with how one bears his sin in death and notes that the blasphemer is put to death by all the congregation, both sojourner (proselytes or their wives) and native (both male or their wives). The final remark notes that a death penalty also ensues for the one who "curses his father or his mother" (המקלל אביו ואמו), but only if they invoke the divine name (שיקללם בשם). It is interesting to note the juxtaposition here of the two types of blasphemy (cursing of God and of parents), just like was present in *m Sch^eb* 4.13. In both of these midrashic texts, the dominating expression for cursing uses the stem קלל. The texts from *Sifra* reflect by now familiar disputes and discuss them in ways parallel to discussions in other Jewish sources, noting similar analogous situations along the way.

In the next two texts, the variations of the verb גדף along with its noun form appear seven times. Four times it is in the Numbers text (2x- מגדף; 2x- גדפה), while three appearances are in the Deuteronomy text (2x- מגדף; 1x- המגדף).

Sifre § 112 on Numbers 15:30-31. This text considers the "audacious acts," or sins with a high hand against Torah.[94] The great example in the passage is Manasseh, who is said to have mocked Torah (2 Kgs 21; 2 Chron 33:1-9). Twice the text says that he blasphemed the Lord (את ה' הוא מגדף//מגדף שהיה). Among the other sins mentioned are profaning holy things and idolatry. In the exposition, the act is compared to scrapping a bowl clean leaving nothing behind.[95] In Num 15:31, the action is called despising the Word of the Lord and the examples are Sadducees and Epicureans. The issue, which also includes the way worship is conducted, is seen as a violation of the first commandment.[96] The guilt is said to remain on the offender even after death. Apparently the violator is not among the righteous in the end.

This text is important, because it relates and compares blasphemy to a series of sins that deal more with actions than words. Manasseh as the prime example is chosen not for what he says, but what he does. It indicates a kind of fluidity in the approach taken to blasphemy. Technically it requires the pronunciation of the Name, but practically it can involve actions that reflect total unfaithfulness. In other words, there can be blasphemy that involves utterance as well as blasphemy that includes actions. This is similar to what the discussions in Josephus and Philo indicated. The pattern of a broad usage for blasphemy continues and is spread widely across the strands of tradition.

Sifre § 221 on Deuteronomy 21:22. This text is very similar to *m Sanh* 6.4.[97] It considers the issue of the penalty of hanging for blasphemy and whether women are hanged as well as men. Only two rabbis (Eliezar [c. 90 CE] and Judah [c 200 CE]) are noted as favoring hanging for women. The famous incident involving 80 women is noted, a text also discussed in *m Sanh* 6.4.[98] There are numerous references to blasphemers (2x- מגדף; 1x- המגדף). The

[94]Karl George Kuhn, *Der Tannaitische Midrasch: Sifre zu Numeri* RT Zweite Reihe: Tannaitische Midrashim, Band 3 (Stuttgart: W. Kohlhammer, 1959), pp. 319-34, esp., pp. 324-34.

[95]This imagery uses a wordplay as the verb גרף is used.

[96]K. Kuhn, *Der Tannaitische Midrasch: Sifre zu Numeri*, p. 330: "Denn es heißt: *Den das Wort (דבר) des Herrn hat er veractet*, d.h. er hat das 1. Gebot (דיבור) nicht beachtet, das Mose aus dem Munde der Macht gesagt worden ist: "Ich bin der Herr, dein Gott . . .du sollst keine andern Götter haben neben mir " (Exod 20, 2-3).

[97]It also will be paralleled conceptually in *b. Sanh* 45b-46a and 63a. The most readily available access to a summary of this text comes from Strack-Billerbeck, *Kommentar*, 1:1013, R. Hammer, *Sifre: A Tannaitic Commentary on the Book of Deuteronomy*. YJS 24 (New Haven: Yale University Press, 1986), pp. 231-32, 467, and H. Bietenhard, *Sifre Deuteronomium*. Judaica et Christiana 8 (Frankfurt: Peter Lang, 1984), pp. 523-26.

[98]On this text and its probable symbolic meaning originally as referring to idolators, see Martin Hengel, *Rabbinische Legende und frühpharisäische Geschichte: Schimeon b.*

key remark for this survey is the remark that only blasphemers and those who threaten "the fundamental principle of the faith" are subject to hanging, a probable allusion to idolatry (*b Sanh* 45b). The exposition notes that cursing the name of God (שקלל את השם) is a special kind of case, since it explains that God's name is not to be profaned (ונמצא שם שמים מתחלל). The text earlier detailed how hanging takes place after dying, but that a simultaneous hanging like Roman practice is also possible. The person is hanged for profaning the Name of God.

This passage is like many others we have seen. Blasphemy is seen as among the worst of sins, which is why it is worthy of death. To see a violation of a fundamental of the faith is very similar to pointing out that blasphemy violates the first commandment.

Mekilta has five uses of גדף. Four appear in Mishpatim (= Nezikin) on Exod 21.12 (1x- במגדף; 3x- למגדף).[99] The other use is in Beshallaḥ on Exod 14.8 (ומגדפים).[100]

Mekilta Beshallaḥ on Exodus 14.8. This text is an exposition of the defeat of Egypt as the Israelites flee out of Egypt heading for the Promised Land. The Egyptians are said to have been "scorning, reviling, and blaspheming" (מנאצים ומחרפים ומגדפים) as they chased the Israelites, while Israel was engaged in praise, just like texts such as Ps 149:6; 57:6, and Isa 25:1 call on the nation to do. Here are three great verbs of derision. The remarks explain how Egypt went out "with high hand." It also suggests why their corporate judgment was just, since the fortunes of war lie in God's hands. No more detail about the blasphemy appears.

Mekilta Nezikin on Exodus 21.12. This passage explains who shall surely be put to death by staging a rhetorical debate. The question is whether death by the sword (decapitation) is meant or death by strangulation. A rhetorical opponent makes a case for strangulation by appealing to the parallel with the adulterer of Lev 20:10. But the exposition prefers a comparison to the blasphemer of Lev 24:16, referring simply to the case of the blasphemer (במגדף). The exposition notes three times a comparison with the blasphemer (למגדף), who also shall surely be put to death. The exposition goes on to argue from the Gen 9:6 reference to shedding of blood and from the example of the

Schetach und die achtig Hexen von Askalon, AHAW (Heidelberg: Carl Winter/Universitätsverlag, 1984).

[99] J. Z. Lauterbach, *Mekilta de-Rabbi Ishmael* (Philadelphia: Jewish Publication Society, 1949), vol. 3, p. 34; J. Winter and A. Wünsche, *Mechiltha: Ein tannaitischer Midrasch zu Exodus*, p. 88.

[100] For this text, J. Z. Lauterbach, *Mekilta de-Rabbi Ishmael* (Philadelphia: Jewish Publication Society, 1933), vol. 1, p. 203; J. Winter and A. Wünsche, *Mechiltha: Ein tannaitischer Midrasch zu Exodus* (Leipzig: J. C. Hinrichs'sche Buchhandlung, 1909), pp. 248-50.

breaking of the heifer's neck in Deut 21:4 that decapitation is meant. Serious crime needs a serious penalty. Murder is the topic here and blasphemy as a serious crime is only mentioned as a point of comparison. No other detail about blasphemy is present here.

The *Mekilta* references are only illustrative. Nothing of additional significance emerges from these references.

Amoraic Midrashim

The *Midrash Rabbah* texts are full of examples and developed discussions of blasphemy. Though these texts are late, they exhibit a certain consistency in the nature of the illustrations that reflect the presence of older tradition. Of particular interest is the development of a fixed phase in this material, since these texts often describe blasphemy with the intensive expression "revilings and blasphemies," where חרף and גדף appear together.

Genesis Rabbah 16.6. This is the more significant of two texts in *GenR*.[101] It involves a discussion of six precepts allegedly given to Adam in Gen 2:16, a tradition also noted in *DeutR* 2.25.[102] Blasphemy is mentioned as related to the reference to the "Lord" in 2:16, which is then related to Lev 24:16. The six precepts involve idolatry, blasphemy, appointing judges, bloodshed, incest, and theft.[103] The key line discussing Gen 2:16 and blasphemy uses a euphemism and reads, "THE LORD alludes to blasphemy ("blessing the Name;" י' על ברכת השם), as you read, *And he that blasphemes the name of the Lord* (ונוקב שם י'; Lev. 24:16)." The passage indicates that the prohibition of blasphemy comes as early as any commandment, so its age indicates its importance. Interestingly as well, the authority of judges as possessing early historical roots is also noted as Exod 22:27 is also cited next. The argument is that judges should be respected (אלהים לא תקלל).

---

[101]The other text is *GenR* 1.13, where a remark is made in discussing sacrifices to the Lord. It says that those who revile, blaspheme, and engage in idolatry (המחרפים ומגדפים והעובדים) are blotted out of the world. After citing Lev 1:2, the text reads, "Now you can surely argue from this: If when one is going to dedicate a sacrifice the Torah directs, let him cause the Divine Name to be related to nothing but the sacrifice, then they who revile, blaspheme, and engage in idolatry, will surely be blotted out from the world!" For *GenR* texts, see H. Freeman and M. Simon, eds., *Midrash Rabbah*, 2nd ed., 10 vols. (London: Soncino, 1951). These passages are in vol. 1, pp. 12, 131.

[102]b. *Sanh* 56b has a similar discussion. For the *DeutR* text, see H. Freeman and M. Simon, eds., *Midrash Rabbah*, vol. 5, pp. 52-55. The Deuteronomy discussion parallels almost exactly the *GenR* text and so is not discussed separately. There the key phrase is ועל חלול השם.

[103]In all likelihood incest includes adultery, pedastry and bestiality.

Exodus Rabbah 41.1. The exposition involves the golden calf incident of Exod 32:17-18.[104] The act is condemned not only because there was idolatry but also because God had graciously continued to give manna, despite the presence of the idols (Neh 9:18; Ezek 16:19). God was also seen as gracious in that although the nation engraved an idol, he sat in heaven engraving the two tablets of testimony. The contrast in activity between God and Israel is part of the passage's poignant call to faithfulness. In mentioning Exod 32:18 and discussing the meaning of "the noise of them that sing I do hear," the reply comes that what is heard is,

> the noise of reproach and blasphemy (קול הרופין וגדופין). This was explained by the men of the Great Synagogue thus: *Yes, when they made them a molten calf and said: this is your God that brought you out of Egypt* (Neh 9:18). Is this not sufficient provocation? Then why does the verse continue *And had wrought great provocations?* (Neh 9:18). Because, in addition reproaches and blasphemy (הרופין וגדופין) were uttered there.

Here is a text where corporate blasphemy is taking place. Once again it involves both utterance and action. The golden calf is often the great rabbinical example of national blasphemy. We also see here the first of several uses of the fixed phrase where reviling and blasphemy appear together. It appears to point to particularly offensive speech accompanying disrespectful action.

Leviticus Rabbah 7.6, 10.6-7, 32.2. These passages can be covered more briefly.[105] *LevR* 7.6 reviews some of the nations that God has judged as it expounds the fate of fire for the unrighteous. Among those discussed are the Sodomites, Pharaoh, Sisera, Sennacherib, Nebuchadnezzar, and finally, Rome. Rome is simply called the "wicked state." In contrasting Rome to Israel, the following remark appears:

> The wicked state, because it blasphemes and reviles (מהרפת ומגדפת), saying, Whom have I in heaven . . .? (Ps 73:25), is to be punished with fire, I beheld even till the beast was slain, and its body destroyed and it was given to be burned with fire (Dan 7:11). — Israel, however, who are despised and lowly in this world, will be comforted by means of fire, as it is said, For I, says the Lord, will be to her a wall of fire round about, and I will be the glory in the midst of her (Zech 2:9).

Once again God punishes corporate blasphemy, but this time it is from a pagan nation. Blasphemy here is more than utterance, but a national state of

---

[104]For the passage, see H. Freeman and M. Simon, eds. *Midrash Rabbah*, vol. 2, pp. 468-69.

[105]H. Freeman and M. Simon, eds., *Midrash Rabbah*, vol. 3, pp. 98-99, 130-31, 407-11.

mind against God, as the citation from the Psalter shows that disregard of God is read as blasphemy.

LevR 10.6-7 is considering the topic of atonement for serious sin and is presenting the symbolism involved in the priestly garments. The forehead plate represents atoning for blasphemy: "The forehead-plate was to atone, some say, for the shameless, others say for blasphemy . . . He who said for blasphemers (על מגדפים) [derived it] from the case of Goliath." The example of Goliath is applied because he is seen to have blasphemed and he was struck with a stone on the forehead, a common type of associative rabbinical exposition. In commenting further on Goliath, the text notes that he fell upon his face upon collapsing to the earth. The explanation follows: "Why upon his face? — Let the mouth that taunted and blasphemed (והרף וגדף) be put in the dust, as it is written, *Hide them in the dust together, bind their faces in the hidden place (Job 40:13).*" The text points to Goliath as an example of a blasphemer as he challenged the people of God.[106]

LevR 32.2 comes in the midst of a consideration of the Lev 24 incident and is citing Eccle 10:20, where the exhortation is not to curse the king. The Rabbah text here parallels the Rabbah discussion of Eccle 10:20.[107] Rabbi Abin (c. 325 CE) says that a man should not use the intelligence God gave him to rule over cattle, beasts, and birds to revile and blaspheme Him (לפני מחרף ומגדף). So the exposition becomes not only an exhortation not to curse the earthly king, but also the king of the Universe. The exposition rebukes such lack of understanding.

These midrashim considered as a unit exhibit a certain broader view of blasphemy, though many of the examples are corporate in character. Nonetheless, a figure like Goliath shows an individual blaspheming without being involved in a more narrow use of the Name.

Numbers Rabbah 10.2, 13.3. These two passages also look back to models of those who blasphemed and the fate of judgment that came against them.[108] In 10.2, the example is a figure not raised in detail before, Sisera of Judg 4:3. He is part of a discussion where the exposition surveys the nation's history to show how the wicked receive measure for measure in judgment. Among others in the listing are Pharaoh (Exod 15:8) and Haman (Esth 9:25). Of Sisera it was said, "What was his end? Because he abused and reviled (ומגדפם מחרפם) while also oppressing them he died an ignominious death, for He

---

[106]See the discussion above on Rabshekah in Isa 37 = 2 Kgs 19 and n. 22 in that discussion, which is similar conceptually.

[107]See *EccleR* 10.19 § 1 on Eccles 10:20. These texts are so similar, I will not comment separately on the *EcclesR* passage. For it, see H. Freeman and M. Simon, eds., *Midrash Rabbah*, vol. 8, pp. 280-83. In *EcclesR*, the exhortation adds a note about not cursing the rich, but the exhortation at the start about the use of intellect is the same except it is attributed to Rabbi Judah b. Rabbi Simon (c. 320 CE).

[108]H. Freeman and M. Simon, eds., *Midrash Rabbah*, vol. 4, pp. 342-43, 506-07.

delivered him into the hand of a woman." The text presents another example of a blasphemer who also sought to destroy the people of the nation, so that God responded with judgment.

In 13.3 the text is also contrasting the righteous and unrighteous. Here numerous figures are said to have blasphemed. Of Adam, the text declares, "Rabbi Simeon b. Laḳish (c. 250 CE) said: As soon as Adam came away from the judgment he began to revile and blaspheme (התחיל מהרף ומגדף)." Then follows an analogy that suggests this judgment in the mind of the expositor,

> It mentions cherubim in this text: *And He placed at the east of the garden of Eden the cherubim* (Gen 2:24) and it mentions cherubim in connection with Sennacherib: *O Lord of hosts, who sits upon the cherubim* (Isa 37:16). As in the latter cases there were revilings and blasphemings (חרופים וגדופים), so the cherubim mentioned here point to revilings and blasphemies (חרופים וגדופים).

So the text has two examples, one drawn directly from the Hebrew Scriptures (Sennacherib) and one inferred (Adam). After discussing Pharaoh, the text moves on to consider Amalek. The exposition now considers Prov 29:23, that "a man's pride shall bring him low," which actually is the main text of the entire exposition of 13.3. Of Amalek, the passage declares,

> Another exposition: '*A man's pride*' applies to Amalek, who displayed haughtiness towards the Holy One, blessed be He, by his reviling and blasphemies (בחרופיו וגדופיו), putting the branch[109] to his nose and taking the phallai of Israelites and casting them towards heaven and uttering revilings and blasphemies (ומחרף ומגדף) saying" 'Here is what you delight in.'

The inference is said to come from Deut 15:18 and closes citing Joshua's victory over him in Exod 17:13. This rather graphic and offensive example is significant, since the blasphemy is surely a combination of word and deed without formal utterance of the divine Name.

Lamentations Rabbah 4.16-18. This passage considers another moment of failure within the nation.[110] In 4.16 the slaying of Zechariah in the Temple is said to be one of the seven transgressions committed by Israel on that day. For "they killed a priest, a prophet, and a judge, they shed innocent blood, the profaned the divine Name, the defiled the Temple court, and it happened on the Sabbath which was also the Day of Atonement." The listing of seven sins probably suggests the full presence of sin. This case involves the use of blasphemy with the divine Name.

In 4.18 the exposition continues on the theme that the unfaithfulness of prophets and priests led to exile. The example is the horrid slaying of Zechariah and the nation's ignoring the word of Jeremiah. The result is a

---

[109]See Ezek 8:17.
[110]H. Freeman and M. Simon, eds., *Midrash Rabbah*, vol. 6, pp. 226, 230.

nation sent into wandering. Why did it happen? "Rabbi Ḥanina (c 225 CE) said, The Israelites were not exiled until they blasphemed[111] the Holy One, blessed by He. Rabbi Simeon[112] said: The Israelites were not exiled until they became quarrelsome towards the Holy One, blessed be He." Once again blasphemy is seen more in terms of action and attitude than specific speech. The rejection of a prophet's word and the slaying of a prophet are the acts that touch off God's judgment.

Canticles Rabbah 2.13 § 4; 2.16 § 1; 3.4 § 2; 4.4 § 5. These texts cover other incidents from Israel's history.[113] In 2.13 the exposition simply involves a discussion of the conditions under which Messiah will appear. Using Ps 89:52 as proof, it is argued that it will be in an era when one generation after another blasphemes. So the era of blessing comes after an era of taunting. The text reads,

> The scion of David will come only in a generation, which is full of impudence and deserves to be exterminated. Rabbi Janna (c. 220 CE) said: If you see one generation after another cursing and blaspheming (מחרף ומגדף), look out for the coming of the Messiah, as it says, Wherewith your enemies have taunted the footsteps of your anointed (Ps 89:52) and immediately afterwards it is written, Blessed be the Lord forevermore. Amen and amen.

Since it is the character of a period that is discussed here, little is learned about the nature of the blasphemy in this text.

In 2.16 the exposition is discussing the Song of Songs and is treating it as a picture of God's care for Israel. In the survey of God's care for the nation, the insults and blasphemies that fell from Sisera (Judg 4:3) are noted.[114] The protection of the Lord against Sisera's army is noted,

> When I was in distress I sought assistance only from him: And the children of Israel cried unto the Lord; for he had nine hundred chariots of iron; and . . . he mightily oppressed the children of Israel (Judg 4:3). What is meant by 'mightily'? With insults and blasphemies (בהירופין ונידופין). When he required something He sought it only from me as it says, And let them make me a sanctuary (Exod 25:8).

This text reveals an example like those involving Sennacherib and Goliath, where insulting God's people and power are taken as one act.[115]

---

[111]This is *ni'aẓu* and could be translated "condemned." See J. Neusner, *Lamentations Rabbah*, BJS 193 (Atlanta: Scholars Press, 1989), p. 318.

[112]Which Simeon is meant here is unclear, so no date is given for this figure. If it is Gamaliel II, then the date is c 140 CE.

[113]H. Freeman and M. Simon, eds., *Midrash Rabbah*, vol. 10, pp. 127, 139-40, 147, 190

[114]See *NumR* 10.2, which also uses this example.

[115]See 2 Kgs 19 = Isa 37and Josephus, *Ant* 6.183.

In 3.4 the topic is the presence of burden and judgment on Israel as she awaits deliverance during the time of Daniel. Judgment from the wilderness is said to be harsher than judgment from the sea. Nebuchadnezzar came from the wilderness to judge the nation. Belshazzar becomes an example of the blasphemer. The text reads,

> — the sound of the blasphemies and insults of the wicked (חירופין וגידופין של רשע קול), as it says, But you have lifted yourself against the Lord of heaven; and they have brought vessels of his house, etc. (Dan 5:23). 'I am affrighted so I cannot see ' — the prosperity of that wicked one, as it says, Belshazzar the king made a great feast (Dan 5:1). What is meant by 'great'? Rabbi Ḥama (c 250 CE) ben Rabbi Ḥanina (c 220 CE) said: It means, greater than that of his God. He said to them: 'How often was your 'omer refined before it was offered?' They replied: 'It was passed through the sieve thirteen times. He said to them, 'Mine is passed fourteen times.'

A discussion follows regarding God's judgment against Belshazzar's arrogance. This example is also particularly graphic for it shows that arrogance against God is seen as blasphemous. The example here is like that noted in Josephus, *Ant* 10.233, 242.

In 4.4 there comes a more developed version of the discussion of Goliath and blasphemers like that in *LevR* 10.6. In the *Canticles* version, the plate on the forehead is said to represent possible atonement for blasphemers (2x-על הגודפנין). Not only are Exod 28:38 and 1 Sam 17:49 mentioned, but then there is the elaboration that Dagon, the god of Goliath, was in the warrior's heart. His defeat by David is seen as judgment for his blasphemy as he fell on his face and returned to the earth. The judgment comes, "In order that the foul mouth which blasphemed and cursed (שהירף וגידף) might be buried in the earth, in accordance with the verse, *Hide them in the dust together* (Job 40:13)." David is said to have trod upon Goliath's neck in fulfillment of the verse in Deut 33:29, which says, "you shall tred on their high places." Goliath's sin of blasphemy was to challenge God's people and power, an example like that of Sisera in *CanR* 2.16 and its parallels.

These Rabbah examples, even though some of them are quite late, are significant because they reflect a pattern of illustration of blasphemy that extends beyond merely mentioning the divine Name. Numerous figures of old are seen as having paid for their blasphemy through God's intervention or the use of intermediaries. Among the examples are Adam, Amelek (slain by Joshua), Sisera (judged by a woman), Goliath (slain by David), and Belshazzar (overrun by Cyrus and Darius). The nation is also subject to judgment for rejecting the prophets. The examples bring together words and attitudes that show themselves in deeds, especially the arrogance of claiming to possess power greater than God or the ability to oppose God's people. The pattern is so consistent that it suggests a view deeply held by this period.

Midrash on the Psalms 109.2 on v. 2. This midrashic text is quite late and does not use the term blasphemy, but describes a scene that comes very close to it conceptually.[116] The midrash is considering Ps 109:2, which says "the mouth of the wicked and the mouth of the deceitful are opened against me (ופי מרמה עלי פתחו)." The midrash then asks what this verse means. The reply is,

> It means that when the wicked came into the Temple, they said: 'Where is their god? Let him come down and maintain their cause now, as is said, *Where are their gods, the rock in whom they have trusted . . . Let him rise up and help you* (Deut 32:37-38).' Thus they spoke in the Holy Temple and even more, boasting: *Our high hand and not the Lord has done all this!* (Deut 32:27). Now is not all this an open mouthing against the Lord (אין זה פתחון פה)? Hence it is said, *For the mouth of the wicked and the mouth of the deceitful are opened against me* (פי רשע ופי מרמה עלי פתחו; Ps 109:2).

Here is an example of a euphemism, "open mouthing against the Lord." It describes blasphemy as a sin of arrogant remarks and recalls claims made by figures like Rabsehkah and Goliath. Total arrogance before the Lord and a claim to have power like God is seen as blasphemous.

The midrashic expositions of blasphemy reveal the sense of revulsion that blasphemy produced for the faithful. They also supply an array of illustrations of blasphemous speech and acts. Profaning the Name is certainly seen as blasphemy, an emphasis that has appeared throughout the textual survey. There are also numerous examples of figures that are said to have blasphemed, usually with acts of high arrogance challenging God or His people. Such examples include Adam, Pharaoh, Amalek, Sisera, Goliath, Rabshekah, and Belshazzar. Most come from outside the nation, but they all issue a challenge either to God's power or to the honor of his name. In many cases, it is action that speaks as loud as words. Again the appeal to words and action fits the pattern within Judaism.

10. The Palestinian Talmud

The Key Terminology

This commentary on the Mishnah was produced in Galilee and was completed in the first half of the fifth century. It contains only a few discussions of

---

[116]William G. Braude, *The Midrash on the Psalms*, 2 vols., YJS 13 and 14 (New Haven: Yale University Press, 1959), 2:202-03. It dates from 750-800 CE.

blasphemy. Versification is not as standardized with this Talmud, so both the traditional enumeration and the Neusner numbering are used when passages are discussed, while the terminology survey uses a shorthand version of the traditional enumeration.

Once again, the dominating term in this material is גדף, which appears 36x. Five uses involve the noun, while the rest involve the verb. Twenty-six of these uses are concentrated in a few passages (*y Sanh* 23c, 25a-b, and *y Sh*^e*b* 34b). In addition, it appears in parts of *y MKatan* 83b = *y Sanh* 25b, and *y Meg* 70c = *y Taan* 66a. Two uses of חרף are relevant (*y Meg* 70c = *y Taan* 66a).[117] Finally, the term נאץ also appears in *y Meg* 70c = *y Taan* 66a, as well as in *y Sanh* 18b.

y Terumot 1.40d (Neusner 1.6)

This passage is considering when valid heave offerings are being made and who can make the appropriate separation required of the offering.[118] Among those who should not make such a separation is a drunkard. There is debate over whether a drunkard's prayer is valid or not. Abba bar Rabbi Huna (c 290 CE) argues that such a prayer should not be made, but if he should pray, his intercession is still valid. The anonymous reply is that the drunkard should not pray. If he does, his prayer is deemed "blasphemy" (גדופין). The view represented in this rejection of the prayer seems to be that prayer offered by someone in an unworthy mental state while making sacrifices is dishonoring to God. More interesting is that to call such a prayer blasphemous does not seem to require the use of the divine Name, but rather reflects the dishonorable condition of one who addresses God and tries to worship him in such a state. Thus blasphemy is used in this text in a broader sense than its technical legal usage in *m Sanh* 7.5.

y Yoma 7.44c (Neusner 7.3)

This text presents a tradition that was already seen above in *LevR* 10.6.[119] It is the discussion of the symbolism of the frontlet piece of the high priest. The Goliath incident is noted as the basis of the symbolism (1 Sam 17:49 in combination with a reference to Exod 28:38). The debate centers on whether it symbolizes the sins of "those who blaspheme" (על חגודפנים) or "those who sins are presumptuous." Those who favor presumption cite Jer 3:3 as support.

---

[117]Uses in *y Ber* 7d, *y Yeb* 7b, *y Naz* 57a, and *y Kidd* 59a are not relevant.

[118]Jacob Neusner, ed., *TLI* vol. 6 CSHJ (Chicago: Chicago University Press, 1988), pp. 89-90; Gerd A. Wevers, *Terumot: Priesterhebe* ÜTY I/6 (Tübingen: J. C. B. Mohr [Paul Siebeck], 1985), p. 28.

[119]Jacob Neusner, ed., *TLI* vol. 14 (1990), p. 201; Friedrich Avemarie, *Yoma: Versöhnungstag* ÜTY II/10 (Tübingen: J. C. B. Mohr [Paul Siebeck], 1995), p. 195. Brackets in the translations represent Neusner's commentary. His translations have been checked against the German versions as well.

The debate is never resolved, only noted. The importance of the text is that Goliath is again seen as an example of the blasphemer. His blasphemy involves an attack on the people of God.

y Megillah 1.70c (Neusner 1.4) = y Taanit 2.66a (Neusner 2.12)

This passage discusses the thirteenth of Adar as "Nicanor's day" (1 Macc 7:26-50; 2 Macc 14:11-15, 36; Josephus, *Ant* 12.402-12).[120] This ruler of Greece was going through Jerusalem on his way to Alexandria when "he saw Jerusalem and broke out into cursing, blasphemy, and insult (*Meg* - וניאץ וגידף וחירף; *Taan*- וחירף וגידף וניאץ), saying, "When I come back, I shall break down that tower." The passage goes on to note that the Hasmoneans undertook the king in battle, cut off his hand and head and displayed them in Jerusalem on a pole saying, "the mouth that spoke shamefully and the hand that stretched out arrogantly." Here the attack of the people of God is again seen as an attack on God, like the Sennacherib incident. The stacking up of terms of vilification, like that seen in *Midrash Rabbah*, is also found here. The account's point is not only to explain the day, but also to show that blasphemers get their just rewards.

y Mo'ed Ḳaṭan 3.83b (Neusner 3.7)

This text considers in great detail the issue of rending garments.[121] Included in the discussion is who rends garments, the ten occasions when "rejoined at the seam" garments are not to be torn, and how much they must be torn. One of the occasions when tearing a rejoined garment is prohibited is upon "hearing the Name of God cursed." Blasphemy is also raised as the discussion turns to the question of blasphemy by a Gentile. The teaching is said to derive from the Rabshekah incident (of 2 Kgs 19:1). One view argues that clothes are torn "on hearing the curse of an idolater of the Name of God." Another view argues that, if Rabshekah was an Israelite, then clothes are not torn. Still another opinion stated by Rabbi Hoshaiah[122] is that the law is the same for both Israelites and others who curse the Divine Name: one rends their clothes. The support is God's claim that He is the "God of all flesh" from Jer 32:27.

The question then becomes whether one should rend garments at the present time (of the writing of the Talmud). Four rabbis are noted who argue:

---

[120]Jacob Neusner, ed., *TLI* vol. 18 Besha and Taanit (1987), p. 202, and vol. 19 Megillah (1987), p. 26; Frowald G. Hüttenmeister, *Megilla: Schriftrolle*. ÜTY II/10 (Tübingen: J. C .B. Mohr [Paul Siebeck], 1987), p. 20.

[121]Jacob Neusner, ed., *TLI* vol. 20, Hagigah and Moed Qatan, 1986, pp. 213-17, esp. 214, 216-17. See also *b Mo'ed Ḳaṭan* 26a. It also discusses 2 Kgs 19:1. Heinz-Peter Tilly, *Moed Qatan: Halbfeiertage*, ÜTY II/12 (Tübingen: J. C. B. Mohr [Paul Siebeck], 1988), pp. 108-09. Parts of this passage overlap with *y Sanh* 25b. The key term in this text is מדף.

[122]Which Hoshaiah is meant is not clear, but he is either a figure of the third (c 225 CE) or fourth (c 300 CE) centuries.

"Once blasphemers became many, they have ceased from tearing their clothes upon hearing blasphemy." A second question concerns blasphemy through euphemism. Then comes a short anecdote to answer the question. Rabbi Simeon ben Laqish (c. 250 CE) is riding along the road and encounters a Samaritan who is cursing. So the rabbi dutifully tore his clothes. The Samaritan cursed again, so the rabbi did his "rending" duty a second time. The rabbi got off his beast of burden and punched the Samaritan in the chest, saying to him, "Evil one! Does your mother have enough clothes to give me?" The story teaches that "they do tear their clothing when they hear God cursed through euphemisms, and they also tear their clothing at this time." So the story resolves both questions.[123] What is important to note is that euphemism is treated as an equal offense to cursing the Name. Both acts are responded to as reflecting blasphemy.

y Sanhedrin 1.18b (Neusner 1.1)

This passage discusses arbitration in legal matters.[124] The text exhorts that one should not compliment an arbitrator as an opportunity to gain advantage neither should one seek someone to make an arbitration after a judgment has already been made. Rabbi Eleazar (c. 150 CE), son of Rabbi Jose the Galilean (c. 110 CE) said that a person who praises the arbitrator is like one whom "curses the Eminent one." Then Ps 10:3 is cited in a variation of its original form. The Talmud reads, "He who blesses the arbitrator blasphemes the Lord." The syntactically obscure MT reads, "The one who is greedy blesses and reviles Yahweh" (The text could read, "he blesses the one who is greedy and reviles the Lord"). The talmudic rendering follows the former sense. The talmudic citation appears to argue that the remarks really try to sway an arbitrator through compliments motivated from greed, not sincerity. So the rabbi issues his warning. Blasphemy is used as an example to show the severity of the act and to describe the "praise for gain" as misused as well as misleading speech.

y Sanhedrin 5.22d (Neusner 5.1)

This text is considering the topic of profaning the Sabbath.[125] Num 15:32-36 is discussed. The violation was gathering sticks and not harvesting. The text is said to make the violation clear. The violator was executed by stoning, as Heaven demanded. Rabbi Hiyya (c 280 CE) explains: "The Lord said to Moses, 'Bring out of the camp him who cursed; and let all who heard him lay

---

[123]The story of Simeon ben Laqish also appears in *y Sanh 7.25a* (Neusner 7.5).

[124]Jacob Neusner, ed., *TLI*, vol. 31 Sanhedrin and Makkot, 1984, p. 16. Gerd A. Wevers, *Sanhedrin: Gerichtshof*, ÜTB IV/4, 1981, p. 7. Here the key term is במאץ.

[125]Jacob Neusner, ed., *TLI*, vol. 31 Sanhedrin and Makkot, 1984, pp. 151-56, esp. 154-55. Gerd A. Wevers, *Sanhedrin: Gerichtshof*, ÜTY IV/4, 1981, pp. 127.

their hands upon his head, and let all the congregation stone him (Lev 24:13-14).'" Now the point of the exposition is that the citation of Lev 24 shows that the Sabbath violator is treated as the blasphemer. Moses was asked to inquire of Heaven how to execute the man, not if he should be executed. The assumption of the text is that the sticks were being gathered to prepare to worship an idol like Peor or Mercury. The text shows how easily Num 15 and Lev 24 were associated with each other, since they share the same penalty.[126] Though none of the key terms for blasphemy appear, the passage operates conceptually in the same area because of the citation of Lev 24.

y Sanhedrin 6.23b (Neusner 6.1)

This discussion considers the command to stone in Lev 24:14 along with the proper location of such stoning.[127] That account deals briefly with the question of where one is stoned in a case where Gentiles populate a town. He is stoned in the place that "accords with either Rabbi or sages in regard to the provision to be made in the case of towns populated by Gentiles." The remark alludes to *m Sanh* 6.1. This means the outside gates of the city in which he performed the act of worship, unless the town is totally Gentile. In that case, they stone him at the door of the Israelite court. This example shows that a text on blasphemy was applied to cases of idolatry, the exact reverse of the previous text where appeal using Numbers ran from Sabbath-idolatry to blasphemy. Again, blasphemy terminology is absent, but the use of Lev 24 is significant in showing how idolatry and blasphemy were treated as similar crimes.

y Sanhedrin 6.23c (Neusner 6.6)

This exposition considers the question of how blasphemers and idolaters are hung, drawing quite directly from the discussion of the Mishnah.[128] The principle is stated from *m Sanh* 6.4: "Only the blasphemer and the one who worships an idol are hung." Then consideration is given to the views of Rabbi Eliezar (c 90 CE) that "just as the blasphemer, who is stoned, is hung (Deut 21:23), so I encompass all others who are stoned, that they too are to be hung." The majority of rabbis reason differently: "Just as the blasphemer (המגדף), because he struck out at the fundamental principle, is hung, so I encompass all those who have struck out at the fundamental principle, that they too be hung." Only violating a fundamental principle leads to hanging.

---

[126]The argument here is like what is seen in *m Ker* 1.1-2, *b. Ker* 7a-b, and *TNeofiti* on Lev 24:11-23, with some dissent noted in the *b Ker* text.

[127]Jacob Neusner, ed., *TLI*, vol. 31 Sanhedrin and Makkot, 1984, p. 170; Gerd A. Wevers, *Sanhedrin: Gerichtshof*, ÜTY IV/4, 1981, p. 144. Another, somewhat different discussion of the same issue occurs in *b Sanh* 42b, where being taken outside three camps is the point.

[128]Jacob Neusner, ed., *TLI*, vol. 31 Sanhedrin and Makkot, 1984, p. 180-81; Gerd A. Wevers, *Sanhedrin: Gerichtshof*, ÜTY IV/4, 1981, pp. 146-47. A similar discussion occurs in *b Sanh* 50a, where violating a fundamental principle of the faith is a cause for execution.

Blasphemy is seen as a basic and serious violation of faith, an explicit interpretive understanding of it that stretches back at least to Philo.[129]

y Sanhedrin 6.23c (Neusner 6.7)

In presenting the rule of hanging, there is consideration of the severity of punishment by stoning in comparison to other punishments.[130] Deut 21:23 is cited from *m Sanh* 6.4 along with its remark that the violator was hanged because "he cursed the Name, so the Name of Heaven came to be profaned." The argument is developed by Rabbi Eliezer ben Jacob (c 90 CE) since he is cited as teaching:

> The rule governing the one who disgraces the divine name is stricter than the one covering the one who blasphemes (מבמגדף), and the rule governing the one who blasphemes (במגדף) is stricter than the one who disgraces the divine name. In regard to the one who blasphemes (במגדף), it is written, "His body shall not remain all night on a tree [Deut 21:23]," while in regard to the one who disgraces the divine name it is written, "Then Rizpah, daughter of Aiah, took sackcloth, and spread it for herself on the rock, from the beginning of the harvest until rain fell upon them from the heavens (thus leaving out the bones of Saul and Jonathan) [2 Sam 21:10]." [So a stricter rule covers the bones of a blasphemer].

The remark in effect closes the basic argument, though the discussion is not finished. This passage and its argument are complicated since the discussion starts with the citation of Deut 21 and is cut off in mid-stream with the cited portion above.[131] The argument resumes later in 6.7, where the ultimate argument is made that "greater is the sanctification of the divine name than profanation of the divine name."[132] Again Deuteronomy and 2 Samuel are compared. So it appears that the discussion reports a dispute on the relative merits of two kinds of sin, but in such a confused way that it is not entirely clear how the dispute is resolved. The way this account compares and reverses the comparison between blasphemy and disgracing the name shows that the point is debated. But the example of Rizpah indicates that blasphemy

---

[129]*Migration of Abraham* 115-17.

[130]Jacob Neusner, ed., *TLI*, vol. 31 Sanhedrin and Makkot, 1984, p. 184; Gerd A. Wevers, *Sanhedrin: Gerichtshof*, ÜTY IV/4, 1981, pp. 150-51. This discussion is similar to *y Sanh 9.27b* and *b Sanh 49b-50b*. For *y Sanhedrin* 9.27b (Neusner 9.5), see Jacob Neusner, ed., *TLI*, vol. 31 Sanhedrin and Makkot, 1984, p. 302. It merely cites, *m Sanh* 9.3 that stoning is the more severe punishment, because it is used on the blasphemer and idolater. I will not note this text separately, because it reflects the standard rabbinic view on the issue of severity of punishment.

[131]Jacob Neusner, ed., *TLI*, vol. 31 Sanhedrin and Makkot, 1984, pp. 185 and the note after 6.7 I.C.

[132]Jacob Neusner, ed., *TLI*, vol. 31 Sanhedrin and Makkot, 1984, pp. 188-89, see esp. [VV]-[AAA].

is the more severe offense, requiring more careful care of the body. The passage does not tell us very much about blasphemy, other than to indicate that it is seen as a quite serious offense.

y Sanhedrin 7.24c (Neusner 7.5)

The key reference to blasphemy in the following passage is set up in 24c by a twice-noted citation from the list of thirty-six transgressions out of *m Ker* 1.1.[133]

y Sanhedrin 7.25a-b (Neusner 7.8-9)

This is the most detailed passage in this talmud.[134] It is a discussion of *m Sanh* 7.5 and is similar to a discussion in *b Sanh* 55b-56a. The text notes that the warning against blasphemy (למגדף) appears in Exod 22:27, where God is not to be reviled, and the penalty of extirpation is taught by Lev 24:15-16, since "whomever curses God shall bear his sin." The penalty is, "He who blasphemes the name of the Lord shall be put to death." Then comes a discussion of how these conclusions fit the exegetical methods of Rabbi Ishmael (c 120 CE). Reading the second part of Exodus 22:27 as about judges, the principle is extended in the following manner:

> If Scripture warns against cursing the judges, is it not an argument *a fortiori* that there should be a warning against cursing God with euphemisms. If for cursing God with euphemisms, one suffers the penalty of extirpation, if one does so with the fully expressed name of God, is it not an argument *a fortiori* [that the penalty should be extirpation]?

The exposition argues from the penalty resulting from insulting judges back to blasphemy for substitute names. The argument appears to be a lesser to greater argument. If one suffers extirpation for the abuse of humans, how much more one should suffer for insulting God, even with a substitute name? The argument also works in the reverse direction as well. If one suffers extirpation for using the Name, then one does as well for substitutes. In other words, since substitute names fall between the judges and the blasphemy of the Name, and both of those crimes have a penalty of extirpation, so the crime that comes between is liable to the same penalty. But the question whether one is liable only if one pronounces the Name or whether euphemisms can also lead to a guilty verdict is still noted and elaborated. The discussion presents this debate in a way that has already been noted in our survey:

---

[133]Jacob Neusner, ed., *TLI*, vol. 31 Sanhedrin and Makkot, 1984, p. 205; Gerd A. Wevers, *Sanhedrin: Gerichtshof*, ÜTY IV/4, 1981, p. 168.

[134]Jacob Neusner, ed., *TLI*, vol. 31 Sanhedrin and Makkot, 1984, pp. 230-37; Gerd A. Wevers, *Sanhedrin: Gerichtshof*, ÜTY IV/4, 1981, pp. 187-92. There are two citations of forms of נדף here.

there are Tannaim who teach that there is warning and extirpation because of cursing God with euphemisms, and for cursing God with the fully expressed name of God one is subject to the death penalty. And there are Tannaim who teach that, on account of cursing with euphemisms, one is subject to a warning, and for cursing with the fully expressed Name of God, one is subject to the death penalty and extirpation.

With this remark, the discussion notes the arguments on both sides, with both sides appealing to Exod 22 and Lev 24. Again, no resolution is present, only the case for each side is given; though the bulk of the teaching suggests that euphemisms do make one liable. Later in 7.8 (= 25b), there is discussion about rending one's garments that largely parallels *y. Mo'ed Ḳaṭan* 3.83b.[135]

Here the rabbinical debate focuses on extirpation, which is dependent upon distinguishing in part blasphemy with euphemism from blasphemy of the Name. The text also appears to distinguish the death penalty from extirpation, given that in this talmudic text being "cut off" looks like exclusion from the community. Does extirpation come for euphemisms or not? The center of the debate, as the subsequent exposition shows, revolves around the different readings of Lev 24:15-16 and whether the verses describe parallel offenses or distinct offenses. This debate has been traced throughout the textual survey of blasphemy material and its continuing presence is the result of a decided ambiguity in the original text of Leviticus.

Then comes a discussion of extirpation for idolatry which leads into a treatment of Num 15:30. It is regarded that Num 15 refers to a blasphemer and not to an idolater. So a defense for giving extirpation to an idolater comes on the following basis:

[Blasphemers and idolaters are equivalent to one another,] like a man who says to his fellow, 'You have scraped out the whole plate and left nothing in it,' [likewise the idolater completes what the blasphemer starts]. There is a parable [illustrating the same point]. Rabbi Simeon ben Eleazar (c 165 CE) says, 'It is comparable to two people sitting with a plate of beans between them. One of them stuck out his hand and scrapped off the whole plate and left nothing on it. So are the blasphemer and idolater: he leaves not a single religious duty after him.'[136]

The significant feature about this final portion of the passage is the equation it makes between idolatry and blasphemy. These are seen as virtually equivalent sins, sharing the same penalty. The debate over euphemism also shows up again here, with various positions being advocated. It is not clear that this debate is ever resolved in this passage.

---

[135]There are seven appearances of נדף in various forms in this passage.

[136]On this illustration, see *b Ker* 7a-b and *Sifre* § 112 and the discussions of these passages.

This key text suggests that debate about the fate of a blasphemer who used a euphemism was quite alive at this later period. It seems to reflect an old debate about a decidedly ambiguous text. At the least, there was a warning for the person who used a euphemism. But this text suggests that many made the argument that a euphemism left one liable, just as blaspheming with the Name or blaspheming a judge did.

y Sh^ebuoth 3.34b (Neusner 3.1)

This text surveys a disputed tradition involving Rabbi Aqiba (c 135 CE).[137] Should a blasphemer bring an offering, since he has not committed an act? Once again the key term appearing four times is המגדף (or in two cases, מגדף). The discussion opens with the note that a blasphemer should bring an offering, so how can Aqiba challenge this? Associates replying in the name of Rabbi Simeon ben Lachish (c. 250 CE) ask for proof from an example. The response simply notes that Aqiba has inconsistent statements on the topic. The response attributes the difference to two Tannas that represent different traditions in the name of Rabbi Aqiba. The debate, which is not resolved in terms of a decision one way or the other, is wrestling with the question of whether blasphemy is seen as an action, a debate that also shows up in *b Sanh* 65a.[138] This text, discussed below, also involves Aqiba but mentions other rabbis. This text, reflecting as it does, a debate over whether blasphemy as an utterance is seen as an action, shows its special and ambiguous character within Judaism.

The Palestinian talmudic texts fit well with the pattern of what has already been seen within Judaism. In one text, blasphemy is seen in a sense clearly broader than the use of the divine Name (*y Ter* 1.40d). Once again there are examples of blasphemers, like Nicanor and Goliath, who threaten God's people. There is a tendency in this material to show how similar blasphemy and idolatry are in terms of penalty. Also there is debate when the blasphemy is seen as an act demanding an offering or merely an utterance that does not require an offering (*y Sh^eb* 3.34b). In addition, the intense rabbinical debate around blasphemy and euphemism is noted with some detail in one text (*y Sanh* 7.25a). This passage seems to make the case that euphemism does make one liable. At the least, euphemism brings a warning and separation from the community. If the warning goes unheeded, then the repeat offense leads to a death conviction on the principle already noted from *m Sanh* 8.4, namely, that

[137]Jacob Neusner, ed., *TLI*, vol. 32 Shebuot, 1984, pp. 76-77; Gerd A. Wevers, *Makkot: Geißelung/Shevuot: Schwüre*, ÜTY IV/5-6, 1983, pp. 114-15.
[138]The Aqiba view is also noted in *b Sanh* 63a and *b Ker* 7a-b. On these texts, see discussion of the Babylonian Talmud below.

failure to heed a warning about being an incorrigible son can lead to death
with the second offense.

11. The Babylonian Talmud and *Aboth de Rabbi Nathan*

The Key Terminology

The Babylonian Talmud, finalized in the first half of the sixth century, and
one of its supplemental tractates, *Aboth (ARN),* possess numerous references
to blasphemy. Many of them merely mention the term without elaboration, or
the discussion largely overlaps with what has already been shown or will be
discussed in more detail in other texts.[139] The numerous examples of
blasphemy in these texts add to or reinforce several of the examples already
discussed, reflecting a pattern of understanding, which itself is evidence of an
older tradition.

---

[139]This survey will not discuss these largely redundant texts. They include: *b 'Er* 13a, *b
Pesaḥ* 93b, *b Yom* 67b, *b Ḥag11b*, *b BQam* 38a, *b Sanh* 42b-43a, 48b, 53a, 63a, 71b, 78a,
79b, 82b, *b Sheb* 22a, *b 'AbZ* 2b, *b 'Arak* 6b, and *b Ker* 2a-4a. Of these texts, *b Sanh* 79b is
like the argument seen in *m Sanh* 9.5 and one to be discussed in *b Sanh* 49b-50a; *b Sanh* 63a
is like *b Sheb* 22a, where both discuss the possibility of a blasphemer bringing an offering
like *b Ker* 7a-b discussed below, as well as *y Sheb* 3.34b discussed above; *b 'AbZ* 2b is like *b
Sanh* 56a, another text to be considered; *b Ker* 2a-4a names blasphemy as one of thirty six
sins that require extirpation (*m Ker* 1.1) and repeats the discussion of *b Sanh* 63a, which also
considers the issue of possible sacrifices for blasphemers; and *b Yoma* 67b considers a list of
sins that all should understand, a list that includes blasphemy, idolatry, immorality, bloodshed
and robbery and looks very much like the list of Noachian laws discussed in *b Sanh* 56a and
60a. Other texts add little to the discussion other than to mention blasphemy. Among such
texts are *b Shab* 75a, where there is a debate whether magianism, a priestcraft in Persia, is
sorcery (Samuel- c 220 CE) or blasphemy (Rab- c 220CE); *b Shab* 118b, where one rabbi
(Master- c. 165 CE) holds that one who reads the *Hallel* every day "blasphemes and
reproaches;" *b Meg* 24b, where a levite who is old and deformed should not pronounce the
blessing or else he is "a reviler and blasphemer;" *b Kid* 49a, where to add to a translation is to
be "a blasphemer and libeler" (see the parallel in *t Meg* 3.41 above); *b BBat* 15b, where Job is
mentioned as an example of one who "began to curse and blaspheme;" and *b Nid* 31a, where
there is an illustration of a man who was stuck with a thorn on a trip, so that he blasphemed
and reviled until he found his injury had spared him a sea journey in which another was
killed. A final example, *b BQam* 38a considers the retort of Rabbi Samuel b. Judah (c 280
CE) about receiving consolation from the Babylonian rabbis when his daughter died. He
argued that this was tantamount to blasphemy. Here an action is described in a metaphorical
use that shows how much one detests any connection to people from a certain geographic
region. Many of the briefly noted examples use forms of גדף. Those that use other terms are: *b
'Er* 13a; *b Yom* 67b; *b Ḥag 11b*, *b Sanh* 42b-43a, 48b, 53a, 71b, 79b, 82b; *b 'AbZ* 2b, *b 'Arak*
6b, and *b Ker* 2a. These texts also show the variety of situations to which the rabbis applied
the concept, but they do not add to the portrait that the other more detailed talmudic examples
will provide.

The central term once again is גדף, which appears 55x. In both *b Sanh* and *b Ker*, the term appears 17x. Some uses are strictly secular, as in some passages the term simply means to reject or ridicule a stated rabbinical view (*b Shab* 62b; *b Sanh* 3b, 40b; *b Zeb* 12a; *b AbZ* 35a, 43a). Other terms, as noted below, will appear in a few other important texts, of which קלל, is the next most frequent.

b Mo'ed Ḳaṭan 26a

This passage discusses the rending of garments when God's name is blasphemed, along with other acts that require rending, such as the death of a parent or teacher, hearing evil tidings, when a scroll of the Law is burned, or at the sight of the cities of Judea, the temple, or Jerusalem sitting in ruins.[140] The practice for blasphemy is defended by appeal to 2 Kgs 18:37 and 19:1. The key phrase, introduced earlier in the discussion, is rending garments on hearing "God's Name blasphemed (ועל ברכת השם)." Rending occurs whether one hears the blasphemy or hears it reported. The only exception is for witnesses who report a blasphemy and have already ripped their garments earlier. This text shows that the reaction to blasphemy continued to include this act of mourning. The argument is similar to one made in *y Mo'ed Ḳaṭan* 3.83b, which also appeals to 2 Kgs 19.

b Nedarim 87a

This tractate also discusses when rending of garments is required, particularly its timing.[141] It discusses rending when someone dies as well as other situations calling for such mourning. The discussion is extremely complicated and mentions blasphemy only at the end. The principle being argued appears to be that rending must come with the event or just after it, even if the rending involves making an incorrect identification (i.e., a father for a son or the reverse). But to rend and then have the action does not work. Rending can happen with an action (and even include a misidentification), but it cannot anticipate an event. There are exceptions. They are "blasphemy, idolatry, betrothal, and divorce." These offenses, which are not described in any more detail, are not retractable. The exception appears to work this way: a blasphemy once uttered cannot be taken back; but must be, if there is a desire to retract, atoned for; just as consent to a divorce, once made, cannot be taken back. This text actually adds little to our understanding of blasphemy itself,

---

[140]The texts for this section comes from I. Epstein, *The Babylonian Talmud*, 35 vols (London: Soncino, 1935-48). This passage is found in the *Seder Mo'ed Ḳaṭan*, vol. 10, pp. 163-68. Talmudic original texts reflect the readings in L. Goldschmidt, *Der Babylonishche Talmud* 9 vols. (Haag: Martinus Nijoff, 1933-35).

[141]I. Epstein, *The Babylonian Talmud: Seder Nedarim*, vol. 33, pp. 268-69.

though it does show that blasphemy once committed is to be dealt with and cannot be ignored.

b Giṭṭin 56b

This text is similar to *ARN B* 7, which is to be considered shortly.[142] Titus is sent by Vespasian to take Jerusalem. Titus is reported to have said, *"Where is their God, the rock in whom you trusted* (Deut 32:37)?" Then he is described as one "who blasphemed and insulted Heaven (שחירף וגידף כלפי מעלה)." What did he do? He took a harlot by the hand and entered the Holy of Holies and spread out a scroll of the Law and committed a sin on it. He then took a sword and slashed the curtain. Though quite distinct in its detail and tone, the slashing of the curtain shows an invasion of temple sanctity like that of Mk 15:38. With an economy of expression and sensitivity to the details, the gemara reveals, in effect, a rash blasphemy of action that accompanied whatever Titus is alleged to have said.

The account goes on to note the praise of Abba Ḥanan (c 140 CE) for God's restraint in punishment: "Who is like you, mighty in self-restraint, that you heard the blaspheming of the wicked man (שומע ניאוצו וגידופו של אותו רשע) and keep silent?" Then Titus is said to have taken the curtain and formed a basket out of it in order to carry the vessels home by ship so that he could celebrate his victory. The sea voyage home was not a good one since a gale kicked up that threatened the leader. Titus arrogantly comments that God only has power over the water and mentions the cases of Pharaoh and Sisera. God replies, addressing him as "Sinner, son of a sinner, descendant of Esau the sinner, I have a tiny creature called a gnat." Upon landing, the gnat is said to have entered Titus through his nose and eats away at his brain for seven (!) years. Upon Titus' death, Rabbi Phineas ben 'Aruba (c 70 CE) reported that he was there when they split open the skull and found "something like a sparrow two *selas* in weight." This text not only details the blasphemy, revealing it to be tied up with a series of arrogant actions, but also graphically teaches that it does not pay. The text's clear point is that if man does not judge blasphemy, it will be judged eventually by God.

b Sanhedrin 38b

This is one version of a very famous text, where rabbi Akiba claims that the seat at the right hand of God belongs to David.[143] The context is a discussion of Rabbi Joḥanan's dictum (c 80 CE) that, "the Holy One, blessed be He, does nothing without consulting his heavenly court." The discussion turns to the phrase *till thrones were placed* from Dan 7:9-10. The views are then recorded:

---

[142]I. Epstein, *The Babylonian Talmud: Seder Giṭṭin*, vol. 17, pp. 259-61.

[143]I. Epstein, *The Babylonian Talmud: Seder Sanhedrin*, vol. 23, pp. 245-46.

One was for Himself and one for David. Even as it has been taught: One was for Himself and one for David: this is Rabbi Akiba's (c 100 CE) view. Rabbi Jose (c 90 CE) protested to him: Akiba, how long will you profane (עושה שכינה) the Shekinah? Rather one for justice and the other for mercy. Did he accept this answer or not? — Come and hear! For it has been taught: One for justice and the other for charity; this is rabbi Akiba's view. Said Rabbi Eleazar ben Azariah (c 100 CE) to him: Akiba who have you to do with *Haggadah*? Confine yourself to the study of *Nega'im* and *Ohalot*.[144] But one was a throne, the other a footstool: a throne for a seat and a footstool in support of his feet.

This key text accuses Akiba of risking offense to God, of profaning the Shekinah, that is, blaspheming, by suggesting "a human being sits beside Him."[145] Now Akiba is not put at risk of suffering a penalty, because he is expressing an interpretive view and his motives are not seen as hostile. What he gets instead is a serious rabbinical warning. He takes the rebuke to heart and changes his view, but not to the satisfaction of a second rabbi, who issues an interpretation that even prevents, through an appeal to Isa 66:1, any type of personification as being the explanation. The entire discussion shows how God's honor was protected as unique. It also indicates that offense could emerge from a remark not using the Name of God and that the offense could be accompanied by a warning.[146]

b Sanhedrin 45b-46b

This passage is discussing *m Sanh* 6.4, which rules that "the blasphemer and idolater (המגדף והעובד) are hanged."[147] In the gemara, the remark is made about the blasphemers of God (קללת אלהים) that, "Just as the blasphemer (מקלל) in question is executed by stoning, so all who are stoned [must be subsequently hanged]." This is the view of Rabbi Eliezer.[148] The Sages have another view, arguing not all who are stoned are hanged, but only some: "Just as the blasphemer (מקלל) in question denied the fundamental principle [of faith] (שכפר בעיקר), so all who deny the fundamental principle (אף כל שכפר בעיקר)."

---

[144]These two sections are treatise names in the Seder Tohoroth, which was regarded as the most difficult of the Talmud. Akiba had a reputation for handling this material well, but his *Haggadic* rulings were often disputed. See Epstein, *The Babylonian Talmud: Seder Sanhedrin*, p. 245, n. 8.

[145]Epstein, *The Babylonian Talmud: Seder Sanhedrin*, p. 245, n. 7. This issue of exaltation and being seated in heaven is the topic of the next chapter.

[146]This anecdote also appears in *b Ḥag* 14a. For a discussion of this text in more detail, see Alan Segal, *Two Powers in Heaven: Early Rabbinic Reports about Christianity and Gnosticism*, SJLA 25, ed. Jacob Neusner (Leiden: E. J. Brill, 1977), pp. 47-51.

[147]Epstein, *The Babylonian Talmud: Seder Sanhedrin*, p.300. A similar discussion appears in *Sifre Deuteronomy* § 221, as was noted above.

[148]Which Eliezar is meant here is not specified. The only Eliezar who was a leader of a school is Eliezar b. Pᵉdath from c 270 CE. Usually such figures appear without any additional identification.

For the rabbis this fundamental violation would apply only to a few sins, namely idolatry and blasphemy, given the section of the discussion. The rabbis are said to apply a rule of general to particular and Eliezer is said to use the rule of extension and limitation to get to his more wide ranging conclusion. The exposition goes on to argue that the penalty applies to an idolater, who is a particular kind of offender, but who also is like the blasphemer in every respect. So the penalty of hanging also applies to this second offense for the rabbis. On the other hand, Eliezer argues that the separation of the clause on hanging and cursing in Deut 21:23 extends the application of hanging to all who suffer a curse.

In 46a the argument notes that a person is hanged because they have cursed and profaned the Name of God (נמצא שם שמים/קללת אלהים), citing a later portion of *m Sanh* 6.4.[149] The mishnah receives elaboration in 46b, where a parable is told that involves twins, one became a king and the other a robber.[150] When the robber was hanged, the people said, it was the king. So the king commanded the body be taken down. So the point of the teaching is that man made in God's image is not to be left hanging. Here is another text highlighting how blasphemy is a fundamental violation of faith, punishable by death and public display. This passage is a major discussion of the topic as the full variety of terminology that is used for blasphemy shows. The three major terms for the concept appear in this discussion.

b Sanhedrin 49b-50b

This passage considers the four types of death entrusted to the Beth Din as noted in *m Sanh* 7.1: stoning, burning, slaying by the sword, and strangulation.[151] As in mishnaic texts where these various forms of punishment are named, the discussion turns to which punishment is most severe. In response to the view of Rabbi Simeon (c 200 CE) that burning is the most severe, the rabbis argue that only blasphemers and idolaters are stoned for violating a fundamental belief of the faith: "Stoning is severer than burning, since in this manner the blasphemer and the idol worshipper (למגדף ולעובד)[152] are executed. Wherein lies the particular enormity of these offenses? — Because they raised their hand against God (שכן פושט ידו בעיקר)."[153] The argument is then applied to the other types of punishment: "Stoning is severer than strangulation, since it is the penalty of the blasphemer and the idol

[149]Epstein, *The Babylonian Talmud: Seder Sanhedrin*, p.304.

[150]Epstein, *The Babylonian Talmud: Seder Sanhedrin*, p.306

[151]Epstein, *The Babylonian Talmud: Seder Sanhedrin*, p. 330-38. Similar discussion appears in *m Sanh* 9.3 and *y Sanh* 6.23c.

[152]This combination appears five times in the passage, often as an explanation looking back to this first use. In addition, מגדף appears once more by itself.

[153]See *b Sanh* 45b-46b above. The phrase here recalls the use of שכפר בעיקר there.

worshipper, the enormity of whose offense has already been stated."[154] As with many of the talmudic texts, the major point focuses on the basic nature of the violation of blasphemy and its ranking as the worst of sins. In Judaism's view blasphemy is an attack against the one and only true God.[155]

b Sanhedrin 55b-57a

This extensive passage may be the most important talmudic text.[156] The passage comments on *m Sanh* 7.5, which specifies stoning only if the blasphemer utters the divine Name. The comment uses the first of many euphemisms to describe the crime: "[The blasphemer (מגדף) is not punished, unless he 'blesses' the Name (שיפרש השם)."[157] The comment then cites Lev 24:16. Interestingly, the comment then goes on to talk about cursing and reviling God (קרא ונקב שם),[158] an indication of some of the conceptual synonyms that point to blasphemy. Later the phrase תקלל is used from Exod 22:27, for not cursing God. So once again Lev 24 and Exod 22 are used side by side. There is then a long aside on the various ways one might use the divine Name (in writing, engraving, or pronunciation). Then the discussion returns to discuss Lev 24 with what is described as an alternative view,

> The Scripture says, "*[And the Israelitish woman's son] blasphemed and cursed* (ויקב ויקלל), proving that blasphemy denotes cursing (דנוקב קללה). But perhaps it teaches that both offenses must be perpetuated? You cannot think so, because it is written, *Bring forth him that has cursed,* and not 'him that has blasphemed and cursed' (את הנוקב והמקלל), proving that only one offense is alluded to."

In an argument a modern linguist might make, it is argued that both blasphemy and cursing are treated as part of a single offense, since both verbs are interchanged to summarize the violation.

The topic then shifts to whether heathens are subject to blasphemy. The query is whether the prohibition of blasphemy can be deduced to apply to heathens from this verse or from another passage, since the reference in Lev 24:16 to "any man" had already been noted: "What is taught by the expression *any man?* The inclusion of heathens, to whom blasphemy (השם

---

[154]So also with slaying: "Stoning is severer than slaying, being the penalty of a blasphemer, etc."

[155]The note on this text in Epstein, *The Babylonian Talmud: Seder Sanhedrin*, pp. 332-33, n. 7, states, "there can be no doubt that the rejection of idolatry is a *sine qua non* of Judaism."

[156]Epstein, *The Babylonian Talmud: Seder Sanhedrin*, pp. 378-90.

[157]This phrase could be just as easily be translated "sings the Name." It connotes a worshipful tone, a worship that the blasphemer abuses.

[158]Later in the passage, this combination of verbs appears with ויקלל added. See next citation below.

(ברכה)[159] is prohibited just as to Israelites; and they are executed by decapitation; for every death penalty decreed for the sons of Noah is only by decapitation." This allusion to the shedding of blood for murder in Gen 9:6 is read quite literally. The response comes that Gen 2:16 is the source of the belief that blasphemy is also a crime for the heathen, since it mentions "the Lord," the divine Name to Adam, showing that respect for the Name goes back to the earliest period of humanity's creation. This key argument will be raised again in *b Sanh* 56b and was noted already in *GenR* 16.6 and *DeutR* 2.25.

Rabbi Isaac the smith[160] goes on to argue that substitutes for the divine Name also apply. Again Lev 24:15-16 is cited. Then comes his comment:

> Whence do I know that all substitutes are included [in this law]? From the verse, *Any man that curses his God* (יקלל אלהיו)—showing culpability for any manner of blasphemy: this is the view of Rabbi Meir (c 140 CE). But the Sages maintain: [Blasphemy] with the use of the ineffable Name is punishable by death; with the employment of substitutes, it is an object of an injunction, [but not punishable by death].

Here is the conflict on the issue of whether the Name alone is required for capital blasphemy or whether substitutes are allowed. The debate recalls a similar discussion in *m Sch^eb* 4.13, where alternate letters were used for the Name or attributes of God were named instead of the specific Name.

The dispute continues as Rabbi Miyasha (c 300 CE) argues that a heathen using a substitute name is to be slain: "If a heathen blasphemed (את השם שבירך),[161] employing substitutes of the ineffable Name, he is in the opinion of the Sages punishable by death." Lev 24 is again cited as noting that the penalty is for native born and "the stranger." Then an explanatory comment follows, noting that the ruling means that proselytes and natives are culpable only if the divine Name is pronounced, but "the heathen is punished even for a substitute only." Rabbi Meir (c 140 CE) is said to hold that strangers (proselytes) and citizens are stoned, but a heathen is decapitated. All of this is based on the seven precepts taught the sons of Noah: obedience to authority, to refrain from blasphemy (ברכת השם), idolatry, adultery, bloodshed, robbery and eating flesh of a living animal.

In 56b, as a review of the Noachian commands is given, the argument from Gen 2:16 is repeated, also using Gen 18:19, since both texts mention the

---

[159]Note the use of yet another term for blasphemy, the now more frequent "bless" euphemism. Decapitation alludes to the use of a sword, a view stated more explicitly in the parallel *Sifra* 19. For that text, see discussion above.

[160]He apparently comes from the talmudic period, see Epstein, *The Babylonian Talmud: Seder Sanhedrin*, p. 380, n.7

[161]Note the euphemism again, which also appears below in the listing of the Noachian law.

Lord: "*The Lord*—is [a prohibition against] blasphemy (ברכת השם), and thus it is written, *and he that blasphemes the name* (ונקב שם) *of the Lord, he shall surely be put to death.*" Later in the same section a note is added that one of the Tanna of the school of Manasseh omitted reference to blasphemy and obedience to authority, while Rabbi Judah ben Bathyra (c 110 CE) did add blasphemy to the list. A long discussion of this school's approach follows with some arguing that adultery, bloodshed and blasphemy are punishable for heathen and others questioning this or that category.

This entire long section is as full a presentation of the rabbinical variety of views on blasphemy as we have. It shows a great degree of discussion surrounding the use of alternatives to the Name and the issue of the heathen and blasphemy. The discussion's length and detail indicate that there was much debate over the scope of blasphemy. Many held that the use of substitutes for the Name was as severe an offense as using the Name. Thus, despite the limitations seen in *m Sanh* 7.5, it is clear that for some the limitation of blasphemy to pronunciation of the Name alone was too narrow. Although it is recorded as a minority view in the material, it had a strong enough presence to receive full attention, suggesting it was a well-received counter view.

b Sanhedrin 60a

This passage also develops *m Sanh* 7.5.[162] Again the debate swirls around the issue of substitutes for the divine Name. Rabbi Joshua ben Ḳarḥa (c 150 CE) and company say, along with Rabbi Aha b. Jacob (c 320 CE), "He is not guilty unless he cursed the Tetragrammaton, excluding a biliteral Name, the blaspheming of which is not punishable."[163] Appeal for support comes from the use of the euphemism "may Jose smite Jose." In this euphemism the substitution four letter name of Jose indicates by its nature the previous use of the divine Name, otherwise the four letter euphemistic substitution would not have been made. Then follows a discussion of when rending garments takes place. Both the one "who hears [the Name blasphemed]" and who hears it from the person who first heard it must rend garments. But other witnesses need not rend the garment.[164] The example of rending is from 2 Kgs 18:37 and involves Hezekiah's response to Rabshekah. Rabbi Judah (c 165 CE) argues that "he who hears [the divine Name blasphemed-השומע] by a Gentile need not rend his clothes." The rabbi argues that Rabshekah was an apostate Israelite to defend his minority position and more limited application. This identification responds to an objection against a limitation for Gentiles, by arguing that

---

[162]Epstein, *The Babylonian Talmud: Seder Sanhedrin*, pp. 407-09.

[163]A biliteral Name only uses some of the letters of the divine Name like EL or YH. The phrase is שיברך שם בן ארבע.

[164]This discussion is like *b Moed Qatan* 26a and *y Moed Qatan* 3.83b.

Rabshekah is not Gentile. He also held that rending only involved hearing the "*Shem hameyuḥad* (or the unique Name blasphemed)." Rabbi Ḥiyya (c 200 CE) argued another view, that rending need no longer occur. He suggested that all one's clothes would be reduced to tatters since blasphemy was now so prevalent! He also argued that formerly substitutes would have also required rending.

Once again, lively debate surrounds the discussion of what is required in terms of rending. Questions included when had a captial offense of blasphemy occurred, and were heathen included in such legal questions. The care and detail with which blasphemy is discussed and the variety of opinions spanning several figures are other key indications of its importance and of the controversy surrounding it.

b Sanhedrin 64b-65a

The topic has shifted to discussing how the idolater and sorcerer are handled.[165] In 64b there is a very brief comparison between the idolater and blasphemer (במגדף/מגדף is used later in the sentence), where the two practices are equated. This comparison was seen above in *b Sanh* 45b-46b. The remarks here add little to what was seen there. Next in 65a-b comes a discussion of sorcery and its penalty of stoning. In discussing the death penalty, the question is raised whether action is required for a sin offering to be necessary. The teaching of Akiba from *b Ker* 2a is noted, namely, that action is not necessary before a sacrifice is required. Blasphemy is mentioned as an example: "But Resh Laḳish (c 250 CE) maintains: Granted that Rabbi Akiba (c 100 CE) does not require a great action, but he requires at least a small one. But what action is there in the blasphemer (מגדף) [which is included in the enumeration]?—The movement of the lips."

The discussion then goes on to consider the actions of a sorcerer, who "knocks his arms." But later Raba (c 200 CE) argues that "Blasphemy (מגדף) is different, since the offense lies in the intention." In other words, the action is not as important as the intent, a principle noted as early as Philo.[166] In this talmudic text, assessing the intent behind the blasphemous remark is seen as important.

b Sanhedrin 81b

This difficult passage is considering the use of a curse or enchantment. In the midst of naming various curses that can be used, one of the curses discussed is, "May the *Kosem*[167] slay him [his enemy], his Master and his Provider,

---

[165]Epstein, *The Babylonian Talmud: Seder Sanhedrin*, pp. 441-44.

[166]See the Balaam illustration in *The Migration of Abraham* 115-17 noted above.

[167]This term, which was noted above in *m Sanh* 9.6, has a disputed meaning. It is either an indirect way to refer to God or refers to a charmer of some kind, probably using such a name.

etc."[168] Now the reference to the Creator-Provider is an allusion to God. A man using such a curse is "to be punished by Zealots" (i.e., pious men). The punishment, which is citing *m Sanh* 9.6, involves death. It appears that the sentence is seen as a response to blasphemy, and includes an utterance which makes a reference to divine attributes. The problem with being certain of this likely conclusion is that the text is too brief and contains no explicitly developed explanation. If the conclusion is correct, then another passage gives evidence of blasphemy not using the divine Name.

b Sanhedrin 94a-b

Here is another significant text as it gives examples of those who blasphemed by speaking against the land of Israel.[169] Here is the full, relevant passage:

> A Tanna taught in the name of Rabbi Joshua ben Ḳarḥa (c 150 CE): Pharaoh, who personally blasphemed (שהירף), was punished by the Holy One, blessed be He in Person; Sennacherib, who blasphemed (שהירף) [94b] through an agent [Rabshekah], was punished by the Holy One, blessed be He, through an agent. [Thus:] Pharaoh, of whom it is written, [and who said,] *Who is the Lord, that I should obey His voice?* [Exod 5:2] was punished by the Holy One, blessed be He, in person, as it is written, *And* the Lord *overthrew the Egyptians in the midst of the sea* [Exod 14:27] and it is also written, *You did walk through the sea with Your horses* [Hab 3:15]. But Sennacherib, of whom it is written, *By* your messengers *have you reproached the Lord* [2 Kings 19:23], was punished by the Holy One, blessed be He, through an angel, as it is said, *And an angel of the Lord went out, and smote in the camp of the Assyrians an hundred fourscore and five thousand* [2 Kings 19:35].

This passage comes back to two standard examples of blasphemy: Pharaoh and Sennacherib. It should be noted that both blasphemed the Lord by actions and words that reflected great arrogance rather than through using a specific term.

b Shebuoth 35a, 36a

This passage considers oaths and again discusses which uses of the Name make one accountable.[170] The discussion develops *m Sheb* 4.13, citing the view of Rabbi Meir (c 140 CE) that any substitutes make the blasphemer (המקלל) liable, while the Sages exempt anyone who uses a substitute. Other situations are also considered, such as slandering the father and mother also using המקלל. What follows is a long exposition on the various names. Which

---

[168]Epstein, *The Babylonian Talmud: Seder Sanhedrin*, vol. 24, pp. 542-43.

[169]Epstein, *The Babylonian Talmud: Seder Sanhedrin*, p. 634.

[170]Epstein, *The Babylonian Talmud: Seder Shebu'oth*, vol. 26, pp. 202-205, 211.

of them can be erased (because they are not just used of God and so are not sacred) and which cannot be erased?[171]

In 36a another key passage appears summarizing the disagreement between Rabbi Meir (140 CE) and the Sages. It reads beginning with the citation of the Mishnah from *Sh^ebuoth*:

> HE WHO BLASPHEMES BY ANY OF THEM (המקלל) IS LIABLE: THIS IS THE OPINION OF RABBI MEIR; BUT THE SAGES EXEMPT HIM. Our rabbi taught: *Whosoever curses his God* (יקלל אלהיו) *shall bear his sin* [Lev 24:15]. Why is it written? Is it not already said: *And he that blasphemes the name of the Lord* ('ונקב שם ה) *shall surely be put to death?* [Lev 24:16]—I might think that he should be liable only for the actual Name; from where do we know to include the substitutes? Therefore it is said: *whoever curses his God* (יקלל אלהיו) [Lev 24:15]—in any manner; this is the opinion of Rabbi Meir; but the sages say: for his actual Name, death; for the substitutes, there is a warning.[172]

Here is a resolution of the debate on the use of substitute names. Death is automatic for use of the Name, as has been consistently advocated throughout these texts. A substitute name is still seen as a violation, but it gets a warning. What happens after a warning is not clear. This text does not say, but on analogy with the incorrigible son in *m Sanh* 8.4, it is conceivable that a second violation could bring death. The passage goes on to note that slaying someone for cursing his parents also requires use of the Name. In making the point, Rabbi Menaḥem ben Jose (c 180 CE) appeals to Lev 24:16. The text reflects the prevailing rabbinic view.

b Kerithoth 7a-b

This complicated passage reveals debates over whether one can bring an offering to deal with liability for blasphemy and when does extirpation apply to someone who blasphemes.[173] The discussion is considering when one should be subject to extirpation so they are cut off. Rabbi Akiba (c 120 CE), appealing to Num 15:30 and a discussion on offerings for unintentional sins,

---

[171]The sacred names include: El Eloha', Elohim, Your God, I am that I am, Alef Daleth, Yod He, Shaddai, and Ẓebaoth. So, names are tied to figures like Abraham, Naboth, and the names Solomon used in the Song of Songs.

[172]The note in Epstein, *The Babylonian Talmud: Seder Shebu'oth*, pp. 211, n. 11, indicates that a warning comes with the penalty of flogging. Though a distinct situation in Mark, this detail is interesting in light of the New Testament account of Pilate's flogging (Mk 15:15- in preparation for crucifixion, but see Lk 23:16, where an initial request to warn through flogging is rejected). Of course, failure to heed the warning would lead to death on the second violation.

[173]Epstein, *The Babylonian Talmud: Seder Kerithoth*, vol. 32, pp. 51-58. The discussion here is paralleled in *b Sh^eb* 22a, where the point is made that one who speaks blasphemy is to bring an offering; see also *y Sh^eb* 3.34b.

allows for an offering in the case of one who blasphemes (מגדף) in error.[174] The Sages disagree arguing that there is no action in the case of blasphemy, so no sacrifice is required. The Sages continue their case by arguing that Num 15:30 does not apply to a blasphemer, but to an idolater. The blasphemer who blasphemes the Name is subject to being cut off. The debate over Num 15 continues in the unit with opinions moving back and forth between rabbis who hold it applies to idolatry (Eleazar ben Azariah- c 100 CE) and others who see it as referring to blasphemy (Issi ben Judah [c 170 CE] on behalf of the rabbis). The discussion closes with the resolution: "Another [Baraitha] teaches: '[*The same blasphemes*][175]*the Lord* [Num 15:30]': Rabbi Eleazar ben Azariah says: the text speaks of one who worships idols, while the Sages say: The text intends only to pronounce *kareth* for him who blasphemes the Name (למברך השם)." Thus the passage also reflects the standard rabbinic approach to the issue, where blasphemy of the Name means death. The debate over leniency for unintentional sin is but a sub-point in the face of the larger agreement over offense against God's name.

Aboth de Rabbi NathanB 3, 7, 32, 35

These additional tractates to the Babylonian Talmud contain some of the most developed pictures of blasphemy through extensively illustrated examples.[176] The first passage in chapter 3 is explaining why the Sages are said to make a hedge around their words. One of the explanations reads,

> Another interpretation. 'He who digs a pit will fall into it; and a serpent will bite him who breaks through a wall.' This is the blasphemer (המקלל), as Scripture says: 'and the !sraelite woman's son blasphemed the Name (השם את)[177] and cursed (Lev 24:11).' Who is the serpent who bit him? It was Moses, as Scripture says: 'So Moses spoke to the people of Israel; and they brought

---

[174]This argument is also used in *b Sanh* 63a. This term for blasphemer appears several times in this discussion.

[175]The citation here is a kind of shorthand reference to the Lord, as Num 15:30 was cited in full earlier in the passage, where the phrase is את ה' [הוא] מגדף. Thus the expanded translation here as well.

[176]Anthony J. Saldarini, *The Fathers according to Rabbi Nathan: Aboth de Rabbi Nathan Version B*, Studies in Judaism in Late Antiquity, ed. Jacob Neusner, vol. 11 (Leiden: E. J. Brill, 1985), pp. 49-50, 67-69, 188, 210. Citations of the original reflect the version edited by Salomon Schechter, *Aboth de Rabbi Nathan* (Hiledesheim: George Olms, 1979 [Wien: 1887ed.])

[177]Here the original has only an object and lacks a verb, allowing it to be supplied from the context, so that there is no expression of blaspheming the Name.

him who had cursed out of the camp, and stoned him with stones (Lev 24:23).'
for stoning and pushing.[178]

This text contains a rather traditional interpretation of Lev 24 and the son's use of the Name to blaspheme. What is interesting to note, however, is the care with which the crime is stated, even though it is only summarized.

Aboth de Rabbi NathanB 7 treats the fall of Jerusalem and contains one of the most developed examples of blasphemy in this survey. It describes the various blasphemous acts of "a wicked man, Titus, son of Vespasian's wife."[179] Titus, "defiantly entered" the temple, slashed the curtain, dragged a prostitute into the Holy of Holies "and he began to blaspheme, curse, vilify and spit toward Him on high (מחרף ומגדף ומנאץ ומרכך כלפי מעלה) saying: So this is the one who you say slaughtered Sisera and Sennacherib. Here I am in his house and in his domain. If he has any power; let him come out and face me." What is fascinating about this text is that Titus is said to pick two of the prime examples of arrogance against God in Sisera and Sennacherib and repeats their sin of arrogance, only he does so in a more sacred location, in the Holy of Holies at the temple. Titus is portrayed as a blasphemer with no limits, and it is clearly both action and word that offend. In addition the description of his action uses almost every negative term available, piling all the actions on top of one another.

The passage continues as the rabbis comment on the scene. Abba Hanan (c 140 CE) considers the patience of the Lord and says, "'O Lord God of Hosts, who is mighty as you are, O Lord (Ps 89:9)?' You are mighty because you hear the blasphemy, curses and vilification (שומע חירופו וגידופו וניאוצו) of this wicked man and you keep silent." Again the blasphemy is summarized and its scope indicated by the stacking up of verbs that describe it. Both cursing and vilification appear here and in the original description of the act. God's restraint is praised, but the story is not finished.

Titus packed up the candlesticks and collected the vessels from the Temple. He then boarded a ship to return home to Rome in triumph. But a fierce gale arose on the sea. Again Titus arose "to blaspheme, curse, vilify, and spit (התחיל מגדף ומחרף ונאץ ומרקק) toward Him on high." He complains that

---

[178]The unconnected phrase ending this citation "for stoning and pushing" is not clear in its force. It apparently alludes to the fact that the one stoned was stoned and pushed into a pit (*m Sanh 6.4*; *b Sanh* 42b-43).

[179]As was noted above, this example with some variation also appears in *b Giṭ* 56b. It also is alluded to in *LevR* 22.3; *GenR* 10.7, and *EcclesR* 5.8. A shorter version is noted in *ARN A*, see Judah Goldin, *The Fathers according to Rabbi Nathan*, Yale Judaica Series, ed. Julian Obermann, vol. 10 (New Haven: Yale University Press, 1956), p. 9. This text discusses "the wicked Titus, blast his bones!" It lacks many of the details of version B, noting only how he struck the altar and cried out to Lycos. The remark about Vespasian is probably a rhetorical rebuke, rather than historical fact, see Salderini, *The Fathers according to Rabbi Nathan: Aboth de Rabbi Nathan Version B*, p. 68, n. 15.

God did not meet him in the house, but is coming forth now. Titus confidently claims that God's power is limited only to the water as the Roman leader recalls the flood and the death of Pharaoh, while alluding to Jonah 1:15. The Lord replies by promising that he will fight Titus with the most insignificant of created things, the mosquito. Titus arrives home safely to his celebration. He is praised as "Conqueror of the Barbarians!" He goes into the baths, and emerges to be handed a cup of wine. As he was drinking a mosquito is said to have entered his nose. The little creature began eating away at the inside of his brain. This became clear when doctors examined him after his death and found " a mosquito the size of a baby pigeon, weighing two liters." Rabbi Eliezar (c 90 CE) is said to have witnessed the mosquito weighed on the scale. The anecdote closes with "to fulfill what Scripture says, 'Evil shall slay the wicked (Ps 34:22).'" A final note describes how Rabbi Johanan ben Zakkai (c 80 CE) upon seeing the temple destroyed and the sanctuary burned rose and "tore his clothes, removed his phylacteries and sat down to mourn with his disciples."

This account, so full of detail and graphic drama, shows how blasphemy was viewed, especially when God was opposed and the people were overwhelmed by an opponent who is portrayed as possessing total arrogance. The judgment that comes from the hand of God is seen as a fully justified reward for such insolence. Blasphemy here is not just word, but deed, so that God acts to show the folly of the wicked.

The next passage in *Aboth* 32 has perplexed those who have studied it.[180] It reads, "Rabbi Johanan ben Baroka (c 110 CE) says, 'If one profanes the Name (המחלל שם) of heaven in public, he shall be punished in secret; and if the name is profaned (והשם מתחלל) he is punished only in public.'" The passage is clear that blaspheming the Name gets punished when it occurs. It appears to suggest, given the contrast in the verse, that public blasphemy is punished privately, while private blasphemy is punished publicly. Fortunately the resolution of the dilemma is not significant to our study, since the point is that blasphemy, which is not described beyond profaning the name, is punished.

The final *Aboth* text from chapter 35 warns the blasphemer, much like chapter 32 appears to do, in the midst of expounding the value of studying Torah and honoring it. "Those who insult in secret and blaspheme in public (המנאצים בסתר), those who sneer in public and those who quarrel will suffer the same fate as Korah and his congregation, as Scripture says: 'And the earth closed over them . . . . (Num 16:33).'" Later in the chapter, those who profane Torah are also said not to have a share in the world to come. Such warnings

---

[180]See, for example, the comment of Saldarini, *The Fathers according to Rabbi Nathan: Aboth de Rabbi Nathan Version B*, p. 188, n. 9. Version A of Rabbi Nathan lacks the text. For the view of another text making a similar point, see the discussion of *Pirke Aboth* 4.5 above.

about the fate of blasphemers are common in the midrashim, of which the Titus saga is the prime example.

The talmudic texts show that blaspheming the Name is consistently seen as a sin punishable by death. It also reflects debate over whether substitute names make one liable, though the rabbinic position limits automatic death to the specific offense using the Name. The indication of detailed debate on the point might suggest an old difference of opinion on the matter (*b Sanh* 55b-57a). In addition, a few texts indicate an array of examples that suggest a broader definition for blasphemy. Such examples include Pharaoh (*b Sanh* 94a-b), Sennacherib (*b MKaṭ* 26a; *b Sanh* 60a), and Titus (*b Giṭ* 56b; *ARN* 7). Even the example involving the rebuke of Akiba for arguing that David sits by God has a similar concern (*b Sanh* 38b). All these illustrations treat cases where there is an inherent, direct challenge to God's unique authority.

12. Conclusion

Summarizing such an extensive survey is not easy, especially given its many twists and turns. But a summary of the key elements is possible.

There is little discussion of formal judicial examples of blasphemy. Trials for blasphemy are not present in these texts, though *m Sanh* 7.5 does define a procedure for examining a charge and limits the offense to speaking the very Name of God. Lev 24:10-16 is the one passage that many of the texts discuss where blasphemy is presented (note Josephus, *Ant* 4.202). It possessed ambiguities that made defining blasphemy, especially where euphemisms were used, a subject of some rabbinic debate. Num 15:30-31 is often cited as a similar situation to blasphemy with its Sabbath violation followed by a death penalty. To use the divine Name in an inappropriate way is certainly blasphemy and is punishable by death (Lev 24:10-16; *m Sanh* 6.4 and 7.5; Philo, *On the Life of Moses* 2.203-06). At the base of these ideas about blasphemy lies the command of Exod 22:27 not to revile God nor the leaders he appointed for the nation.

Debate exists whether use of an alternative name for such an utterance is blasphemy, though some sentiment exists for including these examples (*m Sch*e*b* 4.13; *b Sch*e*b* 35a; *b Sanh* 55b-57a, 60a). Warnings were certainly issued in such cases where a range of euphemisms was used for utterances, but it does not appear, at least in the rabbinic period, to have carried an automatic death sentence.

What happened if a warning was ignored seems easy to determine, given the parallel with another warning involving the incorrigible son in *m Sanh* 8.4. An unheeded warning would lead to potential liability on the second offence.

The official rabbinic position is that the use of the divine Name constitutes the only clear case of capital blasphemy (*m Sanh* 7.5). One is even to avoid blaspheming foreign deities as a sign of respect for the name of God, texts that certainly reflect an apologetic stance taken with outsiders (Josephus, *Ant* 4.207; Philo, *On the Life of Moses* 2.205; *Special Laws* 1.53).

Yet beyond utterances of blasphemy involving the Name, there is also a whole category of acts of blasphemy. These examples move beyond mere utterance of the Name, though often including it. Here one can start with of the use of a range of substitute titles. But beyond these offensive utterances one can see discussed a whole range of actions offensive to God. Such actions would have been perceived by all as blasphemous, even if they were not specifically addressed by any formal, ideal legal statute. Their existence suggests a category of cultural blasphemy that all would recognize as representing an offense against God.

Acts of blasphemy seem to concentrate on idolatry, a show of arrogant disrespect toward God, or the insulting of his chosen leaders. Often those who blasphemed verbally went further and acted on their feelings as well. God manages to judge such offenses one way or another. Examples in Jewish exposition are Sisera (Judg 4:3 and *NumR* 10.2; disrespect toward God's people), Goliath (1 Sam 17 and Josephus, *Ant* 6.183; disrespect towards God's people and worship of Dagon), Sennacherib (2 Kgs 18 – 19 = Isa 37:6, 23; disrespect for God's power), Belshazzar (Dan 3:29 Θ [96] and Josephus, *Ant* 10.233, 242, disrespect for God's presence in the use of temple utensils at a party), Manasseh (acting against the Torah; *Sifre* § 112) and Titus (*b Giṭ* 56 and *ARN B* 7; entering, defaming the temple, slicing open the curtain and taking the utensils away). Acting against the temple is also blasphemous (1 Macc 2:6; Josephus, *Ant* 12.406). Significantly, comparing oneself to God is also blasphemous according to Philo and reflects an arrogance like that seen in other acts of blasphemy just noted above (*On Dreams* 2.130-31; *Decalogue* 13-14.61-64). At Qumran, unfaithfulness in moral action by those who pretend to lead the people (*CD* 5.12) or the act of speaking against God's people (*1QpHab* 10.13) are blasphemous. In the Mishnah and Talmud, idolatry and blasphemy are seen as very similar, while in a few texts they are said to be virtually the same (*y Sanh* 7.25a). Still other examples treated more briefly in this rabbinic material are: Adam, the generation of the flood, Sodomites, Pharaoh, Naboth, Korah, Amalek, Nebuchadnezzar, and Rome, as well as Tabor and Carmel as false locales of worship. Within Israel, the outstanding example is the golden calf incident, where idolatry is offensive to the holiness of Israel's God (Philo, *On the Life of Moses* 2.159-66).

Blasphemy represents an offense against God and a violation of a fundamental principle of the faith. Sometimes God alone punishes the blasphemer (e.g., Pharaoh, Korah, Titus), while at other times judgment is to be carried out by the community (the Israelite woman's son). But a second important level of blasphemy is attacking God's people verbally, as Sennacherib or Goliath did. Here Exod 22:27 has a special role to play. Those who challenge the leadership God has put in place for his people are also seen as attacking God himself. So blasphemy operates in a rather wide range of insulting speech or activity.

How this view of blasphemy in Judaism relates to the leadership's examination of Jesus requires careful consideration of one other important topic, namely, the highest Jewish forms of exaltation. By "high" exaltation is meant a very specific kind of activity, going directly into God's presence. The question does not involve merely the ability to go into heaven as a righteous one. The possibility of a heavenly abode offended no Jew who believed in an after life for the righteous. Rather the crucial question concerns the possibility of going directly into God's presence to be or serve at his side. Did Jews consider God's holiness to be so unique that such a place would be inappropriate for anyone, human or angelic? Thus, the next chapter considers in detail the question of who gets to go into the presence of God and labor at his side. It is only when the themes of blasphemy and exaltation within Judaism are carefully understood that one can then ask about the basis for the leadership's reaction to Jesus' remarks at his examination as presented in Mk 14.

Chapter III

Exalted Figures in Judaism

Assessing the background to the Jewish examination of Jesus means considering not just what blasphemy was in Judaism, but also considering how the claim to sit at God's right hand fits into Jewish expectation concerning exaltation. This chapter covers some wide ground. It asks some simple questions of the Jewish tradition: Who is exalted before God? Who gets to go into directly into God's presence?[1] What do they do there? How long do they stay? Are there any preparations or pre-conditions for going? This study also considers more than who sits in God's presence (though this is certainly the most directly relevant category), because to look at a slightly broader set of examples will help to show how unusual being seated with God is. It also gives a better sense of what the conceptual options were when early Judaism contemplated someone going into God's presence. It is when one sees how many other types of contact with God existed, and how those were mediated, that one senses how special being seated with him is.

Our survey will stay focused on these key questions. Many other interesting issues exist, especially as they relate to the tradition history of the various texts, as well as the debates concerning the meaning of some of the titles, and the significance of some of the figures that appear. However, such questions will only be treated as they fall within the scope of our study. Though many detailed studies exist on particular individual figures, I am not aware of the existence of such a general survey of exalted figures asking these specific questions about their exaltation.[2]

---

[1] A listing of who has visions of God does not receive treatment. Only those cases where the seer discusses the nature of their journey into God's presence are noted. If a particular vision of God simply presents revelatory content, then it is not discussed in this survey.

[2] Two studies come close but have other concerns. They are Larry Hurtado, *One God, One Lord: Early Christian Devotion and Ancient Jewish Monotheism* (Philadelphia: Fortress, 1988), and Jarl E. Fossum, *The Name of God and the Angel of the Lord: Samaritan and Jewish Concepts of Intermediation and the Origin of Gnosticism*, WUNT 36 (Tübingen: J. C. B. Mohr [Paul Siebeck], 1985). Hurtado's examination is a survey like this one, but he tends to stay focused on the categories of higher exaltation that relate to his theme of monotheism and how exalted mediators fit into it. Fossum highlights angelic figures, since his topic treats the Angel of the Lord. Thus these treatments are somewhat more narrow than our examination will be. One other article is significant for dividing these texts along temporal lines and comparing them with the New Testament's portrait of Jesus. See P. G. Davis, "Divine Agents, Mediators, and New Testament Christology," JTS 45 (1994):479-503. Davis

The survey proceeds one figure at a time, trying to give some sequence to the dating, where possible, within the treatment of each individual. Two general classes of exalted figures exist: exalted human figures and exalted angelic (or angelic-like) figures.[3] This division is considered to be more useful than merely surveying the topic by given texts, because some figures have several distinct functions, depending on which work discusses them. It will be easier to see the range of possibilities, if one groups all the portraits of a given figure together in a single discussion. It will also allow us to see if human figures are handled in a way similar to angelic ones. In addition, this structure enables us to see quickly which figures were the object of the greatest and most wide ranging reflection. For those few cases where figures work across both major categories, some overlap will take place in the presentation.[4] In such cases, the discussion in a category highlights what is presented about that figure when they have the name under consideration. A summary of whom sits under what circumstances will conclude the chapter. Since the dating of many of these texts overlaps or in some cases is disputed over quite a range of time, there is no attempt to put all of the figures into any comprehensive chronology. They are simply taken one figure at a time.[5] The survey is limited to Jewish material, focusing mostly on earlier material (i.e.,

---

divides divine mediation texts in Judaism into three types: past–legacy texts; present–mediator/intervention texts; future–consummation/judgment figures. He notes that the New Testament is unique in presenting Jesus with a constancy of operating at several levels at once. Other figures who have multiple roles in Judaism are Michael and Enoch, as this survey shall also show, but the constancy of the New Testament presentation stands out as exceptional. My survey is unique in focusing upon "in his immediate presence" texts.

[3]The survey will not discuss in detail texts where divine attributes are given exalted status, categories like Wisdom or the Word, because the primary issue of this survey involves the exaltation of figures who have their own clear, distinct identity. The phrase "angelic-like" designates those figures who are seen ultimately as glorified human figures and who now function in heaven like angels. For this category, see Hurtado, *One God, One Lord*, pp. 41-50.

[4]In the few cases, where a figure overlaps categories because an exalted human figure is transformed into an angelic-like one (e.g., Similitudes Son of Man-Enoch; Metatron-Enoch), the discussion will consider the figure in both categories noting their interrelationships. In both these cases, it is the "transformed, transcendent" figure who is the dominant element of the portrait, though the ultimate human roots of the figure are also extremely important for our particular set of questions. In these cases there is value in being sensitive to how the figure is revealed at a literary level, that is, how the transfer from one sphere to another is described and developed. It is important also to be sensitive to how that figure is seen ultimately when all the pieces of the resultant portrait are brought together.

[5]The listing of human figures will proceed in a largely canonical historical order. Angelic figures are covered discussing named angels like Gabriel and Michael first. The other angelic figures of the tradition then follow. Since many of the angelic examples are often equated with Michael, they will be covered after he is covered, so the rationale for the connections can be more clearly understood. A brief survey of angels as a group closes the treatment of this subcategory.

pre 3rd Century). Rabbinic references from the Midrashim or Talmud are limited to those cases where some earlier roots exist that make tracing a figure's later development of value. Jewish elements in Christian texts are only noted if the likelihood is good that the material is Jewish or the connection is worthwhile mentioning.

1. Exalted Human Figures

Adam

Several traditions treat Adam as an exalted viceroy figure, giving him regal-like qualities.[6] For example, Philo in *On the Creation* 148 nicely spells out the honor given to Adam at the creation:

> And with great beauty Moses has attributed the giving of names to the different animals to the first created man, for it is a work of wisdom and indicative of royal authority, and man was full of intuitive wisdom and self-taught, having been created by the grace of God, and, moreover, was a king. And it is proper for a ruler to give names to each of his subjects. And, as was very natural, the power of domination was excessive in that first-created man, whom God formed with great care and thought worthy of the second rank in the creation, making him his own viceroy and the ruler of all other creatures.

Similar in thrust is the earlier[7] *Wis* 9:2-3 where the fundamental place of humanity in Adam is described in a prayer of Solomon. In the prayer, the petitioner notes that God gave Adam a key role because "by your wisdom [you] have formed humankind to have dominion over the creatures you have made, and rule the world in holiness and righteousness, and pronounce judgment in uprightness of soul."[8] In *Wis* 10:1-2, Wisdom is said to have protected the "first-formed father" of the world when he alone had been created. Wisdom also delivered him from his transgression and "gave him

---

[6]This figure is not developed by Hurtado at all, but Fossum, *The Name of God and the Angel of the Lord*, pp. 271-78, has a nice summary discussion, though his discussion is not very date sensitive, mixing the order of earlier and later texts as it proceeds.

[7]Wisdom is usually dated in the 1st Century BCE, while Philo lived from about 20 BCE-50 CE. Wisdom is often connected with Alexandria as well. See C. A. Evans, *Noncanonical Writings and New Testament Interpretation* (Peabody, MA: Hendrickson, 1992), p. 13, for a summary and a short bibliography of the key works treating Wisdom. Evans' work is the best quick reference handbook for the wide variety of extra-canonical texts available in English. Citations from the deutero-canonical books come from the *NRSV* unless otherwise noted.

[8]Interestingly, Solomon asks in v. 4 for "wisdom that sits by your throne;" an example of a personification of a divine attribute which he can then dispatch graciously as an expression of his mercy. Wisdom and Logos are the two major attributes portrayed as mediated to humanity in parts of Judaism.

strength to rule all things." Thus, Adam's role in creation stands at the base of the development of his exalted role.

A few texts compare Adam to his descendants, taking the view that what was true of Adam in the beginning is also true of him within a larger frame of divine history. For example, *Sir* 49:14-16 (2nd Cent BCE) concludes its "Hymn to the Witnesses" (44:1 — 49:16), an ode to Israel's great men, with this summary, "Few have ever been created on the earth like Enoch, for he was taken up from the earth. Nor was anyone ever born like Joseph; even his bones were cared for. Shem and Seth and Enoch were honored, but above every other created living being was Adam."

Such high regard for Adam's role at the creation and in history led to a variety of expectations concerning future honor for him. In the *Life of Adam and Eve* 47:3, Adam is called to sit "on the throne" of the one who overthrew you.[9] According to *Life* 12 — 16, this throne is his rightful place. It was taken from the "seducer" and given to Adam, when the now fallen angel refused to give it up. His refusal was motivated by jealousy as he rejected the command, given by Michael, that he should give worship to Adam because he was made in the image of God. The devil argues that he is superior and was created earlier so he should not and would not worship Adam. According to this work, jealousy of this sort motivated his temptation of Eve and Adam. Thus, this passage looks for a reinstatement of Adam to an exalted position of second rank, a position he was created for in the beginning. As such, it is a significant text for our theme, though we are not told where this throne is located or what Adam will do from it. Adam is seated in heaven on a throne once apparently occupied by a key angel.[10] The text is designed to show a restoration to humanity of what was lost at the fall. It thus appears that Adam is seen in the text as the representative man who fulfills his originally created, vice regent function and shares in the rule of creation.

Such a view of Adam seems to be an early one, as Qumran speaks of the כבוד אדם, the glory of Adam (or man), that will be given to those God has

---

[9]All citations of the work of Old Testament Pseudepigrapha will come from the various translations in James H. Charlesworth, ed., *The Old Testament Pseudepigrapha*. 2 vols. (New York: Doubleday, 1983, 1985), unless otherwise noted. This citation is on 2:290 and reads, "Then he shall sit on the throne of him who overthrew him." Hereafter this work is abbreviated as *OTP*. For the first century CE date of the *Life of Adam and Eve*, see M. D. Johnson, *OTP* 2:252.

[10]The *Apoc Moses* 39:2-3 from the second to fourth century CE has a similar statement: "I will establish you on the throne of your dominion on the throne of your seducer" (see *OTP* 2:291). Subsequent chapters of this work indicate the reinstatement comes with resurrection. The initial judgment, given after the Fall, appears in *Life of Adam and Eve* 25 — 29, which depicts an initial visit to the heavenly throne-room. Adam and Eve are escorted by Michael to see the Lord sitting in Paradise with an appearance of flaming fire. Afterwards Adam is expelled from Paradise.

chosen, i.e., the righteous (*1QS* 423; *CD* 3.20; *1QH* 17.15). Each of these texts speaks of an eschatological reward that is grounded in the position and honor given to the creation of the first person.[11]

Similar themes appear in the more mysterious *2 En* J, though here we return to the original creation.[12] In 30:11-13 Adam is a second angel, who is assigned at the original creation to be a king, a ruler over the earth with God's wisdom. V. 14 makes it explicit that Adam is in view and not simply the race as a whole. No other creature is like him. Other portions of this work put him in charge of Eden, which is now in the third heaven (cf., *2 En* 8 with 31:1-2). From his throne, which sits in the open heaven, Enoch can see that the angels and the earth were "subjected to Adam . . . to rule and reign over it." (31:3). This text depicts Adam's original glory.

A slightly different kind of reinstatement appears in the *TAbr*.[13] Here Adam is more observer than participant. *TAbr* 11:10-12 has a scene we shall discuss a few times as it refers to Michael and Abel as well as Abraham and Adam. In this passage, Abraham sees Adam in heaven as an observer at the final judgment. Adam himself is "in glory" and is said to watch because everyone comes from him as "the first-formed Adam." Enthroned at the entrance to paradise, the first man sees two gates, one narrow and the other broad. All souls pass through one or the other. He rejoices when one goes through the door of the righteous and falls from his throne and wails when a sinner receives judgment. There is much wailing as scarcely one in seven thousand[14] are saved. As we shall see, the issue of a throne in heaven is complicated, as Adam is not the only glorified person enthroned. In 13:2-3, Abel sits on a throne as well, executing judgment. This text presents the first attempt to describe what Adam does on his throne. He, as the great ancestor, is witness to the judgment. The text is also important since it shows that one cannot simply assume that the mention of a throne in heaven or a reference to someone sitting on such a throne automatically indicates the honoree is seated

---

[11]For example, *1QH* 17.15 speaks of an inheritance to be received by the righteous God who forgives as he confirms his covenant.

[12]This text, also known as Slavonic Enoch, has a disputed date, with suggestions ranging from the first century CE to the ninth century CE! It is dated very cautiously to the late first century by F. I. Andersen, *OTP* 1:94-96, but is attributed, if Jewish, to a "fringe Jewish sect" or perhaps to a group of god-fearers. J is the long recension of *2 Enoch* and could well be later in date.

[13]This text may date from c 100 CE plus or minus twenty-five years, so E. P. Sanders, *OTP* 1:874-75, who also notes that the "reasonable conjecture" is not certain. Other suggestions range from second century BCE to mid second century CE.

[14]See 1 Kgs 19:18.

next to God or that the honor is uniquely his. More must be said about the throne in question to be certain of either of these conclusions.[15]

We now move to some much later texts, which go in a similar direction. One passage appears in a fourth century Christian Coptic text that may have Jewish roots, *Discourse on Abbaton* 13a.[16] The Christian nature of this passage is clear as the report of what happened in heaven comes from Christ, but what is said about Adam is similar to what we have already seen. Adam is set upon a "great throne" and given a "crown of glory" and a "royal sceptre." The angels were commanded to come and worship him, "whether angel or archangel." After worshipping God, Adam is honored with "Hail, you image and likeness of God!" Similar is *PesiktaR* 48.2.[17] The teaching about Adam in the sermon is attributed to the fourth century Rabbi Tanḥuma bar Abba. He said, God "had intended to make Adam ruler over his world, and to set him up as king over all God's creatures in the world. 'I am king in the worlds above;' the Holy One, blessed be He, said, 'and Adam will be king in the worlds below.'" The passage then notes that Adam is put in the Garden of Eden and is made king there. This text is about the original creation, not a later reinstatement, since the rabbi is discussing God's intent that Adam was to live forever, like a ministering angel. The *Abbaton* text appears to have the same time frame.

Nonetheless, these exalted texts about Adam did produce some reaction in later materials. Some of this Adamic speculation left some Jews uncomfortable. One example comes from the fifth century *GenR*.[18] In 8.10, the ministering angels are said to have "mistook him [for a divine being] and wished to exclaim 'Holy' before him." An illustration follows of a king and a governor riding in a chariot together. The subjects wish to give homage to the king, but do not know which man is the king. As a result the sovereign pushes the governor from the chariot, so they know. In the same way God, the passage argues, put Adam to sleep, so the angels could know the man was the mortal. The passage shows that there was some "divine" speculation

---

[15]See, for example, the *AscIsa* 7:13-17, where a throne sits in the first heaven to which praise is given in honor of God who is in the seventh heaven. In fact, each level of heaven is structured this way with a representative angel of greater glory than his counterparts sitting on the throne in the second through fifth heavens (7:18-37). One should not assume that the view of the *Testament* is that of the *AscIsa*, but neither can it be excluded that something of similar complexity might be in the background.

[16]Fossum, *The Angel of the Lord*, p. 272.

[17]The date of this work is 550-650 CE, Evans, *Noncanonical Writings*, pp. 135. Translations from the *Pesikta* are from William G. Braude, *Pesikta Rabbati*, 2 vols. (New Haven: Yale University Press, 1968). For this text, see vol. 2:813.

[18]Evans, *Noncanonical Writings*, pp. 133-34. The following *Midrash Rabbah* translations are from H. Freedman and M. Simon, eds., *The Midrash Rabbah*, 10 vols (London: Soncino, 1983). For the following passage, see *Genesis Rabbah*, pp. 61.

surrounding Adam and the greatness of his original position, no doubt grounded in Adam's being made in God's image. However, official Judaism wanted to make sure that no matter how exalted Adam was, he was not confused with a divine figure. Apparently the vice regent role of Adam was asserted strongly enough in some quarters that one might be led by inference to this disturbing conclusion.

In sum, these Adamic texts do reveal that some reflection on Adam saw him as a highly exalted, ruling figure. Most of the references deal with his original creation, something that was marred by the Fall. A few texts argue for some type of reinstatement for him at the resurrection or as an observer at the judgment. It is not prudent to simply coalesce all of this imagery, but the pattern does show, despite some differences of detail, that in the view of some Jews, Adam either had or would have a throne of authority in heaven as the first human. Though he is a "ruler" in the original creation, his role in those texts that look to reinstatement is less clear. The image bothered some later Jews enough that comment was made to clarify just how limited that authority was. Where in heaven the throne is or how close to God Adam sits is never said, though in one text (*Life of Adam and Eve* 47:3) he gets the throne of a major angel, namely, that of his seducer.

Abel

Abel appears in heaven in two texts. His portrait is also quite striking. In the first example, he is simply placed among the righteous, sharing the heavenly glory of the righteous that comes when flesh is put aside for glorious, heavenly clothes. This note appears in the *AscIsa* 9:8-10.[19] In the seventh heaven, Isaiah sees "the holy Abel and all the righteous. And there I saw Enoch and all who were with him, stripped of (their) robes of the flesh; and I saw them in their robes of above, and they were like angels who stand there in great glory. But they were not sitting on their thrones, nor were their crowns of glory on them."[20] In 9:18 the description continues, "then indeed they will receive their robes and their thrones and their crowns, when he has ascended

---

[19]For the date of *Ascension*, see M. A. Knibb, *OTP* 2:149. This text is part of a larger composite work, and the vision section of the ascension is a later Christian work that probably dates from the mid-second century CE. On the debate about whether this portion of the text may have undergone Christian redaction, see the discussion immediately below and n. 21. It does seem likely that the text as we have it has been subject to substantial redaction by Christians at certain points, as n. 22 below makes clear. Nonetheless, the conception of a heavenly journey may be rooted in Jewish expectation, since it is paralleled in other Jewish materials, as this chapter will show.

[20]Other texts mentioning the heavenly garb include 7:22 and 8:26. See Joseph P. Schultz, "Angelic Opposition to the Ascension of Moses and the Revelation of the Law," *JQR* 61 (1970-71):290-91.

into the seventh heaven." This text is potentially important, because it attributes to the righteous thrones in heaven, a figure of vindication and shared authority, like that seen already in chapter 7, except that there it was for some angels. The texts about receiving crowns are under some suspicion of being a Christian addition.[21] But that claim is not at all certain for this detail. The thrones for the righteous are not unlike the thrones some angels possess, according to *AscIsa* 7:13-37. Since the righteous are "equal to the angels who (are) in the seventh heaven" (8:15), it is not impossible that the original author of the work saw the righteous as receiving crowns. But one should be cautious of making too much of this text, given its uncertain origin. In sum, Abel is one glorified among many, and he may have access to a heavenly throne as a result. If he does, he shares it with all the righteous.

As far as Isaiah is concerned, he takes a standard role for one who sees heaven. He is transformed (9:30) and could not see the Glory after initially glimpsing it "in spirit", while the righteous could (9:37-38). He also hears the song of praise (9:40-42), and sees the future victory of a descending and ascending Messiah (10:7-31)[22].

The second text has a more exalted role for the one descended from Adam. The text comes from the *TAbr*, which is also to be dated around 100 CE.[23] Numerous figures take part in this scene. The angel Michael has escorted Abraham to heaven to see what is taking place. As was already noted, Adam is present as a witness to the judgment. The key portion concerning Abel in 13:1-3 reads:

> And Abraham said, "My lord, Commander-in-chief, who is this all-wondrous judge? And who are the angels who are recording? And who is the sunlike angel who holds the balance? And who is the fiery angel who holds the fire?" The Commander-in-chief said, "Do you see, all-pious Abraham, the frightful man who is seated on the throne? This is the son of Adam, the first-formed,

---

[21]Ithamar Gruenwald, *Apocalyptic and Merkavah Mysticism*, AGAJU 14 (Leiden: E. J. Brill, 1980), p. 61.

[22]This last section is certainly subject to Christian addition as Jesus is named in 10:8. The reference to glimpsing goes, "And I saw the Great glory while the eyes of my spirit were open. But I could not thereafter see . . . ."

[23]For this date, see n. 13 above. The text in question has different citation numbers, which makes locating it confusing, but this is because of the two recensions A and B. The verses in question are 13:21-27 in H. F. D. Sparks, ed., *The Apocryphal Old Testament* (Oxford: Clarendon Press, 1984), p. 413. He says that he is following recension A, but with a few exceptions. Apparently this has impacted his numeration. Turning to E. P. Sanders' translation in *OTP* 1:900, the verses in recension B are 11:1-8, while for recension A, they are 13:1-8 (*OTP* 1:889-90). In the above discussion I shall follow Sanders' numeration in recension A, citing 13:1-3 first, then recension B 11:1-3. For another discussion of this text, see Andrew Chester, "Jewish Messianic Expectations and Mediatorial Figures and Pauline Christianity," in *Paulus und das antike Judentum*, ed. Martin Hengel and Ulrich Heckel, WUNT 58 (Tübingen: J.C.B. Mohr (Paul Siebeck), 1991), p. 57. He discusses recension A.

who is called Abel, whom Cain the wicked killed. And he sits here to judge the entire creation, examining both righteous and sinners . . ..'

The text goes on to describe Adam as witness, and notes a second judgment by Israel, and then a third and final judgment by God. Two angels, one on the left and another on the right, record righteous deeds (the angel on the right) and sins (the angel on the left) respectively. The angel with the balance is Dokiel and the one with fire is Purouel. It is not said that these angels sit, but it appears unlikely as they each hold something and are busily engaged in the activity of helping in the judgment, holding a balance and fire as they record. The throne for Abel appears to be unique.

Another version of the scene appears in a separate version of this book. In 11:1-4B the text reads,

> And Abraham said to Michael, "Lord, who is this judge? And who is the other one who brings charges of sins?" And Michael said to Abraham, "Do you see the judge? This is Abel, who first bore witness, and God brought him here to judge. And the one who produces (the evidence) is the teacher of heaven and earth and the scribe of righteousness, Enoch. For the Lord sent them here in order that they might record the sins and the righteous deeds of each person."

Later the text makes it clear that Enoch does not give the judgment, God does (vv. 6-8). Enoch is only a scribe. There are no angelic helpers in this version either. The simpler version here may give signs of being more original.[24]

The role of Abel in both versions is the same, though it is more exalted in A. In B, Abel judges, while in A, he sits on a throne as well. The authority is clearly granted by God, while in B, it is made clear that the ultimate judge is God. Enoch's role in B is carefully circumscribed as well. He is in his typical role, as we shall see shortly, of heavenly scribe. However, Enoch is absent from A, since that scene has an explicitly angelic cast of helpers. Here is great authority granted to Abel for a single moment. It is important to note that the more complex version in A has three judgments, so that Abel's role is preliminary and temporary. Israel and God finish what he starts.

In sum, Abel's exalted function, though high, is only for a season, even in the more extensive account in A. In B, it is circumscribed as well by the latter

---

[24]Sanders, *OTP* 1:875 and n. 27 mentions that the judgment scene in A might not be original. The date for recension B is not clear, but Sanders suggests an Egyptian provenance as well. One cannot be sure which version is more original. As shall often be the case, any conclusions about the order of versions must be tentative. Fortunately, the decision has no bearing on this study's major concerns.

remark that God, not Enoch, judges–a point that seems to limit Abel's role in this version to a status of third rank.[25]

Enoch

Enoch is the first of several figures to be considered who experience an ascension.[26] A rich and varied tradition grew up around this figure.[27] With the simple description of an ascension in Gen 5:24 as the base, the question became what happened to this figure when he arrived in heaven, not having died previously. What emerges is a glorified figure who functions as the great heavenly scribe and is said also to take on various other more exalted roles, like that of the Son of Man/Chosen One. The portrait is so exalted that it becomes a subject of dispute for later rabbis.

By far the most common description of Enoch is as heavenly scribe and seer, "the scribe of righteousness" as *1 En* 12:3-4, 15:1, 51:3 (without the title), 82:1-3 (described without the title) and 92:1 portray him (note also especially *1 En* 14).[28] In this role he records "the secrets of wisdom" (51:3)

---

[25]My view of this text is thus more limited than Chester's characterization in "Jewish Messianic Expectations and Mediatorial Figures and Pauline Christianity," in *Paulus und das antike Judentum*, p. 57. His claims seem exaggerated both with respect to Abel and Adam. The later judgments are underplayed by him, though he is correct that Abel has "an extraordinarily exalted status" here. The qualification, however, that his judgmental responsibilities are temporary is surely quite significant. Chester's description of Adam as "very close to that of a divine figure," seems especially overdrawn. As a glorified witness, he may only be representative of all glorified humanity, exalted and singled out because he is their father.

[26]Alan Segal, "Heavenly Ascent in Hellenistic Judaism, Early Christianity and their Environment," in *ANRW* 23.2 (Berlin: Walter De Gruyter, 1980), p. 1354 and n. 76. For Enoch, the key, early ascension passages include Gen 5:24; *Jub* 4:23; *Sir* 44:16; 49:14; *Wis* 4:10-11 — this is a general reference, "some were taken up"; *1 En* 39:3-14; 70 — 71; and much of *2 Enoch* (Both A and J versions, esp. *2 En* 3), attesting to a wide spread and well known tradition.

[27]For surveys of this figure, see Larry Hurtado, *One God, One Lord*, pp. 51-56; D. S. Russell, *The Method and Message of Jewish Apocalyptic*, OTL (Philadelphia: Westminster Press, 1964), pp. 327-31; 348-50; and P. Grelot, "La Légende d'Hénoch dans les Apocryphes et dans la Bible: Origine et Signification," RSR 46 (1958):5-26, 180-210, esp. 14-26.

[28]On a date for much of *1 En* as second century BCE, see E. Isaac, *OTP* 1:7. The date of the more controversial Similitudes section will be discussed later along with its Son of Man figure. The bulk of these references come from the recognized early sections of the work. The major scene where Enoch enters heaven is *1 En 14*, which has roots in Ezek 1:22, 26 and Isa 43:2, especially in the images of crystal throne associated with the throne and the presence of fire associated with judgment and testing. This scene will be developed when the Son of Man imagery is discussed. On this scene, see especially, Gruenwald, *Apocalyptic and Merkavah Mysticism*, pp. 32-36. The reading of 51:3 is disputed. It either reads, "all the secrets of wisdom will flow out from the counsel of his mouth" or "his mouth shall pour forth all the secrets of wisdom and counsel." Both stress the reporting and revealing of what he sees as the Elect One exercises judgment. This reading sees an ultimate identification between Enoch

and passes on the results of his important transcription to Methuselah (82:1-3; 91:1). In 51:3, he also functions as one who reveals eschatological judgment from the wisdom he received from God, a role to be examined more closely below. He also reveals judgment against the heavenly Watchers who sinned in Gen 6:1-4 (12:3-4; 15:1). What Enoch gains from his visit to God's presence is insight into God's plan.

Jub 4:17-23 is similar.[29] Here is the first figure who learned "writing and knowledge and wisdom" (v. 17). He is taken up to heaven for "six jubilees of years" (vv. 21-23) and "he is there writing condemnation and judgment of the world, and all of the evils of the children of men." This man of wisdom is a "witness to the generations of the world so that he might report every deed of each generation in the day of judgment (10:17)." Only one with a consummate sense of righteousness is worthy for such a task. The ascension testifies to his qualifications for this role.

TAbr was already considered in the survey of Adam and Abel. In recension B 11:3-8 Enoch has recorded the judgment and produces the record against a woman being examined for murdering her child and committing adultery. She denies it, but Enoch's record is brought forward against her. Enoch does not judge here,[30] but is only responsible for the evidence that helps judgment take place.

A version of the slightly later *2 En* (or, Slavonic Enoch) 10:1-7 has the prophet responsible for writing some 360-66 books.[31] 11:37-38 describes him as a witness of all that is done, while 13:57 says he is a recorder of man's deeds. This leads to an exhortation in 13:72-77 that he has made this recording that cannot be destroyed. The record has been passed on, so that one might keep one's heart from wickedness and prepare for that day with the possibility of experiencing peace.

---

and the Elect One in *1 En* 70 — 71; see discussion of this below. On this verse, see Black, *The Book of Enoch*, p. 214.

[29]This work is dated to the second century BCE as well. See O. S. Wintermute, *OTP* 2:43-44.

[30]*1 En* is very different in this regard, causing some to wonder if this is not an alternate approach to the figure designed to curb what some might have seen as an excessive view of Enoch's exaltation; Hurtado, *One God, One Lord*, pp. 148-49, n. 7. *TAbr* is dated to around 100 CE; see nn. 13, 23 above. For later, clearer effort to limit the portrait of Enoch, see the discussion later in this section on *TOnq* on Gen 5:24 and from *GenR* 25.1 on Gen 5:24.

[31]The variation in the number of books reflects a disputed textual tradition. The appearance of this specific theme appears to be limited to the short recension as reflected in manuscript U. On the citations from the paragraph, see H. F. D. Sparks ed., *The Apocryphal Old Testament*, pp. 321-26, and the translation and discussion of A. Pennington in that volume. He dates the work to the end of the first century.

Coming to another version of *2 En*, we see a similar role as heavenly scribe.[32] In 22:8, he is given "clothes of glory" (A) or "clothes of my glory" (J). In 22:1, he has a pen and is given the books from the storehouse. Most interesting of all is that he is placed at God's left hand, where he sits to record what God tells him (24:1). He sits on the left "with Gabriel" (J) or "closer than Gabriel" (A). No one is mentioned as sitting on the right. Here the heavenly scribe is exalted to a position very close to God as the ultimate amanuensis. God simply "explains" to Enoch what is taking place (25:1 J).

By far the majority of the early Enoch tradition gives him this unique role as the stenographer of heaven. Fitting in with this are a few additional traditions, some of which may be influenced by Christian interpolation. One example of possible interpolation is found in the *ApocElijah* 4:11-19, where he appears with Elijah pointing to the judgment of one called "the shameless one (v 17)."[33] Here Enoch, with Elijah, functions more as an accuser. The other texts simply portray Elijah as clothed like the righteous in heaven, "into clothes of [my-J] glory" (*2 En* 22:8-9) or "like an angel" (*AscIsa* 9:9). In these texts Enoch is simply functioning as a prophet of judgment or as one prophet among many.

A much more controversial role for Enoch is seen in texts that give him a much more comprehensive function than "scribe of righteousness." Two passages call for special attention here. One text identifies Enoch as Son of Man (*1 En* 71:14). It is probably an early text, while the other, the Metatron portrait in *3 En*, is much later.[34]

---

[32]At this point I am working with versions J and A in *OTP*, vol. 1. Both versions are cited as specified.

[33]The range of dating for this work is rather wide, first to fourth century, see O. S. Wintermute, *OTP* 1:729-30. It also is a composite work and the section involving Elijah looks to be influenced by Rev. 11:8-9.

[34]The issue of the date of the *Similitudes* section of *1 En* is a much discussed question with many stressing the fact that this material was missing at Qumran. Among those treating it as not belonging with early versions of *1 En* and placing it in the late first- early second century CE are J. C. Hindley, "Towards a Date for the Similitudes of Enoch. An Historical Approach," NTS 14 (1968): 551-65 and M. A. Knibb, "The Date of the Parables of Enoch: A Critical Review," NTS 25 (1979): 345-59. On the other hand, others argue for a date in the mid-first century, C. L. Mearns, "Dating the Similitudes of Enoch," NTS 25 (1979): 360-69. J. J. Collins, "The Son of Man in First Century Judaism," NTS 38 (1992): 451-52, has noted that not much should be made of the absence of these manuscripts at Qumran, since *Ps Sol* and *TMos* are also unattested in the scrolls. He also suggests that this section might be unacceptable to the Qumranians, because of the near equality of the sun and moon in *1 En* 41. Collins argues that the strong Son of Man-messianic portrait would more likely be earlier than later among Jews. Finally, he points out that there is no evidence of the fall of Jerusalem. So he prefers a pre-70 CE date. Thus, a mid-first century date (40-70 CE) is quite possible for this material. See also J. Theisohn, *Der auserwählte Richter: Untersuchungen zum Traditionsgeschitlichen Ort der Menschensohngestalt den Bilderreden des äthiopischen Henoch*, StUNT 12 (Göttingen: Vandenhoeck & Ruprecht, 1975), pp. 152-201 and S. Uhlig,

Given the controversy over the identification of Enoch with the Son of Man in this book, we shall leave for later the majority of discussion about the identification of the transcendent judging figure who sits on a heavenly throne. That question will appear below under the separate category of Son of Man/Chosen One, since this is where the bulk of the image is presented. Here I seek only to consider the great likelihood that these two figures are identified in the work. If this identification is correct, then all that is said of the Son of Man in *1 Enoch* is ultimately applied to the OT luminary Enoch.

1 En 71:14 has been a source of controversy for most of this century. The text reads:

> Then an angel came to me and greeted me and said to me, "You, son of man, who art born in righteousness and upon whom righteousness has dwelt, the righteousness of the Antecedent of Time will not forsake you."

The text goes on in vv. 16-17 to note that everyone shall follow in "your path." Together with him shall be "their dwelling places" and "their portion." They shall never be separated from him. It closes, "So there shall be length of days with that Son of Man and peace to the righteous ones; his path is upright for the righteous, in the name of the Lord of the Spirits forever and ever."

The identification of a transcendent, and possibly pre-existent figure, who as an exalted human sits by God was so difficult for R. H. Charles that he amended the key text.[35] J. J. Collins has argued differently by making a distinction in the identification of Son of Man with Enoch.[36] He argues that Enoch is portrayed in the text, not as *the* Son of Man, but *a* Son of Man, a representative of the righteous who in turn the Son of Man also represents as a collective figure.[37] The major problem with this approach is that it totally underplays the mention of righteousness in v. 14 and the pronouns in vv. 16-17 that look back to that verse. The text gives the impression that the Son of

---

Das äthiopische Henochbuch. JSHRZ V/6 (Gütersloher Verlagshaus Gerd Mohn, 1984), pp. 573-75. Uhlig notes the absence of Esther from Qumran as evidence against the argument from silence concerning the lack of *Similitudes'* manuscripts and sees references to the "Parthians and Medes" in 56:5-7 as important evidence of a c. 40 CE date. For *3 En*, see P. S. Alexander, "The Historical Setting of the Hebrew Book of Enoch," JJS 28 (1977):156-80. He opts for a date range from 450-850 CE. For the text in German translation with many helpful notes about the original, see Peter Schäfer and Klaus Herrmann, *Übersetzung der Hekhalot-Literatur I §§1-80*, TSAT 46 (Tübingen: J. C. B. Mohr [Paul Siebeck], 1995).

[35]R. H. Charles, ed., *The Apocrypha and Pseudepigrapha of the Old Testament* (Oxford: Clarendon Press, 1913), 2:237. This solution is categorically rejected today as too harsh.

[36] J. J. Collins, "The Son of Man in First Century Judaism," NTS 38 (1992):453-59.

[37]Collins cites and builds on the view of S. Mowinckel, *He That Cometh*. trans. G. W. Anderson (Oxford: Basil Blackwell, 1956), pp. 442-43. His position looks like a variation of one critiqued by E. Sjöberg, *Der Menschensohn im äthiopischen Henochbuch* (Lund: Gleerup, 1946), pp. 148-55, that was held by Hoffmann and Dillmann.

Man figure present, who is Enoch, is also the focal point for the rest of the righteous. Thus we are confident that Enoch should be identified with the Son of Man in this text, as Sjöberg argued long ago.[38]

What the presence of this text means is that Enoch, in this one case, is transformed not just into a scribe to carry on scribal activity, but into the eschatological judge himself, a "vizier of the royal court" as Hurtado puts it (*1 En* 45:3; 51:3; 55:4; 61:8; 62:2-8; 69:27, 29).[39] Three of these key texts place this figure on God's throne or on the throne of glory.[40] In 51:3, we read "in those days" the Elect One sits on "my throne, and from the conscience of his mouth shall come out all the secrets of wisdom (Isa 11:2-4), for the Lord of the Spirits has given them to him and glorified him." Here the wisdom otherwise tied to Enoch as scribe and the glorification associated with him are present alongside the seating.[41] In 55:4, kings, potentates and all who dwell on the earth "see my Elect One, how he sits in the throne of glory (v. 1, my glory)." From this throne he judges Azazel, all his company, and his army in the name of the Lord of the Spirits. Thus this rule has this figure judging the evil angelic hosts. In 61:8, The Lord of the Spirits (God) "placed the Elect One on the throne of glory; and he shall judge all the works of the holy ones in heaven above, weighing in the balance their deeds." These texts present this figure as the eschatological judge on behalf of the righteous. In 62:2 the Lord of the Spirits himself sits down on the throne. The image, when the whole section is considered, is of a shared judgment, though where God is when the Son of Man sits in 51:3, 55:4 and 61:8 is not clear.[42] Is God at his side or has he given over the throne for a time as judgment is mediated? Either way, Enoch-Son of Man in this setting is a highly exalted figure, given almost unprecedented authority. It will take our later survey of the Son of Man to complete this image and better assess its significance.

Much later comes the portrait of Enoch as Metatron in *3 En*.[43] One reason for noting this later text is that it confirms that an angelic-Enoch connection

---

[38]Sjöberg goes on to argue in *Der Menschensohn im Äthiopischen Henochbuch*, pp. 159-72 how these chapters fit as a unit with *1 En* as we now have it. I also find these arguments compelling. See also Rudolf Otto, *Reich Gottes und Menschensohn: Ein religionsgeschichtlicher Versuch* (München: C. H. Beck'sche Verlagsbuchhandlung, 1954 [1933]), pp. 132-70, who also argues for the identification. On *1 En* 51:3, see n. 28 above.

[39]Hurtado, *One God, One Lord*, p. 54.

[40]M. Hengel, *Studies in Early Christology* (Edinburgh: T & T Clark, 1995), pp. 185-89. He notes the influence of both Isa 11:1-5 and Ps 110:1 on this portrait, a point of significance as these are regal texts describing a form of comprehensive rule.

[41]Note how this language also seems almost to ignore anything said about pre-existence by speaking of a glorification "in those days."

[42]One should recall *TAbr B* 11:3-8 and its explicit denial of this role to Enoch.

[43]On these passages, see Fossum, *The Name of God and the Angel of the Lord*, pp. 292, 297-98; Christopher Rowland, *The Open Heaven: A Study of Apocalyptic in Judaism and*

was made within Judaism, suggesting such a reading of *1 En* is correct.[44] In *3 En* 4:2-3, Metatron is answering the question how he came to be called "Youth." He responds,

> Because I am Enoch, the son of Jared. When the generation of the Flood sinned and turned to evil deeds, and said to God, 'Go away! We do not choose to learn your ways,' the Holy One, blessed be he, took me from their midst to be a witness against them in the heavenly height to all who should come into the world.

This figure's description looks like portions of *1 En* 12, where Enoch declares judgment against the sins of the angelic "watchers" of Genesis 6. The difference is that in *3 En* it is the human generation of the flood that is the object of his report. But a major role of the Enoch figure is to give witness to the sins of the creation. Metatron-Enoch gets a throne in 10:1-2, "a throne like the throne of glory." It is placed at the door of the "seventh palace" (seventh heaven). Now it is significant to note that this is apparently not the same throne as God's, but one *like* the throne of God.[45] So the exaltation here does not seem to be quite as intimate as that of the Son of Man in Enoch, but the figure still has a major role. In 12:1-5, this figure is given a crown with the title "Lesser YHWH," because God explained, "My name is in him." Enoch-Metatron is a vice regent figure, who receives homage in *3 En* 14. After receiving his crown, "all the princes of kingdoms who are in the height of the heaven of ʾArabot and all the legions of every heaven trembled at me (14:1)." Even "Sammaʾel, the Prince of the Accusers," shudders (14:2). They, and all those who guide the world, fall prostrate upon seeing him and the glory of his crown (14:5). His transformation from flesh to glory is discussed in *3 En* 15. In 48D, he receives seventy names, much as God did in 48B, both texts of even later origin. So *3 En* gives a second example of an exalted Enoch, who receives great honor before God. He is seated with him in the seventh heaven and receives authority and honor, even to the extent that angels bow to him. More will be said of this book's portrait of this figure later when angelic-like figures are considered.

Enoch-Metatron is also mentioned in *TPs-J* to Gen 5:24. The verse reads, "Enoch worshiped in truth before the Lord, and behold he was not with the

---

Early Christianity (New York: Crossroad, 1982), p. 344, and Russell, *The Method and Message of Jewish Apocalyptic*, p. 348.

[44]At the least, it suggests others read that work this way.

[45]Alexander in *OTP* 1:263, n. 10b even points out how texts like *b Ḥag* 15a say that no one is allowed to sit in heaven but God, so that having a throne is a privilege. This survey has already noted several thrones in heaven, so this "prohibition" appears to be a later position. The later rabbis who came to control official Judaism appear to have formulated such restrictions to prevent speculation like that seen in many of these texts. In their view by doing so, God's honor and uniqueness were protected.

inhabitants of the earth because he was taken away and he ascended to the firmament at the command of the Lord, and he was called Metatron, the Great Scribe."[46] This portrait combines exaltation and his role as scribe. It confirms that the association of Enoch-Metatron had spread far enough to be noted in a targum.

But this reading of this figure was also controversial. The older *TOnq* to Gen 5:24 reads, "And Enoch walked in reverence of the Lord, then was no more, for the Lord had caused him to die."[47] Here Enoch is paid the respect of living a righteous life, but is denied an ascension, so the ground for an unusual exaltation is removed. Even more limiting and critical of him is the portrait of *GenR* 25.1, which discusses Gen 5:24.[48] Here R. Hama b. R. Hoshaya (c 260 CE) argues that "he was not" in the verse means that Enoch "was not inscribed in the roll of the righteous but in the roll of the wicked." R. Aibu (c 320 CE) calls Enoch "a hypocrite, acting sometimes as a righteous, sometimes as a wicked man." God removes him while he is righteous and judges him. The midrash also notes the view of those who think Enoch was translated, but replies with a citation from Ezek 24:16 that to "take" can mean to take away in death. The midrash also presents a second account where it is insisted that the additional remark "God took him" means that he "was no more in the world" because he had died. R Jose (c 350 CE) argues that if Genesis had merely said, "And Enoch walked with God," then one could say that Enoch had not died. But the issue of being taken alive to heaven is precluded by the additional remark. All of this counter tradition shows that the Enoch speculation produced a strong reaction because of the great role given to him.

In sum, Enoch is one of the most exalted figures in Judaism. He is seen as a revelatory seer in most cases, but in at least one early text he gets as close to God as any figure, sharing in his judgment in the end and being seated on a

---

[46]The translation is from Michael Maher, *Targum Pseudo-Jonathan: Genesis: Translated, with Introduction and Notes*. ArB 1b (Edinburgh: T & T Clark, 1992), pp. 36-37. Note 10 suggests that the identification came before 450 CE. See also I. Gruenwald, *Apocalyptic and Merkavah Mysticism*, pp. 235-41.

[47]This translation is from Bernard Grossfeld, *The Targum Onqelos to Genesis: Translated, with a Critical Introduction, Apparatus, and Notes*, ArB 6 (Edinburgh: T & T Clark, 1988), p. 51. In n. 3, Grossfeld remarks that the reading is "an attempt to counter the sectarian tendency to glorify Enoch who was said to have been translated to heaven alive and to have been transformed into an angel. The anti-sectarian Rabbinic attitude reduced Enoch to more human proportions, with human failings, alleging that he had died before his time because his righteousness was not expected to endure." See also David J. Halperin, *The Faces of the Chariot: Early Jewish Responses to Ezekiel's Vision*, TSAJ 16 (Tübingen: J. C. B. Mohr (Paul Siebeck), 1988), p. 67.

[48]This text can be found in the Soncino edition of the *Midrash Rabbah*, *Genesis Rabbah* II, p. 205.

throne God uses. He assumes this role, because God himself extends the invitation to him to sit and receive such honor. His translation into heaven while still alive indicates the act of God's selection of him. Only the direct initiative of God could permit such a role to exist for a member of his creation. Other seatings of Enoch also take place in other texts, but these only reflect his more common role as scribe, where his proximity only underlines the fact that he received revelation directly from God. The later image of Metatron in *3 En* really does not represent a major advance on the Son of Man image of *1 En*. The picture of the angelic honor given to Metatron is a natural extension of the fact that he holds a position so near to God. The portrait is also a source of controversy, as later rabbis try to curb its development, either by challenging the idea that Enoch was translated at all or by noting the punishment of a figure like Metatron for letting himself be seen as too much like God.[49] Not everyone is comfortable with the idea that a creature can get this close to God.

Abraham

One might expect that Abraham, as holder of one of the foundational covenants of God, would be a major figure with a long row of references, but this is not the case. For him, there are two early texts and two late ones. The first passage comes from the *TAbr*.[50] In chapters 9 — 11, Michael brings Abraham by chariot up to the first gate of heaven (11:1). Here he sees people in two groups, one going through a straight and narrow gate and the other proceeding through a broad and spacious gate (11:2-7). In a passage already considered, Abraham asks who the man is that reacts to where the people are sent. That man was Adam (11:8-12).[51] Next he sees two angels handing out judgment and recompense to those who had passed through the broad gate (12:1-18). Included in the scene is a reference to books that contain the sins of each person. When the sins and righteous acts are evenly balanced, then the person is "set in the middle" and not sent either way. Chapter 13 mentions the work of judgment that Abel performs, something already discussed above. Each person's work is tested by fire. Those who survive are placed with the righteous. Abraham asks about the soul in the middle, and the angel suggests praying for it. They pray, after which God judges, and the soul is no longer in the middle. It is carried up to paradise, as the angel reports that it was "saved through your righteous prayer" (14:8). A further long intercession saves those who were headed for judgment (14:9-15). Then Abraham is returned to the earth to await his death (15:1-15).

---

[49]This punishment incident from *3 En* 16:1-5 is discussed in more detail below in the angelic section, when Metatron is covered.

[50]For its c. 100 CE date, see n. 13 above.

[51]In the edited edition by Sparks, *The Apocryphal Old Testament,* this scene is *TAbr* 13.

Abraham is a typical apocalyptic figure in this passage. He is the witness of judgment in heaven and also serves as a persuasive intercessor for the potentially lost. His heavenly visit is temporary. He is escorted by Michael, but never sits. He is a revelatory seer, much as Enoch usually is.

The second text comes from the *ApocAbr*.[52] In chapters 18 — 19, there is an expanded version of Gen 15. The journey to heaven is announced in chapters 9 — 10, as Abraham must offer a sacrifice and then is escorted above by the angel Iaoel, whose appearance is described in glorious terms (11:1-3). After a forty day fast and a sacrifice, Abraham is finally led up to heaven, where he hears God praised in song (17:1-21). There Abraham sees and hears the fiery voice of God, but does not see him (17:1; 18:1-3). He sees the angels around the throne and describes them in terms very much like Ezek 1 (18:4-14). Fire and "indescribable light" surrounded the crowd (18:13). Standing on the seventh firmament, Abraham sees the heavens open up (19:1-4). He could look down to the sixth firmament and could observe the angels of the sixth firmament carrying out the orders of the angels of the eighth firmament (19:5-8). Then a fresh angelic order gives him a glimpse of the fifth firmament of the hosts of stars (19:9). Next the "Eternal and Mighty One" promises Abraham his protection (20:5) and shows him what is planned for the ages (21:1). The vision, which lasts several chapters, presents an overview of history until the end. Once again, Abraham visits heaven during his life as a revelatory seer to observe God's plan.

Two texts are much later and give Abraham a more exalted role. The first passage is highly figurative. In *Midrash to Ps* 110.4, the exposition concerns the battles of Gen 14 and answers the question, "Who, then, fought all the battles?" Abraham is seated at God's right hand according to Ps 110:1, because the Lord fights his battles for him.[53] The text applies Isa 41:2-3 to the ruler. This shall also be done for Messiah in the end. This midrash is not about a heavenly seating, but refers instead to the close relationship Abraham and Messiah have to God that allows the Lord to fight on earth for those he has appointed. Seating here is merely a metaphor for being close to God as his regal agent.

The final text is also from *Midrash to the Ps*. The text comes from Ps 18.29.[54] Here Rabbi Yudan (c 350 CE) reports remarks from Rabbi Ḥama (c 260 CE). He notes that in the time to come, lord Messiah will be seated "at his right hand," as the exposition then cites Ps 110:1. And he also will seat

---

[52]This work dates from between 70 CE and the mid-second century. See R. Rubinkiewicz, *OTP* 1:683.

[53]William G. Braude, *The Midrash on the Psalms*, 2 vols., YJS 13 and 14 (New Haven: Yale University Press, 1959), 2:206-07. These texts, though they may contain older tradition, are to be dated to the eighth century.

[54]William G. Braude, *The Midrash on the Psalms*, 1:261.

"Abraham at his left." This causes Abraham's face "to pale" as he states with some apparent shock, "My son's son sits at the right, and I at the left!" The right side was the side of higher honor, so Abraham is asking how he, as the ancestor, could have a lower place. The Holy One "comforts" Abraham by saying "Your son's son is at my right, but I, in a manner of speaking, am at your right!" Then Ps 110:5 is cited.

The exchange is shown to give honor to Abraham and relieve his complaint. The text has no discussion of what takes place as a result of the seating. The exposition is intended to show the relationship between promise and Messiah, with Abraham representing the start of the promise. Again in this late text, it is luminaries who get to sit at God's direct instigation.

In sum, the picture of Abraham is rather typical of other heavenly visitations in the early Jewish texts. He is a seer who gets to see what the final judgment looks like. In one late text, he sits by God, but Messiah has the place at God's right hand. This single, brief, and late reference tells us little else, other than the fact that both are deeply honored by the act.

Jacob

One might also expect that the one from whom Israel derives it name would be a popular figure for exaltation, but there is only one text that gives such a role to him. It is, however, a curious text. In a fragment of the *Prayer of Joseph* cited by Origen in his commentary on John, there is discussion of a chief angel and ruling spirit, Jacob (Frag. A, 1).[55] It reads, "I, Jacob, who am speaking to you, am also Israel, an angel of God and a ruling spirit." Smith's note on this passage indicates that Israel is often portrayed as an angel in magical and mystical literature.[56] Smith also notes that the expression "ruling spirit" appears in astrological literature.[57]

---

[55]This work dates from the second century, and possibly the first, see J. Z. Smith, *OTP* 2:700. The fragment comes from Origen's *Commentary on John* Book 2 (25). For the Greek text in Origen, see Minge, ed., *Patrologia Graeco-Latina* 14 (Origenes, vol. 4), cols. 168-69 (= PG14, 168-69). For another English translation, see R. E. Heine, *Origen: Commentary on the Gospel according to John Books 1-10*. The Fathers of the Church (Washington DC: Catholic University of America, 1989), sections 189-90, pp. 145-46. Smith calls the work "a myth of the mystery of Israel" in *OTP* 2:704 and there is discussion whether this figure should be seen as thoroughly docetic. The fragment has only nine verses. One reference to be discussed also has a trace in fragment C, which is a paraphrase of Fragment A and is in Origen's *Philocalia* 33:19. Another discussion of these texts appears in Fossum, *The Name of God and the Angel of the Lord*, pp. 188-89, 315-17, as well as in M. Hengel, *Der Sohn Gottes: Die Entstehung der Christologie und die jüdisch-hellenistische Religionsgeschichte* (Tübingen: J. C. B. Mohr [Paul Siebeck], 1975), pp. 76-77, who notes the connection to the language of Exod 4:22.

[56]*OTP* 2:713, n. **A** b. In the introduction to the book, he notes *b Ḥull* 91b and Hekhalot literature, both much later material than this passage from the *Prayer of Joseph*. See *OTP*

Frag. A, v. 2 observes that Abraham and Isaac were created before any work. But Jacob is more unique than the two seemingly older patriarchs. Verse 3 reads, "But, I, Jacob, who men call Jacob but whose name is Israel, am he who God called Israel which means, a man seeing God, because I am the firstborn of every living thing to whom God gives life." Then in v. 4, Jacob is said to have "descended to earth and I had tabernacled among men and that I had been called by the name of Jacob." This leads in vv. 7-8 to a final description of the figure in a discussion with the angel Uriel, "Are you not Uriel, the eighth after me? and I, Israel, the archangel of the power of the Lord and the chief captain among the sons of God? Am I not Israel, the first minister before the face of God?" Frag. C says that "Jacob was greater than man, . . . he was a chief captain of the power of the Lord and had, from of old, the name of Israel . . .."

In sum, Jacob in this text seems to be some form of an incarnated angelic figure.[58] Though he is highly exalted and sees God, we are not told anything else about his heavenly activity. Nor are we told he sits, only that he serves before and sees God. The description of this figure will remind us of Michael when he is surveyed. Michael never sits in heaven but is always busy doing God's bidding. Nonetheless, here is another example of a highly exalted figure. It is also important to note that this figure has a transcendent-human mix, as is apparently the case with Enoch-Son of Man. The difference between the two appears to be that Enoch is somehow transformed into Son of Man, while this Jacob example appears to involve an incarnation or, at least, a descent to earth. In both cases, however, what one was as a human is not how one ended up being seen.

Levi

For Levi there is also only one text, the second century BCE *TLevi*, which is probably from the Maccabean period.[59] As part of a vision, this son of Jacob stands at the throne of God in the third heaven, where mysteries are revealed to him while he serves God as an appointed priest (2:9-10). Levi's call is to

---

2:702. Fossum, *The Name of God and the Angel of the Lord*, p. 189, cites a coptic magical papyrus from Christian circles that uses Israel-El of Jesus.

[57]*OTP* 2:713, n. **A** c. Unfortunately, he gives us no references for this parallel.

[58]This portrait could have been considered in the angelic section, but it is here because the dominating ground of the description is Jacob. The mystery emerges in his angelic-like roots. Fossum, *The Name of God and the Angel of the Lord*, p. 314, suggests an angel of the Lord figure. When he goes on to suggest demiurgic qualities, however, nothing in the texts conclusively argues for this. "First born from every living thing" in Frag. A, v. 3 can suggest priority, and not necessarily a cosmological role. See Ps. 89:27.

[59]See H. C. Kee, *OTP* 1:777-78. This work has some Christian interpolations as well from the second century CE.

"tell forth his mysteries to men (2:10). He is told, "You shall announce the one who is to redeem Israel" (2:10). This is some type of visionary experience as it occurs after Levi falls asleep (2:5). After this he is on a high mountain and passes through the first and second heavens before receiving his commission (2:6-8). In 5:1, Levi gets a glimpse of the Most High: "At this moment the angel opened for me the gates of heaven and I saw the Holy Most High sitting on the throne." There he hears from God his commission of the priesthood, which is to remain until the Lord comes to dwell in the midst of Israel. After a brief discussion with the escorting angel, who makes intercession for Israel but whose name is not given, Levi awakens (5:7).[60] This brief heavenly experience points to a revelatory seer, functions already applied to Enoch and Abraham.

Moses

By far the most developed exalted human figure in Judaism is Moses.[61] There appear to be four reasons for this emphasis.[62] First, no figure is more important to the establishment of the nation or of its community of Law than Moses. Second, he encountered God at the bush (Exod 3). Third, his unique time on Sinai, face to face with God, leaves room for reflecting on what took place there (Exod 19 — 34, esp. 33:12-23). Third, his death was also shrouded in a degree of mystery as he passed away in a secluded place, alone (Deut 34).[63] As Deut 34:10 states, the belief was that Moses "knew the Lord

---

[60]This angelic function is often given to Michael: Dan 10:13, 21; 12:1; *1 En* 20:5.

[61]Only Enoch and possibly the Messiah come anywhere close to the scope of treatment Moses receives.

[62]The portrait of Moses is discussed in detail by Wayne A. Meeks, *The Prophet-King: Moses Traditions and the Johannine Christology*, SNovT14 (Leiden: E. J. Brill, 1967), esp. pp. 100-285. Of particular significance is a study by W. Hall Harris, III, *The Descent of Christ: Ephesians 4:7-11 and Traditional Hebrew Imagery* AGAJU 32 (Leiden: Brill, 1996). I thank him for interaction on this material and providing proof pages of his study. Harris carefully analyzes Jewish Moses traditions in chapters 3-4 of that work (pp. 66-142). Chapter 3 treats mostly later Jewish works, though *TPs* 68:19, which merely says that Prophet Moses "ascended to the firmament" seems aware of traditions like those to be considered. Shorter surveys are present in Wayne A. Meeks, "Moses as God and King," in *Religions in Antiquity: Essays in Memory of Erwin Ramsdell Goodenough*, ed. Jacob Neusner, SHR 14 (Leiden: E. J. Brill, 1968), pp. 354-71; Hurtado, *One God, One Lord*, pp. 56-63, and Fossum, *The Name of God and the Angel of the Lord*, pp. 111-44. The key *Exagoge* text is treated in the full study by Howard Jacobson, *The Exagoge of Ezekiel* (Cambridge: Cambridge University Press, 1983); and in two key articles by Pieter W. van der Horst in his collected studies, *Essays on the Jewish World of Early Christianity*, NTOA 14 (Göttingen: Vandenhoeck & Ruprecht, 1990), pp. 63-93, entitled "Moses' Throne Vision in Ezekiel the Dramatist" and "Some Notes on the *Exagoge* of Ezekiel." Our survey concentrates on early texts, since too many discussions of Moses indiscriminately mix older and later texts.

[63]The speculations were even discussed by Josephus, *Ant* 3.96-97 and 4.326. As 3.96-97 asks, did Moses fall among wild beasts? Or perhaps it was as "others said that he was

face to face." No one else is like him in this regard. As a result, a whole series of reflections about his encounters with God developed, mostly around the two events of Sinai and Moses' death. Some treat him as a revelatory seer, just like other figures, while others give him an array of other heavenly functions, from mediator to full vice regent.[64]

Moses was seen as a heavenly seer in several texts. In the second century BCE *Sirach* he is said to be "equal in glory to the holy ones" (45:2) and that God "allowed him to hear his voice, and led him into the dark cloud; and gave him the commandments face to face (45:5)." This second citation is commentary on Exod 33:12-23. But none of this indicates that Moses went up to heaven, only that God revealed himself directly to Moses on the mountain. Though v. 2 might indicate an exaltation in that Moses possesses a place equal to angelic glory, it probably is only a summary of the glory Moses received as the revelatory agent through whom God ministered powerfully. The question is whether God came to the mountain or Moses was "taken up" to see God. At most, an ascension has to be inferred from this text.

Yet another version of the Sinai encounter is in *Ps-Philo* 11 — 12.[65] In 11:14, the text states that, "For behold today we know that God speaks to a man face to face and that man may live." It is earth that has "borne the voice of God." In 12:1 the glory Moses reflected as a result of his visit is noted as he passed through "the place where the light of the sun and the moon are." This may well suggest transport into heaven. One other item in this text, namely, the seeing of the tree of life in 11:15 and a cutting off of the portion

---

departed [i.e., taken up], and gone to God; but the wiser sort were led by their reason to embrace neither of those opinions with any satisfaction. . . ." More interesting is 4.326, which declares "a cloud stood over him on the [= all of a] sudden, and he disappeared in a certain valley, although he wrote in the holy books that he died, which was done out of fear, lest they should venture to say that, because of his extraordinary virtue, he went to God." As the survey shall show, such reflections did surround Moses, though Josephus seems not to hold to it.

[64]Meeks, *The Prophet-King: Moses Traditions and the Johannine Christology*, pp. 100-75, notes Ruler, High Priest, Divine Man, Prophet-King, King, Prophet, Heavenly-Ascents, Intercessor, and "signs and wonders" as the broad categories of the speculations about his entire career.

[65]This work dates from the first century, see D. Harrington, *OTP* 2:299. Meeks, *The Prophet-King: Moses Traditions and the Johannine Christology*, p. 157-58, also treats this passage as giving a heavenly ascent. This book describes Moses' glimpse of heaven again at 32:9, where Moses seems to be given a more authoritative role over the heavenly bodies. Meeks' translation of the key line in 32:9 is "the heaven where you have entered," while Harrington's translation has "are about to enter," a difference that may indicate a difference of locale as well. Meeks read *Jubilees* prologue, 1:4, 26, the same way, but this may also only involve revelation on the mountain and not a heavenly journey. See W. Hall Harris, *The Descent of Christ: Ephesians 4:7-11 and Traditional Hebrew Imagery*, pp. 131-33 on *Pseudo-Philo*. Harris also rejects 19:10-12 as involving ascension. Harris also sees 11:15; 12:1; and 32:9 as describing an ascension. Of these, only 11:15 seems doubtful.

of the tree by Moses, may also suggest transport to heaven. However, the visionary feel of this particular detail makes this import not entirely certain. The cloud may have been brought to him so that what he saw here was like what he sees next about the temple. For the text says he showed him the tree of life, not that he was taken anywhere. In fact the bulk of the imagery is the exact opposite. God came to earth. It is earth that bore God's voice. It must be said, however, that 12:1 does look to imply a journey, though the stress is on his subsequent descent not an ascent. If one reads 11:15 in light of 12:1, then it might be possible to see a heavenly setting. In other words, 11:15 is a close call as to the locale portrayed. The import of the experience, regardless, is strictly revelatory, the most common result of such a visit.

The much later *3 En* 15B v. 2 is similar. Moses fasts 121 times and is praying for the nation before receiving the law. God comes to meet him with the angel Metatron. His prayer is announced as heard and Moses emerges from the meeting with a glorious face.

In *4 Ezra* 14:9, God gives a revelation of secrets to Moses about the structure of the ages to come. It is a revelation kept secret until it is reported to Ezra. This experience for Moses also apparently took place on the mountain. So several texts appear to have Moses meet God face to face, but the meetings take place on the earth as the cloud covers the mountain. In some cases, like in *Ps-Philo*, it is possible the meeting included a journey to heaven. Nevertheless, such trips had only revelatory aims.

In contrast to this earthly setting stands the picture of *b. Shab* 88b.[66] As Moses came to the mountain to receive the Law, a great protest broke out from among the angels that such "secret treasure" should be given to "one born of woman," especially something hidden for "nine hundred and seventy-four generations." They complain that something like this should be given "to flesh and blood." Then the discussion cites Ps 8:5 and then v. 2. The midrash argues that God is mindful of man, which this event and the Psalmic citation prove. Moses fears being consumed by the fiery breath of the angels. So God replies, "Hold on to the Throne of Glory" (בכסא כבודי). Later God says to Moses, "And return them an answer, as it is said, He makes him to hold on to the face of his throne (פני כסא). And spread his cloud over him" (Job 26:9). The comment of the exposition follows, "Whereon R. Naḥman (c 400 CE) observed: This teaches that the Almighty spread the lustre of His Shekinah and cast it as a protection over him." The image of holding onto the face of the throne is not a seating, but appears to give Moses access to the front of the

---

[66]The Talmud, though it can contain older traditions, dates from c. 500-550 CE. See Evans, *Noncanonical Writings and New Testament Interpretation*, p. 126. The talmudic references in English translation can be found in the relevant volume of the Soncino edition. See *Shabbath*, in *Seder Mo'ed* 1, pp. 421-22. For a discussion of this text, see Halperin, *The Faces of the Chariot*, pp. 298-301.

throne as he bows before it. God, from above, casts his presence over him. So Moses does not sit by God as he comes.

This text does suggest that Moses traveled to heaven briefly to receive the revelation and that the angels protested vigorously. Yet God protected him and he lived through it. Moses' ability to get so close to God was directed and protected by God himself. An alternate interpretation might argue the entire entourage, both angelic and divine, came down to earth. Either way, what is important to see is that Moses got access to the divine throne, speaking directly to God from beneath the throne, and was even allowed to hold onto it for protection. This was a brief glimpse of the throne. Moses operates in the now common category of revelatory seer, though here he does not see the future judgment, but receives the Law. Moses and the Law are elevated by this portrayal.

Moses also functions like standard apocalyptic seers who see judgment. In *2 Bar* 59:4-12, Moses receives the Law and also sees the "end of time" (59:4), as well as the abyss, fire, wrath, judgment, wisdom, Paradise, and worlds which have not yet come (59:5-12).[67] This is quite familiar apocalyptic imagery.

TMos provides yet another text that portrays Moses as mediator.[68] At this book's start, Moses gives his departing remarks to his successor, Joshua. Like many important figures, Moses was formed by God in his plan at the beginning: "he did design and devise me, who (was) prepared from the beginning of the world, to be mediator of his covenant (1:14)." Then Moses explains what Joshua will do for the people and what will happen to the nation after him as the nation divides into two parts and suffers exile. The predictions will cause the people to "remember me . . .. Is this not that which was made known to us in prophecies by Moses, who suffered many things in Egypt and at the Red Sea and in the wilderness for forty years (when) he solemnly called heaven and earth as witnesses against us that we should not transgress God's commandments of which he had become the mediator for us (3:10-12)?" Moses is a mediator-prophet for the people, as the text recalls Moses' reaction to Israel's unfaithfulness. The rest of the work looks to the eventual deliverance of the nation and depicts Joshua's farewell to Moses. Joshua complains that "there is (now) no advocate for them (*non est defensor illis*) who will bear messages to the Lord on their behalf in the way that Moses was the great messenger" (11:17). Moses comforts Joshua and assures

[67]This work dates from early second century CE. See M. A. Knibb, *OTP* 1:616-17. A reference to seeing the New Jerusalem in 4:2-7 is probably just a vision.

[68]On the date of this work, see J. Priest, *OTP* 1:920-21, who places it in the first century CE, but with the possibility that portions of the book are older, and Johannes Tromp, *The Assumption of Moses: A Critical Edition with Commentary*. SVTP 10 (Leiden: E. J. Brill, 1993), pp. 116-17, who argues for the first quarter of the century.

him of God's sovereignty. This text simply reviews Moses' career as an advocate for the people. There is no ascension or anything remotely apocalyptic in this material.[69]

Similar in thrust but attributing a similar role to Moses now in heaven is *Sifre Deut* 34:5 §357.[70] The Piska covers the death of Moses, where Moses sees both the line of kings who will descend from David and the land the nation is about to receive. In discussing Moses' death, another opinion is given to the effect that he did not die: "Others say: Moses never died, and he stands and serves on high, as is shown by the use of the adverb *there* in this verse (Exod 34:5 is meant) and in the verse, *And he was there with the Lord* (Exod 34:28)."[71] Though it is presented as a minority opinion, this rabbinic text testifies to a view that Moses was exalted at the end to continue to serve as a mediator in heaven. Later in the passage, before Moses dies he sees God's back, a reading that conflates Exod 34 with 33:12-23. The revelation is not presented as a particularly unique experience, because it proves that "the dead do see (God's glory)." This later text is obviously much more restrained in its handling of Moses than some of the earlier texts about to be considered. It simply treats Moses as one of the interceding and serving righteous.

So in this cluster of texts on Moses, we see trips to heaven that make him a seer who receives the Law (*Sir* 45; *Pseudo-Philo* 11–12; *3 En* 15B v. 2; *b Shab* 88b) or sees the future (*4 Ezra* 14:9). He also sees judgment to come (*2 Bar* 59:4-12). He serves in one text as a constant, heavenly advocate for the people (*Sifre Deut* 34:5 § 357). All of these roles are basic functions related to exaltation. Only *b Shab* 88b mentions God's throne explicitly. In this text, Moses clings to the base of the throne for protection from the angels.

But how did those who highlight him as an exalted figure see Moses? Here it is best to begin with Philo. In his *Life of Moses* from the early first century,

---

[69]This remark is made contra Segal, "Heavenly Ascent in Hellenistic Judaism, Early Christianity and their Environment," p. 1354, n. 76, who lists this text as one involving an ascension of Moses, as well as against Meeks, *The Prophet-King: Moses Traditions and the Johannine Christology*, pp. 203, 125 n. 3. See now Hall Harris, *The Descent of Christ: Ephesians 4:7-11 and Traditional Hebrew Imagery*, pp. 133-36 on *TMos* (= *AsMos*) and J. Tromp, *The Assumption of Moses*, pp. 256-57, 265-66, who in discussing 12:6 specifically challenges Meeks' claim of a future intercessory role for Moses. He notes in handling 11:17 that the Latin *defensor* appears in Jud 6:13, Sir 30:6, and 2 Macc 4:2, but it renders a Greek term only in this last Maccabean text (κηδεμών). See also Philo, *Life of Moses* 2.166, where the Greek term also appears. Moses is seen as a mediator who makes the case for his people before God.

[70]Reuven Hammer, *Sifre: A Tannaitic Commentary on the Book of Deuteronomy* (London: Yale University Press, 1986), pp. 378-83. It dates from the second half of the fourth century CE.

[71]Hammer, *Sifre*, p. 381. A similar division of opinion is noted in *b Sot* 13b, with ascension being a minority opinion. In fact, this Piska and the talmudic text read very similarly.

he depicts Moses as a king and vice regent figure, who even bears the name god.[72] Several remarks in the passage stress how close Moses was to God. "For, since God judged him worthy to appear as a partner of His own possessions, He gave into his hand the whole world as a portion well fitted for his heir (1.155)." Given that they held things in common, Moses as "the prophet is called the friend of God (1.156)."

The next passage indicates just how exalted the view of Moses was. It is one of several Philonic texts on Moses that have stirred controversy:

> Again, was not the joy of his partnership with the Father and Maker of all magnified also by the honour of being deemed worthy to bear the same title? For he was named god and king of the whole nation and entered, we are told, into the darkness, where God was, that is into the unseen, invisible, incorporeal, and archetypal essence of existing things (1.158)."

He also is the bearer of much wisdom and righteousness: "Perhaps, too, since he was destined to be a legislator, the providence of God which afterwards appointed him without his knowledge to that work, caused him long before that day to be the reasonable and living impersonation of the law (1.162)."

Just what is meant by the fact that he was called god shall be considered shortly, but the remark has its roots in Exod 7:1. What is clear is that Moses is seen as a regal-like figure, a king-prophet who is given broad authority by God. This view is reinforced in Philo's portrait of Moses' death in *Life of Moses* 2.288-91, where "he had to make pilgrimage (ἀποικίαν) from earth to heaven, and leave this mortal life for immortality, summoned there by the Father Who resolved his twofold nature of soul and body into a single unity, transforming his whole being into mind, pure as sunlight (2.288)." Philo appears to see Moses as a figure who ascended to heaven "for when he was already being exalted and stood at the very barrier, ready at the signal to direct his upward flight to heaven, the divine spirit fell on him and he prophesied with discernment the story of his own death, told at the end how the end came; told how he was buried with none present, surely by no mortal hands but by immortal powers . . . (2.291)." Moses is the object of transformation and exaltation, and is buried by "immortal powers" [angels]. His earthly body is left in the grave, while his real soul and body emerge

---

[72]Citations of Philo are from the Loeb collection of Cohn-Wendland with only a few stylistic alterations. See a full selection of Philo citations on this theme in W. Hall Harris, *The Descent of Christ: Ephesians 4:7-11 and Traditional Hebrew Imagery*, pp. 127-31 on Philo of Alexandria. He notes especially: *De Somniis* 1.36, where Moses in an incorporeal state listens to divine music; *Questiones et Solutiones in Exodum* 2.29, which says Moses "was changed into the divine" and became "kin to God;" *Legum Allegoriae* 3.141-43, which explains how Moses could survive a forty day fast; *De Mutatione Nomimum* 7, as he was taken into incorporeal existence; *Questiones et Solutiones in Exodum* 2.40, where on Sinai he went beyond heaven and abided with God, and the discussion of *Vita Moses* 1.158.

unified and glorified. Such is the story of "Moses, king, lawgiver, high priest, prophet" (2.292).

Though some of this language is ambiguous as to whether a translation took place, other Philonic texts seem to confirm it as the Jewish historian-philosopher's view. The *Sacrifices of Abel and Cain* 8 — 10 speak of some God has trained to soar above "species and genus alike and stationed them beside himself . . . And so when Moses was about to die we do not hear of him 'leaving' or 'being added' like those others. No reason exists in him for adding or taking away. But through the 'Word' of the Supreme Cause he is translated (Deut 34:5), even through that Word by which also the whole universe was formed. (§ 8). The language of divinity appears yet again with this text from § 9:

> And even when he sent him as a loan to the earthly sphere and suffered him to dwell therein, He gifted him with no ordinary excellence, such as that which kings and rulers have, wherewith to hold sway and sovereignty over the passions of the soul, but he appointed him as god, placing all the bodily region and the mind which rules it in subjection and slavery to him. 'I give thee,' he says, 'as god to Pharoah' (Exod 7:1); but God is not susceptible of addition or diminution, being fully and unchangeably himself. And therefore we are told that no man knows his grave (Deut 34:6).

For Philo, the vice regency of Moses gave him a unique status among men and led to his exaltation into heaven. Philo gives no details about what Moses does in heaven, as the portrait emerges entirely from the events of his earthly career. In this sense Moses is unlike other portraits of heavenly figures we have seen thus far. Undoubtedly this is because Moses is the one figure who is portrayed as having seen God directly in this life without having been translated or without the aid of a vision.

This "divine" emphasis is not unique to Philo. The later *DeutR*, which dates from about 900 CE but has older tradition embedded in it, has an explanatory passage on how Moses was god. In 11.4, it covers the various ways that Moses was god, when he is also called a man. The answer to the dilemma is seen in the explanation that when the river became blood, when Pharoah drowned, and when Moses was taken up into heaven and made like the angels not eating or drinking, "he was as God," a refrain repeated four times in the passage.[73] The rabbinic explanation is that Moses functioned with divine power and served, in effect, as god for Pharoah, being rewarded afterward with exaltation to heaven.

---

[73]*Midrash Deuteronomy*, H. Freedman and M. Simon, eds. (London: Soncino, 1983) pp. 175-76. For this date, see C. A. Evans, *Noncanonical Writings and New Testament Interpretation*, p. 133.

Philo would probably have agreed with this type of description of Moses's role. In his *Worse Attacks the Better* 160 – 62, he explains how Moses is deified in a figurative sense, saying "he did not become such in reality, but only by convention is supposed to be such." Later in the same text he comments that "the wise man is said to be god to the foolish man."[74] In *Every Good Man Is Free* 43, he comments that Moses was one "having passed from a man into a god, though indeed, a god to men, not to the different parts of nature, thus leaving the Father of all the place of King and God of gods."

Only one text is slightly more ambiguous, but it needs to be understood in light of these other numerous references. It is *Questions on Exodus* 2.29. It reads,

> For when the prophetic mind becomes divinely inspired and filled with God, it becomes like the monad, not being at all mixed with any of those things that are associated with duality. But he who is resolved into the nature of unity, is said to have come near God in a kind of family relation, for having given up and left behind all mortal kinds, he is changed into the divine, so that such men become kin to God and truly divine.

Moses, as prophet, is brought so close to God *when he is inspired* that he can be said to be divine. The emphasis is mine and highlights the passage's point. It is a way to explain how Moses' revelation has divine authority, because he becomes a thoroughly divine vessel when God fills him.[75] God is working through Moses intimately, which means that Moses acts in conjunction with divine authority. So "divinity" for Philo, as for most later Jews who comment on Exod 7:1, describes either the extensive ruling function and power Moses possesses or the way in which he is a vessel for divine revelation.

These texts on Moses concentrate almost exclusively on his earthly career. The explicit Moses ascension texts are tied either to giving the Law or to Moses' death. The texts that do mention ascension simply note that it took place at his death or upon his visit to the mountain to receive the law, though one also senses a conflation of the death scene with Exod 33:12-23 at points. Four apparent examples of explicit ascension exist and have already been

---

[74]Similar is his *On the Change of Names* 19, 24-26, 127-29, where he cites Exod 7:1, speaks of Moses benefiting from God's assistance, and reuses the wise-fool example.

[75]Similar is the later *Midrash Tanḥuma* on Num 10:1-2, an exposition mirrored in *NumR* 15.13. God is said "to give a share of his own glory to those who fear him." Moses is the example, as the exposition cites Exod 7:1 to explain Ps 24:8. The concluding remarks note that God said to Moses, "I have made you king." *Tanḥuma* was probably written around 800 CE, but it has material from the fourth century; see Evans, *Noncanonical Writings and New Testament Interpretation*, p. 136; H. Bietenhard, *Midrasch Tanḥuma B* (Bern: Peter Lang, 1982) 2:263; J. T. Townsend, *Midrash Tanḥuma: Translated into English with Introduction, Indices, and Brief Notes (S. Buber Recension)*, vol. 1- Genesis (Hoboken, NJ: KTAV, 1989), p. xii, and Freedman and Simon, *Numbers Midrash*, p. 654-55.

noted above: Philo's teaching, *Ps-Philo* 12:1 along side of 32:9; *2 Bar* 59, where the standard revelatory seer emphasis appears; and *b Shab* 88b, where Moses clings to God's throne to get protection from the angels.[76] These texts seem to assume a heavenly visit, but they still stay focused on the function of Moses *during his career and not at some later eschatological point.* All of this must be remembered as examination turns to the early second century BCE *Exagoge of Ezekiel.*[77]

The portrait of Moses has been given careful attention, because this *Exagoge* text needs to be placed in context. It is among the oldest, and most important, passages in our entire survey. It also gives Moses one of the most unusual roles to be considered. This interesting and controversial text certainly describes a highly exalted Moses. It is a role similar to one we have already seen, the sitting judge figure who possesses considerable authority. It is a disputed text, with a wide range of views being held concerning it. In many ways, the passage is unique with its explicit invitation to Moses to sit upon the divine throne. Our knowledge of this text is entirely second hand. We know of this poetic, tragic drama only through Eusebius, Clement of Alexandria, and Pseudo-Eustathius as they record what Alexander Polyhistor passed on.[78] The key portion is lines 68-89. It is cited in full following mostly Robertson's *OTP* rendering.[79] Moses speaks in lines 68-82, while Moses' father-in-law, Raguel (Jethro) speaks from lines 83 on, a point noted by a break in the rendering.

(68) On Sinai's peak I saw what seemed a throne

---

[76]If one includes the Samaritan tradition, then a fifth clear example exists. In the second to fourth century *Memar Markah* mention is made of Moses' ascension. He received God's secrets through an angel at the bush as the "illuminator of the family of mankind (1.1-2)." He is told in the same passage to "take from me (God) divinity and make it with your prophethood strong." Manuscript A has only "power" here, not divinity. He is also called "my Second in the lower world." In 6.6, he is seen as a heavenly scribe. In the *Liturgies*, he is given a throne and entrusted with the unseen world. On the Samaritan passages, see J. Mac Donald, *Memar Marqah: The Teaching of Marqah vol. II: The Translation* (Berlin: Alfred Töpelmann, 1963), pp. 3-5, 12.

[77]For this work, see Jacobson, *The Exagoge of Ezekiel* (= *Ezekiel the Tragedian*, trans. R. G. Robertson, *OTP* 2:803-04, who discusses the date).

[78]Eusebius, *Praeparatio Evangelica* 9, 28-29; Clement of Alexandria, *Stromata* 1.23.155-56; and Pseudo-Eustathius, *Commentaries in Hexaemeron* (for this, see PG 18, 729). For the Clement text in translation, see *Clement of Alexandria: Stromateis Books One to Three.* The Fathers of the Church, vol. 85. trans. John Ferguson (Washington DC: Catholic University of America, 1991), pp. 137-39. The Clement text only treats another portion of *Exagoge,* which discusses Moses' birth and his defense of the Israelite.

[79]I have compared the Robertson translation with the text from Jacobson and the notes from van der Horst, "Some Notes on the *Exagoge* of Ezekiel," in *Essays on the Jewish World of Early Christianity,* pp. 81-87. Scriptural parallels are noted in parenthesis.

so great in size it touched the clouds of heaven.
(70) Upon it sat a noble man (Dan 7; Ezek 1),
with a crown, and with a sceptre in the left hand
while with the right hand he did beckon me.
I made approach and stood before the throne.
He handed over the sceptre and bade
(75) me mount the throne, and gave to me the crown;
then he himself withdrew from off of the thrones (Dan 7:9)[80].
I gazed upon the whole earth round about;
things under it, and high above the skies.
Then at my feet a multitude of stars
(80) fell down, and I reckoned their number (Ps 147:4).
They passed by me like armed ranks of men.
Then in terror I awakened from the dream.

(83) My friend, God gave you this as a sign for good.
Would that I might live to see these things transpire.
(85) for you shall cause a mighty throne to rise,
and you yourself shall rule and govern men.
As for beholding all the peopled earth,
and things below and things above God's heaven —
things present, past, and future you shall see.

The text clearly involves an enthronement of Moses (lines 68-76) and, if one reads the beginning parallels to Dan 7 and Ezek 1 correctly, it is God who gives him the throne. The creation also gives him honor at the end of the text. What does this scene mean?

Three views of this text exist. (1) The first, advocated by Jacobson, is that the scene is actually a polemic against Moses' exaltation.[81] Key to this view is that the scene takes place as a dream, so it is an imaginary event, a mere vision. He appeals to Numbers 12:6-8 for support, where it is said that Moses was *not* spoken to in dreams. Jacobson argues that a revelation that comes by means of a dream is automatically suspect in light of the Numbers text. So what appears to be asserted about Moses is, in fact, rejected.

---

[80]Here is one place where our rendering differs in a significant way. The term here is plural and recalls the language of Dan 7:9 with its scene involving the Son of Man. See William Horbury, "The Messianic Associations of 'the Son of Man'," JTS 36 (1985): 42-43.

[81]"Mysticism and Apocalyptic in Ezekiel the Tragedian," ICS 6 (1981):272-93, esp. 277. These views are not noted in the section on the dream in Jacobson's, *The Exagōgē of Ezekiel*.

(2) Van der Horst, who takes a second and diametrically opposed view, challenges the polemical reading.[82] Van der Horst argues that most of the audience, probably Greek, would not know, and much less appreciate, a subtle reference to Numbers. Other problems with the first view also exist. For example, nothing in the context of the *Exagoge* indicates that this scene is a negative one. In addition, nothing about Num 12 makes the point that dreams in themselves are negative. The passage merely distinguishes between other revelation and the direct revelation Moses received at Sinai. So it is not clear that Numbers teaches that dreams in themselves are an inadequate means for revelation. For his part, van der Horst takes the vision more straight forwardly and argues that it is a throne-vision based on Ezek 1 with its human figure appearing on a divine throne.[83] Beyond this, van der Horst claims, that the "highest angel" in some circles of Judaism was allowed to share God's divinity and, further, a human hero could ascend to become one with this figure. He notes Enoch in this regard and sees Moses as the second example. As he says, "This scene is unique in early Jewish literature and certainly implies a deification of Moses."[84] The explicitness of a complete exchange on the throne is certainly unique among the texts we shall examine. But is deification the point?

(3) Martin Hengel briefly states a third view.[85] Though he recognizes the text's uniqueness, Hengel argues that a deification of Moses and God's leaving the throne would "have as a consequence the 'abdication of God.'" This apparently would be unacceptable in any Jewish view. He also objects to van der Horst's bringing Exod 4:16 and 7:1 into the *Exagoge* discussion, when they are not mentioned in the work. For Hengel, Moses "appears as a — certainly unique — judge, ruler and recipient of divine revelation." So something less than a full deification is in view.

I favor this third option. One reason that shall become clear later in this survey is that it is not evident that the "angel of the Lord," who in this period would probably be equated with Michael, ever sits on his own by God. So van der Horst's description of what kind of honor goes to God's lead angel appears overdrawn. This highly exalted angelic figure may do God's bidding and share his name, but God does not seat him. The only possible exception

---

[82]P. van der Horst, "Some Notes on the *Exagoge* of Ezekiel," in *Essays on the Jewish World of Early Christianity*, pp. 82-85. So also W. Hall Harris, *The Descent of Christ: Ephesians 4:7-11 and Traditional Hebrew Imagery*, pp. 123-27 on *Exagoge*.

[83]For the complex history of Jewish interpretation of Ezek 1, see David J. Halperin, *The Faces of the Chariot: Early Jewish Responses to Ezekiel's Vision*, TSAJ (Tübingen: J. C. B. Mohr [Paul Siebeck], 1988).

[84]P. W. van der Horst, "Moses' Throne Vision in Ezekiel the Dramatist," in *Essays on the Jewish World of Early Christianity*, p. 67.

[85]*Studies in Early Christianity*, pp. 190-91.

might be the very cryptic Son of Man figure in Dan 7:13-14, whom some see as originally being an angelic figure, possibly Michael.[86] If so, any clear traces of such an explicit connection of seating in heaven to Michael are lacking in later Judaism as will be made clear. If one removes this implicit background, then the conclusion of a deification is weakened. There is no indication in this text that Moses becomes someone else or any indication of a transfiguration of Moses in this scene. I think it better to see Moses' enthronement, in terms of function, along the lines of Enoch's Son of Man — an exaltation to heavenly vice-regency. He serves as God's exalted right hand man, an image that suggests not only Dan 7 but also Ps 110:1. To put it another way, what Moses is pictured as becoming in heaven is what Moses is to be *in his ministry* on earth, namely, God's vice regent. Even the response of creation can be seen as a figurative way to allude to its submission to him in the miracles that accompany the signs and wonders that lead to the Exodus.

The emphasis in the previous sentences raises another point about this text that needs attention. This image does not appear to be eschatological at all, but a portrayal of Moses' work that summarizes his earthly career. The rest of the *Exagoge* depicts what Moses did in the Exodus. The forward-looking perspective of the vision appears to be directed only toward those events. In this sense, the text is not like Dan 7 or *1 En*. In other words, this glorification to vice regency can be read as a graphic description of the magnificent role Moses had when he led Israel into freedom. If this is correct, the portrait of Moses is not as comprehensive as the Enoch-Son of Man figure of *1 En*. It fits in rather more neatly with the other Mosaic portraits already surveyed, including explanations like those of Philo in Exod 7:1. Here is a regal "godlike" figure, who exercises exceptional power on earth in his ministry. The image may be slightly less exceptional on closer examination than it originally appears once its scope is properly defined.[87]

In sum, Moses is a highly exalted figure in Judaism. What is surprising is how little he is actually shown to be doing in heaven or from there. Most of the exaltation scenes relate directly to his ministry in leading Israel and receiving the Law. There is little actual future apocalyptic speculation surrounding him. Only his privilege to see the future judgment in *2 Bar* 59:4-12 and his role as heavenly advocate in *Sifre Deut* 34:5 § 357 even approach the edge of this

---

[86]For example, J. J. Collins, "The Son of Man in First Century Judaism," NTS 38 (1992): 450-51. For consideration of the view that the angel is Gabriel, see the Son of Man discussion below. The major obstacle to an identification with either angel in Daniel is that the author of this work is not hesitiant to name the angelic figures he discusses.

[87]It must be stressed that to say this of the early material does not mean this imagery was not capable of expansion and development in terms of later reflection. Our summary applies only to the bulk of the early material.

future boundary. When portrayed as seeing or sitting in heaven, it is to see what will take place in the future as a revelatory seer, a common category, or as a way of depicting the authority of his Exodus ministry. As such, this authority is less extensive than other examples we shall see.

David

The source of Israel's major regal dynasty is not the subject of much reflection, especially in early texts. One passage appears at Qumran in *4Q504* IV, 4-8.[88] The passage rejoices in the selection of Israel and Jerusalem as the elect of God: "For you love Israel more than all people and selected the line of Judah. And you have set up your covenant for David, so he can be a shepherd-ruler for your people, because of that he sits before you every day." The language is standard dynastic-covenental language, but the picture of David seated before God all the time is a sign of the honor David possesses. Interesting to note is that David is not seated next to God, but in front of him. Because the text is fragmentary, it is hard to know much more about what is said here. The text does not describe any activity for David nor can one determine how much figurative force this language might bear. Other texts at Qumran might supply some help to us in understanding this cryptic text. It is possible that it should be read like *4QPBless* 1-4, which promises no lack of a Davidic descendant on the throne and thus honors the line, as v. 4 shows: "For to him and to his seed has been given the covenant of Kingship over his people for eternal generations . . . ."[89] Thus, the *4Q504* passage may represent nothing more than standard hymnic expressions of Davidic, messianic hope. If so, it merely celebrates the nature of this dynastic line.

The remaining texts come from much later. The seating of David in heaven is controversially advocated by Rabbi Aqiba (c 120 CE), a view that appears in two similar texts in the talmud, *b Ḥag* 14a and *b Sanh* 38b. In *b Ḥag*, Akiba discusses Dan 7:9 and its plural reference to thrones. After citing the text, he says, "There is no contradiction: one [throne] for him, and one for David; this is the view of Rabbi Akiba. Said Rabbi Jose the Galilean to him, Akiba, how long will you treat the Divine presence as profane! Rather one for justice and one for grace."[90] This text was discussed in the previous chapter on

---

[88]The citation in German can be found in J. Maier, *Die Qumran-Essener: Die Texte vom Toten Meer*, 2:608. The rendering is mine. This text was copied around 150 BCE.

[89]On this passage, see Andrew Chester, "Jewish Messianic Expectations and Mediatorial Figures and Pauline Christianity," in *Paulus und das antike Judentum*, p. 23.

[90]The version in *b Sanh* is virtually identical. Rather than mentioning a contradiction, it reads, "Even as it has been taught: One was for God Himself, one was for David." The retort of Rabbi Jose is expressed as, "Akiba, how long will you profane the *Shekinah*?" Sanhedrin was discussed above in chapter two and the wording of the two texts for profaning is the same (עושה שכינה). For the *b Sanh* text, see the Soncino *Sanhedrin* vol. 23, p. 245. The *b Ḥag*

blasphemy. The view that David sits by God in heaven on a throne associated with Dan 7:9 is present, but also is challenged as an offense to God.[91]

In a still later text from the Hekhalot collection, the *Hekhalot Rabbati* §§ 125-26, David is crowned and ascends to the heavenly house as head of the kings of nations, a concept that sounds like a variation of Ps 89:27.[92] There is a procession of the kings/messengers[93] of the house of David before God with David's crown being the brightest and most precious. Its brightness shone from one end of the world to the other. He sits on his[94] throne opposite God and shares in praise of the heavenly Sovereign. Metatron shares in this praise with the angels. Here is a fully honored David leading the dynastic line of the righteous in worship of God. David appears to do little here beyond what the righteous do in heaven, sharing in the praise of God. It is clear, however, that he has been honored with a special throne as all the other kings bow before him.

In sum, David's presence before God in heaven is not a topic that has a clear line of development. He appears briefly in a Qumranian text that may well have only figurative force and possibly refers to the dynasty. Another rabbi rebukes the claim of Akiba that he sits by God in heaven. Only in the late mystical texts of the *Hekhalot* does he appear clearly as an exalted figure opposite God, sharing in giving praise to the Almighty with a lead seat of honor. There is no development of his activity there outside of praise.

Isaiah

The visit of this prophet, who is the famous recipient of a heavenly vision in Isaiah 6:1-9, is chronicled in the composite *Mart and AscIsaiah*.[95] The prophet in this text takes the standard role of the revelatory seer, but it should

---

text is in the Soncino *Ḥagigah* vol. 10, pp. 83-84. For why Akiba might have associated this seat with a human, see Rowland, *The Open Heaven*, p. 497, n. 66.

[91]It should be noted that the *Midrash to Ps 110* expresses two approaches to the seating language of v. 1. One view is that Abraham and Messiah sit on the right of God, as God fights their battles for them. The text applies to one figure in the past and to another in the time to come. This text was noted in covering Abraham. It makes no heavenly claims. The second view takes the seating as a reference to David's selection by God to rule over Israel, a very historically grounded reading. According to this exposition, David said his rule had to wait until Saul was no longer on the throne.

[92]On this text, see Peter Schäfer, *Übersetzung der Hekhalot-Literatur II §§ 81-334*. TSAJ 17 (Tübingen: Mohr [Siebeck], 1987), 2:56-59.

[93]The texts here differ between a reference to messengers or kings.

[94]A few manuscripts say simply "a throne."

[95]The dating of this work is divided into three portions: the martyrdom, 3:13 — 4:22, and the Vision of Isaiah. The Vision, which is the relevant portion for us, dates from the second century CE. See M. A. Knibb, *OTP* 2:149-50. The vision portion is Christian, as 9:1-5 indicates.

be noted that this portrait of the Isaiah 6 event is probably Christian, not Jewish.[96] In 11:34, Isaiah is told, just before he is returned to earth, that he has "observed what no one born of flesh has observed." What he has seen is the sequence of the seven heavens (7:1 — 9:18), the procession of the righteous (9:6-18), the opening of the books along with the promise of crowns and reward (9:19-26), the heavenly worship of God (9:27 — 10:6), as well as a review of the life of the Lord Jesus (10:7 — 11:33), a point that indicates the Christian character of the portrait. So the picture of Isaiah as heavenly seer is fully in keeping with what normally happens with an ascended figure.

Elijah, Ezra, and Baruch

These three figures are treated together, because their portraits are very brief. Elijah is translated in 2 Kings 2:1-12, but no details are given beyond his being taken up. This event is noted in 1 Macc 2:58, Sir 48:9, and is discussed more figuratively in *1 En* 89:52. Elijah is also the key figure in the *ApocElijah*.[97] The work is probably a misnomer. Elijah has "the word of the Lord come to him" in 1:1. This is standard prophetic language as opposed to an indication of a vision or preparation for an ascent. Thus, though he receives a revelation of the end, there is no heavenly journey associated with it. In 4:11-19, he and Enoch call for judgment on earth against "the shameless one," a purely prophetic function that he shares with the only other figure to be clearly translated in the ancient scripture besides him.

Ezra is exalted in *4 Ezra* 14:8-9 to live with the Son (Messiah) along with others allied to him.[98] So this is a mere exaltation of the righteous. He is a revelatory seer as he is told in the verses: "Lay up in your heart the signs that I have shown you, the dreams that you have seen, and the interpretations that you have heard; for you shall be taken up from among men, and henceforth you shall live with my Son and with those who are like you, until the times are ended."

Another revelatory seer is Baruch, but there is no heavenly visit in at least one of the works often cited as containing one. Two texts picture him receiving revelation. In *2 Bar* 13:1-3, he stands on Mount Zion and hears a voice from heaven announce to him the judgment of the nations.[99] This does

---

[96]See the discussion of this text under Abel, where 9:9 was treated. This example shows how some Christians handled this theme in reference to a famous biblical example.

[97]This also is a composite work, as its Jewish stratum dates from before 117 CE. See O. S. Wintermute, *OTP* 1:729-30.

[98]This work dates to the late first century CE. See B. M. Metzger, *OTP* 1:520.

[99]This work dates from the early second century CE. See A. F. J. Klijn, *OTP* 1:616-17. I note some of these texts, even though a heavenly scene is not involved, because some treat the material as presenting an ascension. See, for example, Segal, "Heavenly Ascent in Hellenistic Judaism, Early Christianity and their Environment," in *ANRW*, vol. 23.2, p. 1354, n. 76.

not involve a heavenly journey. Other texts note the promise of an ascension (46:7), but the revelation of this work involves visions, not an ascent (36:1; 81:4).

In *3 Bar*, the situation is different.[100] Here the prophet is clearly escorted through the heavens (2:1; 3:1; 11:1). Baruch sees the fifth heaven and sees Michael bearing the prayers of the saints to heaven and hears their virtues being delivered to God there (11:1 — 12:9; 14:1-2). In the Slavonic version 16:4, Baruch stands to the right and sees the glory of God. He also sees the resting-place of the righteous with its joy and celebration, along with the torture and lamentations of the unrighteous. With this revelatory glimpse, Baruch is returned to earth.

In sum, Elijah is not the object of a revelatory trip to heaven. Ezra and Baruch are standard revelatory seers, who visit heaven for a brief time and see the events of the end. Baruch's glimpse of God's glory is also brief. Their portraits represent standard apocalyptic portrayals of access to God in order to gain insight on the future.

Our next three categories consider deliverance figures to come or portraits associated with the fate of the righteous in the world to come. A distinction has been made between Son of Man/Chosen One and Messiah, though many would overlap the two categories. This distinction allows the consideration of what is emphasized about each.

Son of Man/Chosen One

This figure may be the most significant image to be considered in our survey. The two titles represent the key descriptions used for the central figure of the *Book of the Similitudes* in *1 En* 37 — 71.[101] Many of the basic features of the Son of Man's authority were noted in discussing Enoch, with whom he is

---

[100]This work is also a composite, making dating hard to determine, but its roots appear to go back to the first or second century CE. See H. E. Gaylord, Jr., *OTP* 1:655-56. The texts to be noted have the themes discussed in both the Slavonic and Greek versions unless noted otherwise.

[101]The distribution of these terms is traced by J. C. VanderKam, "Righteous One, Messiah, Chosen One, and Son of Man in 1 Enoch 37-71," in *The Messiah: Developments in Earliest Judaism and Christianity*, ed. James H. Charlesworth (Minneapolis: Fortress, 1992), pp. 169-91. He carefully defends the view that Enoch and Son of Man are to be seen as identified (pp. 177-85). He notes Chosen One is in 39:6; 40:5; 45:3; 45:4; 48:6; 49:2, 4; 51:3, 5; 52:6, 9; 53:6; 55:4; 61:5, 8, 10; 62:1. After 62:1 only Son of Man appears. Son of Man is referred to in three variations that all translate similarly: *walda sab'* - 46:2, 3, 4; 48:2//*walda be'si*- 62:5; 69:29 [2x]; 71:14//*walda 'eg^{w}āla 'emma-ḥeyāw*- 62:7, 9, 14; 63:11; 69:26, 27; 70:1; 71:17. On these variations, see M. Black, *The Book of Enoch or 1 Enoch*. SVTP 7 (Leiden: E. J. Brill, 1985), pp. 206-07.

identified in 71:14.[102] Here is a figure that comes to the rescue of the righteous and executes judgment from God's throne room. He is seated on his throne, leading to a note of triumph for the righteous. The imagery suggests that both the seating and authority are shared between the Chosen One and the Lord of the Spirits [= God] (Chosen One-51:3; 55:4; 61:8; of the Lord of the Spirits-62:2; Enoch as Son of Man leading in the way of peace and praise-71:8-17).[103] Yet the portrait is controversial and the identification between the Son of Man and Enoch is disputed. Though the initial treatment of this dispute was noted above in the discussion on Enoch, a treatment of general issues related to *1 En* precede the taking up of this question in more detail below.

Two issues need careful attention from *1 En*: the vision of heaven and the character of this figure's authority. Both topics show the imagery's uniqueness. In the background, however, lies the problem of Dan 7:9-14, which must be briefly discussed first, as that scene stands behind some of this shared authority imagery.

The Dan 7 image of one riding the clouds who is given authority by the Ancient of Days has always been seen as a perplexing text for a religious faith committed to the idea of one God. Four approaches have been taken to this figure as he is presented in Daniel.

(1) He can be seen as originally angelic. For example, Collins argues for Michael as this key figure, probably because of the pre-eminent role this angel has in the angelic hierarchy.[104] Fossum opts for Gabriel, noting descriptions of this figure as a person in Dan 8:15ff. and 9:21.[105] The view has well known problems that Hartman and DiLella pointed out.[106] Daniel is so open to angelic authority, why be so cryptic here or why excise it? Where else is Son of Man called an angel?

(2) Appeals to traditional Christian exegesis often read the text as exclusively messianic. The problem with this approach is Dan 7:18, 27, where the reference has a collective force.

(3) The most common view is that Son of Man is a corporate reference to the saints. The view gained ascendancy early in this century with articulation of the position like that by S. R. Driver, recently strongly affirmed by

---

[102]For a defense of this identification, see above discussion on Enoch. The factors noted in the current section apply whether one accepts this identification with Elijah or not.

[103]For this summary, see Alan F. Segal, *Two Powers in Heaven: Early Rabbinic Reports about Christianity and Gnosticism*, SJLA 25 (Leiden: E. J. Brill, 1977), p. 202. The texts mentioning the authority of the Chosen One seem to draw on concepts from Ps 110:1, 5-6 and Isa 11:4; see M. Hengel, *Studies in Early Christianity*, pp. 185-86.

[104] J. J. Collins, "The Son of Man in First Century Judaism," NTS 38 (1992): 451.

[105]J. E. Fossum, *The Name of God and the Angel of the Lord*, p. 279, n. 61. So also Rowland, *The Open Heaven*, pp. 181-82.

[106]L. F. Hartman and A. A. Di Lella, *The Book of Daniel*, AB 23 (Garden City, NJ: Doubleday, 1978), pp. 85-102.

Black.[107] As attractive as it is, there are problems with stating the view this way. In Dan 7 there is a universally recognized identity between the four beasts and the kings of certain nations (e.g., the lion = Babylon-Nebuchadnezzar). Thus the imagery has regal-national overtones. The passage suggests worship for the figure in question with its use of פלח in Dan 7:14, a term Driver too softly rendered as "serve" to avoid the theological problem, but one which Black faced up to in seeing a deification here. But where do we have precedent anywhere for a nation worshipped? If this is the meaning, it stands as the one example.

(4) This leads into the view I find most likely. The "Son of Man" is an otherwise, unidentified representative head, just as the other "beast images" have dynastic-national overtones.[108] This keeps the imagery balanced. There is a corporate-individual interplay here, because the figure represents the nation. This intertwining can honor the corporate force of the text in vv. 18, 27 and yet honor the internal interplay within the imagery of kings-kingdoms.

This figure, who shares God's authority, is a regal-like representative for the nation who is given judging authority and divine prerogative, even though he is described in comparison to a human figure. This description is vague and is capable of being developed in many directions, which is precisely what happened in Judaism. He is a transcendent figure[109], which is why many are

---

[107]S. R. Driver, *The Book of Daniel*, CBSC (Cambridge: Cambridge University Press, 1900), pp. 80, 93. Black has argued that this is the one place in the Hebrew Scriptures where Israel is "deified." See his "The Throne-Theophany Prophetic Commission and the 'Son of Man': A Study in Tradition History." in *Jews, Greeks and Christians: Religious Cultures in Late Antiquity: Essays in Honor of William David Davies*. ed R. Hamerton-Kelly and R. Scroggs. SJLA 21 (Leiden: E. J. Brill, 1976), pp. 57-73, esp. pp. 60-63. The position is grounded in the correct observation that riding the clouds is something deity does (Exod 14:20; 34:5; Num 10:34; Ps 104:3; Isa 19:1).

[108]The term in Daniel is a description, not a formal title, so I have put Son of Man in quotes here. Though overstating the interpretation in my view, W. Bittner, "Gott — Menschensohn — Davidssohn: Eine Untersuchungen zur Traditionsgeschichte von Daniel 7,13f.," FZPT 32 (1985):343-72, especially pp. 364-70, has shown the strong contacts between Davidic hope and Dan 7 in the imagery, especially in texts like Ps 110:1; 1 Sam 29:9; 2 Sam 14:17, 20; 19:28; Zech 12:8; Amos 9:11-12; Isa 55:3-5; and Ezek 34:23-25 with Isa 9:6[7]. His view that the Son of Man is God himself in his self-revelation as a ruling Lord overextends the image in my view. What is more likely is a representative ruling figure whose authority and honor comes directly from God. Thus the Son of Man's position can be intimately associated with God. I see the image as a development of Dan 2:44-45 within the argument of the book, representing an extension of royal-kingdom theology to its theological limits.

[109]Driver's description of his coming on the clouds as reflecting a "superhuman majesty and state" is quite apt; *The Book of Daniel*, p. 88.

drawn to an angelic view of him. Yet at the same time this transcendent figure is likened to a person.[110]

Just as Dan 7 is unique, so are aspects of the visions in *1 En* 14:8-25 and 70 — 71, which build one upon another. In *1 En* 14, the prophet is brought up to heaven where he sees "a wall which was built of white marble and surrounded by tongues of fire" (v. 9). Unlike other such ascents, there is no angelic escort for him on the ascent. This adds an element of uniqueness, though it may be nothing more than taking Gen 5:24 as is. He also sees a great house with a floor of crystal and a ceiling like stars and lightning surrounded by cherubim (v. 10; Ezek 1:22, 26). On entering the house, fear overcame him (v. 14).[111] Then Enoch sees a second house built with tongues of fire. It has greater glory than the first house he saw (v. 15). Here he sees a "lofty throne — its appearance was like crystal and its wheels like the shining sun (v. 18)." He sees that "the Great Glory was sitting upon it — as for his gown, which was shining more brightly than the sun, it was whiter than any snow (v 20)." Enoch's honor is greater than any angel since:

> None of the angels was able to come in and see the face of the Excellent and the Glorious One; and no one of the flesh can see him—the flaming fire was round about him, and a great fire stood before him. No one could come near unto him from among those that surrounded the tens of millions (that stood) before him. He needed no council, but the most holy ones who are near to him neither go far away at night nor move away from him (vv. 21-23).

Enoch is prostrate before God at this point, but is told to come, and so he approaches the gate head down (vv. 24-25).

It is clear that this scene is designed to show the inapproachability of God. Some see a contradiction within the verses that say no angel was able to go in and see his face and the reference to millions that stood before him, but this may be over-reading the text. What the glory and flames obscure is the face of God, which is still unseen. The angels that are near him may be seen to be at the gate, not in the house. In this sense the scene is unique, lacking the surrounding angelic hosts of a passage like Isa 6. What is important about *1 En* 14 for our concerns is that Enoch is seen as a unique figure and that,

---

[110]Actually one could read the background as either view (1), (3), or (4) and still make sense of what takes place in *1 En* in this work's development of the imagery. But this final view best explains the transcendent-human mix, which arises in later developments. At the least it does seem to reflect the way the author of *Enoch* read this imagery in that the transcendant figure had a human-individual connection as well.

[111]On this theme in such visions, see Johann Maier, "Das Gefährdungsmotiv bei der Himmelsreise in der Jüdischen Apokalyptik und 'Gnosis'," Kairos 5 (1963): 22-26.

otherwise, God rules alone.[112] What makes Enoch unique is the direct divine invitation to come in and see the God whom flesh cannot see.

The vision of *1 En* 70 — 71 is equally impressive. In 70:1, Enoch is again seen as translated "before that Son of Man and to the Lord." It was his last day on earth. Here he saw the righteous of old (vv. 3-4). Taken up again in 71:1, Enoch falls before the Lord of Spirits only to be lifted up by Michael (vv. 2-3). After seeing secrets of the heavens, he is carried off again to the "heaven of heavens" (vv. 4-5). Once again crystal and fire are present, including rivers of fire that are surrounded by seraphim, cherubim, and ophanim (vv. 6-7). Countless angels surrounded the house (v 8).

All the imagery up to this point is like *1 En* 14, but from here on differences emerge, including some detail that recalls Dan 7. Four angels — Michael, Raphael, Gabriel, Phanuel — plus numerous others are said to go in and out of the house, a point quite different from the earlier vision (cf. 71:9 with 14:21-23). With them is the "Antecedent of Time: His head is white and pure like wool (Dan 7:9) and his garment is indescribable" (v. 10). In another unusual move, the deity comes to meet Enoch. The prophet does not go in. It is at this point that Enoch is transformed in spirit (v. 12). Then in the presence of the angels (v. 13) he is greeted with "You, Son of Man, who are born in righteousness and upon whom righteousness has dwelt, the righteousness of the Antecedent of Time will not forsake you" (v. 14). It is here that he is installed and his role is specified:

> Everyone that will come to exist and walk shall (follow) your path, since righteousness never forsakes you. Together with you shall be their dwelling places; and together with you shall be their portion. They shall not be separated from you forever and ever and ever." So there shall be length of days with that Son of Man, and peace to the righteous ones; his path is upright for the righteous, in the name of the Lord of the Spirits forever and ever (vv. 16-17).

As different as some of the details are from *1 En* 14, it is clear that in this passage, Enoch becomes the focal point of peace and righteousness. It is the climactic reply of his visit to heaven retold because now the issue is not the detailed nature of the mysteries to be revealed, but the revelation of the greatest mystery of all, the identity of the main figure, the Chosen One/Son of Man. He is the head and vindicator of a host of righteous. He is identified with the Son of Man before all the angels. It is the climactic revelation of the

---

[112]Other brief descriptions of heaven occur in 18:8-9, where a sapphire throne is said to be set on a mountain; 25:3, which mentions fire and a mountain; 39:3-6, where Paradise and the righteous along with The Elect One are noted. See Gruenwald, *Apocalyptic and Merkavah Mysticism*, pp. 32-42, for a good summary of these two visions.

Book of the Similitudes.[113] The revelation makes clear why he is seen as such a unique figure, and why both his ascent in *1 En* 14 and his naming in the role with God's meeting him in *1 En* 71 are portrayed in unprecedented ways.

The identification with one who seemed distinct from him in 70:1 should not be seen as unlikely. The vision explains who the figure is with Enoch looking at it from the outside in 70:1. However in *1 En* 71 the climactic transformation brings him into the scene more directly, making the identification as the literary imagery is shifted accordingly. Given all the unusual things that happen in apocalyptic portrayal, this kind of a shift of perspective should not been seen as problematic.

So these visions with their absence of angelic aid to Enoch throughout, and their portrayal of God's uniqueness, and the unique greeting serve only to highlight the unusual nature of Enoch's honor and appointment.

This is why various commentators in assessing the character of this figure have described the nature of this unusual portrait as representing a stretching of the limits of Jewish expectation–a synthesis of significant proportions. A few samples will show the impression this text has produced. Alan Segal summarizes Enoch's Son of Man portrait: "It seems clear that the figure has been human and becomes both divine and messianic, although his heavenly enthronement aspects are far better described than his earthly tasks."[114] The messianic connections emerge from two texts: 48:10 and 52:4. In 48:10, the judgment comes because "they have denied the Lord of the Spirits and his Messiah." In 52:4, the explanation follows that "all these things which you have seen happen by the authority of his Messiah, so that he may give orders and be praised [powerful–C] upon the earth." One result of this portrait is that, as Chester notes, "this composite figure is represented as heavenly, pre-existent, and 'transcendent'. Thus the 'Messiah', to the extent that he is caught up in this chain of developments, is not a Davidic, human figure related to the present world, but belongs to the heavenly realm and takes on a transcendent role."[115] Black summarizes this way: "It must have been a bold mind, perhaps one influenced by Hellenistic ideas, which elevated the immortalized patriarch Enoch to virtually angelic status, and invested him with the powers of the manlike one of Daniel's vision, the role of the Isaianic

---

[113]Morna Hooker, *The Son of Man in Mark* (London: S.P.C.K., 1967), p. 44, describes the conclusion as "like a writer of good detective fiction, he keeps them in suspense until the last page."

[114]Segal, *Two Powers in Heaven: Early Rabbinic Reports about Christianity and Gnosticism*, p. 203.

[115]This summary appears in Chester, "Jewish Messianic Expectations and Mediatorial Figures and Pauline Christianity," in *Paulus und das antike Judentum*, p. 31. To clarify, perhaps, his remark about David, later on that same page he says: "Here the Messiah is not restricted to Davidic categories, and terms such as 'Servant' and 'Son of Man' assume a messianic connotation, even if that is not their primary point of reference."

Servant and the destiny of the Davidic king."[116] So Segal, in introducing the discussion of this figure, says: "But we cannot altogether dismiss the possibility that some apocalyptic groups posited an independent power as early as the first century or that other groups, among them the predecessors of the rabbis, would have called them heretics."[117]

In sum, the significance of the Enoch-Son of Man portrait is two-fold. First, it represents an unusually high level of exaltation for the figures we have examined. Other humans who sit, like Adam, Abel, Abraham, or Moses, do not sit like Enoch-Son of Man does. Enoch-Son of Man participates in shared eschatological authority, not mere elevation into a role for a time or the mere receiving of a position of honor. Enoch is a special figure. What is granted to him is almost unique, and could be contemplated, perhaps, because he was so righteous that he was taken up by God and spared death. Only the greatest of luminaries could even be considered for such a role. However, to take his new role, he still needed to be transformed into a glorious being. And, of course, he required the direct invitation and direction of God to assume his position. It takes an extensive righteousness to even contemplate this possibility.

So, secondly, the very height of his portrayal is significant. Here is a figure that is thoroughly transcendent. What little is said about his earthly function is limited to brief remarks like 52:4. What becomes dominant in the imagery is the greatness, even uniqueness, of this figure and his role. So great was the portrait that others responded negatively to it, as Segal's study has noted. For some, such a seating was too much.[118]

Messiah

The picture of Messiah could include many of the texts of the previous category. However, our attention now turns to explicit references to the promised son of David. The first two references come from Qumran. One passage merely cites a promise and does not allude to a heavenly visit or role,

---

[116]*The Book of Enoch or I Enoch*, p. 189.

[117]*Two Powers in Heaven: Early Rabbinic Reports about Christianity and Gnosticism*, p. 201.

[118]The Son of Man portrait of *4 Ezra* 13 adds nothing to what is seen here. The figure there is also an eschatological judge. However, the rest of the chapter is very different from *1 En.* Even though *4 Ezra* is a vision of what the Son of Man will do in judgment, heaven is not the focal point, earth is. There is no heavenly vision or detail involving the Son of Man other than the emergence of his disclosure before he does his work on earth (v. 52). So this text does not need treatment. On this portrait, see Michael E. Stone, *Fourth Ezra* (Fortress: Minneapolis, 1990), and his excursus on the Redeemer figure, pp. 207-13. He notes the difference in the portraits both within the book and in relation to other treatments of Son of Man imagery.

but speaks only of a permanent rule. It is the famous *4Q174* (or, *Florilegium*).[119] The key lines 7-13 in column III read:

> (7) And concerning that which He said to David, "I [will give] you [rest] from all your enemies (2 Sam 7:11b), (the explanation of this) is that He will give them [i.e., the sons of light] rest from al[l] (8) the sons of Belial who will seek to cause them to stumble that they may destroy them and [swallow] them [up], just as they came with a plot of [Be]l[ial] to cause the s[ons] (9) of ligh[t] to stumble and to devise wicked plots against them, deli[vering] his [s]oul to Belial in their wi[cked] straying. (10) "[And] Yahweh [de]clares to you that He will build you a house; and I will raise up your seed after you, and I will establish his royal throne (11) [forev]er. I wi[ll be] a father to him and he shall be my son." (2 Sam 7:11c, 12b-c, 13, 14a). This is the Branch of David who will arise with the Seeker of the Law and who (12) [will sit][120] on the throne of Zi[on at the end][121] of days; as it is written, 'I will raise up the tabernacle of David which is fallen' (Amos 9:11). This 'tabernacle (13) of David which is fallen' (is) he who will arise to save Israel.

This text from the early Herodian period gives the common messianic expectation of a Davidic deliverer for Israel's righteous at the end (Pss Sol 17 — 18). The Qumranian element is that he comes with an eschatological expounder of the Law. The point of interest to this survey is that this text looks very much to earthly deliverance and to the permanent establishment of a Davidic dynasty through the rebuilding that occurs at the end.

In contrast to that is an enigmatic text that has been seen in various ways, namely, *4Q491*.[122] The passage comes from a text that possesses little context, so that to whom it refers is unclear. Four views are held. (1) Maurice Baillet presented the hymn as a "Canticle to Michael."[123] (2) Morton Smith

---

[119]For translations of the text, see J. Maier, *Die Qumran-Essener: Die Texte vom Toten Meer*, 2:104-05 and A. Dupont-Sommer, *The Essene Writings from Qumran*, pp. 311-313. The text is in J. Allegro, ed., *Qumrân Cave 4 (I 4Q158-4Q186)*, DJDJ 5, (Oxford: Clarendon Press, 1968), pp. 53-54.

[120]Maier presents this portion as missing and reads it as "will be allowed to appear." Dupont-Sommer does not and gives the translation noted above. A check of the text in Allegro shows that Maier has correctly noted the omission of the text, which is missing three radicals at the start of the verse. Allegro gave no translation for the omission. Nonetheless the translation of Dupont-Sommer looks possible. in terms of the passage's sense. So also G. Vermes, *The Dead Sea Scrolls in English*. 3rd ed. (London: Penguin Books, 1987), p. 294.

[121]Another omission noted only by Allegro and Maier.

[122]For this passage, see J. Maier, *Die Qumran-Essener: Die Texte vom Toten Meer*, 2:559-60 and M. Hengel, *Studies in Early Christology*, pp. 201-03. This text is from fragment 11, column 1.

[123]M. Baillet, *Qumrân Grotte 4.3 (4Q482-4Q520)*, DJDJ 7 (Oxford: Clarendon Press, 1982), 12-72, esp. 26-29. So also, apparently, Stuckenbruck, *Angel Veneration and Christology*, pp. 150-51, who takes Baillet's approach over Smith's.

argued for an ascent of an unspecified person.[124] He argued against the view of Baillet that the described figure does not seem to be of heavenly origin, a point that is against the first view. (3) Martin Hengel has argued for a messianic understanding, which he rates as "most probable."[125] He sees in that passage a positive (or reverse) allusion to Isa 14:13-14[126] and an appeal to Isa 50:8-9 in imagery that cannot be a mere collective. In addition, this portrait is stated too positively without reference to persecution or sin to be the messianic high priest or the teacher of righteousness. (4) John Collins has recently held that it refers to the office of an unnamed teacher of the Law who is seen like an exalted Moses figure.[127] He notes the difference in tone that Hengel raises to object to such an application of the text, but sees it fitting into a different period of the sect's history in the late first century BCE. Exactly how that period might lack elements of suffering for this group is not clear; so that this identification is suspect. The glory of "king's sons" in line 18 and the higher position than the "kings of the East" in line 12 more readily suggests a regal figure, not a Mosaic-like teacher, though it must be noted that Moses did function much like a king. The mention of a throne in the passage also points in a more regal direction. Collins objects to a Davidic messianic background by claiming the text speaks of teaching, not of war or victory. However, the hope of a Davidic king who brings wisdom is not without precedent in Israelite hope (Is 9 – 11; Ps Sol 17:26-29, 32, 40-42). Regardless, the point is that it is regal, as well as didactic, imagery that dominates the description and suggests a regal thrust.

This text is enigmatic, so that it is not clear to whom it refers. Either of the latter two views is quite possible. Nevertheless, this passage could be still another messianic text. As Collins has rightly pointed out, it is not an ascent text, but an enthronement passage.[128] What does it say of the figure it describes?

---

[124]"Ascent to the Heavens and Deification in 4Qm[a]," in Morton Smith, *Archaeology and History in the Dead Sea Scrolls: The New York University Conference in Memory of Yigael Yadin*, ed. L. H. Schiffmann, JSPS 8 (Sheffield: Sheffield Academic Press, 1990), pp. 181-88.

[125]Martin Hengel, *Studies in Early Christology*, pp. 201-03.

[126]By a reverse allusion, I mean that what was a negative image in Isa 14 is now a positive image here.

[127]John J. Collins, "A Throne in the Heavens: Apotheosis in Pre-Christian Judaism," in *Death, Ecstasy, and Other Worldly Journeys*, ed. John J. Collins and Michael Fishbane (Albany: State University of New York Press, 1995), pp. 43-58. This essay appears with the same substantive argument in his *The Scepter and the Star: The Messiahs of the Dead Sea Scrolls and Other Ancient Literature*. The Anchor Bible Reference Library (New York: Doubleday, 1995), pp. 136-53.

[128]John J. Collins, "A Throne in the Heavens: Apotheosis in Pre-Christian Judaism," p. 55.

God gives the figure an exalted seat among "those perfect of the eternal beings, a throne of strength in the congregation of the godlike ones (lines 11-12)." "None of the kings of the East" shall sit there. "None shall be exalted save me, nor shall anyone rival me (line 13)." It is a seat among the "congregation of the righteous ones (line 14)." In line 15, he says, "who can compare with me in glory?" The statement of exaltation closes in line 18 with, "I shall be reckoned with the godlike ones, and my glory, with [that of] king's sons."

What appears to be present is an exaltation, enthronement, and transformation into angelic-like glory, apparently to the head of the righteous, having a position of honor that no other ruler can rival. The tone of the entire passage looks to an individual. As exalted as this portrait is, however, the throne is not equated with one belonging to God, but seems to have its own identity. He sits as the head of the righteous. There could be a hint of judicial authority as well in line 17, "in my legal judgments [none will stand against] me." However the line is broken, so one cannot be certain of its reading. The imagery does look similar to the portrait of the Enoch-Son of Man figure and seems to be of a similar quality. The expectation is that a unique eschatological figure will be exalted one day into a unique heavenly role.

The other three messianic texts are much later and can be treated much more briefly. The first text was already noted in considering Abraham, namely, the *Midrash to Ps* 18.29.[129] Here Messiah is on the right hand of God, as Abraham sits on the left. Messiah's position is initially seen as a place of higher honor than Abraham's until God's reply about Abraham's being seated, figuratively speaking, on God's right. The text shows the honor given to Messiah and Abraham; but beyond this, it tells us little.

The second passage is from *Pesikta Rabbati* 37.1.[130] Here Messiah is also exalted to the heaven of heavens. "The Holy One, Blessed be He, will lift the Messiah up to the heaven of heavens, and will cloak him in something of the splendor of His own glory as protection against the nations of the earth, particularly against the wicked Persians."[131] Words of comfort to Messiah come later when the Holy One speaks and says, "My true Messiah, do not be afraid of them [the opposing 140 kingdoms that beset him], for all these will die by the breath of your lips, as is said 'And with the breadth of his lips shall he slay the wicked' "(Isa 11:4).[132] Much of the sermon is devoted to praising God for what Messiah will mean for the nation. This description summarizes what looks like both a type of heavenly exaltation and the earthly victory of

[129]W. Braude, *The Midrash to the Psalms*, p. 261. This work dates to the sixth or seventh century.

[130]W. Braude, *Pesikta Rabbati*, pp. 684-90.

[131]W. Braude, *Pesikta Rabbati*, pp. 686.

[132]W. Braude, *Pesikta Rabbati*, pp. 687.

Messiah. Messiah is again seen in highly exalted terms, exercising judging authority in victory.

The last messianic text is from *TanḥumaB*.[133] This is an exposition of Dan 7:9. We cite Bietenhard's translation and then comment. "In der Zukunft sitzt der Heilige, g.s.er! (da) und die Engel stellen Throne für die Grossen Israels auf, und sie sitzen (darauf) und richten die Völker der Welt mit dem Heiligen, g.s.er!" Then the text cites Isa 3:14 for support. Later explaining the citation of Isa 3:14, it reads, "Denn der Heilige, g.s.er! sitzt mit den Fürsten Israels (da) und richtet die Völker der Welt. Und wem gehören diese Throne? Dem Hause Davids und den Ältesten Israels, wie es heisst: 'Denn dort standen einst Throne zum Gericht, Throne des Hauses Davids' (Ps 122, 5)."

What appears here is another judgment scene. The angel places the eminent of Israel on thrones and they share God's rule as the nations are overthrown. Most visible is the House of David. Strictly speaking, this is not so much a messianic text as a dynastic text. The entire scene is corporate as God vindicates the righteous and the nation by giving them authority over the world in judgment. Unlike other texts, however, the authority is shared. The thrones are heavenly, but are not equated with God's throne. Here is great honor, glory, and power, given in a more corporate manner.

In sum, the portrait of Messiah or of the house of David also involves images of great heavenly glory and authority. The most common feature is the honor of either heading the righteous or judging the nations. Dan 7:9-10, Ps 110:1, or Isa 11:4 seem to be the key images appealed to for this exalted understanding. Messianic or regal figures sit, though only in the late midrashic text on the Psalms is the location given as next to God's side. In one other later text, the honor is shared with the eminent of the nation. The hope of eschatological glory and vindication has led to this exalted description of the deliverer, who in turn is closely associated with the righteous.

Martyrs/Prominent/Righteous

This is the last major category involving human figures.[134] This more collective category is important to consider because it shows how the

---

[133]H. Bietenhard, *Midrasch Tanḥuma B*, p. 104. The text is from *qdsjm* § 1. The text is from c. 800 CE, but its roots could go back to the fourth century. See n. 75 above. See S-B 4:1210.

[134]For completeness, one could note two more passages. The first is a Christian text, *SybOra* 6.1-2, where the Son of the Immortal is given a throne by the Most High before he was born. This text describes the Christ. See *OTP* 1:406. The passage has a date range of second to seventh century, see *OTP* 1:322. The second passage describes Phineas and Elijah as making offerings for Israel in heaven. It comes from *Liq mi-Midrash Shoḥer Ṭov* on Ps 63.

righteous who get to heaven are portrayed. Some of the texts noted are composite texts of mixed Jewish and Christian origin, namely, *ApocElijah* and *TBen*.

4 Macc 17:17-20 pictures the righteous standing beside the throne, living in the blessed age.[135]

> The tyrant himself [Antiochus, see v. 23] and his whole council were astonished at their endurance, on account of which they now stand beside the divine throne and live the life of the age of blessing. For Moses says, 'All the holy ones are under your hands (Deut 33:3).' These then, having consecrated themselves for the sake of God, are now honored not only with this distinction but also by the fact that through them our enemies did not prevail against our nation and the tyrant was punished and our land was purified, since they became, as it were, a ransom for the sin of our nation.

Here the martyrs are portrayed as glorified offerings made on behalf of the nation, but now standing near God and living in his blessing. The passage is the basis of an exhortation to be faithful to the Law and to "your religion" (18:1). We are not told what else the righteous do in heaven. More specific is the Christian portion of the *ApocEn* 5:37-39, which has the righteous share in the millennium with Christ in heaven for one thousand years.[136] Also to be noted here is the portrait of the glorified righteous gathered together in heaven, an image from the *AscIsa* 9:9 already discussed under the section on Abel.

A key example of a righteous figure is Job. In the *TJob* 33, he is described as among the righteous with a throne in heaven.[137] Job is asserting his confidence that he is righteous and that his throne is with God. In v. 2 he begins to describe, "my throne with the splendor of its majesty, which is among the holy ones." This conceptual picture has much in common with texts noted earlier from Qumran, when the Messiah was considered. This is

---

[135]This text probably dates from just before the fall of Jerusalem; see H. Anderson, *OTP* 2:533-34.

[136]These specifics show the Christian nature of this unit; see O. S. Wintermute, *OTP* 1:726. This work dates around the second century, though the Christian additions might come from the second to fourth centuries, *OTP* 1:729-30. A general reference, probably from Judaism, to such themes for the righteous is found in the *ApocElijah* 1:8, as well as in *1 En* 108:12. The picture in *ApocElijah* is the same, except for a lack of reference to a Christian millennium.

[137]For the date of this work, see R. P. Spittler, *OTP* 1:833-34. He argues it belongs somewhere in the period stretching from the first century BCE to the first century CE. He also notes that some portions may reflect a Montanist expansion by someone who knew the Jewish text, a possibility that includes chap. 33, which is discussed below. The reference of one version of 33:3 to the "right hand of the Father" [P] makes such a suggestion possible, as Father is an unusual term for a strictly Jewish text.

not to argue dependence, but to suggest how consistent some of this imagery from this period is.

In v. 3 he says, "My throne is in the upper world, and its splendor and majesty come from the right hand of the Father" [so P; S has "God" and V has "savior"]. The claim that the throne originates from the right hand is not a statement of location, but source, since glory is said to come from the right hand. It is God's sovereign power that has created this place for him. So in v. 5, he continues, "but my throne is in the holy land ["heaven," as the parallel next line shows], and its splendor is in the world of the changeless one." Its permanence is considered next in v. 7 with, "but the rivers of my land, where my throne is, do not dry up nor will they disappear, but they will exist forever." So he concludes the portrait in v. 9 with "but my kingdom is forever and ever, and its splendor and majesty are in the chariots of the Father." The remarks cause Job's friends to want to test his sanity in *TJob* 34 — 38. The reaction is significant as it shows that the exalted portrait was doubted. What is less clear is whether it is because the friends did not number Job among the righteous, because the portrait was too grand, or both. In chapter 34 one of the friends argues that the evidence of Job's condition is a judgment that stands against his claim (34:4). But there is also considerable discussion of heavenly things and things "beyond us" (38:2, 6). In the reply one senses that Job is perceived as trampling on mysteries that cannot be known. A final complaint comes from Elihu in 41:4 that Job speaks "in boastful grandeur, saying he has his throne in heaven." Job then summarizes Elihu's reply as inspired by Satan and full of insulting words. Nothing in these final remarks adds to the understanding of the throne or indicates it is a unique place of honor. Job claims to be among the righteous in heaven, something his friends cannot believe because Job is the object of such a comprehensive judgment from God. So the exalted portrait of Job is unexceptional.

The exaltation of all the righteous appears in *TBen* 10:5-9, especially in v. 6.[138] It is a brief remark that comes in a section exhorting his sons to keep the Law. Starting in v. 5 the passage begins quoting the call for obedience from Abraham, Isaac, and Jacob,

'Keep God's commandments until the Lord reveals his salvation to all the nations.' And then you will see Enoch and Seth and Abraham and Isaac and Jacob being raised up at the right hand in great joy. Then shall we also be raised, each of us over our tribe, and we shall prostrate ourselves before the

---

[138]This work dates to around 150 BCE, except for portions regarded as Christian interpolations; see H. C. Kee, *OTP* 1:777-78. It is possible this passage is an interpolation as the verses are surrounded by Christian allusions in 10:5, 8 (p. 828). On the exposition, see H. W. Hollander, and M. De Jonge, *The Testaments of the Twelve Patriarchs: A Commentary*. SVTP 8 (Leiden: E. J. Brill, 1985), pp. 439-40. They read the reference to the Lord revealing his salvation in v. 5 as being an allusion to Jesus. See 9:2-3.

heavenly king. Then all shall be changed, some destined for glory, others for dishonor, for the Lord first judges Israel for the wrong she has committed and then he shall do the same for all the nations.

Unlike *TJud* 25:4, which merely mentions the hope of resurrection for those who had sorrow and those who were poor, this passage gives little detail about what happens. It merely develops Dan 12:2. All are changed and then judged — some to glory and others to dishonor. There will be a place of honor for some of the luminaries of the past (Enoch-Jacob) as they are at the right hand. Others will rule tribes, but all will worship God. This is fairly standard eschatological hope. Its significance is that the place of the right hand is reserved for the greats of the faith, though we are not told whether they sit or stand there.

The final key text is from *Wis* 5.[139] After describing how the unrighteous are judged, the writer of *Wisdom* turns to consider how the righteous are raised at the last judgment to honor, "to live forever," as "their reward is with the Lord" (v 15). They receive a "glorious crown" and a "beautiful diadem" from his hand (v 16, NRSV; "glorious crown" translates τό βασίλειον τῆς εὐπρεπείας, a rendering the parallelism of the next line makes acceptable). God's right hand will cover them and his arm will shield them (v 16). Taking up his armor (Isa 59:17), God will arm the creation to fight off their enemies (v 17).

Once again, there is not much detail here. The righteous are brought into God's presence and honored with crowns to show their acceptance by God among the righteous.[140]

In sum, the righteous, as exemplified by Job's claims, are given a place in heaven and crowned with honor. They look forward to a life of blessing in contrast to others who are judged. This represents the basic fate of those who are received into heaven. A glorified transformation, position and place is their reward

Summary of Human Figures

The survey of exalted human figures has shown a wide variety of views about who gets into God's presence. Most figures that see God are escorted there by

---

[139]This work dates from the first century BCE; see Evans, *Noncanonical Writings and New Testament Interpretation*, p. 13.

[140]One other later text that shares this theme is *b BBat* 75b. It says that the righteous are called holy "in time to come." In a unit praising God for the hope of the future glory of Jerusalem, the righteous share this position with Messiah and the great city. The remark comes in a saying where three are said to bear the name "righteous": the righteous, Messiah, and Jerusalem. The text cites Isa 43:7. However, it is not clear that a heavenly scene is mentioned at all here.

an angelic figure. The most prominent activities are to record the secrets of the future, to see them, or to receive revelation from God (Adam, Abraham, Enoch, Moses, Isaiah). If one makes a special trip to heaven, then the most prominent role is that of seer. Not surprisingly, worship is a major activity as well, especially for the righteous as a group. The righteous are also seen as present in heaven before God's throne, but to be able to make a visit directly into the divine presence requires more than merely being among the blessed.

Many are said to sit in heaven, though the variety of examples shows that there was no unity about this imagery. Most of the activity relates to events in the future, but even this perspective is not always present. Adam gets to observe the last judgment and react to the fate of his descendants one at a time (*TAbr* 11:10-12). Abel judges in an initial judgment, a temporary role (*TAbr* 13:1-3). Enoch sits to record the secrets of what is to come (*1 En* 12:3-4; 15:1). Abraham sits to the left of God in a position of honor (*Midrash to Ps* 18.29). Moses sits to receive a vision of authority, an enthronement related to his ministry of guiding the nation (*Exagoge of Ezekiel* 68-82). David sits to receive honor (*Hekhalot Rabbati* §§ 125-26), as does Messiah (*Midrash to Ps* 18.29; *Pesikta R* 37.1). Job sits with the righteous (*TJob* 33). The most exalted portrait is that of Son of Man-Enoch, who sits to exercise eschatological judgment with the Lord of the Spirits (*1 En* 39 – 71, esp. 70 – 71). Seating is reserved for a few, the great luminaries of faith. In some cases the location of the seating is not noted (as for example with Adam and Abel). In other cases, the seating is either on God's throne or in a location that is clearly closely connected to him.

The claim to sit at the right hand is rare, as only Akiba's claim for David uses that explicit imagery, and that view is challenged by Rabbi Jose (*b Ḥag* 14a; *b Sanh* 38b). But Enoch-Son of Man shares the same throne as God, though whether God is sitting as he sits is not clear (*1 En* 51:3; 55:4; 61:8). The image of an exalted Enoch appears to have been countered by other Enoch traditions arguing that he only observed and recorded the judgment, was punished as Metatron-Enoch, or even failed to be among the righteous (*TPs-Jon* to Gen 5:24; *3 En* 16:4-5; *TOnq* to Gen 5:24; *Gen R* 25.1). The exalted Moses imagery also seems to have received attention as needing clarification that prevented a misunderstanding (Philo, *Questions on Exodus* 2:29). These counter traditions indicate that some had a degree of discomfort with placing someone so close to God. It shows that though some gave position of exceedingly high honor to some select righteous luminaries, others sought to make sure that God's honor continued to be perceived as unique.

2. Exalted Angelic Figures

The second group of exalted figures, angelic examples, is important. To consider this group is natural, since they would be perceived as having frequent access to God. Though the category of exalted human figures is the closer analogy for our concerns, the way in which angelic access is portrayed adds to our understanding of how God is perceived to relate to those who reside in heaven. The survey begins with the two key angelic figures of the tradition: Gabriel and Michael. Michael's importance will become evident, since several other figures are often identified with him. These additional figures are considered immediately after he is. Then the remaining examples will conclude the survey.

Gabriel

Though Michael is the more prominent figure, Gabriel is also presented as quite an active heavenly being. In Daniel, he is an interpreter of revelatory visions (8:15-27; 9:21-27).[141] But the angel's role in Jewish teaching is not limited to merely passing on God's revelation.

In *1 En* 20:7, he is said to be among the angels who oversee the garden, the serpents, and the cherubim. In this text, he appears with a host of named angels, each of whom has authority over some aspect of heavenly or earthly activity. Among the angels named in this list are Suru'el, Raphael, Raguel, Michael, and Saraqa'el.[142] They are all said to be "holy angels who watch" (see also *1 En* 9:1). The angelic host serves God and helps to administer the carrying out of his will. In this work, Gabriel is one of the most prominent of those servants.

An indication of Gabriel's prominence also appears in a slightly earlier text from Qumran, *1QM9:14-16*.[143] The war scroll describes the various shields

---

[141]Michael Mach, *Entwicklungsstadien des jüdischen Engelglaubens in vorrabbinischer Zeit,* TSAJ 34 (Tübingen: J. C. B. Mohr (Paul Siebeck), 1992, p. 61. A similar "revealer" role appears in Lk 1:19.

[142]Mach, *Entwicklungsstadien des jüdischen Engelglaubens in vorrabbinischer Zeit,* p. 263-64; see also esp. n. 425 for other texts where these figures are named, including magical texts and sources in mysticism. The key group of angels often varies in number from four to seven. A list of seven possibly appears without names, but described just in terms of function at Qumran in 4Q405 (= 4QShir Shabb^f). For a translation, see Florentino García Martínez, *The Dead Sea Scrolls Translated: The Qumran Texts in English.* 2nd ed. (Grand Rapids: Wm. B. Eerdmans, 1996), p. 426. See also *3 En* 18.

[143]J. Maier, *Die Qumran-Essener: Die Texte vom Toten Meer,* 1:138 and Mach, *Entwicklungsstadien des jüdischen Engelglaubens in vorrabbinischer Zeit,* p. 252, though he erroneously cites the reference as 19.14ff.. The text is correctly cited on p. 214. The text is from the Herodian period.

on the towers that are to go out to battle.[144] On one of the shields, three cubits in length, is the portrait of Gabriel. He is given second position after Michael.[145] Apparently the portraits were designed to underscore the presence of the Lord's army and its protection. In this case, the role of protector is shared with other angels, yet there appears to exist a sense of ranking among them.

Yet another role is given to this angel in *2 En* 24:1-2. Here is one of the few cases where an angel is said to sit.[146] In a tantalizingly brief text, the following is said in recension J: "And the Lord called me; and he said to me, 'Enoch, sit to the left of me with Gabriel.'" The version of A merely summarizes: "And the Lord called me; and he placed me to the left of himself closer than Gabriel." As was noted in discussing this key human figure, Enoch is brought to God's side to record the events he sees. Now only the J version is clear in having Gabriel sit, while only A notes that Enoch is closer than the angel. This seating appears to be temporary and is related to the revelatory seer function of Enoch, with Gabriel, his escort, present to observe events with them. So it may well be that the angelic seating, if there is one, is

---

[144]Apparently a "tower" was a type of battle formation. See Dupont-Sommer, *The Essene Writings from Qumran*, p. 183, n. 1. It was a square formation of 300 foot soldiers arranged with a hundred men on each side.

[145]Gabriel's name falls into a lacunae in v. 14, but its presence is guaranteed there by its reappearance in a second listing given in v. 16. Two other angels are mentioned with him, Sariel and Raphael, in third and fourth positions respectively.

[146]In fact, in rabbinic tradition there is a tradition that angels cannot sit. See Gruenwald, *Apocalyptic and Merkavah Mysticism*, p. 66 and n. 137, and p. 60 and n. 113. Gruenwald (p. 60) notes a text in *AscIsa* 7:21, where an angel is said to sit. He argues that this defies Jewish tradition. For this text, he could be correct, since this work is Christian in its current form. See nn. 173-74 below. He sees the only exception as Metatron, and that is because of his connection to Enoch. See *b Ḥag.* 15a. He may overstate the case. For the tradition of no sitting, he cites one passage from *GenR* 65.21 (Theodor-Albeck ed., p. 738; Freedmann, ed., *The Midrash Rabbah,* vol. 1:597-98) and from *y Ber* 2c (= Neusner 1.1 VIII.E). Both texts declare that angels have no joints, while the *GenR* text says that there is no sitting in heaven for angels. Whether these later texts can be projected back into this earlier period is quite uncertain. It is true, however, that angelic heavenly seating is rare, and this view was seen among the later rabbis as dangerous to assert, see Segal, *Two Powers in Heaven*, p. 60-67 on *b Ḥag* 15a. For a full discussion of angelic seating in heaven which qualifies Gruenwald's remarks, see the end of the discussion on Angel of Light, Melchizedek, and the Heavenly Man and nn. 173-75 below. But it also must be noted that the exact origins of the two manuscript traditions of A (the shorter recension) and J (the longer recension) for *2 En* are quite obscure. Only J mentioned below has Gabriel sit, and it should also be noted that *2 En* seems to operate on the fringe of Judaism. See the introduction to *2 En*, by F. I. Andersen, in *OTP* 1:91-100. So even this "clear" text has a divided tradition and roots in a small wing of Judaism.

present because a human figure the angel is escorting is asked to sit. Little else is said including who might be on God's right.[147]

One more text from *2 En* may be relevant. Gabriel is said to be a protector of the righteous, as he is sent to protect a young Melchizedek in 71:28[A]. Interestingly in version J, it is Michael who is sent! In 72:5[A], Gabriel takes the baby from his father Nir and places the child in protection in Eden, a place over which he had responsibility according to *1 En* 20:7.[148]

In sum, we see Gabriel functioning as an active angel, being a vehicle of revelation, a heavenly escort and an honored angel, given a place just behind Michael. In all of this, it is his activity that stands out. The one time he is said to sit, it is with Enoch and is in a place of seemingly less prominence (*2 En* 24:1-2).

Michael

This angel is without a doubt the most prominent of the heavenly servants. So significant is his role that several other titles, like the "Prince of Light," the angelic Melchizedek, and the "Heavenly Man," are often associated with him. The survey will consider each of these titles.

The portrait of Michael begins with his description in Daniel. In 10:13, he is called "one of the chief princes."[149] He aided the man of Daniel's vision in fighting the king of Persia, a protective and battling role that will be common for this figure (see also 10:21). In 12:1, Michael is called "the great prince who protects your people." This seems to be a function of a national guardian

---

[147]Stuckenbruck, *Angel Veneration and Christology*, p. 129, n. 208, notes how the right side is empty and wonders if a Christian redactor has handled the passage at this point. Similar speculation comes from Rowland, *The Open Heaven*, pp. 94; 485, n. 47, where he suspects an interpolation with Christ at the right hand making the text not strictly Jewish. Rowland also cites the Slavonic version of *2 En* 24:1 and *1 En* 71 for showing belief that a human is involved in this scene; see p. 497, n. 66.

[148]Version J has the "Lord's archistratig" perform this role, which was Michael's title in 71:28[J].

[149]Michael Mach, *Entwicklungsstadien des jüdischen Engelglaubens in vorrabbinischer Zeit*, pp. 24-25. Major studies on this figure at Qumran include S. F. Noll, *Angelology in the Qumran Texts*, unpublished PhD thesis (Manchester: Manchester University, 1979), and Maxwell J. Davidson, *Angels at Qumran: A Comparative Study of 1 Enoch 1-36, 72-18 and Sectarian Writings from Qumran*. JSPS 11 (Sheffield: Sheffield Academic Press, 1992). A much older study surveying Michael is W. Lueken, *Michael: Eine Darstellung und Vergleichung der jüdischen und morgenländisch-christlichen Tradition vom Erzengel Michael* (Göttingen: Vandenhoeck & Ruprecht, 1898). This last noted study has been briefly critiqued in Hurtado, *One God, One Lord*, p. 72. The most recent survey on Michael is Johannes P. Rohland, *Der Erzengel Michael: Arzt und Feldherr: Zwei Aspekte des vor- und frühbyzantinischen Michaelskultes*, BZRG 19 (Leiden: E. J. Brill, 1977), pp. 9-33.

angel, a role the rabbis came to debate as they sometimes claimed that Israel's protector was only God.[150]

As chief prince, Michael is often found escorting those honored with a visit to heaven. For example in *TAbr*, he plays a major role in Abraham's journey.[151] He is the "archangel" and "Commander-in-chief" sent to inform Abraham of his approaching death (1:4A). The title "Commander-in-chief" occurs throughout the book. He visits Abraham (2:2-12), takes messages back to heaven (9:3-8A; 8:1-2B), and becomes the patriarch's heavenly escort (11:1-12A; 8:3-5B). There Abraham receives a vision of the future, the typical revelatory seer role for a human figure. Michael is the interpreter of all that he sees in chapters 11 — 14. A vivid scene takes place in chapter 15:11-15A. Here Michael goes before the Most High to report on his fulfilling his command to show Abraham all. This is done before Death is sent to claim Abraham. Michael leads an escort of angels to bring the patriarch's soul to heaven, bury his body at Mamre, and bring him to Paradise (20:10-14A).[152]

A similar role appears for him with Enoch in *2 En* 22:6.[153] Here the archangel escorts the great saint and changes the saint's clothes to those of glory. He also intercedes for him in light of the importance of the revelation Enoch bears (33:10A). Michael is called the "archistratig." The promised protection he will give to Melchizedek according to 71:28J and 72:5J has already been noted in covering Gabriel, who has that role in recension A.

The escort function for Michael brings him into God's presence to receive instructions and carry them out. There is no sitting in association with this role.

Another function present in the earlier material is that of protector, a role noted in Daniel but appearing elsewhere. Some titles appear for Michael in the midst of this role that show his importance. For example, in the *TMos* 10:2, he is called "the messenger, who is in the highest place appointed."[154]

---

[150]See the discussion in Ephraim E. Urbach, *The Sages: Their Concepts and Beliefs.* trans. Israel Abrahams (London: Harvard University Press, 1987), pp. 138-40 and p. 744, n. 17, who cites *Pirke de-R.Eliezer* 42. Urbach's work was originally released in 1975. This chapter is a survey of how the later rabbis dealt with angels, often reducing their role, because of speculations surrounding them.

[151]This work dates from the second century. See E. P. Sanders, *OTP* 1:874-75 and n. 13 above.

[152]In 14:7B, Michael only escorts him to heaven, and he is the lone escort. This is one of the few places recension B calls Michael "Commander-in-chief." This recension has Abraham see a vision of an angel driving six myriad of souls of sinners to destruction (9:5B). See Mach, *Entwicklungsstadien des jüdischen Engelglaubens in vorrabbinischer Zeit*, pp. 151-52.

[153]This is also a late first century work. See F. I. Anderson, *OTP* 1:94-95.

[154]As has been already noted, this work has a first century date. See J. Priest, *OTP* 1:920-21 and n. 68 above.

As the kingdom appears, his role is to avenge the righteous against their enemies. In *1 En* 20:5, he is named as one of the angels who watch, along with Gabriel and others. His function here is said to extend over the people and the nations. In the slightly later *TSol* 1:6, Michael, as archangel, gives Solomon a magical ring with a seal engraved on a precious stone that allows him to face the demonic forces.[155] The gift is said to come from the Lord Sabaoth in heaven.

In another text also noted in the Gabriel discussion, Michael is the angel whose portrait is given the first position among the shields on the tower of the army of the people of God in *1QM* 9:15-16. In addition, his role is defined in 17:6-7 as a ruler of the eschaton as he is said to be sent to the people to offer final comfort through the power of the "great angel," with Michael then named in the parallel line.[156] The raising up of Michael means that Israel will have dominion. But as Stuckenbruck notes, "Nothing here, however, portrays Michael as an object of reverence by the human community."[157]

Besides escort and protector, Michael is sometimes described as an intercessor and looks at times in later material like a priestly figure. In *3 Bar* 11 — 16, he is the interceding angel who goes into God's presence and as the gatekeeper of the fifth heaven, holds "the keys of the kingdom."[158] Michael serves here as the chief angel (ἀρχιστράτηγος) who accepts the prayers of humanity and brings them to God (11:4; 12:1, 7). In the Slavonic version, he brings their prayers (14:2), while in the Greek edition, he brings their "virtues" (11:9). Under Michael are a row of angels who bring him the

---

[155]This text dates from the first to third century. See David Duling, *OTP* 1:940-43.

[156]Maier, *Die Qumran-Essener: Die Texte vom Toten Meer*, 1:152. This text is one of the reasons many equate the "Prince of Light" so prominent as a victorious figure in the scroll with Michael. The role given to Michael here is like that described for the "Prince of Light" in *1QM* 13:9-14 as he helps with all the angels of justice to bring victory to the righteous. I shall return to this passage in more detail when considering the Prince of Light and Melchizedek. The other key texts are: *1QS* 3:18-21; *CD* 5:18; and *11QMelch* (= *11Q13*) II 1:9-10, 13, 16. The Prince of Light is a vindicator of Moses and Aaron, as well as the announcer of deliverance who executes judgment. See J. Fossum, *The Name of God and the Angel of the Lord*, pp. 185-88.

[157]Stuckenbruck, *Angel Veneration and Christology*, p. 150, n. 268. For him, the same applies to the treatment of Melchizedek at Qumran. The only possible exception is the exaltation of the figure of *4Q491*. Stuckenbruck seems to think that if the fragment can be attached to a context like the *War Scroll* then an angelic figure might be in view. I have already argued above that this figure is slightly more likely to be messianic, given that text's internal comparisons to earthly, regal figures.

[158]This text also has a complicated history and could reflect some Christian interpolation in these chapters. It is dated from the first to third centuries. See H. E. Gaylord, Jr., *OTP* 1:655-56. It appears that the Slavonic version is less subject to such alterations than the Greek version. See also Stuckenbruck, *Angel Veneration and Christology*, p. 178, and Mach, *Entwicklungsstadien des jüdischen Engelglaubens in vorrabbinischer Zeit*, pp. 140-41, 217-18, and especially 233.

prayers (12:6). The angel escorting Baruch to the fifth heaven in this book bows before Michael acknowledging him as "chief of our whole regiment." However, Baruch never bows before Michael. The key passage for our concern is 14:1-2, for here Michael goes behind some doors (Greek) or gates (Slavonic) into God's presence to deliver these requests. As he goes Baruch hears "noise like thunder" (Greek) or "thunder as if there (were) forty oxen" (Slavonic). Once again Michael attends the Lord long enough to deliver the message and then departs to do more of God's bidding.

Later materials also show this more priestly function. The new element is that now the angel bears heavenly sacrifices.[159] In the fifth century *b. Ḥag* 12b, Michael, "the great Prince, stands and offers up thereon [at an alter] an offering, for it is said, *I have surely built you a house of habitation, a place for you to dwell in for ever* (1 Kings 8:13).[160] And from whence do we derive that it is called heaven? For it is written: *Look down from heaven, and see, even from Your holy and glorious habitation* (Isa 63:15)." Present also are ministering angels that sing in praise at night but are silent during the day. Other texts also probably present his intercessory work, as *TDan* 6:2 calls him an "intercessory angel" and *TLevi 5:5-6* identifies the same figure as "the angel who makes intercession for the nation Israel." The angel is not named in either case, but the description by Levi looks like a reference to Michael. In *1 En* 40:9 Michael is said to be "set over all disease and every wound of the children of the people." Here he functions as one of four key angels. Raphael, Gabriel, and Phanuel are the other three.

This role had some controversy surrounding it. Some were apparently, as a result of the angel's high position, making sacrifices in the name of Michael the great prince. An interesting text in *b Ḥull* 40a complains about this practice, which is compared to sacrifices made in the name of mountains, hills, rivers, desert places, sun and moon, as well as in the name of the small worm.[161] R. Judan (c 350 CE) in *y Ber* 9.13a-b (= Neusner 9.1 VIII RR-SS) appealed for a different response by those in distress. The rabbi recalls this remark from the Holy One, "he [the one in distress] should not cry out to either Michael or Gabriel; instead he should cry out to me; and I will answer immediately." The passage then cites Joel 3:5. The potential exaltation of the

---

[159]Fossum, *The Name of God and the Angel of the Lord*, pp. 217, 327 and especially p. 321.

[160]In this text it is assumed that the earthly temple is like the heavenly one, which allows the citation of 1 Kings. See the next line of this passage. The great Prince is another way to call him a guardian angel; *b Yoma* 77a.

[161]Stuckenbruck, *Angel Veneration and Christology*, pp. 60-63. For this theme, see also Peter Schäfer, *Rivalität zwischen Engeln und Menschen*, SJ 8 (Berlin: Walter de Gruyter, 1975), pp. 28-29, 62-64, 70.

angels is met again with a critique of the practice as being an insult to the uniqueness of God.

In sum, Michael has a significant ministry in God's presence as the protector of Israel and the chief of the angels (*1QM* 9:15-16; *3 Bar* 11 – 16; *TMos* 10:2). He is so close to him that rabbinic warnings in a later period emerged, urging the faithful not to use him as an intermediary intercessor (*b Ḥull* 40a; *y Ber* 9.13a-b, in response to concepts highlighting a mediatorial role like those in *1 En* 40:9; *b Ḥag* 12b). Yet what is most striking about this survey is that in texts where Michael is explicitly named, he is never seen as stationary or seated in God's presence. He is always moving in and out of God's presence while doing his bidding. Even in texts that declare his involvement in eschatological rule, he is portrayed as active and fighting for the righteous. One has the impression that the angel's responsibility to do God's bidding keeps him quite active and busy! In this sense, the picture of Michael is quite different from some of the exalted human figures we have considered. Michael appears to possess open access to God, but only engages the Holy One when there is business to be done or worship to be performed.

It must be noted, however, that other descriptions of key angelic figures parallel the functions attributed to Michael. Those figures need consideration before completing the assessment of "chief angel" figures. Nonetheless, the scope of heavenly activity noted in the descriptions of Michael when he is explicitly named are important to observe, as is the fact that he does not sit in God's presence.

Prince of Light/Melchizedek/Heavenly Man

We consider these three categories together, because they all share "chief angel characteristics" and are often associated with Michael. These figures all have a major role in heavenly activity. The first two of these titles are prominent in the Qumran material.

The "Prince of Light" is a transcendent being who stands in opposition to Belial (*1QS* 3:18 — 4:1, 15-16).[162] The key portions of this text from 3:18-25 read:

> (18) And He allotted unto man two Spirits that he should walk in them until the time of His Visitation; they are the Spirits (19) of truth and perversity. The origin of Truth is in a fountain of light, and the origin of Perversity is from a fountain of darkness. (20) Dominion over all the sons of righteousness is in the hand of the Prince of light; they walk in the ways of light . . .. (24) And all the spirits of his lot [of the Angel of darkness- v. 21] cause the sons of light to

---

[162]Maier, *Die Qumran-Essener: Die Texte vom Toten Meer*, 1:173-76. The following citation is from Dupont-Sommer, *The Essene Writings of Qumran*, pp. 78-79.

stumble; but the God of Israel and His Angel of truth succour all (25) the sons
of light.

This well-known passage on the two spirits could well refer to Michael. The
parallels to other texts describing his role are striking. For example, in *1QM*
13:10, the righteous receive the help of the Prince of light.[163] In *1QM* 17:6-7,
"final succor" is sent "by the power of the Great Angel to the lot he has
[re]deemed, and to the servant Michael by the everlasting light; to enlighten
the Co[venant of Israel] with joy."[164] Thus the prince looks to be the angel of
the nation who fights their final battle.[165] This image underscores the fact that
this figure is sent by God and is a protector. But there are no detailed
heavenly scenes involving this figure.

More detailed description accompanies the portrait of Melchizedek at
Qumran.[166] These parallels with the Prince of light and Michael make the
identification likely. The key witness to this figure is *11QMelch.* 2:9-13. After
mentioning the first year-week of the Jubilee of the new Jubilium and the
removal of sin in vv. 7-8, it reads,

> For (9) this is the moment of the year of good pleasure (Isa 61:2) for
> Melchizedek, for him to be exalted in the judgment of God's holy ones to a
> rule of justice as it stands written about him (10) in the songs of David, where
> he has said (Ps 82:1), "God (Elohim) stands in the community (council) of
> God; in the midst of the gods he holds judgment;" and about him it is said (Ps
> 7:8-9), "Return (11) to the height above them; God (YHWH) judges the
> people." And when it says (Ps 82:2): "How long will you judge unjustly and
> show partiality to the wicked?" (Selah). (12) Its interpretation concerns Belial
> and the spirits of his lot, who rebelled by turning away from the precepts of
> God . . .. (13) And Melchizedek will execute the revenge of the vengeance of
> God on this day.

Here we see Melchizedek functioning as the executor of divine judgment in
responding to the cry of the people for judgment of the unrighteous. He

---

[163]Maier, *Die Qumran-Essener: Die Texte vom Toten Meer*, 1:145 and Dupont-Sommer,
The Essene Writings of Qumran, p. 189.

[164]Maier, *Die Qumran-Essener: Die Texte vom Toten Meer*, 1:152 and Dupont-Sommer,
The Essene Writings of Qumran, p. 194.

[165]Another possible reference is in *4Q544* 2:1-6, but this text is too broken and unclear to
be sure. See Maier, *Die Qumran-Essener: Die Texte vom Toten Meer*, 2:720.

[166]The key study on this figure is P. J. Kobelski, *Melchizedek and Melcherešaʾ*, CBQMS
10 (Washington, D.C.: Catholic Biblical Association, 1981). See also F. L. Horton, Jr. *The
Melchizedek Tradition: A Critical Examination of the Sources to the Fifth Century A.D. and
in the Epistle to the Hebrews,* SNTMS 30 (Cambridge: Cambridge University Press, 1976).
For the relevant Qumran texts, see Maier, *Die Qumran-Essener: Die Texte vom Toten Meer*
1:361-63 for *11QMelch. = 11Q13* and 2:383-84 for *4Q401*. Maier's translation seems to
obscure the references to Melchizedek. See below, n. 169, and the discussion surrounding it.

proclaims forgiveness[167] and brings the Jubilee. He is God's agent and is close enough to God's authority that he can bear the name of God and have Ps 82:1 cited to describe him, even though it originally described the prominent role of God himself in exercising judgment from within his council. In *11QMelch*, the angel Melchizedek carries out judgment in the divine council and defeats Belial (Satan) and his hosts. In this role, one can see both the parallels to the descriptions of Michael and the high position his calling involves, including descriptions that are more exalted than anything else given to Michael. Yet the parallelism of the roles as executor of the final judgment is why many identify the two, a correlation that is probably correct.

Rowland goes on to claim that the implication of the text is that Melchizedek sits on God's throne and exercises the divine right of judgment.[168] But one must be careful not to import imagery. There is no mention of a throne or allusion to it. Melchizedek does carry out God's judgment and revenge, but, if he is seen as an angelic figure, the execution of that judgment does not involve his sitting, but his coming to earth with the forces that execute the judgment and fight the battles for the righteous as *1QS* 3:24-25, *1QM* 13:10, and 17:6-7 show in the passages we noted for Michael. Nonetheless, there is no doubt that Melchizedek is a highly exalted figure, who is active like God's vice regent. In this role, he has a position like Enoch-Son of Man did in *1 En.*

Melchizedek is also described as a "heavenly High Priest" in *4Q401* 11:2-3 and 22:3. In 11:2-3, he is called a priest twice, while in 22:3 the description of him in association with righteousness recalls 11:3.[169] These texts are so brief that not much can be made from them. However, one can note that this mediatorial function is something that also emerged in the description of Michael (*1 En* 40:8; *b Hag* 12b).

A final mention of Melchizedek occurs in *2 En.*[170] These brief references describe him as the "head of the priests in another generation" (71:33-34A). In 71:34-35J, he is the first of twelve priests, "a great archpriest," who will perform miracles greater and more glorious than previous ones. He is both a

---

[167]See also line 15 and its allusion to Isa 52:7.

[168]Rowland, *The Open Heaven*, p. 109.

[169]Anna Maria Schwemer, "Gott als König und seine Königsherrschaft in den Sabbatliedern aus Qumran," in *Königsherrschaft Gottes und himmlischer Kult im Judentum, Urchristentum und in der hellenistischen Welt.* ed. Martin Hengel and Anna Maria Schwemer, WUNT 55 (Tübingen: J. C. B. Mohr [Paul Siebeck], 1991), p. 89, n. 127.

[170]On this possibly late first century CE work, see F. I. Anderson, *OTP* 1:94-95. The book is hard to date, with ranges running from first century to the ninth! It also is of a possibly composite character, especially in chapters 24 – 33. I shall not consider a much later (6th century?) reference to Melchizedek in a long recension of *2 Enoch* 23. For this reference of a miraculously conceived Melchizedek, who is later taken to Paradise, see Fossum, *The Name of God and the Angel of the Lord*, p. 183.

king and priest. But there is no heavenly visit associated with this office. Nor is he a transcendent figure of angelic nature. This is an exalted, human Melchizedek, making this portrait distinct from the other examples.

Melchizedek is another highly exalted figure in Judaism. Though he is not said to sit, he is a participant in the divine council and is destined to function as the avenging judge of the end. Only Enoch-Son of Man has a similar role, though the Son of Man figure is clearly associated with a throne in a way that Melchizedek is not.

The last portrait that reminds us of Michael is the "Heavenly man" who is the messenger sent to Aseneth in *JosAse* 14:1-12.[171] He is "chief of the house of the Lord and commander of the whole host of the Most High" (14:7). In this work, the angelic figure is merely a messenger, a role seen for both Gabriel and Michael. The descriptions of this angel recall texts like Dan 10:6 with his shining face and eyes like sunshine (14:9). This description of Michael adds nothing to our portrait of him, as it is strictly a messenger role that is in view.

In sum, the parallel Michael images of Prince of Light, Melchizedek, and Heavenly Man also reveal a highly exalted figure. In particular, Melchizedek looks to a figure that has a major function in the eschaton. But what is most interesting to note is that this greatest of angels is nowhere said explicitly to sit by God, whether the descriptions involve Michael or one of the possible alternate titles. As was suggested earlier, this detail may help us understand the Moses figure in *Exagoge* as not involving a deification, and it may have implications for the Son of Man discussion and the portrait of the exalted Jacob as well. The argument would be that if the lead angel of the heavens does not sit with honor in heaven, then any figure that sits by God must belong to some other category. It is not an angelic-like quality that allows them to sit. There is no clear evidence of a purely angelic figure like Michael permanently seated by God. In fact, there is something about the honor bestowed to exemplary humans that seems to be more important. Though angelic-like transformation comes with the seating, it is who the honoree originally was that is a key part of why they are exalted. The seatings of named transcendent figures inevitably involve figures that have been identified as having some human connection (Enoch-Son of Man, Enoch-Metatron). The honor, though great and contemplated as exceedingly rare, is directly bestowed by God and involves shared authority with him, but deification appears to say just a little too much about what is portrayed. It is everything but that. Yet it is so close, that the potential for it being misunderstood leads others to warn against such levels of exaltation. What

---

[171]For the date of the first century BCE to early second century CE work, see C. Burchard, *OTP* 2:187-88.

seems most prominent is the installation into a key function, usually a regal one like the execution of judgment in defense of justice for God's people.

Excursus on the Seating of Angels in Heaven

The issue of the seating of angels also needs some more attention. Three texts discuss seating of angels. The first two examples involve unnamed angels. One example involves the *ApocZeph*, where each angel has a throne that shines brightly in the fifth heaven. This detail is according to version A cited from the Christian writer Clement, *Stromata* 5.11.77.[172] This reading is corroborated in 3:9, where the angels who record the deeds of each person "sit" at the gate of heaven. The standard theme of heavenly recorder accompanies this seating.

The second example comes from the *AscIsa*. It is suspected that this portion of the *MartApocIsa* comes from Christian circles and is possibly of Gnostic character.[173] As such it should be considered only with care, since the detail might not reflect Jewish thinking at all. In chapter 7 there is a reference to a throne in several of the heavens Isaiah visits. In 7:19, one sits on the throne and has a greater glory than the other angels. When Isaiah goes to worship this figure the angel leading him stops him. Once again nervousness is expressed at not giving others honor due alone to God. The same action is repeated at the third, fourth, and fifth heavens (7:24, 29, 33), though here Isaiah make no attempt to worship the seated figure. The prophet apparently has learned his lesson.[174] These thrones seem to symbolize the one in charge of the heaven in question. There is no throne in the sixth heaven. What is interesting to note is that these texts are somewhat exceptional in mentioning angels (or thrones) who sit. Both citations come from sources of recognized conflated character. It means that these exceptions may be exceptional because their origin has roots in an angelology distinct from Judaism. Even if they are Jewish in origin, the fact that they involve unnamed angels shows that their seating is related to their "command" position in a

---

[172]Stuckenbruck, *Angel Veneration and Christology*, p. 97, n. 129 appears to question if this fragment can be attributed to the *Apocalypse*. This portion is discussed by O. S. Wintermute, *OTP* 1:499-500, who notes that the Clement portion is different than Coptic versions. It may reflect "a Christian recension" of the text, though he still connects its ultimate roots to the *Apocalypse*. For the Clement text, see PG 9 (Clemens Alexandrinus 2) cols. 115-16. Here the angels in the fifth heaven opnly call upon God. Nothing is said about their sitting.

[173]See M. A. Knibb, *OTP* 2:154.

[174]The discussion is made more complicated by the fact that "throne" might refer to a special class of angel. See M. A. Knibb, *OTP* 1:166 n. m, and Stuckenbruck, *Angel Veneration and Christology*, p. 94 and n. 120. *TLevi* 3:8 seems to be aware of such a group also. The Isaiah text still attributes a seating to these figures, as 7:19, 24, 27, 29, 31 show. But these angels seem to be of a different class than the figures who are said to sit next to God.

sub-level of heaven and not to some role in close proximity to God. In fact, in both cases, the seated angels clearly are not in proximity to God.

One final example has already been noted in discussing Adam. It is *Life of Adam and Eve* 47:3. Here Adam sits on a throne originally occupied by his seducer. This appears to be the major Jewish exception to the rule that angels do not sit. What is interesting about this text is that an angel does not end up on the throne, as it was reserved in God's plan for a human. Where this throne is or what is done from it is not noted in the text.

These three texts taken together, along with the example of Gabriel in *2 En* 24, show how rare seating for angels is. The human factor in many of the key examples indicates that most expressions in Jewish theologies of exaltation included the idea that eventually some humans might receive greater honor and have a greater presence in heaven than any of the angels.[175]

Yahoel (Iaoel)

Yet another angel who is said to be present around God's throne is Yahoel. He appears in the *ApocAbr*.[176] This angel is a messenger of God, who is to consecrate Abraham and strengthen him after the patriarch had lost the strength to stand upon entering heaven. Abraham comes to heaven in preparation for seeing the things to come (10:3). Yahoel is sent by the voice of God. In 10:8-17, we are told that he resides in the seventh heaven and is charged with keeping the seraphim from fighting with each other, to hold Leviathan, to loosen Hades, and to destroy those who wondered at the dead. He also had judged Abraham's father for honoring the dead. In 11:1-4, he serves as Abraham's escort in this vision and is described in terms like Dan 7 and Ezek 1, possessing hair like snow and a glorious face. His name contains within it the name of God as God (10:3) calls him "Iaoel of the same name". As Stuckenbruck has argued, this characterization falls short of a shared authority status.[177] He sings a song of praise to God with Abraham and worships God with him (17:1-21). He is portrayed as doing God's bidding in a variety of ways. As Stuckenbruck also notes, the description of angels in terms of Dan 7 and Ezek 1 is not unusual, so nothing should be read into that connection.[178] In sum, Iaoel is simply portrayed as one of the many angels active in the presence of God.

---

[175]This brief survey indicates how the claim that angels do not sit needs some qualification. It is quite rare rather than prohibited. See n. 146 above.

[176]This work dates from the first to second century. See R. Rubinkiewicz, *OTP* 1:683.

[177]Stuckenbruck, *Angel Veneration and Christology*, p. 219.

[178]Stuckenbruck, *Angel Veneration and Christology*, p. 219, n. 37 and p. 89, n. 111.

Eremiel

Similar to Yahoel is Eremiel, who appears in the *ApocZeph.*[179] Zephaniah is another apocalyptic seer who sees the judgment (*ApocZeph* 9 — 12). Eremiel is the angel over the abyss and Hades. His appearance is much like God's, in that his face shines like the rays of the sun. As a result, Zephaniah mistakes him for God and is shocked that God would visit him (6:11-15). But the misperception is soon corrected, as Eremiel warns him not to worship: "Take heed. Do not worship me. I am not the Lord Almighty, but I am the great angel, Eremiel, who is over the abyss and Hades . . ." (6:15). This text reveals the heavenly activity of yet another angel and shows how their appearance was so likened to God that an angel could be confused with the Most High.[180] It also indicates that for this author at least, angels were not to be given honor equal to God.

Michael, Surafel, [Uriel, Raphael,] Gabriel, Asuryal[181]

In *1 En* 9:1-11, several angels appear as a group. These "holy ones of heaven" bring the case of the saints before the Holy One as they observe the fallen angels sin against humanity. In alluding to Gen 6:1-4, the angels seek relief for humanity. In response, God sends Asuryal, Raphael, Gabriel, and Michael to execute various aspects of the judgment against the fallen angels, two of whom are named (Azaz'el and Semyaz). Once again angels are seen in their typical role of intercession and carrying out God's bidding with respect to judgment.[182]

---

[179]This work dates from the first century BCE to the first century CE. See O. S. Wintermute, *OTP* 1:500-01.

[180]Still another angel could be added to this list of named angels. Uriel, whose appearance is not described, also functions as an escort and revealer to Enoch in *1 En* 72:1; 74:2; 79:6; and 82:7. This angel shows him the various stars of heaven. For Uriel, see Mach, *Entwicklungsstadien des jüdischen Engelglaubens in vorrabbinischer Zeit*, p. 178.

[181]In the text for this category, the names in the various versions differ slightly. Manuscript A has Suraful. B has Uryan and Suryan. C has Ur'el and Rufa'el. The interceding angels are Michael, and Gabriel. Since the angels in question act in a parallel role as a group, this difference is not significant to our survey. Asuryal appears as one of the commissioned angels responding to the intercession.

[182]Similar to this intercessory portrait is *Tob* 12:15, where mention is made of seven angels who present the prayers of the saints and enter into the presence of the "glory of the Lord" to do it. The angel who reveals this information to Tobit is Raphael, who is one of the seven. He had appeared to Tobit in 5:4, but does not reveal himself until this point. He is sent by God and goes back to him after the announcement. He also makes clear that he is simply doing God's will (12:16-20). This is a typical portrait of an angel, the messenger of God.

Metatron

The last single angel to be considered is one appearing in the later text of *3 En.*[183] Though this text is late, as are others to be noted alongside this portrait, the image that emerges is distinct enough and yet similar enough to what we have seen to deserve consideration. The extent of exaltation for this figure created sufficient controversy that other texts attempt to circumscribe his role.

This angel is known as "the lesser YHWH." This title appears in 12:5; 48C:7; and 48D:1(90). In 12:5, this figure is being crowned and is receiving a robe. As he is crowned, God calls the angel the lesser YHWH before the entire heavenly household, with the explanation that the name is written within him.[184]

In 48C:7, he is called "the lesser YHWH, Prince of the Divine Presence, knower of secrets." This entire chapter has God describe the elevation of Enoch to heaven and his transformation into a large angelic figure of huge stature (70,000 parasangs, v 5; for his diadem, 500 x 500 parasangs, v 7).[185] He is "prince over all the princes" and is made "a minister of the throne of glory." He also is given wisdom and understanding to see the secrets of heaven above and the earth below (48C:3-4). His throne is placed at the door of God's palace (48C:8). God takes seventy of his names and calls him by them to increase his honor. God assigns ruling authority to him over rulers and kings, times and seasons, the arrogant and the humble (48C:9). Metatron is seen to carry out to decrees of the Holy One (48C:10). For three hours a day he sits in the heaven above, over the babes that die in the womb and those that die young, and he teaches them Torah (48C:12). In 48D:1[90], the name appears in a list as one of 93 names the angel possesses. Though the grandeur of this figure is clearly expanded in these later additions to *3 En*, many of the basic elements of the portrait are in the main section of the book (cf. *3 En* 9:2).

The book opens with a citation of Gen 5:24, the exaltation of Enoch.[186] Rabbi Ishmael (c 120 CE) then describes an ascent where he beheld the vision of the chariot. The angel Metatron, "prince of the Divine presence," greets him as his escort to the seventh palace and the camp of the Shekinah.

---

[183] The date of this work has been wrapped in some controversy. Most now put it late, in the fifth to sixth century CE. See P. Alexander, *OTP* 1:225-29, and his article, "The Historical Setting of the Hebrew Book of Enoch," JJS 28 (1977): 156-80.

[184] For the idea of angels who bear the name, see 30:1 and the note by P. Alexander, *OTP* 1:284-85, n. 30d, as well as Schäfer, *Übersetzung der Hekhalot-Literatur* 1 §§ 1-80, (§ 15), pp. 36-37 and n. 28 on p. 36.

[185] This addition to *3 Enoch* is apparently from the *Alphabet of Aqiba*; see *OTP* 1:311, n. **48C** a.

[186] On the competing targumic renderings of Genesis, see the discussion above under Enoch.

Metatron revives him after the rabbi collapses from seeing the glory of the seraphim, cherubim, and ophanim. After an hour of recovery, Ishmael was ready to sing a hymn of praise to God (1:1-12). The angel, who is called "Youth" by those attending the chariot, is asked how he can bring a person ("one born of woman") to see the chariot. The question recalls a theme also seen above in the objection to Moses' presence in *b Shab* 88b. The answer is that Enoch is from Israel and so is worthy (2:1-4). Ishmael then asks the angel about his name. The angel notes that he has seventy names corresponding to the seventy nations of the world, and yet his King (God) calls him "Youth" (3:1-2). When Ishmael observes curiously that this angel is greater than all princes and more exalted than all the angels, yet is called "youth," the angel explains with

> I am Enoch, the son of Jared. When the generation of the Flood sinned and turned to evil deeds, and said to God, 'Go away! We do not choose to learn your ways,' the Holy One, blessed be he, took me from their midst to be a witness against them in the heavenly height to all who should come into the world, so that they should not say, 'The Merciful One is cruel! Did all those multitudes of people sin?' . . . Therefore the Holy One, blessed be he, brought me up in their lifetime, before their very eyes, to the heavenly height, to be a witness against them to future generations. And the Holy One, blessed be he, appointed me in the height as a prince and a ruler among the ministering angels (4:3-5)

The now revealed Metatron-Enoch goes on to relate how other angels ('Uzzah, 'Azzah, and 'Aza'el) laid charges against him as being a human, whom some had advised God not to create. In defending the exalted figure God says, "I have chosen this one in preference to all of you, to be a prince and ruler over you in the heavenly heights" (4:8). After all of this background the answer finally comes to the question of the name "Youth", "Because I am young in their company and a mere youth among them in days and months and years—therefore they call me 'Youth' (4:10).

This text makes clear the unique position of Enoch-Metatron. He is not a pure angelic figure, but an exalted human transformed into an angelic status. He is given a place like that we saw earlier for Enoch-Chosen One-Son of Man. Other descriptions in the book fit this image. In 10:1-6, he is given a throne "like the throne of glory."[187] It is "placed at the door of the seventh palace," where God sits him down. Anyone who wishes to deal with God must speak to him first (v. 4). All the angels tremble at his presence (14:1-4). Later, he is called the "prince of the Divine Presence" who serves the throne of glory, the wheels of the chariot and all the needs of the Shekinah

---

[187]This text is from the Hekhalot material and is equal to Schäfer, *Synopse zur Hekhalot-Literatur,* TSAJ 2 (Tübingen: J. C. B. Mohr [Paul Siebeck]), 1981, § 13.

(15A:1).[188] With this description, he details the transformation of his flesh through fire into a glorious being (15A:1b-2).

The exaltation is so strongly portrayed that it also must be qualified (16:1-5). This text is strongly suspected as being added later as it is the only negative note about Metatron in the entire work.[189] Metatron is later dethroned. It took place when 'Aḥer (c 120 CE) came to see the vision of the chariot. Upon seeing Metatron, he said, "There are indeed two powers in heaven!"[190] God's response is immediate, "Immediately a divine voice came out of the presence of the Shekinah and said, 'Come back to me, apostate sons — apart from 'Aḥer!' Then "'Anapi'el YHWH, the honored, glorified, beloved, wonderful, terrible, and dreadful Prince, came at the command of the Holy One, blessed be he, and struck me with sixty lashes of fire and made me stand to my feet" (16:4-5). The entire account makes it clear that despite Metatron's great authority, there is only one power in heaven.[191]

---

[188]The version in 15B:1 is an expanded account. Here Metatron is the "Prince of all princes" and stands before the one exalted before all gods. He serves before the throne of glory and brings out a deafening fire, so no one may hear the voice of the Almighty. He escorted Moses to heaven on his ascent and bore the news of the nation's forgiveness when Moses interceded for the nation's sin.

[189]P. Alexander, *OTP* 1:268, n. **16** a; P. Schäfer, *Übersetzung der Hekhalot-Literatur* I §§ 1-80 (§§ 19-20), pp. 43-44 and n. 1, as well as esp. pp. 45-48. For the original text, see Schäfer, ed., *Synopse zur Hekhalot-Literatur* TSAJ 2 (Tübingen: J. C. B. Mohr (Paul Siebeck), 1981, pp. 10-11 (§§19-20). The rabbi's name in the *hekhalot* who reports this is Ishmael. If this is Ishmael b. Elisha, then he would also come from the same period (c 135 CE).

[190]'Aḥer was also known as Elisha ben Abuyah. He is a famous heretic in the tradition. These accounts explain how he got that reputation.

[191]Other rabbinical accounts express similar nervousness about this portrait. See *b Ḥag* 15a, *b Sanh* 38b, and *b AZ* 3b. For example, *b. Ḥag*, has Metatron reduced to a scribal role as he is given permission to write down Israel's merit. Then the text notes that there is no sitting in heaven nor are there two powers. The example is Metatron, who received sixty lashes because he failed to rise when 'Aḥer entered into his presence. Apparently Metatron's error was to remain seated, leaving the impression he was God. Note how the punishment in *3 En* 16 results in Metatron standing. On this account and its relationship to *3 En* 16, see Rowland, *The Open Heaven*, pp. 332-40. The version in the Talmud is suspected as being an earlier account than the one in *3 En* 16. On the dispute as to how central "sitting" is in the *b Ḥag* 15a text, see Stuckenbuck, *Angel Veneration and Christology*, p. 71, n. 69. In *b Sanh* 38b, the discussion of Metatron follows the Akiba thrones discussion that we already noted in considering the Son of Man. In 38b, the suggestion comes that Metatron should be worshipped since God's name is in him. The reply is that one should not be rebellious against God. On the history of the two powers debate in Judaism, see Alan F. Segal, *Two Powers in Heaven: Early Rabbinic Reports about Christianity and Gnosticism*. For the debate on the age of this tradition and an attempt to argue for an ongoing and even suppressed tradition here, see C. R. A. Morray-Jones, "Hekhalot Literature and Talmudic Tradition: Alexander's Three Test Cases," JStJud 22 (1991):1-39. This tradition can probably be dated with confidence into the third century, but may well be earlier. On the discussion of the origin of

In sum, Metatron-Enoch deserved to be covered in detail, because his exaltation is described in such detail and clearly produced a counter reaction. Like the Enoch traditions surrounding the Son of Man, the authority of this figure reached such great heights that other traditions qualifying it also emerged. Here is another figure of human-transcendent pedigree who sits executing great ongoing authority. Unlike Enoch-Son of Man this authority is not reserved for some eschatological end, but appears to be extant from the time of enthronement. It is also significant that he has his own throne, protecting the entrance to the seventh heaven and access to God, working as a vice regent-gatekeeper for God. He is not at God's right hand. He does not sit with him, but merely near him in heaven. This portrait also shows how close the major exalted mediator figure came to being described in ways that made him a virtual equal to God. That perception also produced a strong reaction as *3En* 16 shows along with *b Ḥag* 15a, *b Sanh* 38b, and *b AZ* 3b. Those who were placed too close to God or were made too much like him were always subject to a counter claim that attempted to reduce their status.

Angels

The final category for consideration is the angels considered as a group. The functions of the most prominent angels, the "angels of the presence" include intercession (Zech 1:12; Job 5:1; 33:23; *1 En* 39:5; 47:2; 104:1), some who "watch" (Dan 4:17; *1 En* 15:2; 19:1-3; *Jub* 4:15; *2 En* 18:1-9–the "Grigori" are the "watchers"), revealing secrets (*1 En* 60:11; 103:2; 106:19; 108:7; *Jub* 4:18, 21), serving and worshipping God (Dan 7:10; *Jub* 30:18), reporting to God concerning righteousness and evil on earth (*Jub* 4:6), watching over the elements of nature (*1 En* 60:11-23; 85 — 90; *2 En* 4:1-2; 5:1-2; 6:1-2), and protecting either nations or individuals (Dan 10:13, 20-21; 12:1; *1 En* 89:59 — 90:42; 100:5; *Jub* 15:31-32; 35:17).[192] A summary of angelic functions at Qumran is similar: (1) help in eschatological war (*1QM* 1.14-15; 12.4-5, 7-9; 13.10; 17.6), (2) participating with the community in worship (*1QS* 11.8; *1QH* 3.21-23; 6.13; 11.11-13), (3) helping to check the community for the unclean in both battle and worship (*1QM* 7.6; *4Q491* 1-3 1.10), and (4) guarding the community's well being (*1QSa* 2.8-9; *CD* 1.16-17; 15.15-17; *4QFlor* 1.4; *4Q400* 1 i 14).[193] These beings were perceived as a significant

---

Metatron's name, see Stuckenbruck, p. 71, n. 69. In *b AZ* 3, Metatron is a heavenly teacher who sits next to God himself. On this figure, see also Fossum, *The Name of God and the Angel of the Lord*, pp. 297-301, 307-14.

[192]This list is a compilation of the summary description of Russell, *The Method and Message of Jewish Apocalyptic*, OTL, pp. 240-49. Behind much of this imagery of watching or protecting stands Deut 32:8-9, as reflected in the LXX, where an original reference to "sons of God" is read as applying to angels.

[193]This summary is from Stuckenbruck, *Angel Veneration and Christology*, pp. 154-55.

and active liaison between heaven and earth. Some texts are nothing but elaborate detailed lists of angelic functions (*1 En* 9 — 10; 20:1-7; 40:9-10; 71:8-13; *3 Bar* 4:7 [Slavonic version]; *3 En* 17, the angels in charge of each heaven, each star and the sun; *3 En* 35:1 — 36:2, where 496,000 myriads stand before the throne and declare God's holiness).

A special class of angels is placed near God's presence. They are the cherubim, seraphim, and ophanim (*1 En* 61:10- along with "the angels of governance;" 71:7; *3 En* 22C:7; 25:5 [ophanim only]). *1 En* 71:7 is of particular significance, since it describes these angels as "the sleepless ones who guard the throne of his glory."

One gets the sense from these texts of an extensive, not always unified, view of angelic hierarchy. Adding to this sense of a complex hierarchy is a late text from *3 En* 18, where the angels give honor to those angels higher in rank. The list of angels extends for several chapters.

What stands out from these texts is that when one considers the entire angelic host as a group, there is little direct contact with God. They praise God, do his bidding, and are assembled in vast numbers, but only the major angelic figures are said to go into his presence or serve there. The angels as a group function as a vast congregation of witnesses who gather to honor God and serve him. They occupy the various levels of heaven and tend to be responsive to the angels who lead their ranks, as opposed to being directly accountable to God.

In sum, considering the angelic hosts' access to God is important, because it adds to the picture of God's holiness. Though surrounded by thousands upon thousands, only a few get direct access to him. Those that do get to see him serve to strengthen the links between heaven and earth. The rest are engaged as needed. In the case of the watchers who fell, it was their self-serving sin of taking the daughters of men and lying with them (Gen 6:1-4) that brought God's judgment down upon them. These angels stepped out of their role as servants and were judged. Thus the angels as a group serve only to underline how getting direct access to God is a rare honor indeed. His sovereignty is displayed by the rarity of the privilege.

Summary of Angelic Figures

The survey of angelic access to God is quite revealing. In many ways, they have less privilege than the exalted human figures we considered as all their authority is designed to serve God and provide aid to humanity. Key angelic figures include Gabriel, Michael and those titles often associated with him (Prince of Light, Melchizedek), along with the later figure of Enoch-Metatron. They are described as possessing varying degrees of access to God. Michael is most active in this respect as the prince of the angels, but he is so active that he is never clearly portrayed as being seated by God. Even in serving as eschatological judge, he is the leader of battling armies, as opposed to a passive, seated commander (*1QM* 13:9-10; 17:6). Melchizedek judges the evil angels in the council, as does the Prince of Light. Gabriel only sits when he escorts Enoch to the left side of God to record the secrets of heaven (*2 En* 24:1-2). Michael and Gabriel are far more active as escorts, intercessors, or revealers of heavenly secrets. The most exalted portrait is the later one of Enoch-Metatron (*3 En* 10 – 15). Yet his place at the gate of the entrance to God is controversial, bringing a string of other teachings making sure that this role is not misunderstood, if not rejected (*3 En* 16; *b Ḥag* 15a; *b Sanh* 38b; *b AZ* 3b). It also reveals another fascinating feature that was also observed with figures like Enoch-Son of Man and Moses. It is that the more exalted transcendent figures have a strong element of humanity that allows them a place so close to God. The angels were created to serve God and minister to humanity, so that they do not ultimately possess greater honor than the greatest of glorified human figures. It is a glorified human luminary who ends up closest to God, and even those cases are extremely rare.

3. Conclusion

Early Jewish views of heavenly access to God show just how respected and unique the deity was. His presence radiates with a brilliant glory and his honor is protected by an elaborate structure of restricted access, which only his sovereign direction breaks.[194] Though heaven is full of inhabitants who serve and praise him, only a few even get an intimate glimpse of his presence. Those who get to sit in his presence are directed to do so.

The list of those who sit is a select one, consisting either of the great luminaries of the past or of anticipated eschatological luminaries of the future who sometimes represent a mixing of transcendent-human qualities. When it comes to the angels, only Gabriel is said to sit next to God's presence, and that is merely as Enoch's escort (*2 En* 24:1-3). But even this text is not entirely free of suspicion as a Christian interpolation (see n. 147 above).

---

[194]This survey has not even noted how access to God was also restricted by various barriers put in the way of getting to heaven. Not only is there fire, but some texts discuss a variety of obstacles, including a curtain, a host of avenging angels, as well as intense cold and heat. A famous talmudic text on how difficult it is to get access to God appears in *b Ḥag* 14b, 15b, where four rabbis attempt to see God and only one barely survives to tell the story. It discusses the obstacles to getting close to God. The account has several parallels (*t Ḥag* 2.3; *y Ḥag.* 77b). These traditions have not been treated because they appear in later materials. They serve to underscore how rare such access is and that the ascents associated with such visits were only temporary.

Those angels who share in the heavenly council appear to function as a "first among equals" and are sent to carry out a judgment that God has authorized (*11QMelch* 2:9-11, 13-14). When it comes to angels, getting into God's presence relates to service and worship, not sitting.

But what can be said of human figures? Adam, Abel, Enoch, Abraham, Moses, David, Job, the Messiah, Enoch-Son of Man, Enoch-Metatron are said to sit. Enoch sits to receive revelation about the end (*Jub* 4:20; *TAbr* 11:3-8[B]; *2 En* 24:1-3). Adam and Abraham serve as witnesses to the judgment (*TAbr* 10 — 12). Adam is reinstated to the authority he had before the Fall (*Life of Adam and Eve* 47:3; *ApocMos* 39:2-3). Job, whose seating is disputed, argues he gets a seat as one of the righteous (*TJob* 34 — 38). In another text, Abraham also accompanies Messiah for his seating, with Abraham on the left and Messiah on the right (*MidrashPs* 18.29). It is a seating representing honor and reward. Messianic seating is also probably noted at Qumran, as the Messiah is given honor worthy of the deliverer who is seated as the first of kings among the righteous in heaven (*4Q491* 1.13-17). Another Qumranian text has David seated before God on Israel's throne, as an expression of honor to the head of the dynasty and as leader of the righteous (*4Q 504* frag. 2 IV.6). Here is great honor, but it seems to fall short of a vice regency, looking more like a reward for faithfulness. Still another Davidic text comes from a suggestion by Akiba that David sits by God in heaven. This is strongly rejected by another rabbi as a major offense against God (*b Ḥag* 14a; *b Sanh* 38b). Abel exercises a temporary role as a judge in the end (*TAbr* 13:2).

The most significant exaltation scenes involve Moses and the transformed Enoch figures (Son of Man and Metatron). Moses is enthroned with great authority, but his exalted role is merely a metaphorical picture of his authority in establishing the nation (*Exagoge* 68-89). The references to his "deification" appear to be explained by his function as God's powerful agent, so he is "like a god before Pharoah" (Exod 7:1; Philo, *Life of Moses* 1.155-62; *The Worse Attacks the Better* 160-62; *Sacrifices of Abel and Cain* 9 – 10). Thus, the Moses imagery turns out on closer examination to be less exceptional than it first appears.

Enoch-Metatron is given great authority over heavenly affairs, but he also is disciplined when that authority is misused in a way that might confuse him with God (*3 En* 3 — 16). This late text tells us how comprehensive the high exaltation texts could be, especially in some of the later texts. It also indicates the intense fear and reaction such exaltation texts produced when they were seen as giving too exalted a position to someone other than God.

Only Enoch-Son of Man is portrayed as the great eschatological judge of the end, seated next to God (*1 En* 45:3; 51:3; 61:8; 62:2-6; 70:27, especially 46:1-3 and 71:1-17). It is a remarkably unique picture.

As noted, these final two portraits of Enoch-Metatron and Enoch-Son of Man produced controversy. These figures appear in other passages in ways that show great nervousness about the extent of exaltation attributed to them (*TAbr* 11:3-8 [B]- for Enoch; *3 En* 16; *b Ḥag* 15a; *b Sanh* 38b; and *b AZ 3b*- for Metatron). God's honor is unique and is not to be confused with anyone else's status. To equate anyone else with God is to risk thinking blasphemously.

In sum, it is clear that for some within Judaism, being seated by God was possible, but it was limited to very few and usually involved very limited circumstances. With the one exception of Gabriel, all those who sit are human luminaries or humans transformed into a new, glorious heavenly form and role. The highest forms of exaltation apparently also met with some strong opposition or clear qualification of such claims. When one places these few examples of seating around the numerous references to a wide array of other types of heavenly activity and the few texts disputing such claims, it is evident just how rare and privileged the honor is. It takes God's direct intervention and invitation to permit it, and all such authority is still derived authority. Some get close to God at his direction and as an expression of their significance in some key phase in God's plan. But candidates do not apply for the role nor do they claim it for themselves. Only God can direct such a seating.

Now only one set of questions remains. How do the background study of blasphemy and the views surrounding access to God impact the understanding of the Jewish examination of Jesus? How would the Jewish leadership have received his self-claim to be given a seat at the right hand of God?

Chapter IV

Blasphemy and the Jewish Examination of Jesus in Mark

Our study now considers whether the previous examinations of blasphemy and going into God's presence in Judaism help us define the nature of Jesus' blasphemy as outlined in Mark's portrait of the Jewish examination of Jesus in 14:61-62. Our problem and the current state of the discussion is stated most clearly and succinctly by Donald Juel as he reflects upon the mishnaic charge of blasphemy as recorded in *m Sanh* 7.5, which requires pronunciation of the divine name for blasphemy to be present:

> If this second-century conception of blasphemy is an appropriate reflection of early first-century legal standards, it is impossible that Jesus could have been legally condemned for this offence. In fact, his response to the question of the high priest contains clear indications of respectful avoidance of the name of God ("The right hand of power"). Most scholars insist, therefore, that the legal definition of blasphemy must have been considerably broader in the first century. The difficulty with such proposals is the lack of source material for reconstructing legal practice prior to A.D. 70 . . .. Even if the broadest definition of blasphemy be accepted, however, the problem is far from solved. It is still unclear precisely what in the question of the high priest or Jesus' response would constitute a blasphemous statement or claim."[1]

Juel's remark is stated with care. What we lack are sources that give us details of the *legal* practice before 70 CE. However, we do have, as the second chapter above showed, a significant amount of material that describes Jewish views of blasphemy in this period as a *cultural* matter, and with a consistency that suggests it was a widely held view, even among Judaism's religious leaders. This chapter will contend that this cultural background is pervasive enough to indicate what in Jesus' response "would constitute a blasphemous statement or claim" for his distinguished inquisitors.

The consideration of Mark's account proceeds in five major steps, though the first is in many ways a prolegomena. First, I consider the general function of the account in Mark's gospel, apart from issues of detailed historicity. I argue that Mark has two major concerns.

---

[1]Donald Juel, *Messiah and the Temple: The Trial of Jesus in the Gospel of Mark*, SBLDS 31 (Missoula, Mont.: Scholars Press, 1977), pp. 97-98.

(1) There is some interest in detailing how Jesus came to be executed. What issues were at the center of the storm between him and the Jewish officials? Mark does have a broad historical concern in his account to show both Jesus' innocence and the basis of his execution. It follows his attempt to detail the various disputes that have undergirded the ongoing tension between Jesus and the leadership during his ministry. Issues like the authority to heal and forgive sins, purity, legal disputes, the tensions surrounding the temple, and the disputes of the last days in Jerusalem fit in here. Even viewed from the standpoint of a narrative, they set the stage for this decisive meeting. There is even an interesting kind of "Son of Man/blasphemy" bracket in Mark. It binds the first Jewish dispute with Jesus in Mark 2:1-12, which leads to a charge of blasphemy against him for claiming to forgive sin to the final dispute in the examination scene of 14:60-64. In this final text the claim concerning the Son of Man, among other terms, reappears with fresh force in terms that speak of heavenly exaltation. But the very fact the narrative slows down to a crawl at this key point indicates Mark's concern to communicate some detail about these events. I will not develop this point, as it becomes a burden of the rest of the chapter. How careful Mark's work was in more detail is something that requires careful examination. Mark's pastoral concerns, which certainly also exist, do not necessarily rule out the possibility that he also possessed some historical concern as well. Too often the two themes of pastoral theology and history are assumed to be in a kind of exclusive competition, where the presence of one precludes the other. Could the consistent narrative tension also reflect a historical concern? I hope in this chapter to make a case for their union, at least in this section of Mark.

(2) Nevertheless, Mark was also interested in an important pastoral point, portraying Jesus as the model disciple who is unjustly persecuted while trusting God.[2] Disciples can study his experience to see how they should walk and what they might face. Jesus is one who simply offers his powerful confession when asked. In the content, tone, and strength of Jesus' response

---

[2]A specific determination about the date and setting of Mark is part of a long, complex debate that I cannot resolve here. The preponderance of the evidence, mostly external in nature, does suggest that the gospel was written by a companion of Peter, John Mark, in Rome for the largely Gentile community undergoing the threat of significant persecution sometime in the sixties. The external evidence could support any date from the outbreak of the Neronian persecution. For a date of AD 65-67, see C. E. B. Cranfield, *The Gospel according to St Mark*, The Cambridge New Testament Commentary (Cambridge: Cambridge University Press, 1959), pp. 3-9; for a date of AD 68-69, Martin Hengel, *Studies in the Gospel of Mark*, trans. John Bowden (Philadelphia: Fortress Press, 1985), pp. 1-30, has a full discussion of the ancient sources. For our purposes what is important is not fixing the date, but the general setting in the context of persecution, a point about which there is little dispute. As Cranfield states on p 14: "The purposes which are special to Mark would seem to be to supply the catechetical and liturgical needs of the church in Rome, to support its faith in the face of the threat of martyrdom and to provide material for missionary preachers."

lies the example. Both points, history and pastoral theology, are important to Mark's portrayal of these key events. What has produced skepticism about the scene is the way in which christological designations pile up in the interrogation. For many, Mark is simply reflecting the christology of his own time, not that of Jesus at the examination. This issue shall be addressed directly when questions related to possible sources of transmission and authenticity are directly treated in a later section.

With the backdrop of Marcan narrative and pastoral concerns noted, I move to consider the historical elements of Mark's presentation more closely in sections two through five. So secondly, I critique an assumption that has clouded the way many have examined this scene, namely that the scene reports a Jewish capital trial. Thirdly, I consider potential sources for the saying and the blasphemy itself. Here I only ask if it is possible that the saying could reflect knowledge of the Jewish examination of Jesus. Could there exist a chain of transmission for the saying? Fourthly, I consider the saying itself and the issue of blasphemy in it. An attempt will be made to define the various elements of the perceived blasphemy in Jesus' reply. It is here that I apply the historical background already considered in the previous chapters of this study. At the least, the study should indicate what cultural assumptions Mark's presentation of the blasphemy involved and how he saw this key dispute. It would seem clear that this is how Mark framed his argument, whether he got the actual history right or not. Was he playing off of cultural considerations that make some sense of the dispute as he saw it at the time he wrote? If such sensitivities reflect a careful reading of Jewish culture and theological perspective, then might that suggest Mark's framing is rooted in knowledge of the dispute from an earlier time? Finally, come the consideration of the saying as a whole and the nature of its historical character. It is at this point that various issues that are a part of the saying's analysis must be considered: the role and sensibility of the temple charge, the "Jewish" expressions in the scene, the use of Ps 110:1 and Dan 7:13, the apocalyptic Son of Man and Jesus, and the combination and relationship of titles present in the question and the reply. Only within a consideration of these questions can the issue of the actual historical verisimilitude of the scene to an event in the life of Jesus be evaluated.

1. The Pastoral Function of the Examination Scene within Mark

The Jewish examination of Jesus performs a major function in the Marcan narrative.[3] G. B. Caird has put the Marcan question in terms of the purpose of the entire gospel this way: "Why must the followers of Jesus suffer? Why, if he was the promised Messiah, did he suffer, and why should Gentiles believe in him if his own people have rejected him?"[4] Put in this light, the question of the Jewish examination serves to explain the path to suffering and the cross. Jesus as the model disciple is a theme developed by Philip Davis, as he compares what Mark contains versus the omissions in Matthew and Luke.[5] Davis argues that the absence of an infancy account or a detailed presentation of the resurrection leaves the predictions of resurrection in Mk 8:31; 9:9, 31; 10:34 and 14:28 as resolved in the declared accomplishment of resurrection noted in 16:6-7. The effect is a story starting with baptism that moves through various scenes of temptation and opposition and which "culminates in suffering and death toward an as-yet unseen vindication."[6] If God kept his promise for Jesus, he will keep it for the disciple who follows Jesus' path.

The Marcan contrast between Jesus and Peter during the time of the examination in 14:53-72 also underscores this theme, as Jesus refuses to wilt to the pressure of trial as Peter does (esp. vv 66-72).[7] The disciples should be prepared to follow him in suffering (10:39; 13:9; 14:36). The Spirit will give utterance to what one must say when brought before the tribunal (13:9-12). So Jesus' confession in 14:62 is his only statement of defense as he endures his unjust suffering. Hurtado develops this point:

---

[3]Most commentaries do not consider the Marcan account from the standpoint of its narration, being more consumed with questions of the scene's historical detail or the meaning of the scene itself for Mark, especially for his christology. These approaches to the scene where discussed in chapter one. Only recently has focused attention been given to this area of study, which seeks to place the scene more significantly into the whole of Mark's presentation.

[4]G. B. Caird, *New Testament Theology*, completed and edited by L. D. Hurst (Oxford: Clarendon Press, 1994), p. 53.

[5]P. Davis, "Christology, Discipleship, and Self Understanding in the Gospel of Mark," in *Self-Definition and Self-Discovery in Early Christianity: A Case of Shifting Horizons. Essays in Appreciation of Ben F. Meyer from his former Students,* ed. D. Hawkin and T. Robinson (Lewiston: Mellen, 1990), pp. 101-19.

[6]P. Davis, "Christology, Discipleship, and Self Understanding in the Gospel of Mark," p. 109. He notes that the omissions tend to involve events that are not subject to imitation.

[7]For a fuller development of how the theme of Peter's failure fits into Marcan teaching on discipleship and the example of the Twelve in failing to get things right during Jesus' ministry, see L. Hurtado, "Following Jesus in the Gospel of Mark – and Beyond," in *Patterns of Discipleship in the New Testament*, ed. Richard N. Longenecker, McMaster New Testament Series (Grand Rapids. Wm. B. Eerdmans, 1996), pp. 9-29.

Mark writes this passage not only to show Jesus openly affirming who he is, but also to provide the readers with a shining example of how they were to react when put to trial on account of their faith in Jesus. The false witnesses show that this is really a trial based solely on the claim that Jesus is the Son of God and has nothing to do with any illegal behavior of Jesus. By this account, the readers are implicitly instructed to be certain that any trial they undergo stems from their faith and not from any wrongdoing on their part (cf. 1 Pet 3:13-16; 4:12-16). Jesus' forthright acknowledgment of his claim (**I am**. v. 62) exemplifies the unhesitating courage the readers are to show in confessing their faith in Jesus as the Son of God.[8]

The remarks indicate well Mark's pastoral purpose, especially when combined with another note of irony in the passage, which also reflects narrative concerns. There is an interesting interplay within Mark surrounding the charge of blasphemy. A tracing of this ironic theme shows where the remark at the examination fits.

The first major controversy surrounding Jesus in Mark appears in 2:7, where he is charged with blasphemy for claiming to forgive sin. The charge seems to revolve around Jesus' taking up an exclusively divine prerogative with such directness based on his own authority. The offense appears to revolve the fact that forgiveness comes outside any cultic requirements in a mere declaration, an approach that points to Jesus' own authority.[9] But two other relevant blasphemy texts appear in Mark. In each of these cases, it is others who blaspheme or risk blaspheming. In 3:29, Jesus warns about blaspheming the Spirit, as opposed to the other sins and blasphemies the "sons of men" might perform. Those who blaspheme the Spirit are guilty of a sin that cannot be forgiven, for it is an "eternal sin." The remark comes in response to the claim that Jesus casts out demons by Beelzebul in 3:22 or by an unclean spirit in 3:30, texts that form an inclusio around the remark. The combination of 2:7 with 3:29 sets up a "battle of the blasphemies" in Mark, with each side accusing the other of offending God by their appraisal of Jesus.[10] Jesus meets the accusation of the Jewish leadership in 2:7 and in 3:22 with a reciprocal warning. Mark puts at the top of the list of sins an improper assessment of Jesus.

---

[8]Larry W. Hurtado, *Mark*, New International Commentary (Peabody, Mass: Hendrickson, 1989), p. 249.

[9]For this reading of Mk 2, see J. Dunn, *The Parting of the Ways* (London: SCM Press, 1991), pp. 46-47. Forgiveness was possible without recourse to priests or rabbis. The implications for religious authority structures are huge, since these authorities would believe that the way they bestowed forgiveness was in line with divine instruction. See also B. Chilton, *The Temple of Jesus* (University Park: Pennsylvania State University, 1992), pp. 130-33, on Jesus and forgiveness.

[10]I thank David Capes for pointing out this connection to me during a response he gave to a section of my work during the national meeting of the SBL in 1997.

Putting this backdrop next to the examination, we see that while the leadership accuses Jesus of blasphemy in 14:64, he has already warned those doing so of the theological danger of their view. This is later reinforced in 15:29. Those onlookers who insult Jesus are said to blaspheme him, when they deride him for his claim to raise up the temple in three days and as they call for him to save himself.[11] For Mark, the answer to this derision is not only his narrative description of their remarks here, but the vindication that comes in resurrection in 16:6-7, a divine act that answers their retort. Here is Mark's judgment about where God falls in the battle over who blasphemes. The entire narrative exercise is designed to give those confessing Jesus confidence that their confession is valid, even in the face of those who would accuse them otherwise because of their association with Jesus. Thus, the "blasphemy" theme in Mark, viewed strictly from a narrative standpoint, is an important one to which the trial scene contributes significantly. At the very minimum, then, this is how the scene functions for Mark. But the very importance of the difference of opinion about Jesus raises the question whether there is more to the account than mere narratological and pastoral-theological framing. Does a detailed consideration of the text and its cultural background allow us to say anything more?

2. A Jewish Capital Case?

Perhaps one of the most prominent features in the critical examination of this scene is the noting of many "irregularities" in the scene. This feature has been common to the examination of the passage since Lietzmann's study. Lietzmann's examination focused on one complex issue, the right to perform capital execution and that such a Jewish execution would involve stoning.[12] With this focus there crept into the discussion, something that was often assumed by others as well, namely, that this scene involves a Jewish capital case before the Sanhedrin. So more recent studies indicated how the scene does not correspond at all to mishnaic prescriptions. Not only does Jesus fail to utter the divine Name though blasphemy is charged, but also the Mishnah

---

[11]The only other Marcan text to use the term "βλασφημέω" or "βλασφημία" is 7:22, where it appears in a list of those who sin from "the inside." This remark also occurs in the midst of a controversy scene and has implications about how those who followed Jesus related to questions of the Law and purity, but it is not as christologically significant as these other texts using the term. In fact, in this context, given the range of the vices mentioned, it might only mean "slander."

[12]H. Lietzmann, "Der Prozeß Jesu," SPAW 14 (1931). Examination of his thesis of the Jewish right to execute was considered above in chapter one. What is important for us here is that Lietzmann's study emphasized the capital nature of the trial and questioned the scene on that basis.

is violated in several other matters. Just how stable this element of assessment has been can be shown by comparing the essay on the trial of Lohse (1973) to the discussion of the Marcan scene in Reinbold (1994).[13] Lohse's list of irregularities is: a) a capital trial can only be held in the day (*m Sanh* 4.1), 2) it cannot be held on a Sabbath or Feast day (*m Sanh* 4.1, *m Besah* 5.2), 3) no judgment on the day of the trial (*m Sanh* 4.1), 4) blasphemy requires the divine name (*m Sanh* 7.5), and 5) the trial cannot be held in the High Priest's house, but in a gathering room for the council (*m Sanh* 11.2). Reinbold's list is similar except that he adds the additional note that capital cases are to begin with a defense of the one charged (*m Sanh* 4.1), a detail totally lacking in the Marcan scene. He also omits mention of what blasphemy requires. These irregularities are seen as one basis for rejecting the scene and viewing it as Mark's own creation.

A huge side discussion has developed as a result of these claims with some arguing that the Mishnah reflects Pharisaic, not Sadducean practice, a solution made famous by Blinzler.[14] Others have suggested that the more informal scene of Luke, something less than a trial, may be more original account.[15] While others, like Strobel, have argued that the presence of a "deceiver" required an exceptional and more public kind of examination that could include a trial that started and finished on the same day and that could run into the night (*m Sanh* 11.3 [Danby = 11.4]; *t Sanh* 7.11, 10.11).[16]

It may be that Strobel's approach explains the matter, but this is not the only possibility. One could well argue that the entire discussion has contained

[13]E. Lohse, "Der Prozeß Jesu Christi," in *Die Einheit des Neuen Testament: Exegetische Studien zur Theologie des Neuen Testaments,* ed. E. Lohse (Göttingen: Vandenhoeck & Ruprecht, 1973), pp. 96-97. Wolfgang Reinbold, *Der älteste Bericht über den Tod Jesu: Literarische Analyse und historische Kritik der Passionsdarstellungen der Evangelien,* BZW 69 (Berlin: Walter De Gruyter, 1994), p. 252.

[14]Josef Blinzler, *Der Prozeß Jesu,* 4th ed. (Regensberg: Verlag Friedrich Pustet, 1969), pp. 216-29.

[15]David Catchpole, *The Trial of Jesus: A Study in the Gospels and Jewish Historiography from 1770 to the Present Day,* SPB 18 (Leiden: E. J. Brill, 1971), 153-220.

[16]August Strobel, *Die Stunde der Wahrheit,* WUNT 21 (Tübingen: J. C. B. Mohr [Paul Siebeck], 1980), p. 85. Since Danby includes as 11.3, a paragraph not in the Naples 1492 printed edition of the Mishnah, this tractate is alternately numbered as 11.3 or 11.4. The remark in 11.3 notes a feast day execution in Jerusalem for a deceiver. Such a person is to be "put to death at once" with a public announcement of his crime. Other elements in support of Strobel's have been taken up in subsequent studies by D. Neale, "Was Jesus a *Mesith*? Public Response to Jesus and His Ministry," *Tyndale Bulletin* 44 (1993):89-101; G. Stanton, "Jesus of Nazareth: A Magician and a False Prophet Who Deceived God's People?" in *Jesus of Nazareth Lord and Christ: Essays on the Historical Jesus and New Testament Christology* (Grand Rapids: Wm. B. Eerdmans, 1994), pp. 164-80; N. T. Wright, *Jesus and the Victory of God* (Minneapolis: Fortress Press, 1996), pp. 149-474, esp. 439-42. These later studies deal with some of the significant objections others have raised about Strobel's approach. See discussion of Strobel in chapter one above.

a false assumption, namely, that the procedures used were those of a formal Jewish capital trial, since a Jewish trial is what Mark portrays. What if this examination was never intended to be seen as a Jewish capital case or a Jewish trial? Then the entire debate over Mishnaic procedure might be superfluous. Commenting on the legal status of Jews in the Roman province, Betz proposes,

> The Jews did not have the *ius gladii* under the Roman administration; it was reserved for the prefect (*War* 2.117; *Ant* 18.2; Jn 18:31; 19:10). In the provinces, however, the local courts were kept intact and often cooperated with the Roman prefect. Therefore, in the trial of Jesus the Sanhedrin of Jerusalem may have formed a kind of *consilium iudicum* which did the investigation of the case (*cognitio*) and prepared the accusation (*accusatio*) for the court of the prefect. That is why the nocturnal hearing of Jesus, carried through by a commission of the Sanhedrin under the high priest (Mk 14:53-65), and the morning session of the Sanhedrin (Mk 15:1) should not be treated as unhistorical creations of the Christian community; these events fit the legal situation in a Roman province of that time.[17]

In other words, one must reckon with the real possibility that this gathering was never seen or intended as a formal Jewish capital case, but a kind of preliminary hearing to determine if Jesus was as dangerous as the leadership sensed and whether he could be credibly sent to Rome. In turn, a possible false premise has led the discussion of this scene down a distracting path. But a claim for a hearing does not show that a hearing is necessarily present. Is there evidence that Rome was the intended goal for Jesus all along?

Four strands of evidence point to this conclusion. First, the description of the decision in Mark is that Jesus is worthy of death (ἔνοχον εἶναι θανάτου).[18] It asks whether Jesus is worthy to die, or if he qualifies for such a fate. This is described as a condemning judgment (κατέκριναν) in response to a question about how it seems to the council (τί ὑμῖν φαίνεται). This evaluation can function as a statement of an opinion to pass on to Rome, an indictment to continue the process—rather than a final decisive formal legal judgment of guilt. If the text had said, "they condemned him to death," then the statement might have been evidence of

---

[17]Otto Betz, "Jesus and the Temple Scroll," in *Jesus and the Dead Sea Scrolls*, ed. James H. Charlesworth, ABRL (New York: Doubleday, 1992), pp. 87-88. Betz notes the work of A. N. Sherwin-White, *Roman Society and Roman Law in the New Testament* (1963), and S. A. Fusco, *Il dramma del Golgota nei suoi aspetti processuali.*

[18]Some later manuscripts, like A, W, θ , families 1 and 13, and the Byzantine tradition have a different word order, placing the infinitive first in the phrase, but this make no difference to the point. Also noting this as a possibility is Ferdinand Hahn, *Christologische Hoheitstitel: Ihre Geschichte im frühen Christentum,* 5th ed. (Göttingen; Vandenhoeck & Ruprecht, 1995), p. 177. These remarks derive from the 1963 edition.

a formal, decisive verdict. For example, Luke's account has Pilate using the term αἴτιος, which is the legal technical term for guilt (Lk 23:14); and its variation αἰτία does not appear in the Marcan scene.[19] These terms are reserved for formal Roman judgment or descriptions of procedures associated with Rome (Lk 23:4; Jn 18:38; 19:4, 6; Matt 27:37; Mk 15:26; Acts 13:28; 28:18). The one place where the term is used of the Jewish perspective is in Acts 13:28, but even here it is said that they "could not find anything deserving death (μηδεμίαν αἰτίαν θανάτου εὑρόντες), yet they asked Pilate to have him killed." All of this language fits well with the possibility of an examination for cause, rather than a more formal trial.

The Acts 13 text is important, because in v. 27 it is noted that those in Jerusalem and their leaders "condemned" (κρίναντες) him in fulfillment of Scripture. This term looks like the verb in Mk 14:64 and could appear to represent a formal condemnation at a trial, yet it sets up the remarks already noted from Acts 13:28, where the actual condemning procedure is described in terms of seeking death from Pilate. Thus the remarks also fit an examination of Jesus, rather than a formal capital trial. This fits with traditional remarks that describe Jesus as rejected (Lk 9:22; Mk 8:31) or given over to a death sentence (Lk 24:20) or Stephen's charge that the leaders gave over and killed the Just One (Acts 7:52). There is a causative thrust to all of this language, but all of it reflects the awareness that Rome is the ultimate goal. Brown speaks of "the impression of a trial" in Mark and Matthew, citing the convening of authorities, witnesses with specific testimony, interrogation by the high priest, an admission of a messianic claim by Jesus, an indication that blasphemy has been uttered, and a condemnation of the remark as making Jesus worthy of death.[20] But it must be noted that none of these elements or their combination precludes what would take place at a hearing looking for cause. In fact, one could argue that the high priest's direct involvement points more to such an hearing than a formal case where he would likely be silent as chief of the court.[21] Of course, this language could also apply to a formal judgment, as well. It is ambiguous. The problem is that such a hearing, if held, would still be a legal procedure, just not the ultimate one. Now our point is that the rules for examination might differ, when the actual authority for the sentence is present. The kind of hearing can effect the nature of the examination.

---

[19]BAGD, p. 26.

[20]Raymond E. Brown, *The Death of the Messiah*, 2 vol., ABRL (New York: Doubleday, 1994), pp. 423-24. In his discussion, he suggests a less formal feel to both Luke and John, which is the case, but this may be influenced by the fact that causative language has been read as having a more decisive legal thrust of finality.

[21]Pesch, *Das Markusevngelium*, pp. 416-17.

The second strand of evidence is the presence of the temple charge itself in Mk 14:55-59. What was being examined was whether there could be grounds to get Jesus before Rome on political charges, as the Romans would not be interested in a Jewish religious dispute unless it impacted Roman interests or the public peace. One of the things the Romans worked hard to protect was the *Pax Romana*. These remarks about the temple, if they could be proved to the Roman governor, would have made Jesus appear as a serious disturber of the peace in a socially sensitive locale. As a serious threat to provincial peace, Jesus would have to be dealt with as a matter of appropriate Roman stewardship. What on the surface looks like a non-sensical section of the examination scene, the presentation of planned false witnesses who cannot agree on their testimony, is, in fact, a quite important element. The witnesses' testimony had to be solid enough and credible enough to Pilate to have hope of convincing Rome, *not* the leadership, of a dangerous prospect of political instability. It needed to be able to stand up to scrutiny to those outside the Jewish leadership. It is a sign of the strength of the presentation and its lack of anti-Jewish *Tendenz*, when considered as part of a hearing, that these witnesses were judged to be inadequate.[22] In fact, there is no good explanation for why this detail would be created by the community, only to be dropped as inadequate.[23] It does not fit the claim that Mark portrays the trial as unfair, because the inconsistency of the charges is seemingly acknowledged by the examiners as being insufficient, or, at least, as needing something more in addition to make the case. What the council was investigating was legal cause, a charge that had a real chance of being convincing to outsiders and that had a political tinge to it. So the very way in which this temple charge is handled and dropped indicates concern for an outside audience that also will need sufficient cause to convict. This dropped element fits better in a hearing context than as an element in a strictly Jewish capital case, since the pursuit of the temple charge was not merely for internal Jewish purposes but had to be able to work its political effect outside the

---

[22]So quite correctly, Renatus Kempthorne, "Anti-Christian Tendency in Pre-Marcan Traditions of the Sanhedrin Trial," TU 126 (1982): 283-85. For a discussion of the likely background involved in the temple act itself, see Bruce Chilton, *The Temple of Jesus: His Sacrificial Program Within A Cultural History of Sacrifice* (University Park, Penn: Pennsylvania State University, 1992), 91-111.

[23]The inadequacy of the testimony is seen in the fact that the high priest steps in and takes over the questioning, while pushing the discussion in a new, but related direction. The argument that what one has here is early church polemic fails to explain why this charge is never picked up again after this scene. It clearly becomes irrelevant in light of subsequent events. Thus its subordinate role argues for its trustworthiness. It appears to serve as an example of the Jewish leadership attempting to be careful about whether they have real evidence or not.

council. Its lack of development suggests that there was little or no confidence that a case could be made on this temple basis alone.

The third trace of evidence is that there is no effort at a defense from outside witnesses. Now this could simply be the result of a condensation of the scene, but it also would fit with a hearing. Once sufficient evidence existed to bring a charge and ask for death, then any issue of a full defense would be a matter for a later formal trial. In fact, it should not be overlooked that Jesus was asked if he had any reply in Mk 14:60. He simply remained silent. As a result, there is not much that can be made of this absence of a defense, but it does cohere better with a hearing scene.

The last point of evidence looks to earlier motive. The sequence of Mk 12:12-16 shows that the plan to arrest Jesus had Rome in mind, potentially, from an earlier moment. The asking about the payment of taxes to Rome is the first controversy after the noting of the desire to arrest him (Mk 12:12). It is an initial effort to "entrap" him after Jesus' coming to Jerusalem (ἀγρεύσωσιν; Mk 12:13). It shows that an eye is turned toward Rome. Now the "taxes" saying is one of the few in Mark that is seen as authentic by most, though some dispute the setting.[24] But the challenge of a setting in Jerusalem should not be doubted. The question of this tax had to be asked in Jerusalem, since it is here where taxes were paid to Caesar. While in Galilee, it was Herod Antipas who collected the tax. The question is only relevant to someone who lived in Jerusalem. The account itself shows that there was an attempt to see if the prophetic Jesus might be as hostile toward Rome as other prophets had been to outside nations. On the other hand, should the sequence reflect the tumultuous events in Jerusalem, and given the presence of the Herodians and the recent temple controversy this is quite possible, then we have a case of attempting to see if Jesus could be seen as a threat to Rome.[25]

These four elements suggest that the examination that was held was always an attempt to gather charges, so that a case could be made before Rome and Pilate. The haste of the examination, which also indicates this desire, is fueled by two other considerations: 1) the short term presence of Pilate in the city and 2) the danger the leaders would have felt had events dragged out too long

---

[24]For example, Bultmann, *The History of the Synoptic Tradition* (New York: Harper & Row, 1963), p. 26, treats the scene as genuine. The Jesus Seminar accepts the saying as authentic, rating the remark in v. 17 as the only saying in Mark that they see as totally authentic, though they prefer the version of the account in the Egerton Gospel 3:1-6, which means that they regard the rest of the context as inauthentic. Robert W. Funk and Roy W. Hoover, *The Five Gospels: The Search for the Authentic Words of Jesus* (New York: Macmillan, 1993), p. 102. What they cannot explain is why v. 17 would circulate on its own, without some context. By itself the saying makes no sense at all.

[25]As Pesch, *Das Markusevangelium*, p. 226, notes, "Die Alternativfrage, die Jesus gestellt ist, ist eine Falle: Entweder würde Jesus Steuerverweigerung und damit politischen Aufruhr oder Steuerzahlung und damit Götzendienst predigen."

or had they taken place in too public a forum. The city was filled with Galilean pilgrims there for Passover. The night arrest, examination, and early morning sentence lessened the risk of a reaction, as the pilgrims had to journey outside the town overnight (cf., Jesus' own practice [Lk 21:37]). By getting the events to Pilate by daylight and making the legal issue his, security became his problem. A third advantage also resulted from an immediate resolution. Once security was no longer a concern, there was also the advantage of making Jesus a exemplary public example among all those present, if the execution could come quickly while pilgrims were still present. Not only would this be something that was allowed, it was even advised for a figure perceived to be a major deceiver.[26]

3. Potential Sources of the Saying

But what of the key saying then? Before considering it, some attention needs to be given to the potential sources for such a report. Of course, we do not know the source and none of Jesus' disciples at the time were present at whatever examination took place. This reality has led some to argue that there is no potential source for this scene or that, at least, there is no great likelihood of a train of transmission for it.[27] This view is clearly articulated by E. P. Sanders when he claims, "It is hard, though not impossible, to imagine a chain of transmission which would have passed on the exchanges of the supposed trial."[28]

This hesitation to consider sources for the scene seems strongly overdrawn. Numerous potential candidates exist. For example, prominent Jews, who would have had access either to the trial itself or to reports about it, also would have had close contact with the Christian community. Prominent among such figures would be Joseph of Arimathea, who is connected with the burial of Jesus and who apparently had official access to the decision (Mk 15:43).[29] A figure like Nicodemus could also come into play. Any prominent

---

[26]On the case for Jesus being perceived as a deceiver, see n. 16 above and the discussion surrounding n. 68 later in this chapter.

[27]For example, one of the claims of Lietzmann's work is that although the source for Peter's denials was likely to be the disciple himself, this could not be claimed for the trial scene; H. Lietzmann, "Der Prozeß Jesu," SPAW 14 (1931):314-15. On p. 315, Lietzmann argued that ". . . daß uns keine Quelle für diesen Bericht glaubhaft wird. Petrus ist nicht der Gewährsmann, denn er ist, wie zweimal (14, 54.66) ausdrücklich betont wird, nur bis in den Hof des hohenpriesterlichen Palastes vorgedrungen und unten im Hof geblieben. Er kann also von der Verhandlung nichts gehört haben, und einen anderen Zeugen sehen wir nicht."

[28]E. P. Sanders, *Jesus and Judaism* (Philadelphia: Fortress, 1985), p. 298.

[29]It is highly unlikely that Joseph is a figure created by the church. The portrayal of a member of the Sanhedrin as sympathetic to Jesus in the midst of traditions that highlighted

official Jewish leaders who subsequently became Christians would have had access to knowledge about these events. Surely the persecutor Saul fits in this category. His violent opposition to the new sect would have meant he would have known what the Jewish involvement and position on Jesus would have been. Other priests also became a part of the community in Jerusalem (Acts 6:7).

The possible chain of transmission could also have emerged quite naturally out of the flow of everyday events in Jerusalem. What took place with Jesus reflected a heated polemical debate within Judaism that raged in the city because of disputes about Christians "breaking the law," with intense public debate until at least 70 CE.[30] It is hard, if not impossible, to imagine that a Jewish view of the trial did not emerge in the midst of this quite public debate. It is virtually impossible to believe then that the Jewish position on Jesus was never made public. The Annas clan would have justified its role in sending Jesus to Rome as a matter of insuring an understanding of the priesthood's policy concerning the newly emerging, socially disturbing movement. Included in this would have been the reasons Jesus was taken before Pilate. Moreover these debates would have involved the family of the high priest, including the powerful patriarch of the family, Annas. It is significant to note that the same family was involved in the center of this controversy from the time of Jesus until the stoning of James, Jesus' brother in 62 CE, a period of around thirty years.[31] Josephus seems to have had

---

the animosity of the leadership and in the face of the polemical environment in the early church makes the description of his office quite credible. See R. Brown, *The Death of the Messiah*, p. 1240.

[30]See Josephus, *Ant* 20.9.1 §200. The case of James, slain by Annas the younger in 62 CE is especially revealing. Josephus tells us that he was given over to be stoned "for having transgressed the Law" (παρανομησάντων κατηγορίαν παπέδωκε λευσθησομένους). What Law was it James broke, given his reputation within Christians circles as a Jewish-Christian leader who was careful about keeping the Law? It would seem likely that the Law had to relate to his christological allegiances and a charge of blasphemy. This would fit the fact that he was stoned, which was the penalty for such a crime, and parallels how Stephen was handled as well. There is a pattern of treatment that runs through the Jewish-Christians relationship to the Jewish leadership. This public commotion surely also produced public discussion of the original event. The verb for transgression, παρανομέω, which appears 42x in Josephus, is a very broad term as it can refer to acts against another person (*Ant* 12.288). However a string of uses refer to serious transgression against God as numerous kings of Israel are singled out with this term, many of whom are said to follow in the footsteps of Jeroboam (*Ant* 8.245- Jeroboam; 8.253- Rehoboam; 9.168, 170- Joash; 9.18- Ahab like Jeroboam; 9.95- Joram like Jeroboam).

[31]Josephus, *Ant* 20.9.1 §§ 197-203. I thank Martin Hengel for pointing out this argument to me in our numerous enjoyable interactions over this topic. A similar position with regard to Annas's family animosity toward Christians is noted by Brown, *The Death of the Messiah*, p. 409. As he says, ". . . every famous Christian who died violently in Judea before the Jewish Revolt suffered in a tenure of a priest related to Annas." Annas and his five sons all served as

access to reports about the trial of James and the reaction to it. Should we think it was any different with the trial of the one whose movement was at the center of the controversy? And given the continuity within the Jewish leadership during this period, would it be too much to argue that the two sides would have known the views and rationale for opposition much like the leaders of opposing political parties might today? This means that numerous potential, and some quite public, chains of transmission for this scene existed. Surely the events associated with the public spectacle of a trial circulated widely in the city.

The possibility of the saying's being reflective of the real trial scene does not, however, mean that it does come from this event. That requires a careful examination of the key saying itself. Can one specify the nature of the blasphemy as it is reflected in this saying? At the least, one should be able to describe from Mark's (and the early church's) point of view what the nature of the blasphemy was and the cultural assumptions this remark draws upon for that conclusion. Once this is done then consideration can be given to the question whether or not the saying has roots in the actual trial scene.

4. The "Blasphemy" in the Jewish Examination of Jesus

There are three potential elements in the report of Mk 14:61-62 that could have led to the Jewish view that Jesus had blasphemed. As will be made clear, the second and third elements serve as the more likely sources of the evaluation against Jesus. The combination of these elements is important to note, as often the charge is seen to stem from a single factor alone. Yet one must consider the possibility that the reply challenges an array of Jewish cultural assumptions, making the remarks particularly offensive for the leadership. Might it be possible that Jesus' reply was offensive at multiple levels, making the offense even greater in the leadership's view?

The first option was already noted in the discussion of Robert Gundry and Craig Evans in chapter one. It is that Jesus pronounced the divine Name in violation of *m Sanh* 7:5 when he alluded to Ps 110:1. However this citation was suppressed in the public reports of the scene, including that of Mark, so

---

high priests at one time or another in this period, as did one son-in-law (Caiaphas, the high priest during the time of Jesus; Jn 18:13; Josephus, *Ant* 20.9.1 § 198; 18.2.2 §§ 34-35). This family had considerable power for much of a fifty-year period and engaged in a constant battle with the Jewish-Christians in Jerusalem over this time. It should also not be overlooked that when Josephus describes this incident he describes the Sadducees as "more heartless in judging offenders than any of the rest of the Jews (εἰσὶ περὶ τὰς κρίσεις ὠμοὶ παρὰ πάντας τοὺς 'Ιουδαίους §199)." This standard evaluation may mean that Blinzler is right to suggest that the rules of judgment under Sadducean authority were more strict than those that emerged under the Pharisees as reflected in the Mishnah.

as not to repeat the blasphemy and compound the offense.[32] This procedure
would reflect practice noted in the Mishnah, also in *m Sanh* 7.5, where report
of the exact wording of the blasphemy is repeated only in the privacy of a
hearing and not in a public report, so as to avoid repeating the sin.[33] So Jesus
said, "I am, and you will see the Son of Man sitting at the right hand of
Yahweh . . ." but it was reported publicly as "seated at the right hand of
power" as Mk 14 has it.

This explanation is possibly an element of the background, but only with
certain additional assumptions that are not at all a given. It must be noted that
it was common for biblical texts to be pronounced with a substitute for the
divine Name, as also was the case for benedictions with the exception of a
few specified cases. One of the situations with benedictions is noted in *m Sot*
7.6. This text describes how the common priestly benediction of Num 6:24-26
was given to the people. So here we have a scriptural text and a benediction.
In the provinces, each verse was read by itself and the crowd would respond
with an amen in each case, while at the Temple it was read as a whole and
treated as a single verse. But the more important consideration for us comes
next when the issue of the pronunciation of the Name is treated. The text
reads, "in the temple they pronounced the Name as written, but in the
provinces by a substituted word." So it is no guarantee that the presence of the
divine Name in Scripture meant that it would be read.

Another text is *m Yom* 6.2. This text records the confession of the High
Priest as atonement is made over the lamb for the nation's sins on the Day of
Atonement. Included in the saying is the citation of Lev 16:30. This verse
includes a reference to the divine Name, which the High Priest did read, as the
crowd would bow and fall on their faces when "the people which stood in the
Temple court heard the expressed Name come forth from the mouth of the
High Priest." In addition, they responded to the confession and the use of the
Name with a euphemism, "Blessed be the name of the glory of his kingdom
for ever and ever."[34]

Still a third example appears at Qumran, though it is not consistent.[35] In
the Isaiah scroll יהוה is occasionally altered into אדני or reduced in the dual
phrase Lord God (אדני יהוה) to only יהוה (1QIs^a glosses the name in 28:16;
30:15; 65:13, by writing above it- אדוני; and reduces it in 49:22; 52:4; 61:1).[36]

---

[32]Robert Gundry, *Mark: A Commentary on His Apology for the Cross*, pp. 915-18. Craig
Evans, *Jesus and His Contemporaries: Comparative Studies*, p. 412-13. Evans also argues
that this fact alone cannot explain the blasphemy in the scene, a point with which I agree.

[33]For the citation and discussion of this mishnaic text, see the section on it in chapter 2.

[34]The command is also noted in exactly the same way in *m Yom* 3.8.

[35]Stephen Byington, "יהוה and אדני," *JBL* 76 (1957), pp. 58-59.

[36]*Contra* Siegfried Schulz, "Maranatha und Kyrios Jesus," *ZNW* 53 (1962):133, there is
evidence of this type of change in early material. On pp. 132-33, he notes that a shortened

In 1QIsᵃ 50:5, it is replaced with אלהים. The Name is omitted from 1QIsᵃ 45:8, while in 1QIsᵃ 52:5 and 59:21, it is omitted once when it appears twice in the MT. In 1QIsᵃ 3:17, ואדוני appears for the Name, while 3:15 writes אדוני over the Name. In 1QIsᵃ 40:7 and 42:6 a row of dots appears where the Name would be expected, while in 42:5 the term האלהים appears instead of the Name. The same occurs in other texts from Qumran as well.[37] Such changes show that some Jews were careful to avoid writing the divine Name in Scripture, which in turn would prevent it being pronounced as well.

What these examples mean is that it is not certain that even if Jesus cited Ps 110:1 that he would have read the divine Name as written, given the possible variations permitted within oral delivery. Regardless, it also is not certain that the reading of the Name itself from Scripture would have been considered uttering the name "unseasonably," which is a type of blasphemy noted by Philo as worthy of death (*Life of Moses* 2.206, 208). As Evans notes, "Uttering the Divine Name, especially in the context of quoting Scripture and if with all proper reverence, is not blasphemous."[38] Thus, this suggestion by itself is not likely, unless one can argue that what created the charge was a lack of "proper reverence" in the way it was cited. This explanation would

---

from of the divine Name (יהו) appears in the Elephantine papyri of the fifth century BCE (ιαω), but he raises questions about how much can be drawn from this practice. However, the very presence of an alternate and *abbreviated* form of the Name shows that the name is being treated with respect by not being reproduced exactly. The texts at Elephantine can be found in A. Cowley, *Aramaic Paypri of the Fifth Century B.C.* (Oxford: Clarendon, 1923). The passages where יהו appears are: 6.4, 6, 11; 22.1, 123; 25.6; 27.15, 30,6, 15, 24-27 (3x), 31.7, 24-25 (2x), 33.8, 38.1, 45.3-4, and 56.2. Care with regard to speaking the divine Name is also noted in Josephus, *Ant* 2.12. 4 §§ 275-76 and in Philo, *Life of Moses* 2.114. For evidence of a substitution of the name with Lord, one can note the LXX and the examples at Qumran, see next note below. On the use of ιαω, see Ganschinietz, "Iao," in *Paulys Real-Encyclopädie der classischen Altertumswissenschaft* (Stuttgart: J. B. Metzlersche, 1916), vol. 9, cols. 698-721; Menahem Stern, *Greek and Latin Authors on Jews and Judaism* (Jerusalem: Israel Academy of Sciences and Humanities, 1974), vol. 1:98, 171-72, 211-12, and vol. 2:140-41, 410-12, 673; and David Aune, "Iao ('Ιαώ)," RAC, Lieferung 129 (Stuttgart: Anton Hiersemann, 1994), cols. 1-12.

[37]Michael A. Knibb, *The Qumran Community*, pp. 134, 170, 232-33, 250. He notes how the Name is written in old script in *1QpHab* vi.14, while in 1QS VIII.14, the citation of Isa 40:3 leaves only four dots where the name YHWH appeared. Interestingly, in *4QpPsᵃ* ii.13 the reverse is the case, as YHWH appears where Lord was present. Fitzmyer has critiqued Schulz at this point in "The Contribution of Qumran Aramaic to the Study of the New Testament," NTS 20 (1974): 386-91. He notes in the *11QTg Job* the absolute use of מרא, and comments on: 1) the construct chains Schulz mentioned in the Elephantine papyri at 30.15, 2) the use of אלאה for the tetragrammaton in *11QTg Job* 37.3; 38.2 (x), 38.3, and 38.7, and 3) the rendering of שדי twice by מרא in *11QTg Job* 34.5, 7, as well as its likely presence in 36.8. In 34.6-7 he is confident it appears for the divine Name. For a probable other absolute use of the term Lord (מרי), see also *1QapGen* 20.12-13.

[38]Craig Evans, *Jesus and His Contemporaries: Comparative Studies*, p. 413.

require that other, more fundamental and conceptual grounds be raised that formed the essence of the blasphemy, which is possible for this scene as the following options will show.

Nonetheless, this option is important, because it raises the possibility that the circumlocution in the reply, "the power of the blessed One," is sensitive to Jewish practice. Does the reference to "the power of the blessed One" reflect a Marcan rendering, pre-Marcan Christian tradition, a Jewish report of the trial where the allusion to the Divine name is reported in an indirect way, or is it a report of Jesus' words? Someone was aware of potential Jewish sensitivities here. This question concerning "Jewish" expressions in vv. 61-62 is resumed in more detail below.

The second option argues that the major feature of what was seen as blasphemous in the view of the leadership came within Jesus' reply about the Son of Man. After Jesus responds positively to the question whether he is the Christ, the Son of the Blessed, he goes on to speak of the council seeing the Son of Man seated at the right hand of power and coming on the clouds. The key reply reads, "ἐγώ εἰμι, καὶ ὄψεσθε τὸν υἱὸν τοῦ ἀνθρώπου ἐκ δεξιῶν καθήμενον τῆς δυνάμεως καὶ ἐρχόμενον μετὰ τῶν νεφελῶν τοῦ οὐρανοῦ."[39] Now it is contextually plain that within the account the reference to the Son of Man is a self reference to Jesus.[40] The reply combines an allusion to the enthroned authority of a regal figure from Ps 110:1 with the authoritative figure of one like a Son of Man from Dan 7:13.

There has been some debate on what it is Jesus promises the council will see. Some argue that the entire remark is a description only of Jesus' exaltation, an allusion to resurrection to the right hand, a going to God.[41] Jesus promises that the council will see his vindication by God and the effects of his installment into authority. The case for this is grounded in three points. 1) There is the original meaning of Dan 7:13, which portrays one like a Son of Man "going to God" and thus serves as the interpretation of the remark. 2) In addition, Matthew and Luke highlight an instantaneous seeing with Matthew's ἀπ 'ἄρτι (26:64) and Luke's ἀπὸ τοῦ νῦν (22:69). Only a resurrection can fit this near setting. 3) There is the grammatical tightness of a

---

[39]There are no major text critical problems here. A few manuscripts (Θ, family 13, 565, 700) add "you say that" (σὺ εἶπας ὅτι) before the reply, while D omits καὶ ἐρχόμενον. Both these readings are clearly secondary.

[40]I treat only the issue of the passage's meaning here and the nature of the blasphemy charge in the account as it is presented. The discussion of authenticity follows after a description of how the blasphemy is presented in this text.

[41]T. F. Glasson, "The reply to Caiaphas (Mark XIV.62)," *NTS* 7 (1960/61): 88-93. This view is also vigorously defended by Morna Hooker, *The Son of Man in Mark* (London: S.P.C.K., 1967), pp. 166-71.

verb controlling two participles, which one would normally expect to refer to simultaneous events.

However, it is unlikely that resurrection alone is what is meant. Mk 14:28 shows that Mark is not hesitant about alluding directly to resurrection in reporting what Jesus says. What is amazing about this trial scene is the total absence of reference to resurrection. Only an indirect reference to exaltation is mentioned. This could suggest the presence of old tradition and yet mention of exaltation alone seems not to be the only emphasis here. For example, the riding on the clouds, though a heavenly, theomorphic image is not about heavenly activity, but portrays a vindication that involves figures on earth, as even Dan 7 shows. There it is the saints on earth who benefit from the work of the Son of Man.[42] As Müller states of the Dan 7 scene,

> Dabei will bedacht sein, daß nirgends in der alttestamentlichen, frühjüdischen und talmudischen Literatur jemals "Wolken" eine Rolle spielen, solange es darum geht, den Verkehr und die Bewegung der Himmlischen untereinander im Raum ihrer den Augen der Menschen entzogenen Transzendenz ins Wort zu rücken. Erst wenn einer von ihnen aus deren Verborgenheit *heraustritt*, werden Epiphaniewolken und Wolkenvehikel bemüht. Diese Beobachtung legt es nahe, das anhand einer Partizipialkonstruktion pointierte "Kommen" des Menschensohnes als *Abstieg* vom Himmel *zur Erde* zu begreifen.[43]

Now it might be objected that Dan 7:9-13 itself is a heavenly scene, so that Müller is wrong. But this fails to appreciate the fact that the reason for the heavenly installation of the Son of Man who is on the clouds is to vindicate the saints on earth (vv. 21-27). In other words, the reason one is given a glimpse of what is happening in heaven is because it impacts what will happen on earth. Seen in this light, Müller's remarks are appropriate. The allusion, then, anticipates a return to judge and vindicate the saints (In this case, Jesus is including himself as among the vindicated!).

In fact, the claim to come on the clouds is a significant claim, not only alluding to Dan 7:13, but also using imagery that claims a right only deity possesses. Everywhere else in the OT only God or the gods ride the clouds (Exod 14:20; Num 10:34: Ps 104:3; Isa 19:1).[44] Thus comprehensive heavenly authority is present in the image. The picture is of a sovereign, divinely related exercise of power.

---

[42]G. R. Beasley-Murray, *Jesus and the Kingdom of God* (Grand Rapids: Eerdmans, 1986), p. 301; Karlheinz Müller, "Der Menschensohn im Danielzyklus," in *Jesus und der Menschenshohn: Fs. A. Vögtle*, eds. R. Pesch and R. Schnackenburg (Freiburg: Herder, 1975), pp. 37-80, esp. 45.

[43]Karlheinz Müller, "Der Menschensohn im Danielzyklus," p. 45. The emphasis is his.

[44]J. A. Emerton, "The Origin of the Son of Man Imagery," JTS n.s. 9 (1958):225-42.

As for the claim that grammatically one would expect simultaneous events in a verb linked with two participles, it must be remembered that this is a prophetic allusion using metaphorical language, so that a combination of events can be placed in proximity that, in fact, may be quite distant from one another. In addition, the order of these events with seating first and then a mention of coming on the clouds speaks against a reference only to exaltation, as does the earlier allusion to Dan 7 in Mk 13:26, which clearly alludes to a later parousia. If exaltation were meant and the clouds alluded to exaltation, then one would expect the ascension into the clouds to God to lead to the seating. The order of the participles would be reversed. The changes by Matthew and Luke only make explicit what this remark assumes, that a vindication of Jesus is the presupposition for his return, as evidence of his exaltation is seen not only in his return but in the activity among his people that precedes it. The redactional changes by the other evangelists only highlight this additional implied emphasis in the remark. Mark has not made the point quite strongly enough for them, so they develop the implications more fully. Thus the combined allusion is a declaration to total vindication by God that allows Jesus to share authority with God and return functioning with final judgment prerogatives on behalf of God's saints. When he returns it will be as eschatological judge, exercising the judicial power of God on behalf of the righteous. By implication, part of that vindication comes on his own behalf for the judgment being contemplated against him.

Now the problem the leadership would have seen with this remark is probably not that such a figure existed. The portrait of Enoch's Son of Man shows that such a category was contemplated within Judaism. To expect such a glorious figure in the future was possible. What would have caused the offense was that Jesus was making this identification with himself in a *self-claim* to share authority with God. He, as a Galilean preacher, or a wonder worker, or as an eschatological prophet, or even as one making a messianic claim, was extending the claim to the right to share in God's final judgment as the sent judge from heaven. It is the juxtaposition of seating and coming on the clouds that makes clear the transcendent function Jesus gives himself here, with the reference to clouds, making it apparent that more than a purely human and earthly messianic claim is present.[45] There is an implication in this

---

[45] Another possible reading exists, if one does not see a self-claim by Jesus in the allusion to the Son of Man. It would be a claim that a vindicating judgment is coming in the eschaton through such a figure, who remains enigmatically unidentified, and that Jesus is so closely identified with what the Son of Man represents that Jesus will be vindicated in that judgment on behalf of the righteous. Seen in this light, there is still a blasphemy, as the offense to the insight and spiritual discernment of the leadership still stands directly and seriously challenged. So they would be regarded as among the judged. This remark then could be read as a violation of Exod 22:27, since the leadership would be excluded from being among the righteous at the end. The remark would be seen as a subtle anathema against the leadership.

remark as well. If they are contemplating judging him now, he will eventually judge them later.

The self-made claim to sit at the right hand and ride the clouds would be read as a blasphemous utterance, a false claim that equates Jesus in a unique way with God and that reflects an arrogant disrespect toward the one true God. As chapter three showed, a proximate seating next to God might be considered for a privileged few, either a few universally acknowledged greats of the past or the future eschatological figure of judgment. But such honor would never be contemplated by the leadership for a humble, rural Galilean, preacher like Jesus. And yet Jesus seems to claim even more. He will share the throne with the Shekinah and sit next to him at his right hand.[46] Jesus is not only near to God and working with him, he is seated in a way that shares the highest honor with him. Only the figure of Enoch-Son of Man seems close to this imagery, and even his access to God in this way was controversial, despite his translation by God. These remarks would have been read as blasphemous along the lines Philo described in *On Dreams* 2.130-31 or *Decalogue* 13-14.61-64.[47] In *On Dreams*, Philo had said that a man claiming the prerogatives of God is a person who possesses "evil of an extraordinary nature," "a man miserable in every respect," who "has dared to compare himself to the all-blessed God." Such a man utters blasphemies against the creation. In *Decalogue*, he argued that those who give creatures the same honors as those of the creator are "the most foolish and most unjust" of men. Those who think to ascribe to themselves honor like that given to God are possessed with "an insolent and free-spoken madness, as they "make an open

---

See also discussion surrounding n. 55 below. Though I think this option is less likely, for reasons I shall consider in discussing the apocalyptic Son of Man, it is another way in which the tradition could be read and seen as essentially authentic; see the discussion below surrounding nn. 109-16. For this view, see the remarks of C. Colpe, "ὁ υἱὸς τοῦ ἀνθρώπου," TDNT 8:441. He says, "In this respect there is a parallel to what he says about His perfecting to various hearers and also to His proclamation of God's kingdom to the whole people of Israel. Just as the kingdom of God and the Son of Man could not be in competition in this respect, so it is with Jesus and the Son of Man. The apocalyptic Son of Man is a symbol of Jesus' assurance of perfecting. With a shift from the assurance to the one who has it, the whole process may be interpreted as a dynamic and functional equating of Jesus and the coming Son of Man with the future perfecting of Jesus in view. On this view the primitive community then made of it a static personal identification accomplished already in the present Jesus, ..." For Colpe, future perfecting is another way to speak of vindication. He regards Lk 22:69 as authentic, while arguing that the appearance of Dan 7 in Mk 14:62 is a reflection of the early church; see 8:435.

[46]As M. Hengel has argued in *Studies in Early Christology*, pp. 185-203, this claim was unique, though some exaltation imagery comes conceptually close to this. Jesus has chosen to state the point uniquely in the most emphatic way possible.

[47]Detailed treatments of these texts appear in the earlier discussion on blasphemy in chapter 2.

display of the impiety which dwells in their hearts, and venture to blaspheme the deity, whetting an evil tongue, and desiring to vex the pious, who immediately feel an indescribable and irreconcilable affliction." Philo's attitude describes his perception of pagan arrogance, especially against any form of ruler cult. How much more the council would have been offended by Jesus' remarks, made as they were by a Jew. Philo's commentary could explain why the response to this remark was the priest's ripping of the clothes. Afflicted by what he had heard, he gave the clear sign that blasphemy had been uttered (Mk 14:63; *m Sanh* 7.5).

In Jewish perception, what Jesus claims here is like, if not worse than, what other traditional blasphemers of Jewish lore said or did. What the actions of Sisera, Goliath, Sennacherib, Belshazzar, Manasseh, and Titus shared was a disregard for the unique power and honor of God. The chapter on blasphemy in Judaism showed how each of these figures was described and condemned. The midrashim supply particularly interesting additional examples when one considers how Isa 14:12-14 is handled by later rabbis. In these texts, Nebuchadnezzar becomes the illustration of arrogance, though in one major discussion he shares the stage with Pharaoh, Hiram, Joash, king of Judah, and Sennacherib (*ExodR* 8.2). In this midrash, Hiram is condemned as Ezek 28:2 is related to him, while Isa 14 is applied to Nebuchadnezzar who "claimed deity." According to the text, Pharaoh also made such a claim, as the midrash appeals to Ezek 29:3. Joash also fails because he received worship, with 2 Chron 24:17-25 being the key text supplying the evidence. The last example is Sennacherib, noting 2 Kgs 19:35. In the midst of this developed exposition, comes this emotional note. In discussing Zech 4:10 the midrash says, "this refers, however, says R. Berekiah (c 340 CE), to the haughty who declare themselves to be gods, but whom God makes abominations in the world." Here we see a later rabbi's reactions to those who were perceived to have portrayed themselves as too much like God. One can also note, in addition, the tradition involving a son of man claim in *y Taan* 2.65b (Neusner 2.1). Here Rabbi Abbahu (c 300 CE) makes two statements, "If a man should tell you, 'I am God,' he is lying. If he says, 'I am the son of man,' in the end he will regret it: 'I will ascend to heaven,' he said it but he will not carry it out." This tradition is like what is seen in the rabbinic handling of Isa 14.[48] Such statements are to be rejected and subject one to judgment.

---

[48]Nebuchadnezzar is the example in reference to Isa 14:12-14 in several texts like *ExodR* 15.6 and 21.3; *LevR* 18.2; and *NumR* 9.24 and 20.1. In this last text, Solomon is contrasted with Nebuchadnezzar as "the former built the Temple and uttered numerous songs and supplications, while the latter destroyed it and reviled and blasphemed, saying, "I will ascend above the height of the clouds; I will be like the Most High (Isa 14:14)." This is one of the few texts to actually speak of Nebuchadnezzar'a blasphemy while making a point from Isa 14, but the key is not only his action against the temple, which would be seen as a direct attack against God's presence, but the attribution through the application of Isaiah of a heart

The Jewish leadership believed that Jesus' remarks fell into this class. The consistency of these illustrative portraits of the blasphemer reveals a commonly held view of how blasphemy could be perceived in remarks or actions that appeared to reduce God's unique stature. The Jewish reaction to a sense of violation of God's presence, as seen in *Ant* 12.406 or in *1 Macc* 2:6, shows how important the protection of the uniqueness of God's presence was. As our earlier study of figures going into God's presence showed, respect for God's unique presence was jealously guarded. Those who enter gain access by his invitation only. When it is rarely contemplated, it is by invitation only. Jesus' remarks possess a frankness that dissolves such formalities.

In considering Jesus' remarks, some have argued for a type of precedent in texts declaring the vindication of the righteous like *TJob* 33:2-4, *ApocElijah* 37:3-4, and *TBen* 10:5-6.[49] Here are descriptions of figures who receive thrones with imagery that mentions God's right hand. However, these texts speak of honor coming *from* the right hand of God or of a privilege shared *with others*, so that the *TJob* text speaks of a throne from above whose "splendor and majesty are from the right hand," while the Coptic *ApocElijah* text speaks of a host of righteous Christian martyrs set "at God's right hand." These martyrs render thanks for others as they conquer the Son of Iniquity, see the destruction of heaven and earth, and receive the thrones of glory and crowns. In the *TBen*, it is the patriarchs of Enoch, Noah, Shem, Abraham, Isaac, and Jacob who rise (not sit!) "on the right hand in gladness." But Jesus' claim is not to be among the righteous, but to lead them as God's vice regent, a ruling figure like that mentioned in Ps 110:1. There is more in his claim than what we see in these texts about the vindication of the righteous, though what these texts show is a background that parallels to a lesser degree what Jesus claims. If such honor goes to the righteous, how much more honor can be contemplated for the one who brings their vindication. Perhaps this kind of expectation fueled an element of the development of this view within Jesus. As eschatological leader of the to be vindicated righteous, his place in heaven was special.

Morna Hooker summarizes well the leadership's view of the blasphemy charge, a charge that this study has attempted to ground solidly in the

---

attitude that is condemned. If someone was perceived as having made a claim that brought one too close to God or made oneself to be too much like him, these texts help show how such a claim would have been viewed. These Isaiah 14 texts parallel what was seen in chapter two as well, again indicating how consistently these portraits are, as well as the reaction to them. The views of the later rabbis are like those of Philo. The feeling is centuries old. The translation of the Son of Man text can be found in J. Neusner, ed., *TLI* vol. 18, p. 183 or *S-B*, vol. 1, p. 486. On the Son of Man text, see M. Hengel, *Studies in Early Christology*, p. 181 and n. 130.

[49]See, for example, G. R. Beasley-Murray, *Jesus and the Kingdom of God* (Grand Rapids: Eerdmans, 1986), pp. 297-98.

appropriate Jewish religious and cultural background. As she says, *"To claim for oneself* a seat at the right hand of power, however, is to claim a share in the authority of God; *to appropriate to oneself* such authority and *to bestow on oneself* this unique status in the sight of God and man would almost certainly have been regarded as blasphemy."[50] The dispute surrounding Jesus was a debate about his authority as it related to his person and mission. The Marcan text presents this as the essence of the dispute and as central to his conviction to crucifixion.

The leadership handed Jesus over to Roman officials, because they saw in him a dangerous blasphemer and deceiver. But they presented the accusation in political terms, in a form that Pilate could understand and feel enough threatened by to act. Someone like Jesus with such a comprehensive view of his own authority could be portrayed not only as a threat to Israel, but also as a potentially serious problem for Rome. In addition, by subjecting Jesus to crucifixion, the Jewish leadership was making an additional public statement that explicitly turned Jesus' death into one cursed by God, since the current reading of Deut 21:23 would see a crucifixion in such terms.[51] In fact, God would be seen as the source of such a statement by permitting such an act to take place.

At the very least, this is how the church, as reflected by Mark, portrayed the dispute from the Jewish side. But it is significant to note that such a portrayal would be done at great risk to the church, when Mark's gospel emerged in Rome. To blame both the Jewish leadership and the Romans as having a role in Jesus' death meant that two major powerful forces in the early Christians' world would share responsibility for the death. To admit that Jesus was charged as a political subversive and was executed for such a crime put Rome on notice about the Christians, even though the church would have regarded the charge against Jesus as false. To present the account this way suggests that at its base must be roots that motivated such a broad sweep of responsibility. The story had to be told, even if there was risk for the church in terms of who got blamed.

There is also a third option concerning the blasphemy that one ought to note, as it serves as a second feature that adds to the sense of offense. Two elements of potential background illuminate this aspect of the blasphemy. First, when Jesus claims to be a judging figure and that the council will see this exercise of authority, he may well be appealing to martyrdom language background that has already been noted in the expectation of vindication. But the point here is more specific. The idea of "seeing" has been discussed as an allusion to Zech 12:10, "they will look upon (ἐπιβλέψονται) him whom

---

[50]The emphasis in the quotation is ours; Morna Hooker, *The Son of Man in Mark*, p. 173.

[51]On this first century view of crucifixion, see the discussion of the work of Otto Betz in chapter 1, the discussion below of *11Q* 64:6-13, and n. 58 there.

they have pierced ... and will mourn over him."[52] But there is really nothing in this context to suggest an allusion to this text.[53] There is no allusion to "piercing" nor to the need for repentance. Rather the idea of seeing from the martyrdom tradition provides a more likely background. Three texts show the theme. *Wis* 5:2 reads, "When the unrighteous see (ἰδόντες) them, they will be shaken with dreadful fear and they will be amazed at the unexpected salvation of the righteous." *ApocElijah* 35:17 (= 5:28 in Charlesworth, *OTP*) reads, "Then the sinners in torment will see the place of the righteous. And thus grace will occur." This is a composite text, mixing Jewish and Christian elements, but again in an eschatological context, those who see are those who are judged and what they see is the vindication of the righteous. A Christian text with a similar motif is Lk 16:23. The third text is perhaps the most important. It is *1 En 62:3-5*.[54] The text reads

> On the day of judgment, all the kings, governors, the high officials, and landlords, *shall see* and recognize him — how he sits on the throne of his glory and righteousness is judged before him . . .. They shall be terrified and dejected; and pain shall seize them when *they see* that Son of Man sitting on the throne of glory."[55]

Not only does this text repeat the theme of the seeing of vindication, but it includes a reference to the seen Son of Man. As Borsch noted, the three themes of 1) they see, 2) Son of Man, and 3) sitting have a parallel. These three concepts appear in the same order in both texts and reflect "indications of the influence of older common conceptions."[56] The background means that Jesus challenges and warns his accusers that the real authority is not the Jewish council, but Jesus, who will preside over them one day. This future prospect makes their examination a sham.

Second, this aspect of the remark represents an attack on the "divinely appointed" leadership of the nation, at least that is how the leadership would have seen themselves. This attack would be read as a violation of Exod 22:27,

---

[52]Norman Perrin, *Rediscovering the Teaching of Jesus* (New York: Harper & Row, 1976), pp. 181-85.

[53]Correctly Joel Marcus, *The Way of the Lord: Christological Exegesis of the Old Testament in the Gospel of Mark* (Louisville: Westminster/John Knox Press, 1992), pp. 166-67. The following discussion of martyrdom background follows his treatment. See also R. Pesch, *Das Markusevengelium*, vol. 2, p. 438.

[54]This connection was made by F. H. Borsch, "Mark XIV.62 and 1 Enoch LXII.5," NTS 14 (1967-68): 565-67. See also M. Hengel, *Studies in Early Christology*, pp. 185-89. He notes that the seating here is something a little less than being seated at the right hand.

[55]The emphasis is ours.

[56]Borsch, "Mark XIV.62 and 1 Enoch LXII.5," NTS 14 (1967-68), p. 567. For an alternative reading of this emphasis, which also would be seen as blasphemous, see n. 45 above.

which is one of the Torah's prominent blasphemy texts. This makes Jesus both a political and a religious threat. In the leader's view not only was Jesus making a false and religiously dangerous claim by evaporating the distance between himself and God, but he was also challenging the authority of those who had responsibility for the spiritual well being of the nation, suggesting that they would be reckoned among the judged in the end. As such, he raised the prospect of intense political-social unrest, as the temple incident had already suggested. Now anyone who threatened the well being of the people and its political stability before Rome was also subject to reaction by the Jewish authorities, since presenting oneself as a person who might cause the nation to fall into Gentile hands was viewed as a dangerous political act. Such an act could be seen as a criminal offense that carried a penalty of death. Here the key text informing the cultural background is *11QTemple64:6-13*.[57] This text in the key vv. 7-9 reads

> (7) If a man slanders his [= God's] people and delivers his people up to a foreign nation and does evil to his people (8) you shall hang him on a tree, and he shall die. According to the mouth (= testimony) of two witnesses and the mouth of three witnesses (9) he shall be put to death, and they shall hang him on a tree.

Two features of the passage are important. The first is that slandering the people and putting them at risk is what leads to the sentence. Second, it is hanging by a tree, the first century cultural equivalent of which was crucifixion, that is mentioned here. The allusion is to Deut 21:22-23, which described the public display of an offender *after* he was executed on a tree. In the first century, crucifixion was seen as an equivalent of this text, even though the death came simultaneously with the public hanging.[58]

Jesus' remarks were a provocation of the strongest kind. The judges are being threatened with being judged by the accused while he functions as God's intimate representative. His threatening of the leadership with his claim to be eschatological judge and the remark suggesting that the council was unrighteous in having him stand before them was all blasphemous at this second, social level. It seriously challenged their claims for divinely appointed leadership and responsibility for Israel. This element of the charge provided the political grounds the leadership needed to take him to Rome and present him as a threat to public order. So Jesus' claims would not only have been perceived as false, a premise that could allow a very public process as

---

[57]Otto Betz, "Jesus and the Temple Scroll," in *Jesus and the Dead Sea Scrolls*, ed. James H. Charlesworth, ABRL (New York: Doubleday, 1992), pp. 80-81, 87-89.

[58]David J. Halperin, "Crucifixion, the Nahum Pesher, and the Rabbinic Penalty of Strangulation," *JJS* 32 (1981):32-46.

Strobel has noted, but those claims would be seen as potentially dangerous.[59] It is the combination that caused the leadership to act.

Jesus' remark was perceived as blasphemous at two levels. First, his claim to be able to have the prerogative of final judgment and sit next to God in heaven represented a claim to comprehensive authority, a function that the leadership could never contemplate or accept for one of such humble background. Such prerogatives, even when they were rarely contemplated, were reserved for only the very unique. His direct claim to possess such a position would have been automatically offensive. Second, his claim was also an attack on the leadership in violation of the spirit of Exod 22:27, but also an attitude that could put the social structure of the nation at risk before Rome. Jesus was different than a later object of messianic honor, Bar Kockba, as the latter figure at least had the support of some of the social-political leadership in the nation (e.g., Aqiba). So this difference placed Jesus in a category quite different from this later figure. Jesus' claim of authority went beyond political messianic claims in the view of the leadership, as it held them eschatologically accountable for what they would do with him. Such a challenge would not go uncontested. Not only had Jesus made himself too close to God, he had also created a great, irreversible gap between himself and the leadership. At the least, this is how Mark portrays the event. What must be said about this saying is that much within it seems to fit well in the cultural thought world of first century Judaism.

5. The Potential Authenticity of the Saying

The background of the Jewish perception of Jesus' blasphemy has been examined. It now remains to consider if this portrayal and background has the potential to be regarded as an authentic summary of the real scene. This question is stated carefully, for not only are we dealing with a Greek translation, but a text that is about thirty-five years removed from the original scene. This section will treat various elements that have been taken in the past to make the scene a questionable one: the temple charge, the "Jewish" expressions in vv. 61-62—namely, the circumlocutions of God involving εὐλογητός and δύναμις, the use of Ps 110:1 and Dan 7:13, the possibility of Jesus calling himself the apocalyptic Son of Man, and the combination of christological titles that appears in the question and reply. Only after all of the first four subtopics are treated can we consider the presence and relationship of the titles to one another and assess the likelihood of the saying's authenticity.

---

[59]See the discussion above and note 16.

Temple Charge

The movement from the temple charge directly into the christological issue has been seen by many as a problem for the passage. It is argued that the transition into christology is too abrupt to be credible, and thus reflects Mark's work. The scene is designed to heighten the drama, not portray reality. Mark's goal is to get to the theme of Jesus' theologically loaded definition of who he is. The redactional effort is often seen as reflecting a combination of traditional material and material from Mark. For example, Hugh Anderson writes in his comments on vv. 60-65 that

> The question that the **high priest** now puts to Jesus, **Are you the Christ, the Son of the Blessed?** is introduced somewhat abruptly in so far as it has no obvious connection with the foregoing proceedings, certainly not with the alleged prediction of Jesus' part of the destruction of the Temple.[60]

Anderson suggests that perhaps the temple charge goes back to the trial, but the juxtaposition of temple and christology is not credible.[61]

Now the question is whether such a transition is unconnected and abrupt from a historical perspective. In making literary or form judgments about what Mark has done or how he might have summarized what he may have been aware of from tradition, it is important that historical background questions not be underdeveloped or that possibilities which can show the text's unity not be ignored. A striking illustration of this problem is the criticism of Otto Betz in the recent study by W. Reinbold.[62] As he examines the passage historically, he dismisses the entire work of Betz's study, by questioning Betz's suggestion that a morning trial took place in its traditional temple locale.[63] But questioning this detail of his view does not represent a

---

[60]Hugh Anderson, *The Gospel of Mark*, NCC (London: Oliphants, 1976), pp. 330-31.

[61]Anderson, *The Gospel of Mark*, p. 329, argues that Matt 26:60 may reflect history in that a temple saying of Jesus was used at the trial. However, on p. 331, he argues that the high priest's question is a case that "here the church has put its own language on the lips of the high priest." When it comes to Jesus' reply, Anderson argues that "For Mark, the speaker here, the harried and persecuted one, is the very one inseparably connected with God's ultimate triumph." Similar in thrust are E. Linnemann, *Studien zur Passionsgeschichte*, FRLANT 102 (Göttingen: Vandenhoeck & Ruprecht, 1970), pp. 129-30 and E. Lohse, "Der Prozeß Jesu Christi," in *Die Einheit des Neuen Testament: Exegetische Studien zur Theologie des Neuen Testaments*, ed. E. Lohse (Göttingen: Vandenhoeck & Ruprecht, 1973), pp. 99-100, who notes the view of a disjunction is also found in Bultmann and Dibelius. See Lohse's note 42.

[62]Wolfgang Reinbold, *Der älteste Bericht über den Tod Jesu: Literarische Analyse und historische Kritik der Passionsdarstellungen der Evangelien*, BZNW 69 (Berlin: Walter De Gruyter, 1994), p. 256.

[63]Otto Betz, "Probleme des Prozesses Jesu," in *ANRW* II. 25.1 (Berlin: Walter De Gruyter, 1982), pp. 613-44.

careful assessment of the overall argument from historical background, but merely critiques a minor point in the presentation. Nor is his rejection of Strobel entirely compelling.[64] He rejects Strobel's work primarily on the premises that idolatry, which is allegedly the key to a Jewish deceiver charge, is nowhere in view for Jesus, and that the charge of deception is nowhere raised in the NT tradition (a point that is not true when one considers Lk 23:2 with its important reference to Jesus distorting custom in the context of a religion steeped in a commitment to revelation and tradition).

In fact, his assessment is inadequate in a variety of ways. First, there are several NT texts indicating that Jesus was seen as a deceiver explicitly using terms like πλάνος and πλανᾶ (Matt 27:63-64; Jn 7:12, 47).

Second, this testimony also comes from Jewish sources. There is a key traditional text in the Jewish tradition that makes a similar point, saying that Jesus was stoned because he "practiced sorcery and enticed Israel to apostasy" (*b Sanh* 43a- על שכישף והסית והדיח את ישראל). That such a crime was punishable with execution is shown in the list of capital crimes from *m Sanh* 7.4, as the המסית is a crime subject to the death penalty of stoning. It seems likely that the reference to stoning is a figurative way to refer to a capital execution. Another less well known set of texts from Qumran discusses how the high priest is to test for a false prophet and deceiver, using the Umin and Thummin (*4Q375; 4Q376*).[65] Other passages also develop this deceiver theme.[66]

In the texts in the Fathers where there is contention with Jews, the charge against Jesus is consistently that he was a magician or a deceiver, one subject to the evil arts. For example, there is a long discussion in Justin Martyr,

---

[64]August Strobel, *Die Stunde der Wahrheit*, WUNT 21 (Tübingen: J. C. B. Mohr (Paul Siebeck), 1980), pp. 81-92.

[65]On this passage which calls for sacrifices and a test using the Urim and Thummin, see J. Strugnell, "Moses-Pseudepigrapha at Qumran: 4Q375, 4Q376, and Similar Works," in *Archaeology and History in the Dead Sea Scrolls: The New York University Conference in Memory of Yigael Yadin*, Lawrence H. Schiffman, ed., JSPS 8 (Sheffield: Sheffield Academic Press, 1990), pp. 221-56 and Johannes Zimmermann, *Messianische Vorstellungen in den Schriftfunden von Qumran* (unpub. Ph.D. thesis, Tübingen, 1996), pp. 204-16. The text is fragmentary, seems to be an apocryphon of Moses, and has uncertain origins, though it appears not to be from the Qumran community itself. A similar process is discussed by Josephus in *Ant* 3.214-18, though the two sets of passages disagree whether the stone on the left (*4Q376*) or the right (Josephus) shines to give the signal. According to Nehemiah, these stones went out of use by the time of Ezra (Neh 7:65), but Josephus dates their non-use later, at c. 120 BCE; see Strugnell, p. 243. The text is significant because it shows that concern for such issues remained alive to the extent that how such examinations should take place was contemplated with the result that the penalty for such a crime was death.

[66]Martin Hengel, *Nachfolge und Charisma: Eine exegetisch-religionsgeschichtliche Studie zu Mt 8,21f. und Jesu Ruf in die Nachfolge*, BZNW 34 (Berlin: Alfred Töpelmann, 1968), pp. 44-45, n. 14.

Dialogue with Trypho 69.7, where Jesus' miracles are attributed to his abilities in magical arts as they charge him with being "a magician and a deceiver of the people" (μάγον . . . καὶ λαοπλάνον). In 108.2, he is called "a Galilean deceiver" (Γαλιλαίου πλάνου). Origen also dealt with such a claim. In *Contra Celsus* 1.68, there is a long discussion over Jesus' works and ministry. Celsus charges that he is an evil and godless man, while in 1.71, he is a God-hating and unworthy magician (θεομισοῦς ἦν τινος καὶ μοχθηρου γόητος; GCS 1,22). Eusebius repeats the charge in his *Demonstratio Evangelica* 3, 3, 1-4 and 3, 6, 1, where he considers the deceiver (πλάνος) charge (CGS 23, pp. 108-09). The consistent testimony of Christians, Jews and those Christians reporting about the Jewish view is that he was put to death, in part, for deceiving Israel.

Third, Reinbold's assessment also ignores both the relationship and the distinction between idolatry and blasphemy in the Jewish materials already noted. In Judaism, idolatry and blasphemy were comparable and sometimes were seen as interrelated offenses, but they did not have to be such.[67] The punishments for them were often viewed as similar and the way they were assessed was often paralleled.

A fourth point Reinhold also fails to consider is the difference in Betz's position from Strobel's argument, which represented a tightening of Strobel's argument at the places the links were weakest.[68] Whereas Strobel emphasized Jesus the deceiver, Betz highlights how Jesus in his messianic claim is seen as a deceiver. The difference is significant, as it fills in a gap in Strobel's argument, which Reinhold rightly notes but overplays. In sum, Reinhold's critique thoroughly fails to come to grips with the historical evidence on all sides of the controversy that Jesus was slain as a deceiver, a point that lends credibility to the careful historical background work of Strobel and Betz.

What emerges from a careful consideration of Betz's work is that a credible unity to the summarized flow of events emerges that reflects not abruptness but a careful understanding of the conceptual connections that existed at the time. Betz showed how the temple threat could have been interpreted as putting the nation at risk before Rome in a way that demanded response. Here *11QTemple* 64:6-13, already cited above, reflects a sensitivity to the political realities a temple disruption could cause and the need to deal severely with such a challenge, including the prospect of crucifixion for one found guilty of the charge. He also noted a temple-king connection in Jewish tradition, stretching back to 2 Sam 7 and appearing as well in the fourteenth petition of the *Shemoneh Esreh*.

---

[67]See our summary in chapter 2 that distinguishes between acts of blasphemy which *can be* idolatrous acts *and/or* acts of arrogance, from the category of blasphemous utterances.

[68]See the summaries on Strobel and Betz above in chapter 1 and n. 16 above.

But there still could be a minor problem with the argument in this form. It is found in the view that Messiah is possibly not explicitly said to be the builder or destroyer of the temple in these early Jewish texts.[69] Thus the connection may not be an explicit one, but an implicit one. Nonetheless the key to the high priest's transition in the question is not in this detail of building or destroying a temple in our view; it is rather in the authority, the claim of social and structural restoration (whatever it might or might not have been!), and the era that this restorative claim implies is present. Even though this temple charge apparently was dropped and could not be definitively proved, what the potential, but unproven, claim did raise was Jesus' association with some type of golden age restoration from God. Jesus did look for a restoration of the nation, in which he would have a key role. Now the figure that this type of association would suggest was a messianic one. This also made it possible to raise a political question in relationship to Rome. Thus, the transition is a quite natural one and can make good historical sense in the context, whether one takes the more explicit approach of Betz or sees only a conceptual move based on Jesus' claim of bringing restoration here.

---

[69]Robert Gundry, *Mark: A Commentary on His Apology for the Cross* (Grand Rapids: Eerdmans, 1993), pp. 898-901. He notes that it is God who builds the temple in the early key text of *4QFlor* 1-2, 10, where it is also a question whether the temple is meant, the dynasty of regal Davidic rule, or probably both (temple in vv. 1-2, dynasty in v. 10). For views on what Jesus' saying in Mark might have meant, see Gundry's discussion. As shall be argued, it is almost irrelevant what the exact meaning here is, since it was the association related to authority and restoration that led to the more focused personal question that the high priest asked. Gundry' view could perhaps be slightly overstated, if, at this time, texts like Zech 6:12 were read in the way the *Targum Zech* 6:12 and *Targum Isa* 53:5 suggest. Both these later targums suggest that Messiah will build the temple, for the Isaiah targum says that messiah "will build the sanctuary which was profaned for our sins," and the targum to Zechariah speaks of the Anointed who will be revealed, be raised up, and "shall build the temple of the Lord." If such an understanding of Messiah's role existed in this earlier period, then Betz's case is more direct, since the suggestion of a messianic building of the temple would then be explicit. But our point is that even if the connection is more implied, the connection still easily comes to the surface. For other discussions of the relation of the temple to Messiah, see E. E. Ellis, "Deity Christology in Mark 14:58," in *Jesus of Nazareth: Lord and Christ*, ed. Joel B. Green and Max Turner (Grand Rapids: Eerdmann, 1994), p. 200 and nn. 44-45, D. D. Edwards, *Jesus and the Temple* (unpub. Ph.D. dissertation, Southwestern Theological Seminary, 1992), pp. 204-07; J. Dunn, *The Parting of the Ways*, pp. 51-53, who stresses the involvement of the key priests in sending Jesus to his death as part of a dispute over religious authority; and Volker Hampel, *Menschensohn und historischer Jesus: Ein Rätselwort als Schlüssel zum messianischen Selbtsverständnis Jesu* (Neukirchen-Vluyn: Neukirchener, 1990), pp. 174-75, who also notes *LevR* 9 (111a) for this theme. They see a connection between Messiah and temple as possible for this era. The entire Temple pericope as raising the authority question is fully developed by Jostein Ådna, *Jesu Kritik am Temple: Eine Untersuchung zum Verlauf und Sinn der sogenannten Tempelreinigung Jesu, Markus 11,15-17 und Parallelen* (Unpub. Ph.D. thesis: Tübingen/Stavanger, 1993). See esp. his pp. 565-79.

The Issue of "Jewish" Expressions in vv. 61-62

According to Mark, Jesus' silence on the temple charge leads the high priest to step in and ask, σὺ εἶ ὁ χριστὸς ὁ υἱὸς τοῦ εὐλογητοῦ (Are you the Christ, the Son of the blessed One?).[70] The phrase "the Son of the blessed One" is an indirect reference to God, a circumlocution that avoids the pronunciation of God's name out of respect for the deity. In turn Jesus' reply refers to ἐκ δεξιῶν καθήμενον τῆς δυνάμεως (seated at the right hand of power), another circumlocution that describes God through his attributes of power and authority, just as the English name "the Almighty" would. The avoidance of pronouncing God's name is a Jewish custom, but whether these phrases could reflect roots in an authentic tradition has been disputed.

Two examples summarize the reasons raised for questioning the expression's authenticity and regarding it as the work of Mark or the early church. Hugh Anderson writes,

> Although the description **Son of the Blessed** is a typically Jewish reverential circumlocution for 'Son of God', it is quite improbable that a high priest of the Sadducean party would have used this language in collocation with the term 'Christ' or 'Messiah'. The semblance of verisimilitude barely disguises the fact, therefore, that here the Church has put its own language on the lips of the high priest.[71]

Though it is not entirely clear from Anderson's remarks why it is improbable that a high priest of the Sadducees would use such an expression, an explanation is provided by the remarks of Donald Juel as a part of his judgment that "the best explanation of the phrase in Mark is that it is a pseudo-Jewish expression created by the author as appropriate in the mouth of the high priest."[72] Earlier he had noted that 1) the term "'the Blessed One' as a circumlocution for the name of God is almost completely unattested", and 2) that the title "'Son of God' is rarely used as a messianic designation in extant Jewish literature."[73]

Now the tendency of those discussing this problem is to isolate the example of "Son of the blessed One" from a discussion of the "right hand of power," since the "Son" phrase is the more rare and disputed usage. But it could be argued that it is the pair of references that are revealing. The care to

---

[70]This is the Greek text. Only a few manuscripts (Γ, Φ, and a few koine) lack the reference to the Christ.

[71]Hugh Anderson, *The Gospel of Mark*, p. 331. I noted the concluding part of this citation earlier in connection with the claim that the shift to christology was abrupt after the temple discussion; see n. 60 above.

[72]Donald Juel, *Messiah and the Temple: The Trial of Jesus in the Gospel of Mark*, SBLDS 31 (Missoula, Mont.: Scholars Press, 1977), p. 79.

[73]Juel, *Messiah and the Temple*, p. 78.

be reverential by the high priest is respected and repeated by Jesus even as he replies.[74] The detail and the paired response add notes of solemnity to the report. The fact that the two expressions play off of one another should be noted before looking at each expression separately.

It is important to summarize the key linguistic data for both expressions.[75] Traces of the expression "the blessed One" can be found in *m Ber* 7.3 and in *1 En* 77:2.[76] The usage in *1 En* is significant because it refers to "the eternally Blessed." The other Jewish uses of "blessed One" reveal that this phrase is an old synagogue prayer expression, a common respectful way to refer to God, though it is in a dependent, adjectival construction and is not used independently as an isolated name. In fact, there is a long string of traditional discussions about this blessing which invokes God as the one who is to be blessed (המבורך), a phrase tied to a remark by Rabbi Ishmael (c 120 CE), who said the blessing in the synagogue should be, "Bless the Lord who is blessed." The remark concludes a long discussion about the proper benedictions for a variety of situations and audience sizes (*m Ber* 7.3). The development of the

---

[74]This point only applies if the report of the trial did not alter a direct reference to God by Jesus to match the priest's question in order to remove an element of potential blasphemy by naming God directly, a view noted earlier as it was raised by Robert Gundry. My contention is that this is one of the reasons Gundry's suggestion is less than likely at this point. I view the pairing as significant, at least for Mark's portrayal of the event. Though Jesus is making bold claims, he is portrayed as doing so while showing respect for God. Only Mark's version has this pair of circumlocutions, as Matt 26:63 (Are you the Christ, the Son of God?) and Lk 22:67 (If you are the Christ, tell us.) alter the question slightly. The variation means that we are dealing with summaries of the scene here as opposed to the actual wording in at least two of the synoptic gospel portrayals, but a movement away from an almost liturgical-like circumlocution is more likely than the reverse, since a circumlocution is more indirect. Nonetheless, the question remains whether even these summaries are a good general reflection of what took place.

[75]Gustav Dalman, *Die Worte Jesu*, 2th ed. (Darmstadt: Wissenschaftliche Buchgesellschaft, 1965 [1930, 2nd ed]), pp. 163-65, Strack-Billerbeck, 2:51, and Craig A. Evans, *Jesus and His Contemporaries: Comparative Studies*, AGAJU 25 (Leiden: E. J. Brill, 1995), pp. 421-22.

[76]The key expression in the Mishnah is המבורך. See especially, Joseph Heinemann, *Prayer in the Talmud*, SJ 9 (Berlin: Walter de Gruyter, 1977, pp. 100-11, 314, esp. p. 105, n.1. His index contains thirty seven different blessing formulaes involving God. Judiasm was in the habit of showering blessings upon God in its worship. See also *Sifre Deut* § 306 (Finkelstein, p. 342, l. 6). This account has both the blessing ("Bless you the Lord who is to be blessed") and a response that uses the phrase "Bless you the Lord who is to be blessed forever." The two phrases here are: ברכו את ה' המבורך for the blessing and ברוך ה' המבורך לעולם for the response. Though the expression "the eternally Blessed" has not been found in Aramaic fragments of this *1 En* passage, a parallel expression is found in 4Q209 as it reflects *1 En* 23:3-4 (See also Maier's translation, vol. 2, p. 161). The connection to 23:3-4 is noted in Michael Knibb, *The Ethiopic Book of Enoch* (Oxford: Clarendon Press, 1978), p. 179. The Jerushalmi text noted below can be found in P. Schäfer and H.-J. Becker, ed., *Synopse zum Talmud Yerushalmi.* Band I/1-2 (Tübingen: J. C. B. Mohr (Paul Siebeck), 1991), pp. 188-91.

discussion on proper blessing formulaes continues in texts such as *b Ber* 49b-50a (2x), *Mek -Pisḥa* 16 on Exod 13:3 (lines 130-40- Lauterbach), and *y Ber* 11b-c (3x, though the first reference in 11b is only in the London and Paris mss.). The benediction comes to expression in the very old Jewish prayer known as the *Qaddish*.[77] It also was associated with a morning invitation to worship with the call, "Bless you the Lord the one to whom blessing is due."[78] Another Jewish text alludes to this prayer without using the specific benediction (*t Ber* 5.18). So this description is a part of the central prayer life of the nation, an old synagogue prayer. The use of ברך is reserved for God in Judaism. When people are said to be blessed, another term is used (אשרי).[79] So the term ברך is particularly related to God in Judaism. It has overtones of appreciation, prayer, and worship. Its widespread use in the liturgical tradition suggests an old practice.

If the Semitic expression was used at Jesus' examination in a way the Greek reflects, then the priest is speaking of God with great respect as he introduces the question, a point that adds solemnity to its import. Now what is also important in the *1 En* text is that it appears next to a parallel reference to "the Most High," showing that Jews often piled up titles in close proximity to one another when discussing a significant figure. This point is important for the later consideration of the proximity of titles in the Mk 14 setting.

In the Mishnah, the reference to God as blessed comes, as was already noted, from Rabbi Ishmael (c 120 CE), who reports one of the congregational blessings to be, "Bless you the Lord who is to be blessed." Here the expression is adjectival, a reading that also could be applied to the Marcan text as an alternative way to translate what the Semitic could have been behind the text of Mark. So although the exact phrase "Son of the blessed One" is not attested, all of the elements for it are present and parallels of this type of expression do exist in Judaism as the expression "Son of the Most High" in 4QpsDanA[a] shows.[80] In responding to Juel's claim that this is a

---

[77]Ismar Elbogen, *Der jüdische Gottesdienst in seiner geschichtliche Entwicklung* (Hildesheim: Georg Olms, 1962 [1931 ed.]), pp. 92-98. The prayer comes at the end of the reading of Torah or at the end of a public sermon. In *y Sof* 21.6, 10.8, and 19.1, the prayer is associated with the conclusion of the reading of Torah, and comes at the end of the sequence of prayers. These connections appear to be a little more recent in origin. The oldest named rabbi who is tied to the prayer's use is Jose b. Ḥalafta (c 150 CE). See *Sifre Deut* § 306 and *b Ber* 3a. The expression is יהא שמה רבא מברך לעלם. Staerk, *Altjüdiche Liturgiche Gebete* KTVU 58 (Berlin: Walter de Gruyter, 1930), pp. 30-31.

[78]J. Heinemann, *Prayer in the Talmud*, p. 25.

[79]See for example, Ps 1.

[80]For a recent discussion of this Qumranian text, see Émile Puech, "Fragment d'une apocalypse en araméen (4Q246 = pseudo-Dan[d]) et le 'Royaume de Dieu'," RB 99 (1992):98-131. For discussion of its significance for NT studies, see J. Fitzmyer, "The Contribution of Qumran Aramaic to the Study of the New Testament," NTS 20 (1974):382-

"pseudo-Jewish" expression, Marcus cautions, "The fragmentary nature of our sources for first-century Judaism, however, casts doubt on the appropriateness of the prefix 'pseudo-'."[81] Even the fragmentary nature of our sources shows a series of examples that are quite similar to what we have in Mark.

When it comes to the reference to power, things are a little clearer.[82] *1 En* 62:7 has a figurative reference to power, though not as a name, when it says, "For the Son of Man was concealed from the beginning, and the Most High One preserved him in the presence of his power." The expression itself appears throughout the Jewish tradition in *Sifre Num* § 112 [on 15:31], where Rabbi Ishmael (c 120 CE) refers to the mouth of "the Power" (הגבורה). Similar are references to "from the mouth of the Power" in *b 'Er* 54b (מפי הגבורה- 2x); *b Yebam* 105b (מפי הגבורה), and *Tg Job* 5:8 and its reference to "from the Power [תקיפא]." The two talmudic texts describe how Moses received the Law from the Almighty. Similar is *b Shab* 88b, a text already noted above in chapter 3, where the giving of the Law to Moses meant "every single word that went forth from the mouth of the Almighty (מפי הגבורה) was split up into seventy languages." In *b Meg* 31b, Rabbi Abaye (c 335 CE) notes that the curses in Leviticus need to be read one verse at a time because "Moses uttered them from the mouth of the Almighty" (מפי הגבורה). We will see below that this theme appears in other texts as well and is tied to the prohibition to idolatry, an important connection for our topic. A variation on the phrase is "the Power that is above" in *Sifre Deut* §319 [on 32:18], while "from the mouth of the Power" appears again in *ARN* [A] 37.12. An alternate text to *Sifre Deut* § 9 on Deut 1:9 says, "Moses said to Israel, 'I did not speak to you on my own, but out of the mouth of the Almighty.'" *Mek* also has several examples invoking Moses.[83] *Mek-Beshallah 2* (26a) on Exod 14:2 has Moses report on the

---

401 and his "4Q246: The "Son of God" Document from Qumran," Bib 74 (1993):153-74, as well as C. Evans, *Jesus and His Contemporaries*, AGAJU 25, pp. 107-11, who rightly defends a probable messianic reading for this text noting parallels between it, Isa 10:20 — 11:16, and Ps 89:27-28 (= Eng. 26-27) against Fitzmyer's non-messianic reading. This messianic reading is argued in detail by Johannes Zimmermann, *Messianische Vorstellungen in den Schriftfunden von Qumran*, pp. 112-49. He sees a link between Son of Man of Dan 7 and the use of this title here. This text has been alternately numbered 4Q246 and 4Q243 (how Fitzmyer numbered the text in 1974). The recognized designation now is 4Q246.

[81]Joel Marcus, "Mark 14:16: 'Are you the Messiah-Son-of God?'" NovT 31 (1989):127, n. 6.

[82]For brief discussions of these texts, see A. Marmorstein, *The Old Rabbinic Doctrine of God,* vol. 1: The Names and Attributes of God (London: Oxford University Press, 1922), p. 82; G. Dalman, *Die Worte Jesu*, 1:164-65; S-B 1:1006-07; 2:308.

[83]The following *Mekilta* references are keyed to Lauterbach's English translation edition and the numbering system of Finkelstein. See Lauterbach, 26a on 1:190; 54b on 2.147; 59b on 2:182, and 71a on 2:266. For a discussion of this theme, see E. Urbach, *The Sages*, pp. 80-96 and 722-24, esp. 84-86. On p. 86 he closes his survey with this remark, "Without doubt,

freedom of the Israelites that came from "the mouth of the Almighty" (הגבורה מפי). *Mek-Amalek* 4 (59b) on Exod 18:19 calls Moses to seek counsel "with the Power" (בגבורה). *Mek-Baḥodesh* 9 (71a) on Exod 20:18 has Ishmael (c 120 CE) report the words of Akiba (c 120 CE) that speaks of the people hearing the fiery word coming out of the"mouth of the power" (מפי הגבורה). *Mek-Amalek* 1 on Exod 17:13 (54b) has Rabbi Eleazar (c 130 CE) speak of the war being by "the order of the Power" (פי הגבורה). *Mek-Vayassa* 1 on Exod 15:22 has two references coming from Rabbi Eleazar that Moses got the command for the journey "from the mouth of the Almighty" (מפי הגבורה). Later in the same passage while discussing Exod 15:24, the remark is made that when Israel spoke against Moses she was "speaking against the Almighty" (הגבורה על). Both refer to the time of the Exodus and God directing the journey. The term is especially suited to the authority of God and the events associated with the Exodus. This usage is well enough distributed to be seen as common.

In fact the *Sifre Num* § 112 text was noted in the discussion on blasphemy and is a significant text.[84] Here the reference to Moses comes through the teaching of Ishmael (c 120 CE). Idolatry associated with blasphemy is the topic. The act is seen as a violation of the first commandment which "Moses had spoken from the mouth of the Almighty" (מפי הגבורה). Similar in force is *b Mak* 24a, where the command not to have other gods is said by R. Hamnuna (c 290 CE) to have come "from the mouth of the Almighty" (מפי הגבורה). Parallel to that is a reference in *b Hor* 8a, where Ishmael again is the source and again the word about idolatry is "I [am the Lord your God] and you shall not have [any other gods before me]" were heard from the "mouth of the Almighty" (מפי גבורה; the context makes it clear that idolatry is the topic). Now this phrase is showing up consistently as an expression of the revelation to Moses and in a wide range of materials. The association of the term with the authority of God in establishing the nation and giving the Law is significant background.

The expression is almost an idiom. *ARN* 37 elaborates when it notes in comparing Moses and Aaron that "Moses heard the words from the mouth of the Almighty, while Aaron heard them from the mouth of Moses (שמע מפי משה משה שמשה שמע מפי הגבורה ואהרן)."[85] Thus to invoke "the Power" is to speak of the God of the nation who speaks with authority. The expression is so widely attested in the early midrashim that it has a good claim to early roots. The

---

this epithet corresponds to the term δύναμις that occurs also in Matthew xxvi 6. Jesus declares: 'Hereafter shall ye see the Son of Man sitting on the right hand of the *Gevûra* (ἐκ δεξιῶν τῆς δυνάμεως)." He notes it is found by the end of the first century with this force.

[84]Karl G. Kuhn, *Sifre zu Numeri*, RB 2 vol. 3, p. 330, esp. n. 74, and the edition of Horowitz, p. 121, line 9.

[85]For the text, see Salomon Schechter, *Aboth de Rabbi Nathan*, p. 110. I thank Martin Hengel again for putting me on the trail of many of these texts both for blessing and power.

consistency of the usage shows that the expression is full of subtlety and significance. Jesus claims he will sit next to the Almighty, serving beside the true God with full authority as his unique representative. To allude to a description of God that may have been associated with Moses, the Exodus, and the nations' origin surely makes the claim of Jesus even stronger — and more provocative. This kind of involved Jewish expression is unlikely to have its origin in the early church, particularly in a gospel that is written with Gentile concerns in mind.

All of this evidence shows that both expressions fit this setting (*contra* Anderson). But what arguments exist for the likelihood that Mark did not create it? First, Mark has no hesitation in using "Son of God." He does so at various key points, including 1:1 (introduction); 3:11; 5:7; 15:39 (centurion). The middle two cases involve unclean spirits. Interestingly in 5:7, there is the complex expression, Jesus, son of God the Most High (υἱὲ τοῦ θεοῦ τοῦ ὑψίστου). So the expression without a direct reference to God is unusual for Mark. As Kazmierski notes, to attribute its origin to Mark "would be strange in light of his redactional interest in the Hellenistic form of the confession of Sonship."[86] Though I would hesitate to characterize Son of God as a Hellenistic title in light of Qumranian finds (such as 4QFlor 1:10-11) and the tighter inter-relationship between the various cultures, Kazmierski's point about Marcan preferred expression is correct and speaks against Marcan creation.

Second, the very dissimilarity of the expression with Christian titles speaks for "Son of the blessed One" as a non-Christian use, for it requires not only the use of the circumlocution, but an appreciation by Mark's audience of the fact that it substitutes for "Son of God." His audience might not appreciate the subtlety of the indirect reference, regardless of whether Son of God should be read in messianic or in more exalted terms. Significantly, Matthew, writing for a potentially more sociologically sensitive audience opts for the more direct "Son of God" here in 26:63, even doubling the reference by including before the question an oath to the "living God." This indicates that Mark is far less likely to have formed the phrase. Not only was it not his style, it was a hard expression for his audience.

Third, power is not a substitute for God elsewhere in the NT, despite the numerous uses of Ps 110:1 in these texts (Acts 2:34-35; Rm 8:34; Eph 1:20; Col 3:1; Heb. 1:3, 13; 8:1; 10:12; 12:2). All of this points to the exceptional usage as being exactly that, exceptional, and not contrived. Something motivated Mark to write in this indirect style. Neither is it clear that the source would be a creative attempt to echo Jewish tradition perhaps through

---

[86]Carl R. Kazmierski, *Jesus, the Son of God: A Study of the Marcan Tradition and Its Redaction by the Evangelist,* FB 33 (Würzberg: Echter Verlag, 1979), p.171. He prefers to argue that Mark got it from Jewish Christian tradition.

Jewish-Christian sources, since the evangelist Matthew writing for that setting lacks such a reference, though he does retain the reference to power in 26:64 (as does Lk 22:69). When these circumlocutions appear, the evangelists seem motivated by something present in their tradition that causes them to use them. The respect shown to God by the high priest in asking his key question in this sensitive trial setting and the reciprocal response by Jesus are very appropriate for this setting. It is a subtle touch that by its unique character points to authenticity at the root of the trial tradition.

The Use of Psalm 110:1 and Daniel 7:13

This topic and the next one are closely bound together. One could discuss them together, but the availability of these Old Testament images is still a separate discussion from Jesus' use of the Son of Man title. So I will consider issues tied to the question of the apocalyptic Son of Man separately.

In considering authenticity issues tied the use of Ps 110:1, the key text is Mk 12:35-37, where Jesus raised the question why David calls the Christ Lord, if he is supposed to be David's son.[87] If this passage raising the issue of what Messiah should be called is authentic, then there is nothing unusual about its presence in the trial scene.

Now the major objection to the authenticity of this text is its alleged dependence on the LXX to make its argument. It is claimed that the word play involving the title "Lord" is only possible in the LXX, so that this text must be a later christological reflection of the post-Easter, Hellenistic Christian community.[88] Hahn also rejects any attempt to suggest how this text may have been read in Hebrew or Aramaic had there been an attempt to avoid pronunciation of the divine Name, a view Dalman noted years ago.[89]

Two points need to be made here. First, one cannot exclude by mere declaration the likely possibility that the divine Name was not pronounced in an oral setting. The evidence for this likelihood was considered above in the discussion of whether the blasphemy might have entailed pronunciation in the reading of the divine Name. There it was noted as possible, but not certain that the divine Name may not have been pronounced. The minute such a substitution was made, the ambiguity would exist in Aramaic (אמר מריא למראי). Second, even if the substitution was *not* made, the problem the Mk 12 text introduces remains, though with slightly less of an edge. The problem of the Mk 12 text is not that a divine title Lord is used, but that David, an ancestor in

---

[87]For a full treatment of Ps 110:1 and its suitability to this setting, see Darrell Bock, *Luke 9:51 – 24:53*. BECNT, 3b (Grand Rapids: Baker, 1996), 1630-41.

[88]This argument is clearly summarized by Ferdinand Hahn, *Christologische Hoheitstitel.* UTB 1873, 5th ed. (Göttingen: Vandenhoeck & Ruprecht, 1995), pp. 112-15.

[89]Gustav Dalman, *Die Worte Jesu*, 2th ed. (Darmstadt: Wissenschaftliche Buchgesellschaft, 1965 [1930, 2nd ed]), p. 270.

a patriarchal society, calls a descendant his Lord. This problem exists in the text in its Hebrew form as well. In the entire dispute over the later christological significance emerging from this text, it has been forgotten that the dilemma originally rotated around the honor that David gives to the proposed Messiah. Thus it is quite possible that the text in an unaltered Semitic form could raise the dilemma which Jesus points out is present in the text. Why would David call his ancestor Lord? These two considerations mean that Ps 110:1 could be used as a way of probing the authority of the Messiah from the perspective of the one to whom the regal promise, according to Jewish tradition, was given.[90] Nothing in this requires a post-easter reading of this passage.

But there is a final consideration as well that speaks for the authenticity of Jesus' use of Ps 110:1 in Mk 12. It is the very ambiguity and Jewishness of the way Jesus makes his point. The playing down of the Davidic sonship of the messianic figure is counter to the normal post-Easter emphasis as Acts 2:30-36, 13:23-39, Rm 1:2-4 and Heb 1:3-14 show. Those who see a post-Easter creation must deal with this question: would the later, post-Easter community have expressed its conviction about Jesus as Lord in a way that is so ambiguous and that at the same time gives an impression that the long established and quite traditional Son of David title is insignificant? The form of Jesus' query has long been noted to parallel the Jewish style of putting two remarks in opposition to one another. The point is to deny one remark or the other, but to relate them to each other.[91] Jesus is simply affirming that David's calling Messiah Lord is more important than his being called Son of David. The query, which is unanswered in the Mk 12 context, serves to underscore the Messiah's authority and the ancestor's respect for his anticipated great descendant.

Now this issue of Messiah's authority is not a post-easter question. It has been raised by the very nature of the Jerusalem events in which this dispute appears. An earlier query about Jesus' authority came after he cleansed the temple (Mk 11:27-33). Jesus' query here is an answer to the question the leadership posed to him earlier, but with a critical and reflective edge. If David, the one who received the promise, responds to Messiah as Lord, how should others (including you leaders!) view him? Jesus does not make an identification of himself with Messiah here, but merely sets forth the question

---

[90]The one assumption that Jesus and his audience share about the psalm is that David is the speaker, a view that would fit the first century setting. Given that the text is regal and that Israel lacks a king currently, it is also likely that the text would be seen as applying to a king in a restored monarchy, a restoration that could easily conjure up messianic implications.

[91]David Daube, *The New Testament and Rabbinic Judaism* (London: University of London/Athlone, 1956), pp. 158-63.

theoretically and leaves the conclusions to his listeners. Would a post-Easter creation be so subtle?

In sum, the evidence of Mk 12:35-37 indicates that it is far more likely that Ps 110:1 goes back to a period when the issues surrounding Jesus' identity were surfacing than to roots in a community that was openly confessing him in the midst of dispute. As such, its claims to authenticity are strong. This means that the roots of the well attested NT use of Ps 110:1 go back, in all likelihood, to Jesus himself and so this was a text he could use in his defense later, particularly if he contemplated a vindication by God for what was currently taking place. But to show that Ps 110:1 could be used by Jesus, or even was used by him on one occasion, does not indicate if it was used as shown in Mk 14:62. This requires consideration of the text it is paired with, Dan 7, along with some reflection on the Son of Man concept that also is present in the examination scene.

The question of the possibility of Jesus' use of Dan 7:13-14 is closely tied to the issue of the apocalyptic Son of Man. This question is examined now in two steps. Here we consider the conceptual parallels that indicate that during the time of Jesus, speculation about an exalted figure like the Son of Man existed in Judaism. If this is the case, then it can be seriously questioned whether such reflection would have taken place only in a post-Easter context. The next section will consider the issue of the apocalyptic Son of Man and Jesus by looking at the evidence of these sayings themselves, regardless of whether the evidence discussed in this section is deemed as persuasive or not.[92]

It has been a hotly debated question whether one should speak of a Son of Man figure in Judaism, since 1) the expression in Dan 7 is not a title but a metaphor ("one like a son of man") and 2) it was argued that there is no clear evidence in early Jewish texts that such a figure was ever the subject of intense Jewish speculation.[93] More recently the debate has been renewed in a more cautiously stated form. Whether there was *a* Son of Man concept might be debated, but there certainly was speculation about an exalted figure whose roots lie in Dan 7.[94]

---

[92]This two tiered division of the discussion reflects the way the issue is carefully discussed by Raymond Brown, *The Death of the Messiah*, ABRL (New York: Doubleday, 1994), pp. 509-15.

[93]Ragner Leivestad, "Exit the Apocalyptic Son of Man," NTS 18 (1971-72)::243-67. His argument is that only *1 En* gives potential early Jewish evidence for such a title, that it is too late to count, that a title is not certain in the Similitudes, and that a title is not present in Dan 7. One can certainly challenge Leivestad's view of the date of *1 En*. Other points he raises will be addressed shortly.

[94]John J. Collins, "The Son of Man in First-Century Judaism," NTS 38 (1992):448-66 and William Horbury, "The Messianic Associations of 'The Son of Man,'" JTS 36 (1985):34-55.

The summary evidence involves a wide array of sources from Judaism of varying strength. For example, in *11QMel* 2.18, there is reference to the bearer of good tidings who is "the messiah of the spirit of whom Dan[iel] spoke." Now the allusion in the context is probably to Dan 9:25 as seven weeks are mentioned, but Horbury notes that this text was often associated with Dan 2 and 7 in Jewish thinking, so that the same figure may be in view.[95] In *Ezekiel the Tragedian*, a text we examined in detail in chapter 3, it was noted how the throne of exaltation on which Moses sat was associated with the plural expression "thrones," language from Dan 7:9.

Other slightly later texts have even clearer points of contact. *1 Enoch* is filled with Son of Man references (46:2-4; 48:2; 62:5, 7, 9, 14; 63:11; 69:27, 29 [2x]; 70:1; 71:14, 17). His enthronement in 62:2-14 is clearly connected to Dan 7, with its reference to a seat on the "throne of glory."[96] *1 En* 46:1 and 47:3 also seem to allude to Dan 7, as do 63:11; 69:27, 29. The three variations in the way Son of Man is referred to here does not alter the point that it is Dan 7 that is the point of departure for the imagery here.[97] *4 Ezra* 13 is another, later text that also reflects speculation about the figure of Daniel. A rabbinic dispute attributed to the late first century involves Akiba's claim that the "thrones" are reserved for David. It suggests an interesting regal, Dan 7 connection (*b Hag* 14a; *b Sanh* 38b).[98] Some have compared the Melchizedek figure to aspects of Son of Man speculation.[99] Finally, there is the image of the exalted figure in *4Q491*, who also echoes themes of Dan 7.[100] The variety of passages indicates that Dan 7 imagery was a part of first century Jewish eschatological and apocalyptic speculation, apart from the question of the presence of a defined Son of Man figure. This means that Dan 7 was a text that was present in the theologically reflective thinking of Judaism and was

---

[95]William Horbury, "The Messianic Associations of 'The Son of Man,'" JTS 36 (1985):42. Among the texts he notes are *NumR* 13.14 on Num 7:13 and *Tanḥ* (Buber) Gen, *Toledoth* 20, with the second text including a reference to Isa 52:7 as well.

[96]For issues tied to the dating of this material, see the discussion of Enoch in chapter 3 above. It is probably a first century text. On the differences between the Enoch imagery and Ps 110:1-Dan 7 see M. Hengel, *Studies in Early Christology*, pp. 185-89, as Enoch lacks explicit reference to the intimate right hand imagery. However, it must be noted that Enoch's imagery otherwise is very close to these older texts. The issue in all of them is judging authority carried out as the exclusive representative of God from a heavenly throne. The throne and authority are associated directly with God.

[97]*Contra* Leivestad.

[98]These talmudic texts were also discussed in chapter 3 under David, and mention was made of *4 Ezra* in the Son of Man discussion there.

[99]P. J. Kobelski, *Melchizedek and Melcheresa'*, CBQMS 10 (Washington: Catholic Biblical Association, 1981), p. 136.

[100]Martin Hengel, *Studies in Early Christology* (Edinburgh: T & T Clark, 1995), p. 202.

quite available to Jesus once he started thinking in eschatological-vindication terms. There is nothing here that requires a post-Easter scenario.

Now it would seem that only two questions remain with regard to the use of these texts. 1) Did Jesus spoke of himself as the apocalyptic Son of Man? 2) Is the kind of stitching together of Old Testament allusions like the combination in Mk 14:62 possible for Jesus? It is to those questions I now turn, but it must be said before considering them that there is nothing in the evidence about the use and availability of Ps 110:1 or Dan 7:13 that demands that the usage here be seen as post-Easter. When Perrin wrote arguing that Mk 14:62 reflected a Christian pesher tradition, he did not note any of the Jewish texts that reflect traces of Dan 7 that we have just noted.[101] The only question is whether Jesus would have portrayed himself as the authoritative figure described in these texts. We have already argued the case for Ps 110:1 above in discussing Mk 12:35-37, but what of the apocalyptic Son of Man?

Jesus and Apocalyptic Son of Man

The Son of Man title has been the object of intense debate for years and shows no signs of abating.[102] Numerous issues surround the discussion, including an intense debate over whether the expression is representative of a title (like the form of its consistent NT use) or is an idiom. If it is an idiom, then it has been argued that the meaning is either a circumlocution for "I" (Vermes) or an indirect expression with the force of "some person" (Fitzmyer).[103] It seems that for most students of the problem today, a formal title, or at least a unified Son of Man concept, did not yet exist in the early first century and that Fitzmyer has more evidence available for his view on the idiom. It is the idiomatic element in the Aramaic expression and the lack

---

[101]Norman Perrin, "Mark XIV.62: The End Product of a Christian Pesher Tradition?" *NTS* 13 (1965-66):150-55.

[102]Representative of a host of recent mongraphs since 1980 are: A. J. B. Higgins, *The Son of Man in the Teaching of Jesus,* SNTSMS 39 (Cambridge: Cambridge University Press, 1980); Seyoon Kim, *The 'Son of Man' as the Son of God,* WUNT 30 (Tübingen: J. C. B. Mohr [Paul Siebeck], 1983); Barnabas Lindars, *Jesus Son of Man* (Grand Rapids: Eerdmanns, 1983); Chrys C. Caragounis, *The Son of Man: Vision and Interpretation.* WUNT 38 (Tübingen: J.C.B. Mohr [Paul Siebeck], 1986); Volker Hampel, *Menschensohn und historischer Jesus: Ein Rätselwort als Schlüssel zum messianischen Selbtsverständnis Jesu* (Neukirchen-Vluyn: Neukirchener, 1990); Anton Vögtle, *Die „Gretchenfrage" des Menschensohn-Problems: Bilanz und Perspective,* QD 152 (Freiberg: Herder, 1994).

[103]I have already commented on this issue in a special excursus entitled "The Son of Man in Aramaic and Luke (5:24)," in *Luke 1:1 – 9:50* (Grand Rapids Baker, 1994), pp. 924-30 and in "The Son of Man in Luke 5:24," BBR 1 (1991):109-21. For Vermes' argument, see "The Use of בר נשא/בר נש in Jewish Aramaic," *An Aramaic Approach to the Gospels and Acts.* 3rd ed., by M. Black (Oxford Clarendon, 1967), pp. 310-30. For Fitzmyer, "Another View of the 'Son of Man' Debate," JSNT 4 (1979):58-68 and *A Wandering Aramean: Collected Aramaic Essays.* SBLMS 25 (Missoula, Mont.: Scholars Press, 1979), pp. 143-61.

of a fixed concept in Judaism that allow any "son of man" remarks to be ambiguous unless they are tied to a specific passage. This means the term could be an effective vehicle as a cipher for Jesus that he could fill with content and also define as he used it. One can argue that Jesus used the term ambiguously initially and drew out its force as he continued to use it, eventually associating it with Dan 7.[104]

But as was shown above, it is one thing to say that the Son of Man figure was not a given in Judaism and quite another to say that Dan 7 was not the object of reflection in that period. Even if a fixed portrait did not exist, the outlines of such a figure were emerging and was available for reflection and development.

So what is the evidence in the gospels themselves concerning the apocalyptic Son of Man? The designation Son of Man appears 82 times in the gospels and is a self designation of Jesus in all but one case where it reports a claim of Jesus (Jn 12:34).[105] When one sorts out the parallels, it looks as if 51 sayings are involved of which 14 appear to come from Mark and 10 from the sayings source, often called Q.[106] Of the four uses outside the gospels, only one (Act 7:56) has the full phrase with the definite article as it appears in the gospels (Heb 2:6; Rev 1:13; 14:14). In other words the term is very much one associated with Jesus' own speech. In texts where the early church is clearly speaking, the term is rare and the full form of the title almost never appears. The nature of its usage by Jesus and the oddity of the term as a Greek expression is the probable reason the expression appears in this limited way. Other titles like Son of God, Messiah, and Lord were more functional. Jeremias makes the following observation about the pattern of usage,

> How did it come about that at a very early stage the community avoided the title ὁ υἱὸς τοῦ ἀνθρώπου because it was liable to be misunderstood, did not use it in a single confession, yet at the same time handed it down in the sayings of Jesus, in the synoptic gospels virtually as the only title used by Jesus of himself? How is it that the instances of it increase, but the usage is still strictly limited to the sayings of Jesus? There can only be one answer; the title was rooted in the tradition of the sayings of Jesus right from the beginning; as a result, it was sacrosanct, and no-one dared eliminate it.[107]

---

[104]I have made this argument elsewhere already, "The Son of Man in Aramaic and Luke (5:24)," in *Luke 1:1 – 9:50* (Grand Rapids Baker, 1994), pp. 924-30 and in "The Son of Man in Luke 5:24," BBR 1 (1991):109-21.

[105]Mark 2:10 is sometimes seen as an editorial aside by Mark, but the syntax of the verse makes the case for this awkward and quite unlikely. The breakdown is 69 times in the Synoptics (Matt 30; Mk 14; Lk 25), and 13 times in John.

[106]R. Brown, *The Death of the Messiah*, p. 507.

[107]J. Jeremias, *New Testament Theology: The Proclamation of Jesus,* trans. John Bowden (New York: Charles Scribner's Sons, 1971), p. 266.

These factors make a good case for seeing the expression as having roots in Jesus' own use. But such observations only defend the general use of the term. What can be said about the apocalyptic Son of Man sayings?

Turning to the apocalyptic sayings, it is significant to note how multiply attested the apocalyptic Son of Man is within the tradition[108]:

Mark: Mk 8:38 = Matt 16:27 = Lk 9:26
Mk 13:26 = Matt 24:30 = Lk 21:27
Mk 14:62 = Matt 26:64 = Lk 22:69

Q: Matt 24:27 (like Lk 17:24)
Matt 24:37 (like Lk 17:26)
Matt 24:39 (like Lk 17:30)
Lk 12:8 (Matt 10:32 lacks the title)

M: Matt 10:23
Matt 13:41
Matt 19:28 (Lk 22:30 lacks the title) [this could be Q]
Matt 24:44
Matt 25:31

L: Lk 17:22

What the chart clearly shows is that the apocalyptic Son of Man shows up in every level of the synoptic gospel tradition. If the criterion of multiple attestation means anything or has any useful purpose, then the idea that Jesus spoke of himself in these terms should not be doubted. The text that a few of these sayings most naturally reflect is Dan 7:13-14 (triple tradition: Mk 13:26 = Matt 24:30 = Lk 21:27; Mk 14:62 = Matt 26:64 [though Lk 22:69 lacks an allusion to Dan 7]; M: Matt 13:41; Matt 19:28; Matt 25:31; Q: possibly Lk 12:8 [though the parallel in Matthew lacks the title, it does have a vindication-judgment setting]). Though the association to Dan 7 is less widely attested, it is the only biblical text that supplies the elements for those texts that do treat vindication. Once the category of apocalyptic Son of Man is associated with Jesus, then a connection with Dan 7 cannot be very far away.

The idea that this expression was the sole product of the early church faces two significant questions that bring the early church view into doubt. 1) Why was this title so massively retrojected, seemingly being placed on Jesus' lips in an exclusive way unlike any other major title like "Lord," "Son of God," and "Messiah"? 2) If this title was fashioned by the early church and was

---

[108]The following chart is part of a longer apocalyptic Son of Man discussion in my *Luke 9:51 – 24:53*, pp. 1171-72.

created as the self-designation of Jesus, why has it left almost no trace in non-Gospel NT literature, also unlike the other titles?[109] All of this makes it inherently much more likely that Jesus referred to himself as Son of Man in an apocalyptic sense than that the church was responsible for this identification. This means not only that Dan 7 would have been available for Jesus' use, but the evidence also suggests that this text was a significant feature in his thinking by the end of his ministry, since most of the explicit references to Dan 7 appear as Jesus drew near to Jerusalem.

There is one other strand of evidence, which makes a connection between king and Son of Man, that also needs attention. The combination of Son of Man imagery and that of a regal figure, the very combination appearing in Mk 14:62, also has traces in the NT and in Jewish tradition. In the NT the other such text is Mk 2:23-27, where the authority of David appears side by side with an appeal to the authority of the Son of Man, as the famous king is the prototype and justification for Jesus' exceptional activity with his disciples on the Sabbath.[110] In Judaism, it has been noted how the Danielic figure has elements of authority that other texts from the Jewish Scriptures attribute to the great expected king.[111] Bittner notes how the themes of rule, kingdom, and power reflect the presentation of a regal figure, not a prophetic one: "Das Wortfeld von Herrschaft, Königtum, und Macht ist in der altorientalischen Königsvorstellung, wie sie sich in der davidischen Königstradition widerspiegelt, verwurzelt, hat aber mit Prophetenberufungen nichts zu tun."[112] He also notes that such authority, when it involves vindication or the subordination of the nations, points to the regal office (Mic 5:3-4; Zech 9:10; Ps 2; Ps 89). When the issue of duration surfaces, it is kingship that is present (2 Sam 7:16; Isa 9:5MT, vv. 6-7 Eng). The description of the closeness of the Son of Man to God is paralleled most closely by the image of the king (Ps 2:6; Isa 9:5MT, vv 6-7 Eng). As such, the parallels, all of which are a part of the Jewish Scripture and so were available to Jesus, suggest the possibility of making the association present in this text between Messiah and Son of Man.

---

[109]These two penetrating questions are raised by R. Brown, *The Death of the Messiah*, p. 507. If the identification of Jesus with the apocalyptic Son of Man is not correct, one can still defend the authenticity of the saying by appeal to a close, enigmatic use by Jesus, a view I noted above in n. 45 and discuss below in n. 116.

[110]This example is noted in C. A. Evans, *Jesus and His Contemporaries* (Leiden: E. J. Brill, 1995), p. 452. One must be careful here. There is no direct reference to Daniel, only the title is present. Nonetheless, the issue of authority in a major area, the Law, leads one to see the usage as descriptive of one with some form of judicial or discerning authority.

[111]Wolfgang Bittner, "Gott-Menschensohn-Davidssohn: Eine Untersuchungen zur Traditionsgeschichte von Daniel 7,13f.," FZPT 32 (1985):357-64.

[112]Wolfgang Bittner, "Gott-Menschensohn-Davidssohn: Eine Untersuchungen zur Traditionsgeschichte von Daniel 7,13f.," FZPT 32 (1985):358.

A formal question also remains. Is there evidence that Jesus may have combined Old Testament texts in a way like that found in this passage? Objection is often made that Jesus does not combine texts from the Scripture in the way Mk 14:62 does.[113] Yet two texts point to the potential of Jesus conceptually linking texts together like this side by side. In Mk 7:6-10 = Matt 15:4-9 Jesus ties together references to the honoring of parents and the honoring with lips (Isa 29:13; Exod 20:12 [Deut 5:16]; Exod 21:17 [Lev 20:9]) in a way that recalls Jewish midrashic reflection. The concepts of "honor" and "father and mother" appear here. In a second text, Matt 22:33-39 (like Mk 12:29-31), there is a linkage involving the concept of love (Deut 6:4-5; Lev 19:18), resulting in a text on the great commandments of love.[114] These texts, which touch on ethical themes often seen as reflective of Jesus' social emphases, indicate that the style of linking two themes from the Scriptures together could be reflective of Jesus. There is nothing in terms of content or form that prevents this kind of association of texts from reaching back to Jesus. In many cases the evidence that the expression goes back to him is stronger than that the church created it.

Because he has said it so clearly, I cite two of Raymond Brown's remarks about Mk 14:62.[115] One full citation involves one of his key observations as he assesses Perrin's claim that Mk 14:62 is Christian midrash and the other comes from his conclusion on this discussion:

> First, if it seems quite likely that the Gospel picture is developed beyond any single OT or known intertestamental passage or expectation, and that this development probably took place through the interpretative combination of several passages, any affirmation that all this development *must have* come from early Christians and none of it from Jesus reflects one of the peculiar prejudices of modern scholarship. A Jesus who did not reflect on the OT and use the interpretative techniques of his time is an unrealistic projection who surely never existed. *The perception that OT passages were interpreted to give a christological insight does not date the process.* To prove that this could not have been done by Jesus, at least inchoatively, is surely no less difficult than to prove that it was done by him. Hidden behind the attribution to the early church is often the assumption that Jesus had no christology even by way of

---

[113]So for example, Volker Hampel, *Menschensohn und historischer Jesus: Ein Rätselwort als Schlüssel zum messianischen Selbtsverständnis Jesu*, pp. 179-80. He argues that this form of the combination reflects the early church, as does discussion of a returning Son of Man. Against the second point, see above.

[114]A similar teaching appears in the response of a scribe in Lk 10:25-29 to set up the parable of the good Samaritan, but the context is distinct enough that this may well reflect a distinct tradition, not a true parallel. See the discussion of the Lucan pericope in my *Luke 9:51 – 24:53*, pp. 1018-21.

[115]R. Brown, *The Death of the Messiah*, pp. 513-14 is the first citation and the second appears on pp. 514-15. The emphasis in the citation will be his.

reading the Scriptures to discern in what anticipated way he fitted into God's plan. Can one really think that credible?

Later he concludes,

Jesus could have spoken of the "Son of Man" as his understanding of his role in God's plan precisely when he was faced with hostile challenges reflecting the expectations of his contemporaries. Inevitably the Christian record would have crossed the *t's* and dotted the *i's* of the scriptural background of his words. Even though *all* of Mark 14:61-62 and par. is phrased in Christian language of the 60s (language *not* unrelated to issues of AD 30/33), there is reason to believe that in 14:62 we may be close to the mindset and style of Jesus himself.[116]

This study agrees and would make one additional, significant point. There is a far greater likelihood that this text, with all of its sensitivity to Jewish background, goes back to Jesus, or, at the least, reflects an earlier setting than Mark or the early church with which he was associated. One of those elements of sensitivity is present in the way the charge of blasphemy coheres

---

[116]Brown, *The Death of Messiah*, p. 515, n. 55 adds one more point for authenticity in this Marcan text. He notes that the phrase "you will see" is difficult and may favor authenticity, since "Post factum, Christians producing such a statement might have been clearer." A variation on this kind of defense of authenticity, which I believe is less likely is that advocated by Bruce Chilton, who suggests that Jesus taught about the Son of Man as an angel of advocacy in the divine court, who would defend and vindicate the accused because his mission represented the program of God. In this view, the Son of Man, though distinct from Jesus, is inseparably bound with his mission. Thus, at the trial, the remark would still reflect some authenticity and would still be seen by the leadership as a blasphemous rebuke of the leadership's rejection of Jesus' divinely directed announcement of God's program. The Synoptics transform this close association into a purely christological identity. See his "The Son of Man: Human and Heavenly," in *The Four Gospels 1992: Festschrift Fran Neirynck*, vol. 1. BETL vol. C, ed by F. Van Segbroeck, C. M. Tuckett, G. Van Belle, and J. Verheyden (Leuven: Leuven University Press, 1992: 203-18. This reading does defend the essential historicity of the remark, but construes its force differently. Such a view, though possible, seems to leave the issue of the person of Jesus understated and unanswered as the reply in effect becomes, "I am who I claimed, whoever that is, and God will vindicate me through his agent, showing this examination to be in grave error." Chilton argues that Jesus' appeal to the witness of heaven is like an appeal he engages in Mk 9:1, where the idiomatic phrase "to taste death" refers to the immortality of the witnesses Moses and Elijah, to whom Jesus appeals through an oath in the midst of the transfiguration scene. My problem with this view of Mk 9 is that, despite the important linguistic evidence for the possibility of an idiom, it is not clear that Moses was seen in Jewish tradition as one who was taken up while never experiencing death. See the dispute over this in the Moses discussion in chapter 3. For this view, see his, "'Not to Taste Death': A Jewish, Christian and Gnostic Usage," *Studia Biblica 1978: II. Papers on the Gospels, Sixth International Congress on Biblical Studies Oxford 3-7 April 1978*, ed by E. A. Livingston. JSNTS 2 (Sheffield: JSOT Press, 1980), pp. 29-36. For reasons I am arguing, I think a more direct, personally focused reply from Jesus is slightly more likely. Chilton's view is similar to the view discussed in nn. 45 and 109.

with perceptions that would have belonged to the Jewish leadership, a point to which we now return for a final time as we deal with one final argument against authenticity.

The Meaning and Relationship of the Titles

It has been claimed that the stacking up of titles like that in this text is an argument against authenticity.[117] But on formal and conceptual grounds, this claim can be rejected as going beyond the evidence. In discussing the Son of Man it was noted that development is not the private domain of the early church and that combining allusions does not date when such combinations took place. Jesus was capable of formulating an association between Ps 110:1 and Dan 7:13. But this response only deals with the nature of Jesus' reply. What about the way the high priest forms his question with multiple titles? Is the stacking up of titles in his question necessarily artificial?

That the high priest would be concerned about Jesus as Messiah is natural, since a charge is being considered that the leadership feels makes Jesus a candidate to be taken to the Roman authorities. As was also noted, the temple incident and sayings might suggest that Jesus had associated himself with events tied to the return of the Messiah. The Son of Man title is Jesus' way to refer to himself, so both of these elements fit. The only potentially extraneous element is the allusion to Son of the Blessed.

But on formal grounds it is not unusual in Judaism for titles to be piled on one another when one is emphasizing a point. I already noted in an earlier discussion how two names were given for God in *1 En* 77:2, namely "Most High" and "eternally Blessed." One can point to *1 En* 48:2 with its reference to "the Lord of Spirits, the Before-time," a construction much like the one seen in Mk 14. Similar is *Ps Sol 17:21* with its reference to "their king, the son of David." Of course, the outstanding biblical example of the piling up of names is *Isa* 9:6 [Eng], and here also it is a regal figure being named. When this takes place there is something solemn about what is being said. So there is nothing formally odd about the high priest questioning Jesus and doing so with a combined set of titles that suggests the seriousness of the moment.

Read in this light, it appears that the high priest is asking Jesus to confirm his messianic status. Now this point in the question has been challenged in the past because it is not a capital crime in Judaism to claim to be Messiah, that is, it is not blasphemy.[118] The point that messianic confession is not

---

[117]As Donald Juel states about the Mk 14 combination, "The combination of allusions presumes a developed stage of reflection." See his *Messianic Exegesis: Christological Interpretation of the Old Testament in Early Christianity* (Philadelphia, Fortress, 1988), p. 146. Many of the reasons for this view have been noted in the previous section.

[118]See the remarks in Joel Marcus, "Mark 14:61: 'Are you the Messiah-Son-of-God?'" NovT 31 (1989):127-29.

inherently blasphemous is a correct one as the examination of blasphemy showed. But this objection makes an assumption about the question sequence that should be critiqued. The incorrect assumption is that what the examination was seeking and what resulted from the examination were exactly the same thing. It assumes that Jesus' affirmative reply to the high priest's messianic question makes the blasphemous remark revolve around messiahship. But the contention of this study is that this is not the relationship between the priest's question and Jesus' answer. The examination was about messiahship, so that a socio-political issue could be taken to Rome. The threat that Jesus represented to the people in the leadership's view, in a view much like *11QTemple* 64:6-13 expresses, meant that he should be stopped and brought before Rome as a political-social threat, if that danger could be proven. The leadership could have developed real concern about this threat when Jesus uttered the parable of the wicked tenants, which was clearly an attack on the leadership and suggested that Jesus was a "son," whose rejection would be vindicated by God.[119] The threat to Jewish leadership could be translated into a threat to Rome's leadership as well. Jesus believed that he represented God and had authority from above. This could be represented as possessing a claim to independent authority, a risk to all current socio-political structures and a potential source of public instability. This is what the priest's question sought to determine.

But Jesus' reply responds to this messianic query *and yet does even more.* It represents a severe assault on the sensibilities of the Jewish leaders at two levels. First, the reply speaks for an exalted Jesus who sees himself as too close to God in the leadership's view. Second, he makes claims as a judge who one day will render a verdict and/or experience a vindication against the very leadership that sees itself as appointed by God. In the first element of Jesus' affirmation, the leadership sees a dangerous claim to independent authority that they can take to Rome. In both aspects of Jesus' reply there is, in their view, cause for seeing the highest of religious offenses possible, namely, blasphemy. The priest's ripping of his garments says as much. What started out as an investigation about Messiah becomes more than that because of the way Ps 110:1 and Dan 7:13 are woven together. This does not mean that the messianic charge is wrong or even that it is "corrected." It means that Jesus defines who the messiah is in terms of the totality of the authority he possesses. This figure is so close to God that he possesses authority even over the nation's highest religious authorities. That is Jesus' claim. It parallels the claim he made earlier in the parable, except that now God's vindication is to be carried out by and/or on behalf of the very person they are trying to

---

[119]This is perceptively noted by Jack Kingsbury, *The Christology of Mark's Gospel* (Philadlephia: Fortress Press, 1983), pp. 118-19.

condemn. Jesus claims total independence from the authorities of the day. He can be taken to Rome.

One final point needs attention. Recent scholarly debate has surfaced over whether the two titles in the phrase "Christ, Son of the Blessed" are synonymous and what their relationship is within Jesus' Son of Man reply. Some have argued the case that Son of the Blessed or Son of Man limits the Christ title or operates in a distinct way from it.[120] The difference may be summarized in four different options, two for the question and two for the reply. 1) Did the high priest ask about Jesus as the royal messiah (synonyms)? 2) Was he asking about a "Son of God" type Messiah (second title restricts the first)? 3) Was Jesus replying in terms of public function, not making a titular confession (son of man as "this man")? 4) Was Jesus replying by using a title referring to the figure he preferred to highlight (Son of Man = apocalyptic Son of Man)

Arguing for these differences of force is too subtle for the trial setting. Distinctions like these would not be present in the original setting. It certainly would not be present in the question of the high priest. Although it is likely that Mark's readers, given subsequent events, could have raised important distinctions and implications from the terms and may even have read this scene as containing such implications in the titles (i.e., option 2), the original setting is unlikely to have been a confrontation with this distinction. The temple-messiah connection in the pericope argues for an earthly figure as the issue, a royal messianic figure of some kind (option 1). And the Jewish use of the expression "Son of God" as in texts like *4QFlor* 1:10-11 with its connection to 2 Sam 7, does not suggest such a distinction for Son of God. As for Son of Man, the use of Dan 7 points attention immediately to the figure of that text (option 4) and suggests an identification with the messianic figure the priest asks about.

---

[120]Though the phrase Christ, Son of the Blessed is usually seen as making a synonymous connection and Jesus' reference to the Son of Man is seen as simply saying the same thing in a different or more precise way, recently various ways of arguing for a distinction have been presented. Marcus, "Mark 14:61: 'Are You the Messiah-Son-of-God?'" NovT 31 (1989):125-41, prefers a sense of Messiah, the Son of God type. But there is no sense in the text that the high priest is pursuing a fresh line of questioning nor that Son of God *to Jewish ears* would suggest an exalted, transcendent image in distinction to a regal one, unless something else in addition was said to show it was taken as such. Jack Kingsbury, *The Christology of Mark's Gospel* (Philadelphia: Fortress Press, 1983), pp. 118-23, 160-67, argues that Son of God is a confessional title, while Son of Man is a "public" title, showing what Jesus does rather than identifying who he is. So the priest asks who Jesus is, while Jesus replies what he will do as "this man" (= Son of Man). His distinction is designed to question the use of Son of Man as a title. But it is hard, given the allusion to Dan 7, not to see an identification of a figure as present in Jesus' remarks. In fact, it looks like an equation of that figure with the one about whom he is asked.

In sum, Jesus' reply is what leads to his conviction on a charge that had both socio-political elements in it, as well as a religious dimension that constituted blasphemy. None of the objections to the historicity of this scene have persuasive substance. Though one cannot prove absolutely that the scene goes back to Jesus, the evidence makes it likely that the Marcan summary is reflective of what took place or is a reasonable representation of the fundamental conflict of views. It has great verisimilitude with the background that would apply to such a scene. Moreover, the scene possesses clear indications that make it more likely that its details go back to the trial setting than that Mark created it.

6. Conclusion

The following summary brings together the conclusions of this chapter and the entire study. A careful study of the historical background to Jewish views on blasphemy and exaltation does help bring fresh light on a passage that stands near the center of the description of the final events of Jesus' life. In an era when literary study and various exclusively textual approaches to the gospels are on the rise, it is important to recall that such studies cannot replace the need for careful work in the socio-cultural environment of these texts. Literary and formal studies can tell us much about the author and how he tells his story, but they often cannot answer the historical questions the text raises. To assume that they can without a careful philological-conceptual examination of the historical background risks making literary and formal studies roam into an area for which they are not equipped. When it comes to history, the text must be placed in a broader context than mere form and literary analysis. Too much recent study of the historical Jesus has ignored these fundamental limitations in our method or has looked for historical parallels in the wrong milieu as if Jesus had little connection to Judaism at all.

There will always be a need for detailed work in the Jewish environment in which these texts, and the events associated with them, operated. A study like this one shows that there is still room for careful historical work in the sources. In a time when there is renewed interest in the Jewish background to the gospels, a study like this one shows that there is still much to be gained by a careful pursuit of the roots to concepts in these historically significant texts. Some concepts give evidence of a wide distribution in the many sources that explain Judaism. Such distribution indicates that the ideas they possess may have ancient roots in Jewish belief. Both blasphemy and exaltation give evidence of such a wide distribution. Though both areas were debated and discussed, there are fundamental elements of belief that appear alongside the more disputed points.

This study offers the following six conclusions:

1. Blasphemy certainly included the use of the divine Name in an inappropriate way (*m Sanh* 6.4; 7.5; Philo, *On the Life of Moses* 2.203-06). This is blasphemy defined in its most narrow sense. Some suggest that the use of alternate names also constituted verbal blasphemy, though this was heavily debated (*m Sch^eb* 4.13; *b Sch^eb* 35a; *b Sanh* 55b-57a, 60a). Such alternate utterances did produce warnings. Unheeded warnings produced violations and possible full culpability.

But there are also acts of blasphemy, which might or might not include a narrow blasphemous utterance. Acts of idolatry and of arrogant disrespect for God or toward his chosen leaders were seen as blasphemous. Judgment, whether from God or through intermediate agents, was the appropriate response. The list of examples who fit in this category include: Sisera (*NumR* 10.2), Goliath (Josephus, *Ant* 6.183), Sennacherib (2 Kgs 18 — 19 = Isa. 37:6, 23), Belshazzar (Josephus, *Ant* 10.233, 242), Manasseh (*Sifre Numbers* §112), and Titus (*b Giṭṭ* 56; *ARN* 7[B]). Defaming the temple is also seen in such a light. Significantly for this study is the view that comparing oneself to God is blasphemous and is like the other arrogant acts condemned as an affront to God (Philo, *On Dreams* 2.130-31; *Decalogue* 13-14.61-64).

2. God's presence is such that only a few are contemplated as being able to approach him directly. Such figures are great luminaries of the past or anticipated luminaries of the future. Those who sit in his presence constitute an even smaller group. They are directed to do so by God and often sit for a short time.

Of the angels, only Gabriel is said to sit and that is merely as an escort to Enoch (*2 En* 24). In fact, in general, angels do not sit before God. Even Michael, the great archangel, is never portrayed as seated before God. That honor, if it is considered to exist at all, is left to some made "in the image of God." In fact, Metatron-Enoch is punished when he sits in a way that allows him to be confused with God (*3 En* 16).

The list of humans who sit is longer: Adam, Abel, Enoch, Abraham, Moses, David, Job, the Messiah, Enoch-Son of Man, and Enoch-Metatron. Some sit for a time merely to record revelation (Enoch: *Jub* 4:20; *T Abr* 10 — 12; *2 En* 24:1-3). Adam and Abraham sit as witnesses to the final judgment (*T Abr* 10 — 13), while Abel sits for a time and exercises an initial stage of judgment. Adam is returned to the position he had before the fall (*Life of Adam and Eve* 47:3; *ApocMos* 39:2-3 [= later version of *Life of Adam and Eve*; OTP 2:259]). Job argues that he will be restored to a heavenly seat of honor (*T Job* 33). It is possibly a messianic seating that appears in *4Q491* 1.13-17, though it is not certain (an honoring of the Teacher of Righteousness, the end time prophet, or the Eschatological High Priest are other options). What is excluded is an angelic figure. David sits before God on Israel's throne in *4Q504* frag. 2 IV.6. Messiah sits on the right, with Abraham on the left in *Midrash Ps* 18.29, while David sits by God in heaven according to Akiba (*b Ḥag* 14a; *b Sanh* 38b). None of these seatings in God's presence look like the full vice regency that other Jewish texts suggest. Only a few texts reveal a seating that also seems to suggest a significant sharing of authority with heaven.

More exalted portraits appear with Moses (*Exagoge* 68-89), but this looks to portray symbolically his Exodus ministry. Enoch-Metatron is given extensive authority, only to have it removed when it appears that he is confused with sharing power with God (*3 En* 3 — 16). The unique picture in the Jewish material is Enoch-Son of Man (*1 En* 45:3; 46:1-3; 51:3; 61:8; 62:2-8; 70:2; 71:1-17). This figure appears to possess full eschatological power. But the portrait was not without controversy as other traditions strongly counter this portrait, suggesting discomfort with the extensive authority attributed to Enoch (*T AbrB* 11:3-8; *b Sanh* 38b, where reference is to Metatron, who is often associated with Enoch as 3 Enoch 4:2-3 with 16:1-5 show).

Some Jews seem willing to consider the possibility of being seated next to God for a select few great figures and under very limited conditions. Except for perhaps the Enoch-Son of Man portrait, none of these images appears to portray a figure seated at God's right hand or sharing the merkabah throne at the same time God is seated there. To sit at God's right hand on the same throne, as opposed to sitting on a separate throne next to God or somewhere else in heaven, is a higher form of exaltation than merely sitting in heaven. This kind of explicit language never appears concerning any of these figures, although Aqiba's remarks about David are close. Other Jewish material challenges all such forms of exaltation. In the exceptionally rare cases of those who get to go into God's presence, those who go there are divinely directed there. It is not a role one claims for oneself.

3. The examination of Jesus was never intended as a Jewish capital trial. Rome was always the goal. Though we do not know the exact legal procedures for the time of Caiaphas, the discussion of capital authority and procedures for the period of Roman rule would have been an idealized discussion, since Jews did not possess such authority under the Romans. Rules recorded for the Mishnah over a century later might share such an idealized quality as well. Nevertheless, the fact that a hearing and not a final, decisive capital trial was undertaken with Jesus might explain why the procedure of Jesus' examination looks so different from that of a capital trial as it is portrayed in the Mishnah. In fact, certain kinds of cases, where a figure is seen as a deceiver call for a quick and ultimately public procedure (*m Sanh* 11.3 [Danby = 11.4]; *t Sanh* 7.11, 10.11).

4. Numerous potential sources for the trial scene exist. Among the candidates who could have been sources of information are Joseph of Arimathea, Nicodemus, Saul, and the very public polemic against Jewish Christians directed by Annas's family, a battle that ran for more than thirty years. The scene does not lack for sources, even though no disciples of Jesus were present as eyewitnesses.

5. Jesus' blasphemy operated at two levels. 1) There was a claim to possess comprehensive authority from the side of God. Though Judaism might contemplate such a position for a few, the teacher from Galilee was not among the luminaries for whom such a role might be considered. As a result, his remark would have been seen as a self-claim that was an affront to God's presence. 2) He also attacked the leadership, by implicitly claiming to be their future judge (or by claiming a vindication by him). This would be seen as a violation of Exod 22:27, where God's leaders are not to be cursed. A claim that their authority was non-existent and that they would be accounted among the wicked is a total rejection of their authority. To the leadership, this was an affront to God as they were, in their own view, God's established chosen leadership. Jesus' claim to possess comprehensive independent authority would serve as the basis of taking Jesus before Rome on a socio-political charge, as well as constituting a religious offense of blasphemy that would be seen as worthy of the pursuit of the death penalty. In the leadership's view, the socio-political threat to the stability of the Jewish people is an underlying reason why this claim had to be dealt with so comprehensively.

6. The scene as a summary of trial events has a strong claim to authenticity, a stronger claim to it than to the alternative that the scene was created by Mark or by the early church.

The conflict between Jesus and the Jewish leadership two millennia ago was grounded in fundamentally different perceptions of who he was and the authority he possessed for what he was doing. Either he was a blasphemer or the agent of God destined for a unique exaltation/vindication. The claims Jesus apparently made were so significant and the following he gathered was so great that a judgment about him could not be avoided. This study has tried to understand how those who examined Jesus saw his claims in light of their legal-theological categories. Why did the leadership seek to deal decisively Jesus? The checkered trail of history since these events, especially between Jews and Christians, requires that every effort be made to understand what caused a segment of Judaism's leadership to send Jesus to face capital examination by Rome. It is important to consider what claims Jesus made that they saw as so disturbing. Every generation will surely assess these events afresh in light of the new data and methods that may emerge, but it is important that these assessments appreciate how the issues were seen at the time. A study of Jewish views of blasphemy and exaltation brightly illumines the ways in which the Jewish leadership perceived Jesus' claims. The ancient sources also reveal how blasphemy and exaltation clashed during this examination in ways that changed the course of history.

Bibliography of Works Cited

Primary Sources

Allegro, John. *Qurman Cave 4 I (4Q158-4Q186)*. Discoveries in the Judean Desert of Jordan, vol. V. Oxford: Clarendon Press, 1968.

Bietenhard, Hans. *Midrasch Tanhuma B*. Judaica et Christiana, ed. Simon Lauer and Clemens Thoma, vol. 6. Bern: Peter Lang, 1982.

_____. *Sifre Deuteronomium*. Judaica et Christiana, ed. Simon Lauer and Clemens Thoma, vol. 8. Frankfurt: Peter Lang, 1984.

Black, Matthew. *The Book of Enoch or I Enoch: A New English Edition*. Studia in Veteris Testamenti Pseudepigrapha, ed. A. M. Denis and M. De Jonge, vol. 7. Leiden: E. J. Brill, 1985.

Blackman, Philip. *Mishnayoth*. 6 vol. London: Mischna Press, 1951-56.

Braude, William G. *The Midrash on the Psalms,* 2 vols. Yale Judaica Series, ed. Leon Nemoy, vols. 13 and 14. New Haven: Yale University Press, 1959.

_____. *Pesikta Rabbati*. New Haven: Yale University Press, 1968.

Charles, ed., R. H. *The Apocrypha and Pseudepigrapha of the Old Testament*. Oxford: Oxford University Press, 1913.

Charlesworth, James H. *The Dead Sea Scrolls: Hebrew, Aramaic, and Greek Texts with English Translations: Vol. 1- Rule of the Community and Related Documents*. Tübingen: J. C. B. Mohr (Paul Siebeck), 1994.

_____. *The Old Testament Pseudepigrapha*. 2 vol. New York: Doubleday, 1983-85.

Clark, Ernest G. and Martin McNamara and Shirley Magder. *Targum Neofiti 1: Numbers and Targum Pseudo-Jonathan: Numbers*. The Aramaic Bible, ed. Martin McNamara, vol. 4. Edinburgh: T & T Clark, 1995.

Colson, F. H., and G. H. Whitaker, and J. W. Earp, and R. Marcus. *Philo Works, Greek Text and English Translation*. Loeb Classical Library, 10 vols. plus 2 supplementary vols. Cambridge, Mass.: Harvard University Press, 1929-53.

Cowley, A. *Aramaic Paypri of the Fifth Century B.C.* Oxford: Clarendon Press, 1923.

Danby, Herbert Chanan. *The Mishnah: Translated from the Hebrew with Introduction and Brief Explanatory Notes*. Oxford: Oxford University Press, 1933.

Davies, P. R. *The Damascus Document: An Interpretation of the Damascus Document*. Journal for the Study of the Old Testament Monograph Series, vol. 25. Sheffield: JSOT Press, 1983.

Denis, A.-M. *Concordance Grecque des Pseudépigraphes d'Ancien Testament*. Louvain-au-Neuve: Université Catholique de Louvain, 1987.

Diez Macho, Alejandro. *Neophyti 1: Levitico*. Textos Y Estudios, ed. Federico Perez Castro, Madrid: Consejo Superior De Investigaciones Cientificas, 1971.

_____. *Neophyti 1: Numeros*. Textos Y Estudios, ed. Federico Perez Castro, Madrid: Consejo Superior De Investigaciones Cientificas, 1974.

Dos Santos, E. C. *An Expanded Hebrew Index for the Hatch-Redpath Concordance to the Septuagint*. Jerusalem: Dugith Publishers Baptist House, no date.

Dupont-Sommer, A. *The Essene Writings from Qumran*. trans. Geza Vermes. Gloucester, Mass.: Peter Smith, 1973.

Elliger, K. and W. Rudolph, eds., *Biblia Hebraica Stuttgartensia*. Stuttgart: Deutsche Bibelgeschsellbaft, 1997.

Epstein, ed., I. *The Babylonian Talmud*, 35 vol. London: Soncino, 1936-1948.

Finkelstein, Louis. *Siphre ad Deuteronomium*. Corpus Tannaiticum, Berlin: Abteilung, 1939.

Fischer, Bonifatius. *Novae Concordantiae Bibliorum Sacrorum Iuxta Vulgatam Versioem Critice Editam*. Stuttgart: Frommann-holzboog, 1977.

Freedman, H. and M. Simon. *The Midrash Rabbah*, 10 vols. London: Socino, 1983.

Garcia Martinez, Florentino. *The Dead Sea Scrolls Translated: The Qumran Texts in English*. 2nd ed. trans. Wilfred G. E. Watson. Grand Rapids: Eerdmans, 1996.

Goldin, Judah. *The Fathers according to Rabbi Nathan*. Yale Judaica Series, ed. Julian Obermann, vol. 10. New Haven: Yale University Press, 1956.

Goldschmidt, Lazarus, *Der babylonische Talmud*. 8 vols. Berlin: S Calvary & Co, 1897-1909; reprint ed, Haag: Martinus Nijoff, 1933-35.

Grossfeld, Bernard. *The Targum Onqelos to Genesis*. The Aramaic Bible, vol. 6. Edinburgh: T & T Clark, 1988.

_____. *The Targum Onqelos to Exodus*. The Aramaic Bible, vol. 7. Edinburgh: T & T Clark, 1988.

_____. *The Targum Onqelos to Leviticus and The Targum Onqelos to Numbers*. The Aramaic Bible, vol. 8. Edinburgh: T & T Clark, 1988.

Hamm, Winfried. *Der Septuaginta-Text des Buches Daniel: Kap 3-4 nach dem Kölner teil des Papyrus 967*. Tübingen: Rudolf Habelt, 1977.

Hammer, Reuven. *Sifre: A Tannaitic Commentary on the Book of Deuteronomy*. London: Yale University Press, 1986.

Harrington, Daniel J. *Targum Jonathan of the Prophets*. The Aramaic Bible, ed. M. McNamara, vol. 10. Edinburgh: T & T Clark/Anthony J. Saldarini, 1987.

Hatch, Edwin. and Henry A. Redpath. *A Concordance to the Septuagint and the Other Greek Versions of the Old Testament (Including the Apocryphal Books)*. Graz: Akademische Druck, 1954.

Hengel, Martin, and Hans Peter Rüger, and Peter Schäfer, *Übersetzung des Talmud Yerushalmi*. 16 vols. Tübingen: J. C. B. Mohr (Paul Siebeck), 1975-. (= *Der Jerusalemer Talmud in deutscher Übersetzung*, ed. Horowitz, C., 1 vol, *Berakoth*)

Herford, R. Travers. *Pirke Aboth: The Tractate 'Fathers', from the Mishnah, Commonly Called the Sayings of the Fathers*. New York: Bloch Publishing Company, 1925.

Hollander, H. W. and M. De Jonge. *The Testaments of the Twelve Patriarchs: A Commentary*. Studia in Veteris Testamenti Pseudepigrapha, ed. A. M. Denis and M. De Jonge, vol. 8. Leiden: E. J. Brill, 1985.

Horowitz, H. S. *Siphre D'be Rab: Siphre ad Numeros adjecto Siphre zutta*. Corpus Tannaiticum, Leipzig: Gustav Fock, 1917.

Jacobson, Howard. *The Exagoge of Ezekiel*. Cambridge: Cambridge University Press, 1983.

Jastrow, M. *A Dictionary of the Targumim, the Talmud Babli and Yerushalmi and the Midrashic Literature*. New York: Pardes Publishing, 1950 [1903].

Knibb, Michael A. *The Qumran Community*. Cambridge Commentaries on Writings of the Jewish and Christian World 200 BC to AD 200, ed. P. R. Ackroyd, A. R. C. Leaney; J. W. Packer, vol. 2. Cambridge: Cambridge University Press, 1987.

Kuhn, Karl G. *Sifre zu Numeri. Rabbinische Texte- Tannaitische Midraschim*, ed. G. Kittel And K. H. Rengstorf, Zweite Reihe, vol. 3. Stuttgart: W. Kohlhammer, 1959.

Lauterbach, Jacob Z. *Mekilta de-Rabbi Ishmael*. Philadelphia: Jewish Publication Society, 1933-49.

Le Boulluec, A. and P. Sandevoir, ed., *La Bible d' Alexandrie* (Paris: E^{V}ditions du Cerf, 1989)

Lechner-Schmidt, Wilfried. *Wortindex der lateinische erhaltenen Pseudepigraphen zum Alten Testament. Texte und Arbeiten zum neutestamentlichen Zeitalter*, ed. K. Berger, F. Vouga, M. Wolter, D. Zeller, Tübingen: Francke Verlag, 1990.

Levy, J. and H. L. Fleischer and L. Goldschmidt. *Wörterbuch über die Talmudim und Midrashim*. Darmstadt: Wissenschaftliche Buchgesellschaft, 1963.

MacDonald ed., John. *Memar Marqah: the Teaching of Marqah.* Berlin: Alfred Töpelmann, 1963.

Maher, Michael. *Targum Pseudo-Jonathan: Genesis.* The Aramaic Bible, vol. 1B. Edinburgh: T & T Clark, 1992.

Maier, Johann. *Die Qumran-Essener: Die Texte vom Toten Meer,* 2 vols. Uni-Taschenbücher, vol. 1862-63. München: Ernst Reinhardt, 1995.

McNamara, Martin. and Robert Hayward and Michael Maher. *Targum Neofiti 1: Exodus/Targum Pseudo-Jonathan: Exodus.* The Aramaic Bible, ed. Martin McNamara, vol. 2. Edinburgh: T & T Clark, 1994.

McNamara, Martin. and Michael Maher. *Targum Neofiti 1: Leviticus and Targum Pseudo-Jonathan: Leviticus.* The Aramaic Bible, ed. Martin McNamara, vol. 3. Edinburgh: T & T Clark, 1994.

Moulton, James Hope and George Milligan. *The Vocabulary of the Greek Testament: Illustrated from the Papyri and Other Non-Literary Sources.* London: Hodder & Stoughton, Ltd., 1930.

Nestle, Eberhard, and Erwin Nestle, and Barbara Aland, and Kurt Aland, and Johannes Karavidopoulos, and Carlo M. Martini, and Bruce M. Metzger. *Novum Testamentum Graece.* 27th ed. Stuttgart: Deutsche Bibelgesellschaft, 1981.

Neusner, J. *SIFRA: An Analytical Translation.* Brown Judaic Studies, ed. J. Neusner, vol. 140. Atlanta: Scholars Press, 1988.

_____. *The Talmud of the Land of Israel: A Preliminary Translation and Explanation.* 35 vols. Chicago: University of Chicago Press, 1982-89.

Ralphs, A., *Septuaginta: Id est Vetus Testamentum graece iuxta LXX interpretes.* Stuttgart: Deutsche Bibelgesellschaft, c. 1935.

Saldarini, Anthony J. *The Fathers according to Rabbi Nathan; Aboth de Rabbi Nathan Version B.* Studie in Judaism in Late Antiquity, ed. Jacob Neusner, vol. 11. Leiden: E. J. Brill, 1985.

Schäfer, Peter. and Hans-Jürgen Becker. *Synopse zum Talmud Yerushalmi.* Tübingen: J. C. B. Mohr, 1991-.

Schäfer, Peter. and Klaus Herrmann. *Übersetzung der Hekhalot-Literatur I §§ 1-80.* Texte und Studien zum Antiken Judentum, ed. Martin Hengel and Peter Schäfer, vol. 46. Tübingen: J. C. B. Mohr (Paul Siebeck), 1995.

Schechter, Salomon. *Aboth de Rabbi Nathan.* Frankfurt: J. Kauffmann, 1887.

Septuaginta: Vetus Testamentum Graecum Auctoritae Academiae Scientiarum Gottingensis editum. 16 vols. Göttingen: Vandenhoeck & Ruprecht, 1931-.

Sokoloff, M. *Jewish Palestinian Aramaic of the Byzantine Period.* Jerusalem: Bar Ilan University Press, 1990.

Sparks, ed., H. F. D. *The Apocryphal Old Testament.* Oxford: Clarendon Press, 1984.

Taylor, Charles. *Sayings of the Jewish Fathers: Sefer Dibre Aboth Ha-Olam Comprising Pirque Aboth in Hebrew and English with Critical Notes and Excursuses.* Amsterdam: Philo Press, 1970.

Thackeray, H. St. J. and Ralph Marcus and Allen Wikgren and L. H. Feldman. *Josephus.* Loeb Classical Library, 10 vols. Cambridge, Mass.: Harvard University Press, 1926-65.

Townsend, John. *Midrash Tanhuma, Genesis: Translated into English with Introduction, Indices, and Brief Notes (S. Buber Recension).* Hoboken, NJ: KTAV, 1989.

Tromp, Johannes. *The Assumption of Moses: A Critical Edition with Commentary.* Studia in Veteris Testamenti Pseudepigrapha, ed. A. M. Denis and M. De Jonge, vol. 10. Leiden: E. J. Brill, 1993.

Uhlig, Siegbert. *Apokalypsen: Das äthiopische Henochbuch. Jüdische Schriften aus hellenistisch-römanischer Zeit,* vol. 5. Gerd Mohn: Gütersloher Verlagshaus, 1984.

Vermes, Geza. *The Dead Sea Scrolls in English.* 3rd ed. London: Penguin, 1987.

Wahl, Christ. Abrah. *Clavis Liborum Veteris Testamenti Apocryphorum Philoligica: Indicem Verborum in Libris Pseudepigraphia Usurpatorum.* Graz: Akademische Druck, 1972.

Whiston, William. *The Works of Josephus.* Peabody, Mass.: Hendrickson Publishers, 1736/1987.
Winter, Jakob. and Aug. Wünsche. *Mechiltha: Ein tannaitischer Midrasch zu Exodus.* Leipzig: J. C. Hinrichs'sche Buchhandlung, 1909.
Yonge, C. D. *The Works of Philo.* Peabody, Mass.: Hendrickson Publishers, 1854-55/1993.
Zuckermandel, M. S., ed., *Tosephta.* Jerusalem: Wahrmann Books, 1963.

Secondary Sources

Ådna, Jostein. *Jesu Kritik am Temple: Eine Untersuchung zum Verlauf und Sinn der sogenannten Tempelreinigung Jesu, Markus 11,15-17 und Parallelen.* Tübingen/Stavanger: Unpublished PhD, 1993.
Alexander, P. S. "Comparing Merkavah Mysticism and Gnosticism: An Essay in Method." *JJS* 35 (1984): 1-18.
_____. "The Historical Setting of the Hebrew Book of Enoch." *JJS* 28 (1977): 156-80.
Anderson, Hugh. *The Gospel of Mark.* New Century Bible, London: Oliphants, 1976.
Aune, David E. "Iao ('Ιαω)." in *RAC*, vol. 129. Stuttgart: Anton Hiersemann, 1994, cols. 1-12.
Baarlink, Heinrich. *Bist du der Christus, der Sohn des Hochgelobten?: Implizite und explizite Christologie im Markusevangelium.* Serie Kamper Cahiers; vol. 74. Kampen: J. H. Kok, 1992.
Bammel, E. "The Titulus." in *Jesus and the Politics of His Day*, ed. Ernst Bammel and C. F. D. Moule. Cambridge: Cambridge University Press, 1984, 353-64.
_____. "The Trial before Pilate." in *Jesus and the Politics of His Day*, ed. Ernst Bammel and C. F. D. Moule. Cambridge: Cambridge University Press, 1984, 415-51.
_____, ed.. *The Trial of Jesus.* Studies in Biblical Theology, London: SCM, 1970.
Bauckham, Richard. "The Worship of Jesus in Apocalyptic Christianity." *NTS* 27 (1980-81): 322-41.
Baumgarten, Joseph M. "A New Qumran Substitute for the Divine Name and Mishnah Sukkah 4.5." *JQR* 83 (1992): 1-5.
Beasley-Murray, G. R. "Jesus and Apocalyptic: With Special Reference to Mark 14, 62." in *L'Apocalypse johannique et l'Apocalyptique dans le Nouveau Testament*, ed. J. Lambrecht. Bibliotheca Ephemeridun Theologicarum Lovaniensium, vol. 53. Leuven: Leuven University Press, 1980, 415-29.
_____. *Jesus and the Kingdom of God.* Grand Rapids: Eerdmans, 1986.
Bernstein, Moshe J. "כי קללת אלהים תלוי (Deut 21:23): A Study in Early Jewish Exegesis." *JQR* 74 (1983): 21-45.
Benoit, Pierre. "Jesus before the Sanhedrin." in *Jesus and the Gospel*, volume 1, ed. Pierre Benoit. London: Dartman, Longman, & Todd, 1973, 147-66.
Betz, Otto. "Die Frage nach dem Messianischen Bewusstsein Jesu." *NovT* 6 (1963): 20-48.
_____. "Jesus and the Temple Scroll." in *Jesus and the Dead Sea Scrolls*, ed. James H. Charlesworth. The Anchor Bible Reference Library, New York: Doubleday, 1992, 75-103.
_____. "Probleme des Prozesses Jesu." in *Aufstieg und Niedergang der Römanischen Welt*, ed. H. Temporini and W. Hasse. vol. II. 25.1. Berlin: Walter De Gruyter, 1982, 565-647.
_____. "The Death of Chroni-Onias in the Light of the Temple Scroll from Qumran." in *Jerusalem in the Second Temple Period: Abraham Schalit Memorial Volume*, ed. A. Oppenheimer, V. Rappaport, and M. Stern. Library Of The History Of The Yishuv in Eretz Israel, Jerusalem: Yad Izhak Ben-M; Ministry Of Defense, 1980, V.
Bietenhard, Hans. *Die himmlische Welt im Urchristentum und Spätjudentum.* Wissenschaftliche Untersuchungen zum Neuen Testament, ed. Joachim Jeremias and Otto Michel, vol. 2. Tübingen: J. C. B. Mohr (Paul Siebeck), 1951.

Bittner, Wolfgang. "Gott- Menschensohn- Davidssohn: Eine Untersuchung zur Traditionsgeschichte von Daniel 7, 13f.." *Freiburger Zeitschrift für Philosophie und Theologie* 32 (1985): 343-72.

Black, Matthew. *An Aramaic Approach to the Gospels and Acts*. 3rd ed. Oxford: Clarendon Press, 1967.

_____. "The Throne Theophany Prophetic Commission and the 'Son of Man': A Study in Tradition History." in *Jews, Greeks and Christians: Religious Cultures in Late Antiquity: Essays in Honor of William David Davies*, ed. R. Hamerton-Kelly and R. Scroggs. Studies in Judaism in Late Antiquity, ed. , vol. 21. Leiden: E. J. Brill, 1976, 57-73.

"Blasphemy." in *Jewish Encyclopedia*, vol. 4. Jerusalem: Encyclopedia Judaica, 1971, 1073.

Blinzler, Josef. "Das Synedrium von Jerusalem und die Strafprozessordnung der Mischa." *ZNW* 52 (1961): 54-65.

_____. *Der Prozess Jesu*. 4th ed. Regensberg: Verlag Friedrich Pustet, 1969.

_____. *The Trial of Jesus*. Westminster, Maryland: Neuman, 1959.

Bock, Darrell L. *Luke 1:1—9:50*. Baker Exegetical Commentary on the New Testament, ed. Moises Silva, vol. 3a. Grand Rapids: Baker, 1994.

_____. *Luke 9:51—24:53*. Baker Exegetical Commentary on the New Testament, ed. Moises Silva, vol. 3b. Grand Rapids: Baker, 1996.

_____. "The Son of Man in Luke 5:24." *BBR* 1 (1991): 109-21.

_____. "The Son of Man Seated at God's Right Hand and the Debate over Jesus' "Blasphemy"." in *Jesus of Nazareth Lord and Christ: Essays on the Historical Jesus and New Testament Christology*, ed. Joel B. Green and Max Turner. Grand Rapids: Eerdmans, 1994, 181-91.

_____. "When *The Jesus Seminar* Meets *Jesus Under Fire* : On Whose Side Does History Fall?" Princeton Theological Review 4 (1997): 3-8.

Borsch, F. H. "Mark 14.62 and 1 Enoch LXII.5." *NTS* 14 (1967-68): 565-57.

Botterweck, G. Johannes and Helmer Ringgren and Heinz-Josef Fabry. *Theologisches Wörterbuch zum Alten Testament*. Stuttgart: W. Kohlhammer, 1984.

Bowker, J.W. ""Merkabah" Visions and the Visions of Paul." *JSS* 16 (1971): 157-73.

Brichto, Herbert Chanan. *The Problem of "Curse" in the Hebrew Bible*. Journal of Biblical Literature Monograph Series, vol. 13. Philadelphia: Society Of Biblical Literature And Exegesis, 1963.

Broer, Ingo. "Der Prozeß gegen Jesus nach Matthäus." in *Der Prozeß gegen Jesus: Historische Rückfrage und Theologische Deutung*, ed. Karl Kertelge. Questiones Disputatae, vol. 112. Freiburg: Herder, 1988, 84-110.

Brown, Raymond E. *The Death of the Messiah*, 2 vol. The Anchor Bible Reference Library, ed. David Freedman, New York: Doubleday, 1994.

Büchsel, Fredrich. "Die Blutgerichtsbarkeit des Synedrions." *ZNW* 30 (1931): 202-10.

_____. "Noch einmal: Zur Blutgerichtsbarkeit des Synedrions." *ZNW* 33 (1934): 84-87.

Budd, Philip J. *Numbers*. Word Biblical Commentary, vol. 5. Waco: Word, 1984.

Bultmann, Rudolf. *The History of the Synoptic Tradition*. trans. John Marsh. New York: Harper & Row, 1963.

Byington, Stephen. "יהוה and אדני." JBL 76 (1957): 57-58.

Caird, G. B. New Testament Theology. completed and edited by L. D. Hurst. Oxford: Clarendon Press, 1994.

Caragounis, Chrys C. *The Son of Man: Vision and Interpretation*. Wissenschaftliche Untersuchungen zum Neuen Testament, ed. Martin Hengel and Otto Michel, vol. 38. Tübingen: J. C. B. Mohr (Paul Siebeck), 1986.

Cassuto, U. *A Commentary on the Book of Exodus*. trans. Israel Abrahams. Jerusalem: Magnes Press, 1967 Trans. of 1951 Heb. ed..

Catchpole, David. "The Problem of Historicity of the Sanhedrin Trial." in *The Trial of Jesus*, ed. Ernst Bammel. London: SCM, 1970, 45-65.

_____. *The Trial of Jesus: A Study in the Gospels and Jewish Historiography from 1770 to the Present Day*. Studia Post-Biblica, vol. 18. Leiden: E. J. Brill, 1971.

_____. "You Have Heard His Blasphemy." *TynB* 16 (1965): 10-18.

Chernus, Ira. *Mysticism in Rabbinic Judaism: Studies in the History of Midrash*. Studia Judaica: Forschungen zur Wissenschaft des Judentums, ed. E. L. Ehrlich, vol. 11. Berlin: Walter De Gruyter, 1982.

_____. "Visions of God in Merkabah Mysticism." *JSJ* 8 (1982): 123-46.

Chester, Andrew. "Jewish Messianic Expectations and Mediatorial Figures and Pauline Christianity." in *Paulus und das antike Judentum*, ed. Martin Hengel and Ulrich Heckel. Wissenschafliche Untersuchungen zum Neuen Testament, ed. Martin Hengel, vol. 58. Tübingen: J. C. B. Mohr (Paul Siebeck), 1991, 17-89.

Chilton, Bruce. ""Not to Taste Death": A Jewish, Christian, and Gnostic Usage." in *Studia Biblica 1978: II. Papers on The Gospels, Sixth International Congress on Biblical Studies 3-7 April 1978*, ed. E. A. Livingston. Journal for The Study of the New Testament Supplement Series, vol. 2. Sheffield: JSOT Press, 1980, 29-36.

_____. *Pure Kingdom: Jesus' Vision of God*. Studying the Historical Jesus, Grand Rapids: Eerdmans, 1996.

_____. "The Son of Man: Human and Heavenly." in *The Four Gospels 1992: Festschrift Frans Neirynck*, ed. F. Van Segbroeck, C. M. Tuckett, G. Van Belle, J. Verheyden. Bibliotheca Ephemeridun Theologicarum Lovaniensium, vol. C. Leuven: Leuven University Press, 1992, 204-18.

_____. *The Temple of Jesus: His Sacrificial Program Within a Cultural History of Sacrifice*. University Park, Penn: Pennsylvania State University, 1992.

Collins, John J. *The Scepter and the Star: The Messiahs of the Dead Sea Scrolls and Other Ancient Literature*. The Anchor Bible Reference Library, New York: Doubleday, 1995.

_____. "The Son of Man in First Century Judaism." *NTS* 38 (1992): 448-66.

_____. "A Throne in the Heavens: Apotheosis in Pre-Christian Judaism." in *Death, Ecstasy, and Other Worldly Journeys*, ed. John J. Collins and Michael Fishbane. Albany: State University of New York Press, 1995, 43-58.

Colpe, Carsten. "ὁ υἱὸς τοῦ ἀνθρώπου." in *Theological Dictionary of New Testament Theology*, ed. G. Friedrich. vol. 8. Grand Rapids: Eerdmans, 1972, 430-41.

Corley, Bruce. "Trial of Jesus." in *Dictionary of Jesus and the Gospels*, ed. J. B. Green, S. McKnight and I. H. Marshall. Downers Grove, Ill: InterVarsity, 1992, 841-54.

Cranfield, C. E. B. *The Gospel according to St. Mark*. The Cambridge Greek Testament Commentary, ed. C. F. D. Moule, Cambridge: Cambridge University Press, 1959/1977ed..

Dalman, Gustav. *Die Worte Jesu*. 2nd ed. Darmstadt: Wissenschaftliche Buchgesellschaft, 1965 (1930, 2nd ed).

Daube, David. *The New Testament and Rabbinic Judaism*. London: University Of London/Athlone, 1956.

Davidson, Maxwell J. *Angels at Qumran. A Comparative Study of 1 Enoch 1-36, 72-18 and Sectarian Writings from Qumran*. JSPS, vol. 11. Sheffield: Sheffield University Press, 1992.

Davis, P. G. "Divine Agents, Mediators, and New Testament Christology." *JTS* 45 (1994): 479-503.

Davis, Philip. "Christology, Discipleship, and Self Understanding in the Gospel of Mark." in *Self-Definition and Self-Discovery in Early Christianity: A Case of Shifting Horizons. Essays in Appreciation of Ben F. Meyer from his former Students*, ed. D. Hawkin and T. Robinson. Lewiston: Mellen, 1990, 101-19.

de Bruyne, D. A. "Nouveaux Fragments: Des Actes de Pierre, de Paul, de Jean, d'André, et de l'Apocalype d'Élie." *RBen* 25 (1908): 149-61.

De Jonge, M. "The Use of Ο ΧΡΙΣΤΟΣ in the Passion Narratives." in *Jésus aux origines de la christologie*, ed. J. Dupont. Bibliotheca Ephemeridun Theologicarum Lovaniensium, vol. 40. Leuven: Leuven University Press, 1975, 169-92.

Dechent, Hermann. "Der "Gerechte"- eine Bezeichnung für den Messias." *TSK* 100 (1927-28): 439-43.

Derrett, J. M. D. "The Trial of Jesus and the Redemption." in *Law in the New Testament*, J. M. D. Derrett. London: Dartman, Longman, & Todd, 1971, 418-32, 453-55.

Dibelius, Martin. "Das historische Problem der Leidensgeschichte." *ZNW* 30 (1931): 193-201.

Donahue, John R. "Temple, Trial, and Royal Christology (Mark 14:53-65)." in *The Passion in Mark: Studies on Mark 14-16*, ed. Werner H. Kelber. Philiadelphia: Fortress Press, 1976, 61-79.

Dunn, James D. G. *Christology in the Making: A New Testament Inquiry into the Origins of the Doctrine of the Incarnation*. 2nd ed. London: SCM Press LTD, 1989.

_____. *The Parting of the Ways: Between Christianity and Judaism and their Significance for the Character of Christianity*. London: SCM Press LTD, 1991.

Edwards, D. D. *Jesus and the Temple*. Unpub. Ph.D diss.: Southwestern Theological Seminary, 1992.

Ego, Beate. "Der Diener im Palast des himmlischen Königs: Zur Interpretation einer priesterlichen Tradition im rabbinischen Judentum." in *Königsherrschaft Gottes und Himmlischer Kult im Judentum, Urchristentum und in der hellenistischen Welt*, ed. Martin Hengel and Anna Maria Schwemer. Wissenschaftliche Untersuchungen zum Neuen Testament, vol. 55. Tübingen: J. C. B. Mohr (Paul Siebeck), 1991, 361-84.

Elbogen, Ismar. *Der jüdische Gottesdienst in seiner geschichtlichen Entwicklung*. Hildesheim: Georg Olms, 1962 (1931 ed.).

Ellis, E Earle. "Deity Christology in Mark 14:58." in *Jesus of Nazareth Lord and Christ: Essays on the Historical Jesus and New Testament Christology*, ed. Joel B. Green and Max Turner. Grand Rapids: Eerdmans, 1994, 192-203.

Emerton, J. A. "The Origin of the Son of Man Imagery." *JTS* ns 9 (1958): 225-42.

Evans, Craig. "In What Sense 'Blasphemy'? Jesus before Caiaphas in Mark 14:61-64." in *SBL Seminar Papers*, ed. E. H. Lovering, Jr.. Atlanta: Scholars Press, 1991, 215-234.

_____. *Jesus and His Contemporaries: Comparative Studies*. Arbeiten zur Geschichte des Antiken Judentums und des Urchristentums, vol. 25. Leiden: E. J. Brill, 1995.

_____. *Noncanonical Writings and New Testament Interpretation*. Peabody, MA: Hendrickson Publishers, 1992.

Fiebig, Paul. "Der Prozeß Jesu." *TSK* 104 (1932): 211-28.

Fitzmyer, Joseph A. "4Q246: The 'Son of God' Document from Qumran." *Bib* 74 (1993): 153-74.

_____. "Another View of the 'Son of Man' Debate." *JSNT* 4 (1979): 58-68.

_____. *A Wandering Aramean: Collected Aramaic Essays*. Missoula, Mont.: Scholars Press, 1979.

_____. "The Contribution of Qumran Aramaic to the Study of the New Testament." *NTS* 20 (1974): 382-401.

_____. *The Gospel according to Luke*, 2 vol. The Anchor Bible, Garden City, N.Y.: Doubleday, 1981, 1985.

Flusser, David. "At the Right Hand of Power." in *Judaism and the Origins of Christianity*, ed. David Flusser. Jerusalem: Magnes Press, 301-05.

Fossum, Jarl E. *The Name of God and the Angel of the Lord: Samaritan and Jewish Concepts of Intermediation and the Origin of Gnosticism*. Wissenschaftliche Untersuchungen zum Neuen Testament, ed. Martin Hengel and Otfried Hofius, vol. 36. Tübingen: J. C. B. Mohr (Paul Siebeck), 1985.

France, R. T. "The Worship of Jesus: A Neglected Factor in Christological Debate." in *Christ the Lord: Studies in Christology Presented to Donald Guthrie*, ed. Harold H. Rowdon. Leicester: InterVarsity, 1982, 17-36.

Funk, Robert. *The Five Gospels: The Search for the Authentic Words of Jesus*. New York: Macmillan, 1993.

Gabel, J. B., and C. B. Wheeler. "The Redactor's Hand in the Blasphemy Pericope of Leviticus XXIV." *VT* 30 (1980): 227-29.

Gaylord, H. E. "Speculations, Visions, or Sermons." *JSJ* 13 (1982): 187-94.

Glasson, T. F. . "The Reply to Caiaphas (Mark XIV.62)." *NTS* 7 (1960/61): 88-93.

Gnilka, Joachim. *Das Evangelium nach Marcus*. Evangelisch-Katholischer Kommentar zum Neuen Testament, II, 1-2. Zürich: Benzinger, 1978, 1979.

_____. "Der Prozeß Jesu nach den berichten des Markus and Matthäus: mit einer Rekonstruktion des historischen Verlaufs." in *Der Prozeß gegen Jesus: Historische Rückfrage und Theologische Deutung*, ed. Karl Kertelge. Questiones Disputatae, vol. 112. Freiburg: Herder, 1988, 11-40.

_____. *Jesus von Nazareth: Botschaft und Geschichte*. Freiburg: Herder, 1993.

Goldberg, Arnold M. "Sitzend zur Rechten der Kraft: Zur Gottesbezeichnung Gebura in der frühen rabbinischen Literatur." *BZ* n.f. 8 (1964): 284-93.

_____. *Untersuchungen über die Vorstellung von der Schekhinah in der frühen rabbinichen Literatur: Talmud und Midrasch*. Studia Judaica: Forschungen zur Wissenschaft des Judentums, ed. E. L. Ehrlich, vol. 5. Berlin: Walter De Gruyter, 1969.

Goldingay, John E. *Daniel*. Word Biblical Commentary, vol. 30. Dallas: Word, 1989.

Goldstein, Jonathan A. *I Maccabees*. The Anchor Bible, vol. 41. Garden City, N.Y.: Doubleday & Company, 1976.

_____. *II Maccabees*. The Anchor Bible, vol. 42. Garden City, N.Y.: Doubleday & Company, 1983.

Gruenwald, Ithamar. *Apocalyptic and Merkavah Mysticism*. Arbeiten zur Geschichte des Antiken Judentums und des Urchristentums, vol. 14. Leiden: E. J. Brill, 1980.

_____. "Reflections on the Nature and Origins of Jewish Mysticism." in *Gershom Scholem's MAJOR TRENDS IN JEWISH MYSTICISM 50 Years Later: Proceedings on the Sixth International Conference on the History of Jewish Mysticism*, ed. Peter Schäfer and Joseph Dan. Tübingen: J. C. B. Mohr (Paul Siebeck), 1993, 25-48.

Grundmann, Walter. *Das Evangelium nach Markus*. Theologischer Handkommentar zum Neuen Testament, vol. 2. Berlin: Evangelische Verlagsanstalt, 1977.

Gundry, Robert. *Mark: A Commentary on His Apology for the Cross*. Grand Rapids: Eerdmans, 1993.

Hahn, Ferdinand. *Christologische Hoheitstitel*. 5th ed. Uni-Taschenbücher, vol. 1873. Göttingen: Vandenhoeck & Ruprecht, 1995.

Halperin, David J. "Crucifixion, the Nahum Pesher, and the Rabbinic Penalty of Strangulation." *JJS* 32 (1981): 32-46.

_____. *The Faces of the Chariot: Early Jewish Responses to Ezekiel's Vision*. Texte und Studien zum Antiken Judentum, ed. Martin Hengel and Peter Schäfer, Tübingen: J. C. B. Mohr (Paul Siebeck), 1988.

Hampel, Volker. *Menschensohn und historischer Jesus: Ein Rätselwort als Schlüssel zum messianischen Selbtsverständnis Jesu*. Nerkirch-Vluyn: Neukirchener, 1990.

Harris III, W. Hall. *The Descent of Christ: Ephesians 4:7-11 and Traditional Jewish Imagery*. Geschichte des Antiken Judentums und des Urchristentums, vol. 32. Leiden: E. J. Brill, 1996.

Harvey, A. E. *Jesus and the Constraints of History*. Philadelphia: Westminster, 1982.

Hayman, Peter. "Monotheism—A Misused Word in Jewish Studies?" *JJS* 49 (1991): 1-15.

Heil, John Paul. "Reader-Response and the Irony of Jesus before the Sanhedrin in Luke 22:66-71." *CBQ* 51 (1989): 271-84.

Heine, R. E. *Origen: Commentary on the Gospel according to John Books 1-10*. The Fathers of the Church, Washington, DC: Catholic University Of America, 1989.

Heinemann, Joseph. *Prayer in the Talmud: Forms and Patterns*. Studia Judaica, ed. E. L. Ehrlich, vol. 9. Berlin: Walter De Gruyter, 1977.

Hengel, Martin. *Crucifixion in the Ancient World and the Folly of the Message of the Cross*. trans. John Bowden. Philadelphia: Fortress, 1977.

_____. *Der Sohn Gottes: Die Entstehung der Christologie und die jüdisch-hellenistische Religionsgeschchte.* Tübingen: J. C. B. Mohr (Paul Siebeck), 1975.

_____. *Nachfolge und Charisma: Eine exegetisch-religionsgeschichtliche Studie zu Mt 821f. und Jesu Ruf in die Nachfolge.* Beihefte zur Zeitschrift für neutestamentliche Wissenshaft und die Kunde der älteren Kirche, vol. 34. Berlin: Alfred Töpelmann, 1968.

_____. *Rabbinische Legende und frühpharisäische Geschichte: Schimeon b. Schetach und die achtig Hexen von Askalon.* Abhandlungen der Heidelberger Akademie der Wissenschaften Philosophisch-historische Klasse, Heidelberg: Carl Winter/ Universitätsverlag, 1984.

_____. *Studies in Early Christology.* Edinburgh: T & T Clark, 1995.

_____. *Studies in the Gospel of Mark.* trans. John Bowden. Philadelphia: Fortress Press, 1985.

Higgins, A. J. B. *The Son of Man in the Teaching of Jesus.* Society of New Testament Studies Monograph Series, vol. 39. Cambridge: Cambridge University Press, 1980.

Himmelfarb, Martha. *Ascent to Heaven in Jewish & Christian Apocalypses.* Oxford: Oxford University Press, 1993.

_____. "Heavenly Ascent and the Relationship of the Apocalypses and the HEKHALOT Literature." *HUCA* 59 (1988): 73-100.

Hindley, J. C. "Towards a Date for the Similitudes of Enoch: An Historical Approach." *NTS* 14 (1968): 551-65.

Hofius, Otfried. *Der Vorhang vor den Thron Gottes: Eine exegetisch-religionsgeschichtliche Untersuchungen zu Hebrärer 6,19f. und 10, 19f..* Wissenschaftliche Untersuchungen zum Neuen Testament, vol. 14. Tübingen: J. C. B. Mohr (Paul Siebeck), 1972. Pp. 1-27.

Hofrichter, Peter. "Das dreifache Verfahren über Jesus als Gottessohn, König, und Mensch." *Kairos* 30-31 (1988-89): 69-81.

Horbury, William. "The Messianic Associations of 'the Son of Man'." *JTS* 36 (1985): 34-55.

_____. "The Trial of Jesus in Jewish Tradition." in *The Trial of Jesus: Cambridge Studies in Honour of C. F. D. Moule,* ed. Ernst Bammel. Studies in Biblical Theology, 2nd Series, vol. 13. London: SCM, 1970, 103-21.

Horgan, M. P. *Pesharim: Qumran Interpretations of Biblical Books.* Catholic Biblical Quarterly Monograph Series, vol. 8. Washington D.C.: Catholic Biblical Association Of America, 1979.

Horton, Jr., F. L. *The Melchizedek Tradition: A Critical Examination of the Sources to the Fifth Century A.D. and in the Epistle to the Hebrews.* Society for New Testament Studies Monograph Series, vol. 30. Cambridge: Cambridge University Press, 1976.

Hurtado, Larry. "Following Jesus in the Gospel of Mark– and Beyond." in *Patterns of Discipleship in the New Testament,* ed. Richard N. Longenecker. McMaster New Testament Series, ed. Richard N. Longenecker, vol. 1. Grand Rapids: Eerdmans, 1996, 9-29.

_____. *Mark.* New International Biblical Commentary, vol. 2. Peabody, Mass.: Hendrickson Publishers, 1989.

_____. *One God, One Lord: Early Christian Devotion and Ancient Jewish Monotheism.* Philadelphia: Fortress, 1988.

Janowitz, Naomi. *The Poetics of Ascent: Theories of Language in a Rabbinic Ascent Text.* SUNY Series in Judaica: Hermeneutics, Mysticism, and Culture, ed. Michael Fishbane and Arthur Green, Albany: State University Of New York Press, 1989.

Jaubert, A. "Jésus et le Calendrier de Qumrân." *NTS* 7 (1960-61): 1-30.

Jeremias, Joachim. "Zur Geschichtlichkeit des Verhörs Jesu vor dem Hohen Rat." *ZNW* 43 (1950-51): 145-50.

Juel, Donald. *Messiah and the Temple: The Trial of Jesus in the Gospel of Mark.* Society of Biblical Literature Dissertation Series, vol. 31. Missoula, Mont.: Scholars Press, 1977.

_____. *Messianic Exegesis: Christological Interpretation of the Old Testament in Early Christianity*. Philadelphia: Fortress, 1988.

Kazmierski, Carl R. *Jesus, the Son of God: A Study of the Marcan Tradition and Its Redaction by the Evangelist*. Foschung zur Bibel, ed. R. Schnackenburg and Josef Schreiner, vol. 33. Würzberg: Echter Verlag, 1979.

Keck, Leander E. "Toward the Renewal of New Testament Christology." *NTS* 32 (1986): 362-77.

Kempthorne, Renatus. "Anti-Christian Tendency in Pre-Marcan Traditions of the Sanhedrin Trial." *TU* 126 (1982): 283-85.

_____. "The Marcan Text of Jesus' Answer to the High Priest (Mark XIV 62)." *NovT* 19 (1977): 197-208.

Kim, Seyoon. *"The 'Son of Man'" as the Son of God*. Wissenschaftliche Untersuchungen zum Neuen Testament, ed. Martin Hengel and Otfried Hofius, vol. 30. Tübingen: J. C. B. Mohr (Paul Siebeck) , 1983.

Kingsbury, Jack Dean. *The Christology of Mark's Gospel*. Philadelphia: Fortress, 1983.

Klein, Gottlieb. *Ist Jesus eine historische Persönlichkeit?* Tübingen: J. C. B. Mohr (Paul (Siebeck), 1910.

Knibb, M. A. "The Date of the Parables of Enoch." *NTS* 25 (1979): 345-59.

Kobelski, P. J. *Melchizedek and Melchereša'*. Catholic Biblical Quarterly Monograph Series, vol. 10. Washington D.C.: Catholic Biblical Association Of America, 1981.

Kuhn, Heinz-Wolfgang. "Die Kreuzestrafe während der frühen Kaiserzeit." in *Aufstieg und Niedergang der Römanischen Welt*, ed. H. Temporini and W. Hasse. vol. II, 25.1. Berlin: Walter De Gruyter, 1982, 732-36.

_____. "Jesus als Gekreuzigter in der frühchristlichen Verkündigung bis zur Mitte des 2. Jahrhunderts." *ZTK* 72 (1975): 1-46.

Kuyt, Annelies. *The 'Descent' to the Chariot: Towards a Description of the Terminology, Place, Function, and Nature of the Yeridah in Hekahalot Literature*. Texte und Studien zum Antiken Judentum, ed. Martin Hengel and Peter Schäfer, vol. 45. Tübingen: J. C. B. Mohr (Paul Siebeck), 1995.

Lane, William L. *The Gospel according to Mark: The English Text with Exposition, Introduction, and Notes*. The New International Commentary on the New Testament, ed. F. F. Bruce, Grand Rapids: Eerdmans, 1974.

Leaney, A. R. C. *The Rule of Qumran and Its Meaning*. New Testament Library, London: SCM Press LTD, 1966.

Légasse, Simon. *The Trial of Jesus*. trans. John Bowden. London: SCM Press LTD, 1997.

Leivestad, Ragner. "Exit the Apocalyptic Son of Man." *NTS* 18 (1971-72): 243-67.

Lietzmann, Hans. "Der Prozeß Jesu." *SPAW* 14 (1931): 313-22.

_____. "Bemerkungen zum Prozeß Jesu." *ZNW* 30 (1931): 211-15.

Livingston, Dennis H. "The Crime of Leviticus XXIV 11." *VT* 36 (1986): 352-54.

Lindars, Barnabas. *Jesus Son of Man*. Grand Rapids: Eerdmans, 1983.

Linnemann, Eta. *Studien zur Passionsgeschichte*. Forschungen zur Religion und Literatur des Alten und Neuen Testaments, vol. 102. Göttingen: Vandenhoeck & Ruprecht, 1970.

Lohse, E. "Συνέδριον." in *Theological Dictionary of New Testament Theology*, ed. G. Fredrich and G. Kittel. vol. 7. Grand Rapids: Eerdmans, 867-71.

Lueken, W. *Michael. Eine Darstellung und Vergleichung der jüdischen und der morgenländisch-christlichen Tradition vom Erzangel Michael*. Göttingen: Vandenhoeck & Ruprecht, 1898.

Lührmann, Dieter. "Markus 14 53b. 55-64 Christologie und Zerstörung des Tempels im Markusevangelium." *NTS* 27 (1980-81): 457-74.

Mach, Michael. *Entwicklungsstadien des jüdischen Engelglaubens in vorrabbinischer Zeit*. Texte und Studien zum Antiken Judentum, ed. Martin Hengel and Peter Schäfer, vol. 34. Tübingen: J. C. B. Mohr (Paul Siebeck), 1992.

Maddox, Robert. "The Function of the Son of Man According to the Synoptic Gospels." *NTS* 15 (1968-69): 45-74.

Maier, Johann. "Das Gëfahrdungsmotiv bei der Himmelreise in der Jüdischen Apokalyptik und 'Gnosis'." *Kairos* 5 (1963): 18-40.

Marcus, Joel. "Mark 14:61: "Are You the Messiah-Son-of-God?"" *NovT* 31 (1989): 125-41.

_____. *The Way of the Lord: Christological Exegesis of the Old Testament in the Gospel of Mark*. Louisville: Westminster/John Knox Press, 1992.

Marmorstein, A. *The Old Rabbinic Doctrine of God*. Jews' College Publications, vol. 10. London: Oxford University Press, 1927.

Matera, Frank J. *The Kingship of Jesus: Composition and Theology in Mark 15*. SBL Dissertation Series, vol. 66. Chico, Calif.: Scholars Press, 1982.

McKelvey, R. *The New Temple: The Church in the New Testament*. Oxford: Oxford University Press, 1969.

Mearns, C. L. "Dating the Similitudes of Enoch." *NTS* 25 (1979): 360-69.

Meeks, Wayne A. "Moses as God and King." in *Religion in Antiquity: Esays in Momory of Erwin Ramsdell Goodenough*, ed. Jacob Neusner. Studies in the History of Religion: Supplements To NUMEN- Religions in Antiquity, vol. 14. Leiden: E. J. Brill, 1968, 354-71.

_____. *The Prophet-King: Moses Traditions and the Johannine Christology*. Supplements to Novum Testamentum, vol. 14. Leiden: E. J. Brill, 1967.

Meyer, Franz E. "Einige Bemerkungen zur Bedeuteung des Perminus 'Synhedrion' in den Schriften des Neuen Testaments." *NTS* 14 (1967-68): 545-51.

Milgrom, Jacob. *The JPS Torah Commentary: Numbers*. New York: The Jewish Publication Society, 1990.

Millar, Fergus. "Reflections on the Trials of Jesus." in A Tribute to Geza Vermes: *Essays on Jewish and Christian Literature and History*, ed. Philip R. Davies, Richard T. White. Journal for the Study of the Old Testament Supplement Series, vol. 100. Sheffield: Sheffield Academic Press, 1990, 354-81.

Morray-Jones, C. R. A. "Transformational Mysticism in the Apocalyptic-Merkabah Tradition." *JJS* 43 (1992): 1-31.

Moule, C. F. D. "Some Observations on Tendenzkritik." in *Jesus and the Politics of His Day*, ed. Ernst Bammel and C. F. D. Moule. Cambridge: Cambridge University Press, 1984, 91-100.

Mowinckel, Sigmund. *He That Cometh*. trans. G. W. Anderson. Oxford: Basil Blackwell, 1956.

Müller, Karlheinz. "Der Menschensohn im Danielzyklus." in *Jesus und der Menschensohn: für Anton Vögtle*, ed. R. Pesch and R. Schnackenburg. Freiburg: Herder, 1975, 37-80.

_____. "Möglichkeit und Vollzug jüdischer Kapitalgerichtsbarkeit im Prozeß gegen Jesus von Nazaret." in *Der Prozeß gegen Jesus: Historische Rückfrage und Theologische Deutung*, ed. Karl Kertelge. Questiones Disputatae, vol. 112. Freiburg: Herder, 1988, 41-83.

Myllykoski, M. *Die Letzten Tage Jesu: Markus und Johannes, ihre Traditionen und die historische Frage*, vol. 1. Helsinki: Suomalainen Tiedeakatemia, 1991.

Neale, D. "Was Jesus a *Mesith*? Public Response to Jesus and His Ministry." *TynB* 44 (1993): 89-101.

Neusner, Jacob. "The Development of the MERKAVAH Tradition." *JSJ* 2 (1971): 149-60.

Nineham, D. E. *The Gospel of Saint Mark*. The Pelican New Testament Commentaries, ed. D. E. Nineham, London: Penquin Books, 1963.

Noll, S. F. *Angelology in the Qumran Texts*. Manchester: Unpublished PhD, 1979.

O'Neill, J. C. "The Charge of Blasphemy at Jesus' Trial before the Sanhedrin." in *The Trial of Jesus*, ed. Ernst Bammel. Studies in Biblical Theology, 2nd Series, vol. 13. London: SCM, 1970, 72-77.

_____. "The Silence of Jesus." *NTS* 15 (1968-69): 153-67.

Otto, Rudolf. *Reich Gottes und Menschensohn: Ein religionsgeschichtlicher Versuch*. München: C. H. Beck'sche Verlagsbuchhandlung, 1954.

Otzen, Benedikt. "Heavenly Visions in Early Judaism: Origin and Function." in *In the Shelter of Elyon: Essays on Ancient Palestinian Life and Literature in Honor of G. W. Ahlström*, ed. W. Boyd Barrick and John R. Spencer. Journal for the Study of the New Testament Supplement Series, vol. 31. Sheffield: JSOT Press, 1984, 199-215.

Perrin, Norman. "Mark XIV.62: The End Product of a Christian Pesher?" *NTS* 12 (1965-66): 150-55.

_____. *Rediscovering the Teaching of Jesus*. New York: Harper & Row, 1976.

_____. "The High Priest's Question and Jesus' Answer (Mark 14:61-62)." in The *Passion in Mark: Studies on Mark 14-16*, ed. Werner H. Kelber. Philiadelphia: Fortress Press, 1976, 80-95.

Pesch, Rudolf. *Das Markusevangelium*. Herders theologischer Komentar zum Neuen Testament, II, 1-2. Freiburg: Herder, 1976-1977.

_____. "Das Messiasbekennis des Petrus (Mk 8,27-30): Neuverhandlung einer alten Frage." *BZ* n.f. 18 (1974): 20-31.

_____. *Der Prozeß Jesu geht weiter*. Freiburg: Herder, 1988.

_____. "Die Passion des Menschensohnes: Eine Studie zu den Menschensohnworten der vormarkinischen Passionsgeschichte." in *Jesus und der Menschensohn: für Anton Vögtle*, ed. R. Pesch and R. Schnackenburg. Freiburg: Herder, 1975, 166-95.

Plevnik, Joseph. "Son of Man Seated at the Right Hand of God: Luke 22,69 in Lucan Christology." *Bib* 72 (1991): 331-47.

Puech, Emile. "Fragment d'une Apocalypse en Arameen (4Q246=Pseudo-Dan d) et le "Royalume de Dieu". " *RB* 99 (1992): 98-131.

Radl, Walter. "Sonderüberlieferung bei Lukas?: Traditionsgeschichtliche Fragen zu Lk 22,67f; 23,2 und 23,6-12." in *Der Prozeß gegen Jesus: Historische Rückfrage und Theologische Deutung*, ed. Karl Kertelge. Questiones Disputatae, vol. 112. Freiburg: Herder, 1988, 131-47.

Rainbow, Paul A. "Jewish Monotheism as the Matrix for New Testament Christology: A Review Article." *NT* 33 (1991): 79-91.

Reichrath, H. "Der Prozeß Jesu: Vom Leiden und Sterben des 'Königs der Juden'." *Judaica* 20 (1964): 129-55.

Reinbold, Wolfgang. *Der älteste Bericht über den Tod Jesu: Literarische Analyse und historische Kritik der Passionsdarstellungen der Evangelien*. Beihefte zur Zeitschrift für neutestamentliche Wissenshaft und die Kunde der älteren Kirche, ed. Erich Grässer, vol. 69. Berlin: Walter De Gruyter, 1994.

Rohland, J. P. *Der Erzengel Michael: Arzt und Feldherr: Zwei Aspekte des vor- und frühbyzantinischen Michaelskultes*. Leiden: E. J. Brill, 1977.

Rowland, Christopher. *The Open Heaven: A Study of Apocalyptic in Judaism and Early Christianity*. New York: Crossroad, 1982. Pp. 78-123.

_____. "The Vision of the Risen Christ in Rev. 1.13ff.: The Debt of an Early Christology to an Aspect of Jewish Angelology." *JTS* 31 (1980): 1-11.

_____. "The Visions of God in Apocalyptic Literature." *JSJ* 10 (1979): 137-54.

Russell, D. S. *The Method and Message of Jewish Apocalyptic*. The Old Testament Library, Philadelphia: Westminster, 1964.

Sanders, E. P. *Jewish Law from Jesus to Mishnah*. Philadelphia: Trinity Press International, 1990.

_____. *Jesus and Judaism*. Philadelphia: Fortress, 1985.

_____. *Judaism: Practice and Belief 63BCE-66CE*. Philadelphia: Trinity Press International, 1992.

Schaberg, Jane. "Mark 14:62: Early Christian Mekabah Imagery?" in *Apocalyptic and the New Testament: Essays in Honor of J. Louis Martyn*, ed. Joel Marcus and Marion L. Soards. Journal For the Study of The New Testament Supplement Series 24, Sheffield: Sheffield Academic Press, 1989, 69-94.

Schäfer, Peter. "Merkabah Mysticism and Magic." in *Gershom Scholem's MAJOR TRENDS IN JEWISH MYSTICISM 50 Years Later: Proceedings on the Sixth International*

Conference on the History of Jewish Mysticism, ed. Peter Schäfer and Joseph Dan. Tübingen: J. C. B. Mohr (Paul Siebeck), 1993, 59-78.

_____. "New Testament and Hekhalot Literature: The Journey into Heaven in Paul and in Merkavah Mysticism." *JJS* 35 (1984): 19-35.

_____. "Research into Rabbinic Literature: An Attempt to Define the Status Questionis." *JJS* 37 (1986): 139-52.

_____. *Rivalität zwischen Engeln und Menschen: Untersuchungen zur rabbinischen Engelvorstellung.* Studia Judaica: Forschungen zur Wissenschaft des Judentums, ed. E. L. Ehrlich, vol. 8. Berlin: Walter De Gruyter, 1975.

Schenk, Wolfgang. *Der Passionsbericht nach Markus: Untersuchungen zur Überlieferungsgeschichte der Passionstradition.* Gerd Mohn: Gütersloher Verlagshaus, 1974.

Schmithals, Walter. *Das Evangelium nach Markus.* Ökumenischer Taschenbuch-Kommentar zum Neuen Testament, vol. 2. Gütersloh/Würzburg: Gütersloher Verlagshaus/Echter Verlag, 1979.

Schneider, Gerhard. "Das Verfahren gegen Jesus in der Sicht des dritten Evangeliums (Lk 22,54-23,25): Redaktionskritik und historische Rückfrage." in *Der Prozeß gegen Jesus: Historische Rückfrage und Theologische Deutung*, ed. Karl Kertelge. Questiones Disputatae, vol. 112. Freiburg: Herder, 1988, 111-30.

_____. ""Der Menschensohn" in der lukanischen Christologie." in *Jesus und der Menschensohn: für Anton Vögtle*, ed. R. Pesch and R. Schnackenburg. Freiburg: Herder, 1975, 267-282.

_____. "Gab es eine vorsynoptische Szene 'Jesus vor dem Synedrium'?" *NovT* 12 (1970): 22-39.

_____. "Jesus vor dem Synedrium." *Bibel und Leben* 11 (1970): 1-15.

_____. "The Political Charge against Jesus (Luke 23:2)." in *Jesus and the Politics of His Day*, ed. Ernst Bammel and C. F. D. Moule. Cambridge: Cambridge University Press, 1984, 403-14.

Scholem, Gershom. *Die Jüdische Mystik in ihren Hauptströmungen.* 2nd ed. Frankfurt: Suhrkamp Verlag, 1971. Pp. 43-86.

_____. *Jewish Gnosticism, Merkabah Mysticism and Talmudic Tradition.* New York: The Jewish Theological Seminary Of America, 1965.

_____. *Major Trends in Jewish Musticism.* 3rd ed. New York: Schocken Books, 1941, 1954.

Schubert, K. "Biblical criticism criticised: with reference to the Markan Report of Jesus's examination before the Sanhedrin." in *Jesus and the Politics of His Day*, ed. Ernst Bammel and C. F. D. Moule. Cambridge: Cambridge University Press, 1984, 385-402.

Schultz, Joseph P. "Angelic Opposition to the Ascension of Moses and the Revelation of the Law." *JQR* 61 (1970-71): 282-307.

Schulz, Siegfried. "Maranatha und Kyrios Jesus." *ZNW* 53 (1962): 125-44.

Schwemer, Anna Maria. "Gott als König und seine Königsherrschaft in den Sabbatliedern aus Qumran." in *Königsherrschaft Gottes und Himmlischer Kult im Judentum, Urchristentum und in der hellenistischen Welt*, ed. Martin Hengel and Anna Maria Schwemer. Wissenschafliche Untersuchungen zum Neuen Testament, vol. 55. Tübingen: J. C. B. Mohr (Paul Siebeck), 1991, 45-118.

_____. "Irdischer und himmlicher König: Beobachtungen zur sogenannten David-Apokalypse in Hekhalot Rabbati §§ 122-26." in *Königsherrschaft Gottes und Himmlischer Kult im Judentum, Urchristentum und in der hellenistischen Welt*, ed. Martin Hengel and Anna Maria Schwemer. Wissenschafliche Untersuchungen zum Neuen Testament, vol. 55. Tübingen: J. C. B. Mohr (Paul Siebeck), 1991, 309-59.

Segal, Alan. "Heavenly Ascent in Hellenistic Judaism, Early Christianity and their Environment." in *Aufstieg und Niedergang der Römanischen Welt*, ed. H. Temporini and W. Hasse. vol. 23.2. Berlin: Walter De Gruyter, 1980, 1334-88.

_____. "The Risen Christ and the Angelic Mediator Figures in Light of Qumran." in *Jesus and the Dead Sea Scrolls*, ed. James H. Charlesworth. The Anchor Bible Reference Library, New York: Doubleday, 1992, 302-28.

_____. *Two Powers in Heaven: Early Rabbinic Reports about Christianity and Gnosticism*. Studies in Judaism in Late Antiquity, ed. Jacob Neusner, vol. 25. Leiden: E. J. Brill, 1977.

Senior, Donald P. *The Passion Narrative According to Matthew: A Redactional Study*. Bibliotheca Ephmeridum Theologicarum Lovaniensium, vol. 39. Leuven: Leuven University Press, 1975.

Sherwin-White, A. N. *Roman Society and Roman Law in the New Testament*. Oxford: Oxford University Press, 1963. Pp. 24-47.

Sjöberg, Erik. *Der Menschensohn im Äthiopischen Henochbuch*. Lund: Gleerup, 1946.

Smith, Morton. "Ascent to the Heavens and Deification in 4QMª." in *Archaeology and History in the Dead Sea Scrolls: The New York University Conference in Memory of Yigael Yadin*, ed. L. H. Schiffmann. Journal for The Study of the Pseudepigrapha Supplement Series, vol. 8. Sheffield: Sheffield Academic Press, 1990, 181-88.

_____. "Two Ascended to Heaven— Jesus and the Author of 4Q491." in *Jesus and the Dead Sea Scrolls*, ed. James H. Charlesworth. The Anchor Bible Reference Library, New York: Doubleday, 1992, 290-301.

Sommer, Urs. *Die Passionsgeschichte des Markusevangeliums: Überlegungen zur Bedeutung der Geschichte für den Glauben*. Wissenschaftliche Untersuchungen zum Neuen Testament, ed. Martin Hengel and Otfried Hofius, vol. 58. Tübingen: J. C. B. Mohr (Paul Siebeck), 1993.

Staerk, D. W. *Altjüdische Liturgische Gebete*. Kleine Texte für Vorlesungen und Übungen, ed. Hans Lietzmann, vol. 58. Berlin: Walter De Gruyter, 1930.

Stauffer, E. *Jesus and His Story*. New York: Knopf, 1959.

Stern, Menahem. *Greek and Latin Authors on Jews and Judaism*. Jerusalem: Israel Academy Of Sciences And Humanities, 1974.

Stone, Michael Edward. *Fourth Ezra*. Hermenia- A Critical and Historical Commentary on the Bible, Minneapolis: Fortress, 1991.

_____. "The Concept of the Messiah in IV Ezra." in *Religions in Antiquity: Essays in Memory of Erwin Ramsdell Goodenough*, ed. Jacob Neusner. Studies in The History of Religions Supplements To NUMEN, vol. 14. Leiden: E. J. Brill, 1968, 295-312.

Strobel, August. *Die Stunde der Wahrheit*. Wissenschaftliche Untersuchungen zum Neuen Testament, ed. Martin Hengel, Otfried Hofius, Otto Michel, vol. 21. Tübingen: J. C. B. Mohr (Paul Siebeck), 1980.

Strugnell, John. "The Angelic Liturgy at Qumran." *VTSup* 7 (1960): 337.

_____. "Moses-Pseudepigrapha at Qumran: 4Q375, 4Q376, and Similar Works." in *Archaeology and History in the Dead Sea Scrolls: The New York University Conference in Memory of Yigael Yadin,* ed. Lawrence H. Schiffman. Journal for The Study of the Pseudepigrapha Supplement Series, vol. 8. Sheffield: Sheffield Academic Press, 1980, 221-56.

Stuckenbruck, Loren T. *Angel Veneration and Christology*. Wissenschaftliche Untersuchungen zum Neuen Testament, ed. Martin Hengel and Otfried Hofius, vol. 70. Tübingen: J. C. B. Mohr (Paul Siebeck), 1995.

Taylor, Vincent. *The Gospel according to St. Mark: The Greek Text with Introduction, Notes, and Indexes*. 2nd ed. London: Macmillan, 1966.

Theisohn, Johannes. *Der auserwählte Richter: Untersuchungen zum traditionsgeschichlichen Ort den Menschensohngestalt den Bildreden des Ätheopischen Henoch*. Göttingen: Vandenhoeck & Ruprecht, 1975.

Tödt, Heinz Eduard. *Der Menschensohn in der synoptischen Überlieferung*. Gerd Mohn: Gütersloher Verlagshaus, 1959.

Tyson, Joseph B. "The Lucan Version of the Trial of Jesus." *NovT* 3 (1959): 249-58.

Urbach, Ephraim E. *The Sages: Their Concepts and Beliefs.* trans. Israel Abrahams. London: Harvard University Press, 1987.

van der Horst, Pieter W. "Moses' Throne Vision in Ezekiel the Dramatist." in *Essays on the Jewish World of Early Christianity*, ed. Pieter van der Horst. Novum Testamentum Et Orbis Antiquus, ed. Max Küchler and Gerd Theissen, vol. 14. Göttingen: Vandenhoeck & Ruprecht, 1990, 63-71.

_____. "Some Notes on the Exagoge of Ezekiel." in *Essays on the Jewish World of Early Christianity*, ed. Pieter van der Horst. Novum Testamentum Et Orbis Antiquus, ed. Max Küchler and Gerd Theissen, vol. 14. Göttingen: Vandenhoeck & Ruprecht, 1990, 72-93.

Van Unnik, W. C. "Jesus the Christ." *NTS* 8 (1961-62): 101-16.

Vermes, Geza. "Methodology in the Study of Jewish Literature in the Greco-Roman Period." *JJS* 36 (1985): 145-58.

Währisch, H. and C. Brown. "βλασφημέω." in *New International Dictionary of New Testament Theology*, vol. 3. Exeter: Paternoster, 1971, 340-45.

Wallis, "גדף." in *TheologischesWörterbuch zum Alten Testament*, ed. J. Botterweck and H. Ringrenn. vol. 1. Stuttgart: Kohlhammer, 1973, col. 956-58.

Weingreen, J. "The Case of the Blasphemer (Leviticus XXIV 10ff.)." *VT* 22 (1972): 118-23.

Wewers, Gerd A. *Geheimnis und Geheimhaltung im rabbinischen Judentum.* Religionsgeschichtliche Versuche und Vorarbeiten, ed. Walter Burkett And Carsten Colpe, vol. 35. Berlin: Walter De Gruyter, 1975.

Wilcox, Max. ""Upon the Tree"- Deut 21:22-23 in the New Testament." *JBL* 96 (1977): 83-99.

Winter, Paul. "Marginal Notes on the Trial of Jesus." *ZNW* 50 (1959): 14-33, 230-51.

_____. "Markus 14 53b. 55-64: Ein Gebilde des Evengelistin." *ZNW* 53 (1962): 260-63.

_____. *On the Trial of Jesus.* 2d ed., rev. T. A. Burkill and G. Vermes. Studia Judaica, vol. 1. Berlin: DeGruyter, 1974.

_____. "The Trial of Jesus and the Competence of the Sanhedrin." *NTS* 10 (1963-64): 494-99.

Wright, N. T. *Jesus and the Victory of God.* Minneapolis: Fortress, 1996.

Zimmerman, Heinrich. "Das Absolute 'Εγώ εἰμι als die Neutestamentliche Offenbarungsformel (1 und 2 Teil)." *BZ* n.f. 4 (1960): 54-69, 266-276.

_____. "Das absolute 'Ich bin' in der Redeweise Jesus." TrTheZ 2 (1960): 1-20.

Zimmermann, Johannes. *Messianische Vorstellungen in den Schriftfunden von Qumran.* Tübingen: Unpublished PhD, 1996.

Index of Sources

The following index begins with the Old and New Testaments and then discusses categories of Other Ancient Authors and Texts in alphabetical order, grouped according to category or author. Those groupings in order are: Babylonian Talmud, Christian Coptic Texts, Church Writings, Deutero-Canonical Texts, Elephantine Papyri, Greek Papyri, Hekhalot Texts, Jewish Prayers, Josephus, Midrashim, Mishnah, Palestinian Talmud, Philo, Pseudepigrapha, Qumran, Samaritan texts, Targumim, and Tosefta. Units within these groups proceed in numeric and then alphabetical order. Any inconsistencies in citation forms are in order not to disturb how references are cited in sources footnoted.

Old Testament

Genesis			
2:16	81, 102	20:3	35
2:24	84	20:22 – 23:33	33
5:24	122-23, 128, 151,	20:12	36, 228
	176	21:15	62
6	127	21:17	34, 228
6:1-4	123, 175, 180	22	39, 94, 101
8:21	32, 34	22:27	22, 32-35, 37, 39-41,
9:6	80, 102		53-55, 57, 73, 76,
11	60		81, 93, 101, 110,
12:3	32, 34		112, 202-03, 208-09,
14	130		236
15	130	23:13	35
18:19	102	25:8	85
37:29	40	28:38	86, 88
		32:17-18	82
		32:23	35
Exodus		33:12-23	133, 137, 140
3	133	34	137
4:16	143	34:5	137, 150
4:22	131	34:28	137
5:2	105		
7:1	138-39, 143-44, 182	*Leviticus*	
14:8	37		
14:20	150, 201	1:2	81
14:27	105	5:1	75
15:8	83	5:17	75
15:22	218	16:30	198
15:24	218	17:16	75
17:13	84	18:6	46
18:11	35	18:13	46
19 – 34	133	19:8	75
20:2-3	79	19:14	34, 61

New Testament

Other Ancient Authors & Texts

CHRISTIAN COPTIC TEXTS

CHURCH WRITINGS

Clement of Alexandria
Stromata
1.23.155-56   141
5.11.77   173

Egerton Gospel
3:1-6   194

Eusebius
Preparation of the Gospel
(Demonstratio Evangelica)
3, 3, 1-4   212
3, 6, 1   212
9, 28-29   141

Justin Martyr
Dialogue with Trypho
69.7   211-12
108.2   212

Origen
Contra Celsus   212
Philocalia 33:19   131

Pseudo-Eustathius
Commentaries in
Hexaemeron   141

DEUTERO-CANONICAL BOOKS

1 Maccabees
2:1-5   49
2:6   49, 111, 205
2:7-13   49
2:14   49
2:58   147
6:13   50
7:26-43   56
7:26-50   89
7:33-38   57
7:34-35   57
7:37-38   57
7:38   47, 51
7:41   47

2 Maccabees
4:2   137
5:17   49
5:21   49
5:27   50

8:2-4   49
8:4   47, 49
9:13   50
9:28   22, 49-50
10:4   49-50
10:6   50
10:34-36   50
10:35   47
12:14   47, 50
13:11   47
14:11-15   89
14:36   89
15:24   47, 49, 50, 56

Bel
9   50
9 Θ   22

Jubilees
Prologue   134
1:4   134
1:26   134

Sirach
3:16   50
30:6   137
44:1 – 49:16   116
44:16   122
45   137
45:2   134
45:5   134
48:9   147
49:14   122
49:14-16   116

Tobit
1:18S   47
1:21   47
5:4   175
12:15   175
12:16-20   175
13:16   47

Wisdom
1:6   50
4:10-11   122
5   161
5:2   207
5:15   161
5:16   161
5:17   161

Index of Authors

The following index of authors only notes names in the text or names where a discussion is found in the footnotes. It covers authors only. For historical figures, see subject index.

Index of Subjects

284   *Index of Subjects*

Darrell L. Bock (Ph.D., University of Aberdeen) is Research Professor of New Testament Studies at Dallas Theological Seminary. Dr. Bock was the Alexander von Humboldt scholar at the University of Tübingen in 1995–96. He is the author of three commentaries on Luke and coauthor of *Progressive Dispensationalism.*